CW01020254

The Complete Works of John Owen

The Complete Works of John Owen

The Complete Works
of John Owen

THE TRINITY

VOLUME 8

The Holy Spirit—
The Comforter

John Owen

INTRODUCED AND EDITED BY
Andrew S. Ballitch

GENERAL EDITORS
Lee Gatiss and Shawn D. Wright

WHEATON, ILLINOIS

The Holy Spirit—The Comforter

Copyright © 2023 by Crossway

Published by Crossway
    1300 Crescent Street
    Wheaton, Illinois 60187

Cover design: Jordan Singer

Cover image: Custom marble paper by Vanessa Reynoso, Marble Paper Studio

First printing 2023

Printed in China

Hardcover ISBN: 978-1-4335-6021-7
ePub ISBN: 978-1-4335-8579-1
PDF ISBN: 978-1-4335-8577-7
Mobipocket ISBN: 978-1-4335-8578-4

Library of Congress Cataloging-in-Publication Data

Names: Owen, John, 1616-1683, author. | Ballitch, Andrew S., editor.

Title: The Holy Spirit : the Comforter / introduced and edited by Andrew S. Ballitch, Lee Gatiss and Shawn D. Wright, general editors.

Other titles: Pneumatologia. Books VII-IX

Description: Wheaton, Illinois : Crossway, 2023. | Series: The complete works of John Owen ; 8 | Includes bibliographical references and index.

Identifiers: LCCN 2022011798 (print) | LCCN 2022011799 (ebook) | ISBN 9781433560217 (hardcover) | ISBN 9781433585777 (pdf) | ISBN 9781433585784 (mobipocket) | ISBN 9781433585791 (epub)

Subjects: LCSH: Holy Spirit—Early works to 1800

Classification: LCC BT121.3 .O938 2022 (print) | LCC BT121.3 (ebook) | DDC 231/.3—dc23/eng/20220615

LC record available at https://lccn.loc.gov/2022011798

LC ebook record available at https://lccn.loc.gov/2022011799

Crossway is a publishing ministry of Good News Publishers.

RRDS		32	31	30	29	28	27	26	25	24	23
15	14	13	12	11	10	9	8	7	6	5	4	3	2	1

Volume 8

Contents

Works Preface

JOHN OWEN (1616–1683) is one of the most significant, influential, and prolific theologians that England has ever produced. His work is of such a high caliber that it is no surprise to find it still in demand more than four centuries after his birth. As a son of the Church of England, a Puritan preacher, a statesman, a Reformed theologian and Bible commentator, and later a prominent Nonconformist and advocate of toleration, he is widely read and appreciated by Christians of different types all over the globe, not only for the profundity of his thinking but also for the depth of his spiritual insight.

Owen was born in the year that William Shakespeare died, and in terms of his public influence, he was a rising star in the 1640s and at the height of his power in the 1650s. As chaplain to Oliver Cromwell, dean of Christ Church, and vice-chancellor of Oxford University, he wielded a substantial degree of power and influence within the short-lived English republic. Yet he eventually found himself on the losing side of the epic struggles of the seventeenth century and was ousted from his position of national preeminence. The Act of Uniformity in 1662 effectively barred him from any role in the established church, yet it was in the wilderness of those turbulent post-Restoration years that he wrote many of his most momentous contributions to the world of theological literature, despite being burdened by opposition, persecution, family tragedies, and illness.

There was an abortive endeavor to publish a uniform edition of Owen's works in the early eighteenth century, but this progressed no further than a single folio volume in 1721. A century later (1826), Thomas Russell met with much more success when he produced a collection in twenty-one volumes. The appetite for Owen only grew; more than three hundred people had subscribed to the 1721 and 1826 editions of his works, but almost three thousand subscribed to the twenty-four-volume set produced by William H. Goold from 1850 onward. That collection, with Goold's learned introductions and notes, became the standard edition. It was given a new lease on life when the Banner of Truth Trust reprinted it several times beginning in 1965, though without some of Owen's Latin works, which had appeared in Goold's edition, or his massive Hebrews commentary, which Banner did eventually reprint in 1991. Goold corrected various errors in the original seventeenth- and eighteenth-century publications, some of which Owen himself had complained of, as well as certain grammatical errors. He thoroughly revised the punctuation, numeration of points, and Scripture references in Owen and presented him in a way acceptable to nineteenth-century readers without taking liberties with the text.

Since the mid-nineteenth century, and especially since the reprinting of Goold's edition in the mid-twentieth century, there has been a great flowering of interest in seventeenth-century Puritanism and Reformed theology. The recent profusion of scholarship in this area has resulted in a huge increase of attention given to Owen and his contribution to these movements. The time has therefore come to attempt another presentation of Owen's body of work for a new century. This new edition is more than a reprint of earlier collections of Owen's writings. As useful as those have been to us and many others, they fail to meet the needs of modern readers who are often familiar with neither the theological context nor the syntax and rhetorical style of seventeenth-century English divinity.

For that reason, we have returned again to the original editions of Owen's texts to ensure the accuracy of their presentation here but have conformed the spelling to modern American standards, modernized older verb endings, reduced the use of italics where they do not clarify meaning, updated some hyphenation forms, modernized capitalization both for select terms in the text and for titles of Owen's works, refreshed the typesetting, set lengthy quotations in block format, and both checked and added Scripture references in a consistent format where necessary. Owen's quotations of others, however, including the various editions of the Bible he used or translated, are kept as they appear in his original. His marginal notes and footnotes have been clearly marked in footnotes as his (with "—Owen" appearing at the end of his content) to distinguish them from editorial comments. Foreign languages such as Greek, Hebrew, and Latin (which Owen knew and used extensively) have been translated into modern English, with the original languages retained in footnotes for scholarly reference (also followed by "—Owen"). If Goold omitted parts of the original text in his edition, we have restored them to their rightful place. Additionally, we have attempted to regularize the numbering system Owen employed, which was often imprecise and inconsistent; our order is 1, (1), [1], {1}, and 1st. We have also included various features to aid readers' comprehension of Owen's writings, including extensive introductions and outlines by established scholars in the field today, new paragraph breaks marked by a pilcrow (¶), chapter titles and appropriate headings (either entirely new or adapted from Goold), and explanatory footnotes that define archaic or obscure words and point out scriptural and other allusions in the text. On the rare occasions when we have added words to the text for readability, we have clearly marked them using square brackets. Having a team of experts involved, along with the benefit of modern online database technology, has also enabled us to make the prodigious effort to identify sources and citations in Owen that Russell and Goold deliberately avoided or were unable to locate for their editions.

Owen did not use only one English translation of the Bible. At various times, he employed the Great Bible, the Geneva Bible, the Authorized Version (KJV), and his own paraphrases and translations from the original languages. We have not sought to harmonize his biblical quotations to any single version. Similarly, we have left his Hebrew and Greek quotations exactly as he recorded them, including the unpointed Hebrew text. When it appears that he has misspelled the Hebrew or Greek, we have acknowledged that in a footnote with reference to either *Biblia Hebraica Stuttgartensia* or *Novum Testamentum Graece*.

This new edition presents fresh translations of Owen's works that were originally published in Latin, such as his Θεολογούμενα Παντοδαπά (1661) and *A Dissertation on Divine Justice* (which Goold published in an amended eighteenth-century translation). It also includes certain shorter works that have never before been collected in one place, such as Owen's prefaces to other people's works and many of his letters, with an extensive index to the whole set.

Our hope and prayer in presenting this new edition of John Owen's complete works is that it will equip and enable new generations of readers to appreciate the spiritual insights he accumulated over the course of his remarkable life. Those with a merely historical interest will find here a testimony to the exceptional labors of one extraordinary figure from a tumultuous age, in a modern and usable critical edition. Those who seek to learn from Owen about the God he worshiped and served will, we trust, find even greater riches in his doctrine of salvation, his passion for evangelism and missions, his Christ-centered vision of all reality, his realistic pursuit of holiness, his belief that theology matters, his concern for right worship and religious freedom, and his careful exegetical engagement with the text of God's word. We echo the words of the apostle Paul that Owen inscribed on the title page of his book Χριστολογία

(1679), "I count all things but loss for the excellency of the knowledge of Christ Jesus my Lord, for whom I have suffered the loss of all things, and do count them but dung that I may win Christ" (Phil. 3:8).

Lee Gatiss
CAMBRIDGE, ENGLAND

Shawn D. Wright
LOUISVILLE, KENTUCKY, UNITED STATES

Editor's Introduction

Andrew S. Ballitch

FOR A FULL INTRODUCTION to volumes 7 and 8, see the introduction to volume 7. The following introduces key features of volume 8 in particular.

OWEN'S TREATISES

The Work of the Holy Spirit in Prayer (1682)[1]

Owen's treatise on prayer is an attack on set forms of prayer and an argument for free (unwritten and unmemorized) prayer. As previously noted, Owen felt compelled to write on the subject in response to Hugh Cressy's rather abrasive dismissal of the Reformed Protestant position in his *The Church-History of Brittany*. But Owen's project is larger than merely an apologetic against the Church of Rome and its false worship flowing from its composed prayers. Two ideas dominate. Prayers of human composure in the national Restoration Church of England's Book of Common Prayer and the neglect of prayer among other churches are Owen's twin concerns.

Owen begins by asserting the necessity, benefit, and use of prayer in general. This goes without saying, in fact. No true religion exists without prayer. All religion consists principally in prayer. And so the design of his discourse, in Owen's own words, is that when it comes to prayer, "nothing more requisite in our religion than that true apprehensions of its nature and use be preserved in the minds of men, the declaration and defense of them, when they are opposed and unduly traduced, is not only justifiable but necessary also."

---

1 This was published by Nathaniel Ponder, who published several of Owen's works and John Bunyan's *The Pilgrim's Progress*. Owen, in fact, may have introduced Ponder to Bunyan. See N. H. Keeble, "Bunyan's Literary Life," in *The Cambridge Companion to Bunyan*, ed. Anne Dunan-Page (Cambridge: Cambridge University Press, 2010), 18.

Owen understands prayer according to the Spirit to be under attack by the imposition of liturgical forms.

The questions Owen seeks to answer include the nature of the work of the Spirit in aiding and assisting believers in their praying according to the mind of God and the effects and fruit of that work. The sum of what he pleads, from Scripture and experience, is this:

> Whereas *God has graciously promised his Holy Spirit, as a Spirit of grace and supplications, unto them that do believe, enabling them to pray according to his mind and will, in all the circumstances and capacities wherein they are, or which they may be called unto, it is the duty of them who are enlightened with the truth hereof to expect those promised aids and assistances in and unto their prayers, and to pray according to the ability which they receive thereby.*[2]

After summarizing his claim, he lays out eight general principles, which warrant enumerating, since they serve as a foundation for the treatise as a whole:

1. It is the duty of every person to pray for himself or herself. The existence of God simply demands it.
2. It is the duty of some to pray for others. Here, Owen is thinking of fathers, husbands, pastors, and the like.
3. Whoever prays is obligated to pray as well as possible.
4. And the best prayer includes intense, sincere actings of our minds through the greatest assistance we can attain.
5. The duty of prayer is achievable with the aid of God himself.
6. God expressly commands his people to pray, but not to compose written prayers for themselves, much less others.
7. Assistance is promised to believers to enable them to pray according to the will of God. However, at the same time, no help is promised for composing prayers for others.
8. Prayers given in Scripture have everlasting use but give no warrant for compositions unto the same end. This final principle leads Owen to the dominant topic in his preface, an earnest plea against set forms of prayer.

Owen stops short of determining set forms of prayer as inherently sinful, absolutely unlawful, or entirely vitiating of acceptable worship, but neither

---

2   All italics in quotations from Owen appear in the original.

does he have anything positive to say about them. Taking the Missal (or Roman Catholic Mass book) as a case study, he highlights the abuses and corruptions engendered by liturgical forms. While the Missal's development was slow, it eventually imposed worship of human composure as divine and brought with it several unfortunate results. One was the doctrines of the Mass and transubstantiation. The Church of Rome came to believe what it first admitted in prayer. This theology of the Lord's Supper could not have conceivably developed without enforceable set forms of prayer. Another disastrous result was the rise of arbitrary ceremonies that came to adorn the devised prayer forms, leading to superstition and idolatrous practices. A third calamitous outcome was the imposition of the Missal, enforced at times even to the point of death. These consequences further served as catalysts for the cessation of true spiritual and ministerial gifts.

Owen proceeds to build upon the foundation laid in his preface in three movements. In chapters 1–3, he details the biblical evidence for true prayer. Chapters 4–7 exposit the nature of the Spirit's work. And then chapters 8–9 draw out the duties associated with the Spirit's gift of prayer. Owen concludes the treatise with two separate discussions, one on what he calls "mental prayer" and one on prescribed forms, in chapters 10–11, which are significant for historical context and will be handled briefly in turn.

Chapter 1: The Use of Prayer, and the Work of the Holy Spirit Therein

In chapter 1, Owen reasserts the duty of prayer, narrows his subject to the gracious operation of the Holy Spirit in prayer, and argues for the significant relevance of the topic. He observes that the great animosity between different groups on the issue of prayer arises from the fact that prayer is the hinge on which all other differences concerning worship depend. By looking in detail at two passages of Scripture, Owen evinces "that there is promised and actually granted a special work of the Spirit of God in the prayers or praises of believers under the New Testament."

Chapter 2: Zechariah 12:10 Opened and Vindicated

Zechariah 12:10 is the passage upon which Owen's treatise is built. The manner of the fulfillment of what is promised—namely, "the Spirit of grace and supplications"—is expressed by "I will pour out." The pouring out of God's Spirit will be plentiful in the days of the gospel. The promise is addressed to the whole church. The Spirit is efficiently the Spirit of supplication in two ways. One, "by working gracious inclinations and dispositions in us unto this duty." Two, "by giving a gracious ability for the discharge of it in a due manner." For Owen, Zechariah 12:10, properly understood, proves *"that God has promised under the New Testament to give unto believers, in a plentiful manner or measure, the Spirit of grace and of supplications, or his own Holy Spirit, enabling them to pray according to his mind and will."* Next, Owen turns his attention to the witness of the New Testament.

Chapter 3: Galatians 4:6 Opened and Vindicated

Galatians 4:6 reports the fulfillment of the Old Testament promise and expresses the nature of the Spirit's work in prayer. Believers are the subjects of the bestowal of the Spirit's gift, which is the enabling of adopted sons and daughters to act like just that, children of God. What Owen claims from this passage is this: The Spirit "does actually incline, dispose, and enable them to cry 'Abba, Father,' or to call upon God in prayer as their Father by Jesus Christ." Having exegetically underpinned the reality of the Spirit's role in legitimate prayer, Owen turns to a detailed exposition of the nature of the Spirit's work.

Chapter 4: The Nature of Prayer

In chapter 4, Owen outlines human deficiency with regard to the practice of prayer, explaining Romans 8:26. He begins with a definition of prayer, which he articulates as "a gift, ability, or spiritual faculty of exercising faith, love, reverence, fear, delight, and other graces, in a way of vocal requests, supplications, and praises unto God." The fact is, the Spirit supplies and furnishes the mind with what ought to be prayed for in general and in particular. Moreover, without the special aid of the Holy Spirit, none of us knows what to properly pray for. We do not have any accurate estimation of what we need, no conception of the promises of God, which are the measure of prayer, no grasp of the end, goal, or purpose of prayer. The Spirit must supply both the matter and the manner of prayer.

Chapter 5: The Work of the Holy Spirit as to the Matter of Prayer

Owen describes the Spirit's resource of the matter of prayer in chapter 5. In short, "he alone does, and he alone is able to give us such an understanding of our own wants as that we may be able to make our thoughts about them known unto God in prayer and supplication." According to Owen, the principal matter concerns faith and unbelief. Human beings have no conception of either the deprivation of their nature or the grace of God apart from the work of the Spirit. Regarding humanity's perception of this deprivation of nature and the grace of God, Owen memorably states, "Nature is blind, and cannot see them; it is proud, and will not own them; stupid, and is senseless of them." The Spirit acquaints us not only with an impression of our needs but also with the grace and mercy prepared in the promises of God for our relief. These are the measure of prayer, the boundaries within which we pray. Owen argues, "We must pray with our understanding, that is, understand what we pray for. And these things are no other but what God has promised, which if we are not regulated by in our supplications, we ask amiss." Finally, the Spirit supplies the end of prayer. In other words, he guides and directs believers to petition from the right motivations and for proper purposes—namely, the glory of God and the improvement of holiness. In sum, the Spirit teaches believers what to pray for as they ought by furnishing and filling their minds with the matter of prayer.

Chapter 6: The Due Manner of Prayer, Wherein It Does Consist

After supplying the matter of prayer, the Spirit works the manner of prayer in the believer. This consists in the realm of the will and affections. The two are inseparable, for prayer by definition is the obedient acting of the whole soul toward God. The Spirit again does what individuals are unable to do themselves. He conforms the will and works affection in believers suitable for what they are praying about; therefore, he is the fountain of inexpressible fervency and delight. Delight in God as the object of prayer consists in three main things. First, the sight or prospect of God on his throne of grace, ready through Jesus Christ to dispense mercy to supplicant sinners. Second, a sense of God's relation unto us as Father. Third, the boldness and confidence that we have in our access to God in the act of prayer. Delight also flows from a focus on Christ, our access to the Father, the only way and means of our acceptance with God. The Spirit is as much behind how the Christian prays as he is the source of the content of those prayers.

Chapter 7: The Nature of Prayer in General, with
Respect unto Forms of Prayer and Vocal Prayer

Chapter 7 concludes Owen's section on the nature of prayer with a discussion of Ephesians 6:18. Here, Paul does not reference praying by an extraordinary or miraculous gift; rather, praying in the Spirit is the constant duty of all believers, which also illegitimates set forms of prayer. Answering the question "how they are enabled to pray in whose minds the Holy Ghost does thus work as a Spirit of grace and supplication" speaks to both of these faulty notions of prayer. Owen answers the question in brief this way: "Those who are thus affected by him do never want a gracious ability of making their addresses unto God in vocal prayer, so far as is needful unto them in their circumstances, callings, states, and conditions." As a result, set forms are absolutely unnecessary for the believer. And as for the argument that set forms benefit the unregenerate, Owen has another answer: Those unregenerate persons who are given over to sin cry out only when they are in distress. For these people, set forms serve like a charm. Others who attend to prayer out of duty, if their desire becomes sincere, would be hindered by set forms. In all cases, "it cannot be denied but that the constant and unvaried use of set forms of prayer may become a great occasion of quenching the Spirit, and hindering all progress or growth in gifts or graces," just as "those who will never enter the water but with flags or bladders under them will scarce ever learn to swim." Owen will return to prescribed prayer forms in the final chapter of his treatise, but his flow of argument at this point moves from the reality and nature of true prayer to the resulting duties.

Chapter 8: The Duty of External Prayer by Virtue of
a Spiritual Gift Explained and Vindicated

Having expressed the internal, spiritual nature of the duty already, and the exercise of the Spirit's grace therein, Owen transitions to prayer's external performance in chapter 8. His point is this:

> There is a *spiritual ability given unto men by the Holy Ghost, whereby they are enabled to express the matter of prayer, as taught and revealed in the manner before described, in words fitted and suited to lead on their own minds and the minds of others unto a holy communion in the duty, to the honor of God and their own edification.*

So even the words prayed are from the Spirit and therefore are unprescribed. The argument proceeds this way: All people are obligated to pray as they are able, according to their condition, relations, occasion, and duty. All examples of prayer in Scripture are unprescribed. Every command in Scripture to pray is according to one's abilities. And ability includes the conscientious, diligent use of all means—involving the searching of both the heart and the Scriptures—which God has ordained to improve prayer. Abilities also include natural talents of invention, memory, and elocution. Yet external prayer is a gift. Words and expression are an adjunct of the internal gift discussed thus far in Owen's treatise.

Chapter 9: Duties Inferred from the Preceding Discourse

The expression of prayer is a gift inseparable from the internal work of the Spirit. Owen, however, combats the claim that everyone with the grace therefore has the gift, and vice versa. It is true that "all those in whom the Spirit of God does graciously act faith, love, delight, desire, in a way of prayer unto God, have an ability from him to express themselves in vocal prayer." Though it does not follow that everyone who appears to have the gift also has the grace. For instance, the unregenerate can publicly pray unto the edification of others. Interestingly, Owen does explicitly allow for unvocal prayer, but insists that even this must still be expressed in words in the mind. The significance of this point becomes apparent in chapter 10. Like all other spiritual duties, we need the Spirit in prayer's faithful completion, otherwise nothing would exist to separate the regenerate and unregenerate exercise of it. Further, the effects of prayer are so great that it would be impious not to attribute it to God. Prayer is a gift from God from beginning to end.

The duties that follow from Owen's conception of prayer add up to glorifying God for the great privilege the Spirit of grace and supplication brings and its diligent use. Owen describes the appropriate exercise of prayer and divides the topic into three parts. First, it is our duty to use the gift to the inestimable advantage for our own souls. Second, the duty includes our natural faculties. Owen states that prayer "is freely bestowed, but it is carefully to be preserved. It is a gospel talent given to be traded with, and thereby to be increased." This includes constant consideration and observation of ourselves and the Scripture, which serves as a mirror, presenting both what we are and what we ought to be. It entails meditation on God's glorious excellencies and the mediation and intercession of Christ. It requires frequency in exercise and constant fervency and intention of mind and spirit. Third, it is our duty to use prayer unto the ends for which it is bestowed by God. Prayer is a means to stir up faith, love, delight, joy, and the like, as well as to benefit others, specifically our families, churches, and societies. With this exhortation to faithfulness in the duties of prayer, Owen concludes his unified argument regarding the Spirit's role in prayer to focus on two parentheses, mental and prescribed forms of prayer.

Chapter 10: Of Mental Prayer as Pretended
Unto by Some in the Church of Rome

Owen sets his sights in chapter 10 pointedly on mental prayer as it exists in the Church of Rome. Cressy's definition of mental prayer, in *The*

Church-History of Brittany, the work that inspired Owen's treatise, is "pure spiritual prayer, or a quiet repose of contemplation; that which excludes all images of the fancy, and in time all perceptible actuations of the understanding, and is exercised in signal elevations of the will, without any force at all, yet with admirable efficacy." It requires "an entire calmness and even death of the passions, a perfect purity in the spiritual affections of the will, and an entire abstraction from all creatures."[3] In opposition to this concept, Owen insists on the use of the intellect. The experience of true prayer is through the faculties of the soul; it does not circumvent them. It is not as if we can pray in our "will and its affections without any actings of the mind or understanding." Further, so-called mental prayer is impossible to verify, given that it brings no benefit or edification to the church or any member of it. Owen warns, "The use of words is necessary in this duty, from the nature of the duty itself, the command of God, and the edification of the church." Whatever mental prayer is, in Owen's estimation, it is not true prayer.

Chapter 11: Prescribed Forms of Prayer Examined

In his final chapter, Owen handles prescribed forms of prayer, attending to their origin, supposed advantages, and lawfulness. The origin of prescribed forms is clearly human, for the Spirit is not promised to assist in their composition. As to the claimed advantages, for those who have the gift of free prayer by the Spirit, there is none. For those with a comparably low ability to pray for themselves, there is also no benefit, for set forms will only keep them from maturing. For those who do not yet have a desire to pray, other means are at their disposal, including the sincere consideration of themselves and Scripture and the ordinary means of grace. For those that claim personal experience of spiritual advantage, Owen refrains from disputing this, but points rather to God's gracious blessing of his children, even when they fail to order everything according to his word. As to the lawfulness of prescribed forms, Owen comes short of condemning them as unlawful in themselves, at which point he only alludes to the regulative principle of worship but does not pursue it. Owen leaves room for the lawful private use of prescribed forms, though he is suspicious of the benefit even in this setting, while he would prefer their exclusion from public worship.

3 Serenus Cressy, *The Church-History of Brittany, or England, from the Beginning of Christianity to the Norman Conquest* (Rouen, 1668), preface, paras. 42–43; quoted in Owen.

The Holy Spirit as a Comforter (1693)

In his treatise *The Holy Spirit as a Comforter*, Owen handles the signally Puritan topic of assurance. Owen is concerned to offer the believer the comfort in life and in death that can come only from the Spirit himself. At the same time, he elevates ordinary believers through his discussion of the anointing of the Spirit, a conspicuously Protestant motif. This treatise perhaps also best illustrates, in this volume, Owen as expositor of Scripture, as he carefully exegetes what Scripture means in reference to the Spirit as unction, seal, and earnest.

Chapter 1: The Holy Ghost the Comforter of the Church by Way of Office

Owen's work on the Holy Spirit as comforter proceeds in three stages. He first defines the office, then discusses its discharge, and then follows with a description of its effects.

Chapter 1 handles the office, working through the four things that constitute any office. First, there is the trust. The Spirit has the comfort, consolation, and support of believers entrusted to him. Christ's ascension did not mean that he stopped loving and caring for his disciples. He had to go to make intercession for them, which was part of his work that remained toward God. The other part of his remaining work respects the church and individual believers, which he gave to the Spirit. While the Spirit did not commence being comforter when Jesus left, he was at that time promised to be the comforter. Regenerate people were unaware of his ministry or dispensation beforehand. So Christ is still comforter, but by his Spirit.

A mission, name, and work are the three other elements constituting an office. The Spirit's special mission consists of his commissioning to be comforter by the Father and Son. His special name is Paraclete, found first in John 14:16. It is not distinctive with respect to his person, but denominative with respect to his work, used by Jesus as a proper name with respect to his office. The concept of comforter is principally ascribed to the Spirit in this name. The whole context of the promise in John 14–16 verifies this. As our "advocate," as the word is often rendered, he offers consolation—not, of course, as an advocate with God, but for the church in, with, and against the world. The Spirit serves as our advocate by undertaking our protection and defense. And he does so in three primary ways. First, by suggesting and supplying pleas and arguments to witnesses resulting in the conviction of their opponents. Second, in and by his communication of spiritual gifts, both extraordinary and ordinary, with their effects visible to the world. Third, by the internal efficacy of the preached word—namely, conviction, which effects either belief or rejection. The final aspect of an office is a special work. For the Spirit as comforter, this is "to support, cherish, relieve, and comfort the church, in all trials and distresses." This will be more fully expressed in Owen's discussion of particular effects of the office.

Chapter 2: General Adjuncts or Properties of the Office of a Comforter, as Exercised by the Holy Spirit

In chapter 2, Owen treats the discharge of this office, which includes four primary features. One of the properties of the office is infinite condescension. The Spirit's work as comforter is on behalf of men and women, individual human beings, sinful individuals at that. Another property is unspeakable love, as he works by tenderness and compassion. This is fitting given Trinitarian relations:

> In all the actings of the Holy Ghost toward us, and especially in this of his susception of an office on the behalf of the church, which is the foundation of them all, his love is principally to be considered, and that he chooses this way of acting and working toward us to express his peculiar, personal character, as he is the eternal love of the Father and the Son.

Benefits, gifts, or kindnesses bring comfort or consolation only if they proceed from love. And there was indeed infinite love in the acceptation of this office by the Spirit.[4] A third property is power, infinite power as the foundation for unshakable consolation. Only divine power can alleviate consciences and bring full assurance, driving away the disconsolations believers face. Only omnipotence can overcome the opposition from Satan. Finally, an unchangeable dispensation is a feature of the office of comforter. To whom the Spirit is given, he abides with forever, which is true both for individuals and the church unto the consummation of all things.

Chapter 3: Unto Whom the Holy Spirit Is Promised and Given as a Comforter; or the Object of His Acting in This Office

Chapters 3 and 4 transition to the effects of the Spirit's role as comforter with an assertion about whom the Spirit is given to and an explanation of his inhabitation of recipients. Chapter 3 argues that only believers are given the Spirit. Owen says it this way: "All his actings and effects as a comforter

---

4   For a discussion and critique of this Augustinian conception of the Spirit, see Colin Gunton, *Theology through the Theologians: Selected Essays, 1972–1995* (London: T&T Clark, 2003), chap. 7.

are confined unto them that believe, and do all suppose saving faith as ante-cedent unto them." This is not the first saving work, however. Regeneration precedes it, for "he comforts none but those whom he has before sanctified."

Chapter 4: Inhabitation of the Spirit the First Thing Promised

Inhabitation, or indwelling, is the great foundational privilege upon which all others depend. Owen carefully distinguishes what the indwelling of the Spirit is from what it is not. This inhabitation is not the Spirit's essential omnipresence, or an expression of the cause for the effect, or a hypostatic union. Neither is it a union or relation immediately between the Spirit and believers, who are related in such a way to Christ. Rather, it is the actual person of the Holy Spirit who is promised to believers. The fact that he inhabits so many at one time illustriously demonstrates his eternal glory. This indwell-ing is the spring of his gracious operations in us; it is "the hidden spring and cause of that inexpressible distance and difference that is between believers and the rest of the world." The person of the Spirit inhabits believers as the promised comforter.

Chapter 5: Particular Actings of the Holy Spirit as a Comforter

The final three chapters of Owen's treatise describe three particular ways the Spirit comforts—as an unction, a seal, and an earnest. The Spirit as unc-tion, or the Spirit's anointing, is the first in natural order. Owen constructs a biblical argument for what this anointing consists in, contrasting this with arguments that the anointing is the doctrine of the gospel, the testimony of the Spirit to the truth of the gospel, or the chrism (anointing in the rites of baptism, confirmation, and holy orders) and extreme unction (anointing the sick and dying) of the Church of Rome. Owen provides a biblical theology of anointing, beginning with the claim that all things dedicated or consecrated in the Old Testament were anointed with oil. All such types were fulfilled in Jesus Christ, the anointed one, whose anointing was with the Spirit. The unction of Christ consisted in the full communication of the Spirit in all his graces and gifts needed in Christ's human nature and for his work. Though this was essentially a single work, it was carried out, of course, in degrees. Believers have their unction immediately from Christ, consisting in the com-munication of the Spirit. It is like Christ's, but to an inferior degree. The Spirit's "first, peculiar, special effect as an unction"—and here Owen references his previous treatises *The Reason of Faith* and *Causes, Ways, and Means*—"is his teaching of us the truths and mysteries of the gospel by saving illumination." This anointing also dedicates believers as kings and priests, a dedication unto

God, resulting in special privilege. From 1 John 2:20, 27, Owen concludes that the principal benefit of the Spirit as unction is the stability of belief. This anointing is "an effectual means of their preservation, when a trial of their stability in the truth shall befall them." Further, "nothing will give stability in all seasons but the wisdom and knowledge which are the effects of this teaching," teaching which includes "all things," or the whole life of faith, including joy and consolation.

Chapter 6: The Spirit a Seal, and How

Owen is not entirely satisfied with comparisons to human sealing in attempting to understand the Spirit as a seal. For example, discussions of the Spirit putting forth his power in the preservation of believers, as in something highly valuable being sealed up for safety and inviolability, fall short of the rich meaning of sealing. Rather, Owen compares the sealing of believers with the sealing of Christ, which demonstrated God's owning of him, his approbation of him, and manifested that God the Father would take care of Christ and preserve him. He summarizes,

> This sealing of the Son is the communication of the Holy Spirit in all fullness unto him, authorizing him unto, and acting his divine power in, all the acts and duties of his office, so as to evidence the presence of God with him, and his approbation of him, as the only person that was to distribute the spiritual food of their souls unto men.

Owen then defines the Spirit's sealing of believers as God's "gracious communication of the Holy Ghost unto them, so to act his divine power in them as to enable them unto all the duties of their holy calling, evidencing them to be accepted with him both unto themselves and others, and asserting their preservation unto eternal salvation." In both the case of Christ and believers, the sealing is the communication of the Spirit unto them, and the effects are the gracious operations of the Spirit, enabling them to live according to their radical callings. For believers specifically, God, by the sealing of the Spirit, gives testimony that they are his, assurance of that relationship, and evidence to the world, while also protecting them unto final consummation.

Chapter 7: The Spirit an Earnest, and How

When discussing the Spirit as an earnest, Owen is again unsatisfied with human illustrations, this time with transactional language. The Spirit is really neither a pledge or collateral, nor an earnest or down payment, as if God is somehow in anyone's debt or as if a business deal has been struck. Giving security to something future is as far as the metaphor goes. In God's case, he is unilaterally bestowing grace. Believers are given a foretaste of the future now by the Holy Spirit, who also guarantees that future. The Spirit is an "earnest," Owen's preferred term, of our inheritance, which, under forfeiture, needed to be purchased for us by Christ. "The way whereby we come to have an interest in Christ, and thereby a right unto the inheritance, is by the participation of the Spirit of Christ," argues Owen. By communication of the Spirit, we are made joint heirs with Christ; therefore, he is the earnest of our inheritance. He is the firstfruits of the full harvest to come, a spiritual and eternal redemption. In Owen's estimation, nothing could be more comforting.

A Discourse of Spiritual Gifts (1693)

In Owen's analysis of spiritual gifts, he has two primary aims. First, to explain what spiritual gifts are, distinguishing the ordinary from the extraordinary gifts, the latter being no longer operative. And second, to elevate the ordinary gifts as the God-given, sufficient means for building the church. These purposes arose out of the enthusiasm found in the seventeenth-century religious sects, as well as the prevalent charismatic manifestations. They also explain the rise of the Roman Catholic Church, for it was the neglect of the ordinary gifts that resulted in that sacramental institution. And it was the misguided grasping at the extraordinary gifts that occasioned superstition and endless miracle accounts there. As Owen completes his objectives, he protects the balance between the inward and outward call to ministry and insists that the ministry of the gospel cannot be done in human power.

Chapter 1: Spiritual Gifts, Their Names and Significations

Owen's examination of spiritual gifts consists of brief discussions of their name and nature, followed by a treatment of their distribution as both extraordinary and ordinary, which forms the body of the treatise. The definition Owen provides is this: spiritual gifts "are free and undeserved effects of divine bounty." From the human perspective, they are spiritual powers aimed at a certain end. But most basically, they are undeserved gifts. To get at the nature of spiritual gifts, Owen enumerates the similarities and differences with saving graces. The commonalities are three. First, both spiritual gifts and saving graces are purchased by Christ for his church. Christ distributes gifts as the only legitimate weapons of the warfare that consists in the establishing and edifying of the church. Second, they share the same immediate efficient cause. They both are wrought by the power of the Holy Spirit. Third, they both are designed unto the good, benefit, ornament, and glory of the church. Grace gives the church an invisible life; gifts give it a visible profession. In Owen's words, "That profession which renders a church visible according to the mind of Christ, is the orderly exercise of the spiritual gifts bestowed on it, in a conversation evidencing the invisible principle of saving grace."

Chapter 2: Differences between Spiritual Gifts and Saving Grace
The differences between spiritual gifts and saving graces are seven. Graces are the fruit of the Spirit; gifts are the effects of his operation. Graces proceed from electing love, gifts from temporary election. Graces are the essential effects of the covenant; gifts are part of the outward administration. Graces proceed from the priestly office of Christ, gifts from his kingly office. Graces cannot be lost, though they can decay, while gifts can be taken away. Graces are bestowed primarily for the individual's good, gifts for the benefit of others. Principally, graces possess the whole soul, whereas gifts are present in the mind or theoretical intellect, meaning that while grace necessarily transforms the soul and its presence guarantees that one belongs to Christ, the same cannot be said of gifts. Here Owen protects the distinction between the invisible and visible church and makes sense of false professors of Christianity who appear to be saved.

Chapter 3: Of Gifts and Offices Extraordinary; and First of Offices
Transitioning to extraordinary spiritual gifts, Owen explains first extraordinary offices, then the gifts themselves and their origin, duration, use, and end. Offices in general exist whenever there is power and a duty to be performed by it. Extraordinary offices include also an extraordinary call and the bestowal of extraordinary power. The three extraordinary offices are apostle, evangelist, and prophet. Owen explains the special calling and exceptional power attached to each office.

Chapter 4: Of Extraordinary Spiritual Gifts
The extraordinary gifts themselves are listed in 1 Corinthians 12:4–11. At the outset of the discussion of this list, Owen distinguishes between gifts that exceed the whole power and faculties of humanity, including miracles and healings, and endowments and improvements of the faculties of the minds of men, such as wisdom, knowledge, and utterance. This distinction is significant because the latter gifts differ only in degree from the ordinary gifts continually dispensed throughout the history of the church. The first

gift in Paul's list is word of wisdom. Owen understands this as wisdom itself, specifically the wisdom promised to the apostles in the face of adversaries. It also includes special wisdom for the management of gospel truths for the edification of the church. Word of knowledge is "such a peculiar and special insight into the mysteries of the gospel, as whereby those in whom it was were enabled to teach and instruct others." This was initially needed in the church by immediate revelation. Faith, often understood in the context of troubles and trials or suffering, is "a peculiar confidence, boldness, and assurance of mind in the profession of the gospel and the administration of its ordinances." Gifts of healing are referenced in the plural because of their free communication unto many persons. They are distinct from miracles for several reasons. They are a sign unto believers, rather than unbelievers. There is a peculiar goodness and relief toward mankind in them. The kindness, love, and compassion demonstrated in them results in appreciation and obedience flowing from gratitude. Miracles are an immediate effect of divine power exceeding all created abilities. In the context of the early church, Owen claims, "this gift of miracles was exceedingly useful, and necessary unto the propagation of the gospel, the vindication of the truth, and the establishment of them that did believe." Prophecy refers to both the faculty of prediction and the ability to declare the mind of God from the word by the special and immediate revelation of the Holy Spirit. Discerning of spirits was the ability to judge between the Spirit's work and Satan's plagiarized counterfeits. Finally, in reference to tongues and their interpretation, Owen asserts that tongues were sometimes understood by the speakers and the church and at other times not. While tongues were effectual for the propagation of the gospel to unbelievers, interpretation was added that the church might be edified by the gift.

Chapter 5: Of the Origin, Duration, Use, and
End of Extraordinary Spiritual Gifts

The extraordinary gifts and extraordinary offices ended together, coinciding with the establishment of the early church. However, Owen does not rule out the possibility of God continuing to work miraculously. He says, "It is not unlikely but that God might on some occasions, for a longer season, put forth his power in some miraculous operations, and so he yet may do, and perhaps does sometimes." When the extraordinary gifts were operative, they were the glory, honor, and beauty of the church. They were aimed at setting up, planting, advancing, and propagating the kingdom of Christ in the establishment of the church. Those chosen and called for this purpose were enabled by these gifts. Such persons were of course insufficient in themselves, as God purposed the gospel to suffer every disadvantage humanly speaking. It was by the gifts that preaching was rendered effectual. Miracles filled the world with an apprehension of the divine power accompanying the gospel and its preachers. The extraordinary spiritual gifts left no doubt that Christ and the message of his apostles were divine revelation.

Chapter 6: Of Ordinary Gifts of the Spirit

Owen initiates his discussion of the ordinary gifts of the Spirit in the context of the continuation of the ministry of the church. The designation of ordinary must not be understood as in any way pejorative or diminishing. Ordinary simply separates these gifts from the miraculous gifts. They differ only in degree from what the extraordinary office holders possessed. The term also designates the continued supply of gifts throughout the continuation of the ordinary state of the church. Before addressing the gifts themselves, Owen dissects the ministry itself. The ministry is itself Christ's gift to the church, acquired by his humiliation and death, distributed when he ascended unto his exaltation, and consisting in spiritual gifts. The ministerial office continues as the spiritual gifts are continually dispensed and recognized by the church in its calling of ministers. The aim of the ministry is the edification of the church, through protection and the service of the word. The gifts of the Spirit enable ministers to discharge their responsibilities.

Chapter 7: Of Spiritual Gifts Enabling the Ministry to the Exercise and Discharge of Their Trust and Office

The ordinary spiritual gifts are much more than mere natural abilities, and they are antecedently necessary to legitimate a minister. In other words, they come from God, and therefore the outward call of the church alone, though essential, is insufficient. Owen's main claim is this:

> There is a special dispensation and work of the Holy Ghost in providing able ministers of the New Testament for the edification of the church, wherein the continuance of the ministry and being of the church, as to its outward order, does depend; and that herein he does exert his power and exercise his authority in the communication of spiritual gifts unto men, without a participation whereof no man has de jure, any lot or portion in this ministration.

Owen supports this claim with an argument of eight propositions:

1. Christ has promised to be present with his church.
2. This promised presence is by his Spirit.
3. It is secured by an everlasting, unchangeable covenant.
4. The gospel is called the ministration of the Spirit and ministers of it the ministers of the Spirit.
5. The end for which the Spirit is promised is the preservation of the church in the world.
6. The communication of gifts is the means to this end.
7. As such, they are indispensable for gospel administrations.
8. And all of this is demonstrably true in the experience of the church in any age.

But what of the actual ordinary gifts of the Spirit?

Chapter 8: Of the Gifts of the Spirit with Respect
unto Doctrine, Worship, and Rule

Owen concludes his treatise with a taxonomy of ministerial gifts. There are three categories, gifts that pertain to the doctrine, worship, and rule of the church.

First, gifts concerning doctrine help accomplish the primary duty of the ministry—namely, the dispensation of the doctrine of the gospel to the church through preaching. The Spirit gives wisdom, knowledge, or understanding—all designations of the same concept—of the mysteries of the gospel. These can be distinguished, but all speak to acquaintance with and comprehension of doctrine necessary for preaching. In short, the Spirit provides

> such a comprehension of the scope and end of the Scripture, of the reve-
> lation of God therein, such an acquaintance with the systems of particular
> doctrinal truths, in their rise, tendency, and use, such a habit of mind in
> judging of spiritual things, and comparing them one with another, such a
> distinct insight into the springs and course of the mystery of the love, grace,
> and will of God in Christ, as enables them in whom it is to declare the
> counsel of God, to make known the way of life, of faith and obedience unto
> others, and to instruct them in their whole duty to God and man thereon.

The Spirit also gives skill in dividing the word properly, in culling doctrines from the biblical text and applying them. To do this aright, the minister must be well acquainted with his flock and aware of how God's grace operates on minds and hearts, the nature of temptation and the obstacles to faith and obedience, and spiritual diseases and remedies. The last gift concerning preaching is the gift of utterance. Far from natural speaking ability, the gift of utterance is freedom in the declaration of truth—holy confidence, authority, and gravity in expression.

The remaining ministerial gifts are those touching worship and the rule of the church. The gifts concerning worship can be summarized under the heading "prayer," which includes confession, supplication, thanks, and praise. Owen does not treat this in any length but rather points the reader to his *The Work of the Holy Spirit in Prayer*. Gifts concerning the rule of the church are spiritual, with nothing in common with the administration of the powers of the world. They consist in the "humble, holy, spiritual application of the word of God or rules of the gospel" to the church.

The ministry gifts that fall into these three categories are dispensed to church members at large as well. When gifts are attached to duties rather than offices, as in the case of ministers, they are to be exercised in the building up of the body. The gifts are not communicated by extraordinary infusion. They are not attainable in people's diligence alone. But means are ordinarily used in their realization and growth. The gifts ought to be prepared for through the inculcation of humility, meekness, and teachability. They ought to be prayed for and faithfully exercised when granted. Ministry, true ministry, the kind that does in fact build the church and further the cause of the gospel, cannot be done in human power.

A DISCOURSE OF THE WORK OF THE HOLY SPIRIT IN PRAYER

*With a Brief Inquiry into
the Nature and Use of Mental
Prayer and Forms.*

By John Owen, D.D.

———

London, Printed for Nathaniel Ponder,
at the Sign of the Peacock,
in the Poultry, near the Church:
1682

The Work of the Holy Spirit in Prayer
Contents

Preface to the Reader

IT IS ALTOGETHER NEEDLESS to premise anything in this place concerning the necessity, benefit, and use of prayer in general. All men will readily acknowledge that as without it there can be no religion at all, so the life and exercise of all religion does principally consist therein. Wherefore, that way and profession in religion which gives the best directions for it, with the most effectual motives unto it, and most abounds in its observance, has therein the advantage of all others. Hence also it follows, that as all errors which either pervert its nature or countenance a neglect of a due attendance unto it are pernicious in religion; so differences in opinion, and disputes about any of its vital concerns, cannot but be dangerous and of evil consequence. For on each hand these pretend unto an immediate regulation of Christian practice in a matter of the highest importance unto the glory of God and the salvation of the souls of men. Whereas, therefore, there is nothing more requisite in our religion than that true apprehensions of its nature and use be preserved in the minds of men, the declaration and defense of them, when they are opposed or unduly traduced,[1] is not only justifiable but necessary also.

This is the design of the ensuing discourse. There is in the Scripture a promise of the Holy Ghost to be given unto the church as "a Spirit of grace and of supplications."[2] As such, also, there are particular operations ascribed unto him. Mention is likewise frequently made of the aids and assistances which he affords unto believers in and unto their prayers. Hence, they are said to "pray always with all prayer and supplication in the Spirit."[3] Of the want of these aids and assistances to enable them to pray according to the mind of God some do profess that they have experience, as also of their efficacy unto

---

1 I.e., shamed or blamed falsely.
2 Zech. 12:10.
3 Eph. 6:18.

that end when they are received. Accordingly, these regulate themselves in this whole duty in the expectation or improvement of them. And there are those who, being accommodated with other aids of another nature, to the same purpose, which they esteem sufficient for them, do look on the former profession and plea of an ability to pray by the aids and assistances of the Holy Spirit to be a mere empty pretense.

And in the management of these different apprehensions, those at variance seem to be almost barbarians one to another, the one being not able to understand what the other do vehemently affirm. For they are determined in their minds, not merely by notions of truth and falsehood, but by the experience which they have of the things themselves, a sense and understanding whereof they can by no means communicate unto one another. For whereas spiritual experience of truth is above all other demonstrations unto them that do enjoy it, so it cannot be made an argument for the enlightening and conviction of others. Hence those who plead for prayer by virtue of supplies of gifts and grace from the Holy Spirit do admire that the use or necessity of them herein should be contradicted. Nor can they understand what they intend who seem to deny that it is every man's duty, in all his circumstances, to pray as well as he can, and to make use in his so doing of the assistance of the Spirit of God. And by "prayer" they mean that which the most eminent and only proper signification of the word does denote, namely, that which is vocal. Some, on the other side, are so far from the understanding of these things, or a conviction of their reality, that with the highest confidence they despise and reproach the pretense of them. To "pray in the Spirit" is used as a notable expression of scorn, the thing signified being esteemed fond and contemptible.

Moreover, in such cases as this, men are apt to run into excesses in things and ways which they judge expedient, either to countenance their own opinions or to depress and decry those of them from whom they differ. And no instances can be given in this kind of greater extravagances than in that under consideration. For hence it is that some do ascribe the origin of free prayer among us, by the assistance of the Spirit of God, unto an invention of the Jesuits, which is no doubt to make them the authors of the Bible. And others do avow that all forms of prayer used among us in public worship are mere traductions[4] from the Roman Breviaries and Missal.[5] But these things will be afterward spoken unto. They

---

4   I.e., acts of defamation or slander.
5   Breviaries were books of the Latin liturgical rites of the Roman Catholic Church. The Missal was the book containing the prescribed prayers, chants, and instructions for the Catholic celebration of the Mass.

are here mentioned only to evince[6] the use of a sedate[7] inquiry into the truth or the mind of God in this matter, which is the design of the ensuing discourse.

EXPERIENCE REGULATED BY SCRIPTURE

That which should principally guide us in the management of this inquiry is, that it be done unto spiritual advantage and edification, without strife or contention. Now, this cannot be without a diligent and constant attendance unto the two sole rules of judgment herein, namely, Scripture revelation and the experience of them that do believe. For although the latter is to be regulated by the former, yet where it is so, it is a safe rule unto them in whom it is. And in this case, as in water, face answers unto face, so do Scripture revelation and spiritual experience unto one another. All other reasonings, from customs, traditions, and feigned consequences, are here of no use. The inquiries before us are concerning the nature of the work of the Holy Spirit in the aids and assistances which he gives unto believers in and unto their prayers, according unto the mind of God, as also what are the effects and fruits of that work of his, or what are the spiritual abilities which are communicated unto them thereby. Antecedently hereunto it should be inquired whether indeed there be any such thing or not, or whether they are only vainly pretended unto by some that are deceived. But the determination hereof depending absolutely on the foregoing inquiries, it may be handled jointly with them, and needs no distinct consideration. He that would not deceive nor be deceived in his inquiry after these things must diligently attend unto the two forementioned rules of Scripture testimony and experience. Other safe guides he has none. Yet will it also be granted that from the light of nature, from whence[8] this duty springs, wherein it is founded, from whence as unto its essence it cannot vary, as also from generally received principles of religion suited thereunto,[9] with the uncorrupted practice of the church of God in former ages, much direction may be given unto the understanding of those testimonies and examination of that experience.

Wherefore, the foundation of the whole ensuing discourse is laid in the consideration and exposition of some of those texts of Scripture wherein these things are expressly revealed and proposed unto us, for to insist on them all were endless. This we principally labor in, as that whereby not only must the controversy be finally determined, but the persons that manage it

---

6 I.e., provide evidence for.
7 I.e., calm.
8 I.e., where.
9 I.e., in order for this to occur.

be eternally judged. What is added concerning the experience of them that do believe the truth herein claims no more of argument unto them that have it not than it has evidence of proceeding from and being suited unto those divine testimonies. But whereas the things that belong unto it are of great moment unto them who do enjoy it, as containing the principal acts, ways, and means of our intercourse and communion with God by Christ Jesus, they are here somewhat at large, on all occasions, insisted on, for the edification of those whose concern lies only in the practice of the duty itself. Unless, therefore, it can be proved that the testimonies of the Scripture produced and insisted on do not contain that sense and understanding which the words do determinately express, for that only is pleaded, or that some have not an experience of the truth and power of that sense of them, enabling them to live unto God in this duty according to it, all other contests about this matter are vain and useless.

But yet there is no such work of the Holy Spirit pleaded herein as should be absolutely inconsistent with or condemnatory of all those outward aids of prayer by set composed forms which are almost everywhere made use of. For the device being ancient, and in some degree or measure received generally in the Christian world, though a no less general apostasy in many things from the rule of truth at the same time, in the same persons and places, cannot be denied, I shall not judge of what advantage it may be or has been unto the souls of men, nor what acceptance they have found therein, where it is not too much abused. The substance of what we plead from Scripture and experience is only this, that whereas *God has graciously promised his Holy Spirit, as a Spirit of grace and supplications, unto them that do believe, enabling them to pray according to his mind and will, in all the circumstances and capacities wherein they are, or which they may be called unto, it is the duty of them who are enlightened with the truth hereof to expect those promised aids and assistances in and unto their prayers, and to pray according to the ability which they receive thereby.*[10] To deny this to be their duty, or to deprive them of their liberty to discharge it on all occasions, rises up in direct opposition unto the divine instruction of the sacred word.

GENERAL PRINCIPLES

But, moreover, as was before intimated, there are some generally allowed principles, which, though not always duly considered, yet cannot at any time

10 Italics in this treatise are in the original.

be modestly denied, that give direction toward the right performance of our duty herein. And they are these that follow.

1. It is the duty of every man to pray for himself. The light of nature, multiplied divine commands, with our necessary dependence on God and subjection unto him, give life and light unto this principle. To own a Divine Being is to own that which is to be prayed unto, and that it is our duty so to do.

2. It is the duty of some, by virtue of natural relation or of office, to pray with and for others also. So is it the duty of parents and masters of families to pray with and for their children and households. This also derives from those great principles of natural light that God is to be worshiped in all societies of his own erection, and that those in the relations mentioned are obliged to seek the chiefest good of them that are committed unto their care; and so is it frequently enjoined in the Scripture. In like manner, it is the duty of ministers to pray with and for their flocks, by virtue of special institution. These things cannot be, nor, so far as I know of are, questioned by any; but practically the most of men live in an open neglect of their duty herein. Were this but diligently attended unto, from the first instance of natural and moral relations unto the instituted offices of ministers and public teachers, we should have less contests about the nature and manner of praying than at present we have. It is holy practice that must reconcile differences in religion, or they will never be reconciled in this world.

3. Everyone who prays, either by himself and for himself, or with others and for them, is obliged, as unto all the uses, properties, and circumstances of prayer, to pray as well as he is able. For by the light of nature everyone is obliged in all instances to serve God with his best. The confirmation and exemplification hereof was one end of the institution of sacrifices under the Old Testament. For it was ordained in them that the chief and best of every thing was to be offered unto God. Neither the nature of God nor our own duty toward him will admit that we should expect any acceptance with him, unless our design be to serve him with the best that we have, both for matter and manner. So is the mind of God himself declared in the prophet:

"If ye offer the blind for sacrifice, is it not evil? And if ye offer the lame and the sick, is it not evil? [. . .] Ye brought that which was torn, and the lame, and the sick; should I accept this of your hand?" saith the Lord. "But cursed be the deceiver, which hath in his flock a male, and voweth, and sacrificeth unto the Lord a corrupt thing: for I am a great King, saith the Lord of hosts, and my name is dreadful among the heathen." (Mal. 1:8, 13–14)

4. In our reasonable service, the best wherewith[11] we can serve God consists in the intense, sincere actings of the faculties and affections of our minds, according unto their respective powers, through the use of the best assistances we can attain. And if we omit or forego, in any instance, the exercise of them according to the utmost of our present ability, we offer unto God the sick and the lame. If men can take it on themselves, in the sight of God, that the invention and use of set forms of prayer, and other the like outward modes of divine worship, are the best that he has endowed them with for his service, they are free from the force of this consideration.

5. There is no man but, in the use of the aids which God has prepared for that purpose, is able to pray according to the will of God, and as he is in duty obliged, whether he pray by himself and for himself, or with others and for them also. There is not by these means perfection attainable in the performance of any duty, neither can all attain the same measure and degree as unto the usefulness of prayer and manner of praying; but everyone may attain unto that wherein he shall be accepted with God, and according unto the duty whereunto he is obliged, whether personally or by virtue of any relation wherein he stands unto others. To suppose that God requires duties of men which they cannot perform in an acceptable manner, by virtue and in the use of those aids which he has prepared and promised unto that end, is to reflect dishonor on his goodness and wisdom in his commands. Wherefore, no man is obliged to pray, in any circumstances, by virtue of any relation or office, but he is able so to do according unto what is required of him; and what he is not able for he is not called unto.

6. We are expressly commanded to pray, but are nowhere commanded to make prayers for ourselves, much less for others. This is superadded,[12] for a supposed conveniency, unto the light of nature and Scripture institution.

7. There is assistance promised unto believers to enable them to pray according unto the will of God; there is no assistance promised to enable any to make prayers for others. The former part of this assertion is explained and proved in the ensuing discourse, and the latter cannot be disproved. And if it should be granted that the work of composing prayers for others is a good work, falling under the general aids of the Holy Spirit necessary unto every good work whatever, yet are not those aids of the same kind and nature with his actual assistances in and unto prayer as he is the Spirit of grace and supplications. For in the use of those assistances by grace and gifts, every man

11 I.e., by which.
12 I.e., increased in a compounding way.

that uses them does actually pray, nor are they otherwise to be used; but men do not pray in the making and composing forms of prayer, though they may do so in the reading of them afterward.

8. Whatever forms of prayer were given out unto the use of the church by divine authority and inspiration, as the Lord's Prayer and the psalms or prayers of David, they are to have their everlasting use therein, according unto what they were designed unto. And be their end and use what it will, they can give no more warranty for human compositions unto the same end, and the injunction of their use, than for other human writings to be added unto the Scripture.

SET FORMS OF PRAYER: THE BURDEN OF THE MISSAL

These and the like principles, which are evident in their own light and truth, will be of use to direct us in the argument in hand, so far as our present design is concerned therein. For it is the vindication of our own principles and practice that is principally designed, and not an opposition unto those of other men. Wherefore, as was before intimated, neither these principles nor the divine testimonies, which we shall more largely insist upon, are engaged to condemn all use of set forms of prayers as sinful in themselves, or absolutely unlawful, or such as so vitiate[13] the worship of God as to render it wholly unacceptable in them that choose so to worship him. For God will accept the persons of those who sincerely seek him, though, through invincible ignorance, they may mistake in sundry things as unto the way and manner of his worship. And how far, as unto particular instances of miscarriage, this rule may extend, he only knows, and of men, whatever they pretend, not one. And where any do worship God in Christ with an evidence of holy fear and sincerity, and walk in a conversation answerable unto the rule of the gospel, though they have manifold corruptions in the way of their worship, I shall never judge severely either of their present acceptance with God or of their future eternal condition. This is a safe rule with respect unto others; our own is, to attend with all diligence unto what God has revealed concerning his worship, and absolutely comply therewith, without which we can neither please him nor come to the enjoyment of him.

I do acknowledge, also, that the general prevalency of the use of set forms of prayer of human invention in Christian assemblies for many ages, more than any other argument that is urged for their necessity, requires a tenderness

13 I.e., impair.

in judgment as unto the whole nature of them, and the acceptance of their persons in the duty of prayer by whom they are used. Yet no consideration of this usage, seeing it is not warranted by the Scriptures, nor is of apostolic example, nor is countenanced by the practice of the primitive churches, ought to hinder us from discerning and judging of the evils and inconveniences that have ensued thereon,[14] nor from discovering how far they are unwarrantable as unto their imposition. And these evils may be here a little considered.

The beginnings of the introduction of the use of set forms of prayer of human composition into the worship of the church are altogether uncertain, but that the reception of them was progressive, by new additions from time to time, is known to all. For neither Rome nor the present Roman Missal were built in a day. In that and the Breviaries did the whole worship of the church issue, at least in these parts of the world. No man is so fond as to suppose that they were of one entire composition, the work of one age, of one man, or any assembly of men at the same time, unless they be so brutishly devout as to suppose that the Massbook was brought from heaven unto the pope by an angel, as the Alcoran[15] was to Mohammed. It is evident, indeed, that common people, at least of the communion of the papal Church, do believe it to be as much of a divine origin as the Scripture, and that on the same grounds of the proposal of it unto them, as the only means of divine worship, by their Church. Hence is it unto them an idol. But it is well enough known how from small beginnings, by various accessions, it increased unto its present form and station. And this progress, in the reception of devised forms of prayer in the worship of the church carried along with it sundry pernicious concomitants,[16] which we may briefly consider.

Transubstantiation and the Mass

In and by the additions made unto the first received forms, the superstitious and corrupt doctrines of the apostasy in several ages were insinuated into the worship of the church. That such superstitious and corrupt doctrines were gradually introduced into the church is acknowledged by all Protestants, and is sufficiently known; the supposition of it is the sole foundation of the Reformation. And by this artifice of new additions to received forms, they were from time to time admitted into and stated in the worship of the church, by which principally to this very day they preserve their station in the minds

---

14 I.e., as a result.
15 I.e., Koran.
16 I.e., accompaniments.

of men. Were that foundation of them taken away, they would quickly fall to the ground.¶[17]

By this means did those abominations of transubstantiation and the sacrifice of the Mass both leaven and poison the whole worship of the public assemblies, and imposed themselves on the credulity of the people.[18] The disputes of speculative men, superstitious and subtle, about these things, had never infected the minds of the common people of Christians, nor ever been the means of that idolatry which at length spread itself over the whole visible church of these parts of the world, had not this device of prescribed forms of prayer, wherein those abominations were not only expressed but graphically represented and acted, so violently affecting the carnal minds of men superstitious and ignorant, imposed them on their practice, which gradually hardened them with an obdurate credulity. For although they saw no ground or reason doctrinally to believe what was proposed unto them about transubstantiation and the sacrifice of the Mass, and might easily have seen that they were contradictory unto all the conductive[19] principles of men and Christians, namely, faith, reason, and sense, yet they deceived themselves into an obstinate pretense of believing in the notion of truth of what they had admitted in practice. Men, I say, of corrupt minds might have disputed long enough about vagrant forms, accidents without subjects, transmutation of substances without accidents, sacrifices bloody and unbloody, before they had vitiated the whole worship of the church with gross idolatry, had not this engine been made use of for its introduction, and the minds of men by this means been inveigled[20] with the practice of it. But when the whole matter and means of it was gradually insinuated into, and at length comprised in, those forms of prayer which they were obliged continually to use in divine service, their whole souls became leavened and tainted with a confidence in and love unto these abominations.

Hence it was that the doctrines concerning the sacraments, and the whole worship of God in the church, as they became gradually corrupted, were not at once objectively and doctrinally proposed to the minds and considerations

---

17 The ¶ symbol indicates that a paragraph break has been added to Owen's original text.

18 Transubstantiation is the Catholic doctrine of the Eucharist that teaches that the elements of the bread and wine become the body and blood of Jesus. Using Aristotelian categories, the elements change in their "substance," but not in their "accidents," when the priest consecrates them and sacrifices Christ anew. So they are really changed, but the change is imperceptible. This teaching was officially adopted at the Fourth Lateran Council (1215) and reasserted at the Council of Trent (1545–1563).

19 I.e., productive or efficient.

20 I.e., enticed.

of men, to be received or rejected, according to the evidence they had of their truth or error, a method due to the constitution of our nature, but gradually insinuated into their practice by additional forms of prayer, which they esteemed themselves obliged to use and observe. This was the gilding of the poisonous pill, whose operation, when it was swallowed, was to bereave men of their sense, reason, and faith, and make them madly avow that to be true which was contrary unto them all.

Besides, as was before intimated, the things themselves that were the groundwork of idolatry, namely, transubstantiation and the sacrifice of the Mass, were so acted and represented in those forms of worship as to take great impression on the minds of carnal men, until they were mad on their idols. For when all religion and devotion is let into the soul by fancy and imagination, excited by outward spectacles, they will make mad work in the world, as they have done, and yet continue to do. But hereof I shall speak in the next place.

It had, therefore, been utterly impossible that an idolatrous worship should have been introduced into the church in general, had not the opinion of the necessity of devised forms of prayer been first universally received. At least it had not been so introduced and so established as to procure and cause the shedding of the blood of thousands of holy persons for not complying with it. By this means alone was brought in that fatal engine of the church's ruin, from whose murderous efficacy few escaped with their lives or souls. Had all churches continued in the liberty wherein they were placed and left by our Lord Jesus Christ and his apostles,[21] it is possible that many irregularities might have prevailed in some of them, and many mistakes been admitted in their practice; yet this monster of the Mass, devouring the souls of the most, and drinking the blood of many, had never been conceived nor brought forth, at least not nourished into that terrible form and power wherein it appeared and acted for many ages in the world. And upon the account thereof it is not without cause that the Jews say that the Christians received their Tephilloth, or prayer books, from Armilus—that is, Antichrist.

It is true, that when the doctrine of religion is determined and established by civil laws, the laws of the nation where it is professed, as the rule of all outward advantages, liturgies composed in compliance therewith are not so subject to this mischief. But this arises from that external cause alone. Otherwise, wherever those who have the ordering of these things do deviate

---

21 Here Owen is implying his Congregationalism, his church polity that gave local churches autonomy.

from the truth once received, as it is common for the most so to do, forms of prayers answerable unto those deviations would quickly be insinuated. And the present various liturgies that are among the several sorts of Christians in the world are of little other use than to establish their minds in their peculiar errors, which by this means they adhere unto as articles of their faith.

And hereby did God suffer contempt to be cast upon the supposed wisdom of men about his worship and the ways of it. They would not trust unto his institutions and his care of them, but did first put the ark into a cart, and then, like Uzzah, put forth a hand of force to hold it when it seemed to shake. For it is certain that, if not the first invention, yet the first public recommendation and prescription, of devised forms of prayer unto the practice of the churches, were designed to prevent the insinuation of false opinions and corrupt modes of worship into the public administrations. This was feared from persons infected with heresy that might creep into the ministry. So, the orthodox and the Arians composed prayers, hymns, and doxologies, the one against the other, inserting in them passages confirming their own profession and condemning that of their adversaries.[22] Now, however this invention might be approved while it kept within bounds, yet it proved the Trojan horse that brought in all evils into the city of God in its belly. For he who was then at work in the mystery of iniquity laid hold on the engine and occasion to corrupt those prayers, which, by the constitution of them who had obtained power in them, the churches were obliged and confined unto. And this took place effectually in the constitution of the worship of the second race of Christians,[23] or the nations that were converted unto the Christian faith after they had destroyed the western Roman empire.¶[24]

To speak briefly and plainly, it was by this means alone, namely, of the necessary use of devised forms of prayer in the assemblies of the church, and of them alone, that the Mass, with its transubstantiation and sacrifice, and all the idolatrous worship wherewith they are accompanied, were introduced, until the world, inflamed with those idols, drenched itself in the blood of the saints and martyrs of Christ, for their testimony against these abominations. And if it had been sooner discovered that no church was entrusted with power from Christ to frame and impose such devised forms of worship as are not warranted by the Scripture, innumerable evils might have been prevented.

22 This took place during the fourth-century Trinitarian controversies. Arians were followers of the heretic Arius (ca. 250–336), who denied the divinity of Christ.
23 Owen is here referring to New Testament Christians or the church, as distinct from believing Jews in the Old Testament.
24 Rome officially fell in AD 476.

For that there were no liturgies composed, no imposed use of them, in the primitive churches for some ages, is demonstratively proved with the very same arguments whereby we prove that they had neither the Mass nor the use of images in their worship. For besides the utter silence of them in the apostolical writings, and those of the next ensuing ages, which is sufficient to discard their pretense unto any such antiquity, there are such descriptions given of the practice of the churches in their worship as are inconsistent with them and exclusive of them; besides, they give such a new face to divine worship, so different from the portraiture of it delivered in the Scripture, as is hardly reconcilable thereunto, and so not quickly embraced in the church.

I do not say that this fatal consequence of the introduction of humanly devised set forms of prayer in the worship of the church, in the horrible abuse made of it, is sufficient to condemn them as absolutely unlawful. For where the opinions leading unto such idolatrous practices are openly rejected and condemned, as was before intimated, there all the causes, means, and occasions of that idolatry may be taken out of them and separated from them, as it is in the liturgies of the Reformed churches, whether imposed or left free. But it is sufficient to lay in the balance against that veneration which their general observance in many ages may invite or procure. And it is so also to warrant the disciples of Christ to stand fast in the liberty wherewith he has made them free.

Arbitrary Ceremonies

Another evil, which either accompanied or closely followed on the introduction of devised forms of prayer into the church, was a supposed necessity of adorning the observance of them with sundry arbitrary ceremonies. And this also in the end, as is confessed among all Protestants, increased superstition in its worship, with various practices leading unto idolatry. It is evident that the use of free prayer in church administrations can admit of no ceremonies but such as are either of divine institution, or are natural circumstances of the actions wherein the duties of worship do materially consist. Divine institution and natural light are the rules of all that order and decency which is needful unto it.[25] But when these devised forms were introduced, with a supposition of their necessity, and sole use in the church in all acts of immediate worship, men quickly found that it was needful to set them off with adventitious[26]

25 Owen is here defending the regulative principle of worship, the Reformed doctrine that teaches that Scripture has positively prescribed the worship of God, not merely indicated what must be excluded. See the Westminster Confession of Faith (chap. 21) and Savoy Declaration (chap. 22).
26 I.e., accidental; not essential.

ornaments. Hereon there was gradually found out, and prescribed unto constant observation, so many outward postures and gestures, with attires, music, bowings, cringes, crossings, venerations, censings, altars, images, crucifixes, responds,[27] alternatives, and such a rabble of other ceremonies, as rendered the whole worship of the church ludicrous, burdensome, and superstitious. And hereon it came to pass that he who is to officiate in divine service is obliged to learn and practice so many turnings and windings of himself, eastward and westward, to the altar, to the wall, to the people, so many gestures and postures, in kneeling, rising, standings, bowings, less and profound, secret and loud speakings, in a due observance of the interposition of crossings, with removals from one place to another, with provision of attires, in their variety of colors and respect to all the furniture of their altars, as are difficult to learn, and foolishly antic in their practice, above all the preparations of players for the stage. Injunctions for these and the like observances are the subject of the rubric of the Missal and the cautels[28] of the Mass.

That these things have not only no affinity with the purity, simplicity, and spirituality of evangelical worship, but were invented utterly to exclude it out of the church and the minds of men, needs no proof unto any who ever read the Scripture with due consideration. Nor is the office of the ministry less corrupted and destroyed by it. For besides a sorry cunning in this practice, and the reading of some forms of words in an accommodation unto these rites, there was little more than an easy good intention to do what he does, and not the quite contrary, required to make any one man or woman, as it once at least fell out, to administer in all sacred worship.

Having utterly lost the Spirit of grace and supplications, neglecting at best all his aids and assistances, and being void of all experience in their minds of the power and efficacy of prayer by virtue of them, they found it necessary by these means to set off and recommend their dead forms. For the lifeless carcass of their forms merely alone were no more meet[29] to be esteemed prayer than a tree or a log was to be esteemed a god, before it was shaped, fashioned, gilded, and adorned. By this means they taught the image of prayer, which they had made, to speak and act a part to the satisfaction of the spectators. For the bare reading of a form of words, especially as it was ordered in an unknown tongue, could never have given the least contentment unto the multitude, had it not been set off with this variety of ceremonies, composed to make an appearance of devotion and sacred veneration. Yet, when they had

27 I.e., responses.
28 I.e., tricks or trickeries.
29 I.e., fitting; proper.

done their utmost, they could never equal the ceremonies and rites of the old temple worship, in beauty, glory, and order; nor yet those of the heathen, in their sacred Eleusinian Mysteries,[30] for number, solemnity, gravity, and appearance of devotion. Rejecting the true glory of gospel worship, which the apostle expressly declares to consist in the "administration of the Spirit,"[31] they substituted that in the room thereof which debased the profession of Christian religion beneath that of the Jews and Pagans, especially considering that the most of their ceremonies were borrowed of them or stolen from them.¶

But I shall never believe that their conversion of the holy prayers of the church, by an open contempt of the whole work of the Spirit of God in them, into a theatrical, pompous observance of ludicrous rites and ceremonies, can give so much as present satisfaction unto any who are not given up to strong delusions to believe a lie. The exercise of engrafted prevalent superstition will appease a natural conscience; outward forms and representations of things believed will please the fancy, and exercise the imagination; variety, and frequent changes of modes, gestures, and postures, with a sort of prayer always beginning and always ending, will entertain present thoughts and outward senses, so as that men, finding themselves by these means greatly affected, may suppose that they pray very well when they do nothing less. For prayer, consisting in a holy exercise of faith, love, trust, and delight in God, acting themselves in the representation of our wills and desires unto him, through the aid and assistance of the Holy Ghost, may be absent, where all these are most effectually present.

This also produced all the pretended ornaments of their temples, chapels, and oratories, by crucifixes, images, a multiplication of altars, with relics, tapers, vestments, and other utensils.

None of these things, whereby Christian religion is corrupted and debased, would ever have come into the minds of men, had not a necessity of their invention been introduced by the establishment of set forms of prayer, as the only way and means of divine worship. And wherever they are retained, proportionably unto the principles of the doctrine which men profess, some such ceremonies must be retained also. I will not, therefore, deny but that here lies the foundation of all our present differences about the manner of divine worship. Suppose a necessity of confining the solemn worship of the church unto set forms of prayer, and I will grant that sundry rituals and ceremonies may be well judged necessary to accompany their observance. For without them they will quickly grow obsolete and unsatisfactory. And

---

30 The Eleusinian Mysteries were the annual rites performed by the ancient Greeks at the village of Eleusis near Athens in honor of their gods, Demeter and Persephone.
31 2 Cor. 3:8.

if, on the other hand, free prayer in the church be allowed, it is evident that nothing but the grace and gifts of the Holy Ghost, with a due regard unto the decency of natural circumstances, is required in divine service, or can be admitted therein.

Neither yet is this consequent, how inseparable soever it seems from the sole public use of set forms of prayer in sacred administrations, pleaded to prove them either in themselves or their use to be unlawful. The design of this consideration is only to show that they have been so far abused, that they are so subject to be abused, and do so always stand in need to be abused, that they may attain the ends aimed at by them, as much weakens the plea of the necessity of their imposition.

Imposition

For this also is another evil that has attended their invention. The guides of the church, after a while, were not contented to make use of humanly devised forms of prayer, confining themselves unto their use alone in all public administrations, but, moreover, they judged it meet to impose the same practice on all whom they esteemed to be under their power. And this at length they thought lawful, yea, necessary to do on penalties, ecclesiastical and civil, and in the issue capital.[32] When this injunction first found a prevalent entertainment is very uncertain. For the first two or three centuries there were no systems of composed forms of prayer used in any church whatever, as has been proved. Afterward, when they began to be generally received, on such grounds and for such reasons as I shall not here insist on, but may do so in a declaration of the nature and use of spiritual gifts, with their continuance in the church, and an inquiry into the causes of their decay, the authority of some great persons did recommend the use of their compositions unto other churches, even such as had a mind to make use of them, as they saw good.¶

But as unto this device of their imposition, confining churches not only unto the necessary use of them in general, but unto a certain composition and collection of them, we are beholden for all the advantage received thereby unto the popes of Rome alone, among the churches of the second edition.[33] For, from their own good inclination, and by their own authority, without the advice of councils or pretense of traditions, the two Gorgons' heads,[34]

32 This is a reference to capital penalties or execution.
33 "Second edition" is a reference to the churches in the second stage of imposition he is discussing.
34 "The two Gorgons' heads" is an idiomatic description of "councils" and "traditions," indicating they are too horrible to behold. In Greek mythology, Medusa, whose hair was made of snakes the beholding of which would turn one to stone, was the Gorgon killed by Perseus.

whereby in other cases they frighten poor mortals, and turn them into stones, by various degrees they obtained a right to impose them, and did it accordingly. For when the use and benefit of them had been for a while pleaded, and thence a progress made unto their necessity, it was judged needful that they should be imposed on all churches and Christians by their ecclesiastical authority. But when afterward they had insinuated into them, and lodged in their bowels, the two great idols of transubstantiation and the unbloody sacrifice, not only mulcts[35] personal and pecuniary, but capital punishments, were enacted and executed to enforce their observance. This brought fire and fagot[36] into Christian religion, making havoc of the true church of Christ, and shedding the blood of thousands. For the martyrdom of all that have suffered death in the world for their testimony against the idolatries of the Mass derives originally from this spring alone of the necessary imposition of complete liturgical forms of prayer. For this is the sole foundation of the Roman Breviary and Missal, which have been the Abaddons[37] of the church of Christ in these parts of the world, and are ready once more to be so again. Take away this foundation, and they all fall to the ground. And it is worth consideration of what kind that principle is, which was naturally improved unto such pernicious effects, which quickly was found to be a meet and effectual engine in the hand of Satan to destroy and murder the servants of Christ.

Had the churches of Christ been left unto their primitive liberty under the enjoined duties of reading and expounding the Scripture, of singing psalms unto the praise of God, of the administration of the sacraments of baptism and the Lord's Supper, and of diligent preaching the word, all of them with prayer, according unto the abilities and spiritual gifts of them who did preside in them, as it is evident that they were for some ages, it is impossible for any man to imagine what evils would have ensued thereon that might be of any consideration, in comparison of those enormous mischiefs which followed on the contrary practice. And as unto all the inconveniences which, as it is pretended, might ensue on this liberty, there is sufficient evangelical provision for their prevention or cure made in the gospel constitution and communion of all the true churches of Christ.

But this was not the whole of the evil that attended this imposition, for by this means all spiritual ministerial gifts were caused to cease in the church. For as they are talents given to trade with, or manifestations of the Spirit

---

35 I.e., fines or penalties.
36 I.e., a bundle of sticks; kindling.
37 The Hebrew term *Abbadon* in the Bible refers to the place of destruction and also the angel of death or the abyss.

given to profit or edify the church, they will not reside in any subject, they will not abide, if they are by any received, if they are not improved by continual exercise. We see every day what effects the contempt or neglect of them does produce. Wherefore, this exercise of them being restrained and excluded by this imposition, they were utterly lost in the church, so that it was looked on as a rare thing for anyone to be able to pray in the administration of divine worship, yea, the pretense of such an ability was esteemed a crime, and the exercise of it a sin scarce to be pardoned; yet do I not find it in any of the ancient canons reckoned among the faults for which a bishop or a presbyter was to be deposed. But that hereon arose, in those who were called to officiate in public assemblies, as unto the gifts which they had received for the edification of the church in divine administrations, that neglect which has given a fatal wound unto the light and holiness of it, is openly evident. For when the generality of men of that order had provision of prayers made for them, which they purchased at an easy rate, or had them provided for them at the charge of the people, they were contented to be at rest, freed from that labor and travail of mind which are required unto the constant exercise and improvement of spiritual gifts. This imposition was the grave wherein they were buried. For at length, as it is manifest in the event, our Lord Jesus Christ being provoked with their sloth and unbelief, did withhold the communication of such gifts from the generality of those who did officiate in divine worship. And hereby they lost, also, one great evidence of the continuance of his mediatory life in heaven for the preservation of the church.

It is known that this was and is the state of things in the Roman church with reference unto their whole worship in their public assemblies. And, therefore, although they have indulged divers enthusiasts, whose revelations and actings, pretended from the Holy Spirit, have tended to the confirmation of their superstitions, and some of them have ventured at notions about mental prayer which they understand not themselves, yet as unto free prayer by the assistance of the Holy Ghost, in the church assemblies or otherwise, they were the first, and continue to be the fiercest opposers of it; and it is their interest so to be. For shake this foundation of the imposition of an entire system of humanly devised prayers for the only way and means of the worship of the church, and the whole fabric of the Mass, with all the weight of their religion, if vanity and imagination may be said to have any weight, which is laid thereon, will tumble into the pit from whence it came. And, therefore, I must here acquaint the reader that the first occasion of writing this discourse was the perusal of Mr. Cressy's preface to his *Church-History*, wherein, out of a design to advance the pretended mental prayer of some of his enthusiasts, he reflects with much contumely[38] and reproach upon that free praying by the aids of the Spirit of God which we plead for.[39] And he will find that all his pretenses are examined in the latter part of this discourse.

But notwithstanding these things, those of the Roman church do at this day boast themselves of their devotions in their prayers private and public, and have prevailed thereby on many, disposed unto a compliance with them by their own guilt, ignorance, and superstition. The vanity of their pretense has been well detected, by evincing the idolatry whereby all or the most of their devotions are vitiated and rendered unacceptable. But this also is of weight with me, that the provision of the system and order of their whole devotion, and its exercise, are apparently composed and fitted unto the exclusion of the whole work of the Spirit of God in prayer. And yet do they continue under such an incredible delusion as to oppose, revile, and condemn the prayers of others who are not of their communion, on this consideration, that those who make them have not the Holy Spirit nor his aids, which are all confined unto their Church. But if any society of men in the world maintaining the outward profession of Christian religion can do more to exclude the Holy Ghost and all his operations, in prayer and divine worship, than their church has done, I shall acknowledge myself greatly mistaken. It is nothing but ignorance of him and his whole work, with all the ends for which he is promised unto the church, that I say, not a hatred and detestation of them, that causes any to embrace their ways of devotion.

CONCLUSION

But to return. The things pleaded for may be reduced unto the ensuing heads.

1. No persons, no churches, are obliged, by virtue of any divine constitution, precept, or approved example, to confine themselves, in their public or private worship, unto set or humanly devised forms of prayer. If any such constitution, precept, or example can be produced, which hitherto has not been done, it ought to be complied with. And while others are left unto their liberty in their use, this is sufficient to enervate[40] all pleas for their imposition.

2. There is a promise in the Scripture, there are many promises, made and belonging unto the church unto the end of the world, of the communication

---

38 I.e., harsh treatment; contempt.

39 Hugh Paulinus Cressy (1605–1674) was an English convert to Roman Catholicism who became a Benedictine monk. He is remembered for his *The Church-History of Brittany, or England, from the Beginning of Christianity to the Norman Conquest* (Rouen, 1668). No modern edition exists.

40 I.e., weaken.

of the Holy Spirit unto it, as unto peculiar aids and assistances in prayer. To deny this, is to overthrow the foundation of the holiness and comfort of all believers, and to bring present ruin to the souls of men in distress.

3. It is the duty of believers to look after, to pray for, those promised aids and assistances in prayer. Without this all those promises are despised, and looked on as a flourish of words, without truth, power, or efficacy in them. But,

4. This they are commanded to do, and have blessed experience of success therein. The former is plain in the Scripture, and the latter must be left unto their own testimony living and dying.

5. Beyond the divine institution of all the ordinances of worship in the church, with the determination of the matter and form which are essential unto them, contained in the Scripture, and a due attendance unto natural light in outward circumstances, there is nothing needful unto the due and orderly celebration of all public worship in its assembly. If any such thing be pretended, it is what Christ never appointed, nor the apostles ever practiced, nor the first churches after them, nor has it any promise of acceptance.

6. For the preservation of the unity of faith, and the communion of churches among themselves therein, they may express an agreement, as in doctrine by a joint confession of faith, so in a declaration of the material and substantial parts of worship, with the order and method thereof; on which foundation they may in all things communicate with each other as churches, and in the practice of their members.

7. Whereas the differences about prayer under consideration concern Christian practice in the vitals of religion, great respect is to be had unto the experience of them that do believe, where it is not obstructed and clouded by prejudices, sloth, or adverse principles and opinions. Therefore, the substance of the greatest part of the ensuing discourse consists principally in the declaration of those concerns of prayer which relate unto practice and experience. And hence it follows,

8. That the best expedient to compose these differences among us, is for everyone to stir up the gift and grace of God that is in him, and all of us to give up ourselves unto that diligence, frequency, fervency, and perseverance in prayer which God requires of us, especially in such a season as that wherein we live. A time wherein they, whoever they be, who trouble others may, for aught[41] they know, be near unto trouble themselves. This will be the most effectual means to lead us all unto the acknowledgment of the truth, and without which an agreement in notions is of little use or value.

---

41 I.e., everything.

But, I confess, hopes are weak concerning the due application of this remedy unto any of our evils or distempers. The opinions of those who deny all internal, real, efficacious operations of the Holy Spirit on the souls of men, and deride all their effects, have so far diffused and rivetted themselves into the minds of many that little is to be expected from a retreat unto those aids and reliefs. This evil in the profession of religion was reserved for these latter ages. For although the work and grace of the Holy Spirit in divine worship was much neglected and lost in the world, yet no instances can be given in ages past of such contempt cast upon all his internal grace and operations as now abounds in the world. If the Pelagians,[42] who were most guilty, did fall into any such excesses, they have escaped the records and monuments that remain of their deportment. Bold efforts they are of atheistical inclinations in men openly avowing their own ignorance and utter want of all experience in things spiritual and heavenly. Neither does the person of Christ or his office meet with better entertainment among many; and by some they have been treated with scurrility[43] and blasphemy. In the meantime, the contests about communion with churches are great and fierce. But where these things are received and approved, those who live not on a traditionary faith will not forsake Christ and the gospel, or renounce faith and experience, for the communion of any church in the world.

But all flesh almost has corrupted its way. The power of religion, and the experience of it in the souls of men, being generally lost, the profession of it is of no great use, nor will long abide. Yea, multitudes, all the world over, seem to be weary of the religion which themselves profess, so far as it is pleaded to be of divine revelation, be it true or false, unless it be where they have great secular advantages by their profession of it. There is no greater pretense of a flourishing state in religion than that of some churches of the Roman communion, especially one at this day. But if the account which is given us from among themselves concerning it be true, it is not much to be gloried in. For set aside the multitude of atheists, antiscripturists, and avowed disbelievers of the supernatural mysteries of the gospel, and the herd that remains influenced into a hatred and persecution of the truth by a combination of men upholding themselves and their way by extravagant secular interests and advantages, is not very highly considerable. Yea, their present height seems to be on a precipice. What inroads in other places, bold

---

42   Pelagians are those who hold to the heterodox teachings of Pelagius (ca. 354–418), who denied original sin and believed that human beings had the free will to achieve perfection without the aid of divine grace.

43   I.e., coarse language; vulgarity.

opinions concerning the authority of Scripture and the demonstration of it, the person and office of Christ, the Holy Spirit and all his operations, with the advancement of a pretense of morality in opposition to evangelical grace in its nature and efficacy, are made every day is known unto all who consider these things. And although the effects of this poison discover themselves daily, in the decays of piety, the increase of immoralities of all sorts, and the abounding of flagitious[44] sins, exposing nations unto the high displeasure of God, yet the security of most in this state of things proclaims itself in various fruits of it, and can never be sufficiently deplored.

Whereas, therefore, one means of the preservation of the church, and its deliverance out of these evils, is a due attendance unto the discharge of this duty of prayer, the declaration of its nature, with a vindication of the springs and causes from whence it derives its efficacy, which are attempted in the ensuing discourse, may, I hope, through the blessing of God, be of some use unto such whose minds are sincere in their inquiries after truth.

44 I.e., villainous.

The Work of the Holy Spirit in Prayer as the Spirit of Grace and Supplications, and the Duty of Believers Therein

With a Brief Inquiry into the Nature
and Use of Mental Prayer and Forms

The Use of Prayer, and the Work of the Holy Spirit Therein

THE WORKS OF THE SPIRIT OF GOD toward believers are either general, and not confined with a respect unto any one duty more than another, or particular, with respect unto some special duty. Of the first sort are regeneration and sanctification, which, being common unto them all, are the general principles of all actings of grace or particular duties in them. But there are, moreover, sundry special works or operations of this Holy Spirit in and toward the disciples of Christ, which, although they may be reduced unto the general head of sanctification, yet they fall under a special consideration proper unto themselves; of this sort is the aid or assistance which he gives unto us in our prayers and supplications.

I suppose it will be granted that prayer, in the whole compass and extent of it, as comprising meditation, supplication, praise, and thanksgiving, is one of the most signal duties of religion. The light of nature in its most pregnant notions, with its practical language in the consciences of mankind, concurs in its suffrage with the Scripture in this matter. For they both of them jointly witness that it is not only an important duty in religion, but also that without it there neither is nor can be the exercise of any religion in the world. Never any persons lived in the acknowledgment of a deity, but under the conduct of the same apprehension they thought the duty of vows, prayers, and praises, incumbent on them, as they found occasion. Yea, although they found out external, ceremonious ways of solemnizing their devotions, yet it was this duty of prayer alone which was their natural, necessary, fundamental acknowledgment of that divine being which they did own. Neither are there any considerable stories extant recording the monuments of the ancient heathen nations of the world, wherein, to the shame of degenerate Christianity it may be spoken, there are not more frequent accounts given of their sacred invocations and supplications unto their supposed gods than are to be found in any of the historical monuments and stories concerning the actions of Christian nations in these latter ages. This, therefore, is the most natural and most eminent way and means of our converse with God, without which converse we have no present advantage above the beasts that perish but such as will turn unto our eternal disadvantage in that misery whereof they are incapable. This is the way whereby we exercise toward him all that grace which we do receive from him, and render him an acceptable acknowledgment of that homage and revenue of glory which we are never able to exhibit in their due kind and measure. Of what use and advantage the due performance of this duty is unto ourselves no man is able fully to express; everyone can add somewhat of his own experience. But we need not insist on the commendation of prayer, for it will be said, "By whom was it ever discommended?"

And I wish I saw reason to acquiesce[1] in that reply. For not only the practice of the most, but the declared opinions of many, do evidence that neither the excellency of this duty nor its necessity does find such acceptance and esteem in the minds of men as is pretended. But this being not my present design, I shall not farther insist upon it.

For my purpose is not to treat of the nature, necessity, properties, uses, effects, and advantages of this gracious duty, as it is the vital breath of our spiritual life unto God. Its origin in the law of nature, as the first and principal means of the acknowledgment of a divine power, whereof the neglect is a sufficient evidence of practical atheism, for he that prays not says in his heart, "There is no God,"[2] its direction in the Scripture, as to the rule, manner, and proper object of it, the necessity of its constant use and practice, both from special commands and our state in this world, with the whole variety of inward and outward occasions that may befall us, or we may be exercised with, arguments, motives, and encouragements unto constancy, fervency, and perseverance in the performance of the duty of it, with known examples of its mighty efficacy and marvelous success, the certain advantages which the souls of believers do receive thereby, in spiritual aids and supplies of strength, with peace and consolation, with sundry other of its concerns, although much treated of already by many, might yet be further considered and improved. But none of these is my present design. The interest of the Holy Spirit of God by his gracious operations in it is that alone which I shall inquire into.

1   I.e., accept; comply.
2   Ps. 14:1.

And it cannot be denied but that the work and actings of the Spirit of grace in and toward believers with respect unto the duty of prayer are more frequently and expressly asserted in the Scripture than his operations with respect unto any other particular grace or duty whatever. If this should be called into question, the ensuing discourse, I hope, will sufficiently vindicate and confirm its truth. But hereby believers are instructed, as in the importance of the duty itself, so in the use and necessity of the aid and assistance of the Spirit of God in and unto the right discharge or performance of it. For where frequent plain revelations concur, in multiplied commands and directions, with continual experience, as it is with them in this case, their instruction is firm, and in a way of being fixed on their minds. As this renders an inquiry hereinto both necessary and seasonable, for what can be more so than that wherein the spiritual life and comfort of believers are so highly concerned, and which exhibits unto us so gracious a condescension of divine love and goodness? So, moreover, the opposition that is made in the world against the work of the Spirit of God herein, above all other [of] his operations, requires that something be spoken in the vindication of it.

But the enmity hereunto seems to be peculiar unto these latter ages, I mean among such as pretend unto any acquaintance with these things from the Scripture. It will be hard to find an instance in former ages of any unto whom the Spirit of God, as a Spirit of grace and supplication, was a reproach. But as now the contradiction herein is great and fierce; so is there not any difference concerning any practical duty of religion wherein parties at variance are more confident and satisfied in and about their own apprehensions than they are who dissent about the work of the Spirit of God in our prayers and supplications. For those who oppose what is ascribed by others unto him herein are not content to deny and reject it, and to refuse a communion in the faith and practice of the work so ascribed unto him, but, moreover, such is the confidence they have in their conceptions, that they revile and speak evil contemptuously and despitefully of what they do oppose. Hence ability to pray, as is pleaded, by the assistance of the Holy Ghost, is so far from being allowed to be a gift, or a grace, or a duty, or any way useful among men, that it is derided and scorned as a paltry faculty, fit to be exploded from among Christians. And at length it is traduced as an invention and artifice of the Jesuits, to the surprise and offence of many sober persons; the unadvisedness of which insinuation the ensuing discourse will manifest.

Others, again, profess that of all the privileges whereof they are made partakers in this world, of all the aids, assistances, or gifts which they receive from or by the Spirit of God, that which he communicates and helps them with in their prayers and supplications is the most excellent and inestimable. And herein they have, living and dying, in all troubles, distresses, temptations, and persecutions, such assurance and satisfaction in their minds, as that they are not in the least moved with all the scorn and contempt that are cast upon their profession and practice in the exercise of the gift which they have received, but rather judge that they contract the guilt of great sin to themselves by whom this work of the Spirit is reproached. Hence, I know not any difference about religious things that is managed with greater animosities in the minds of men and worse consequents than this which is about the work of the Spirit of God in prayer, which, indeed, is the hinge on which all other differences about divine worship do turn and depend. It may, therefore, be well worth our while, yea, it is our duty, sedately and diligently to inquire into what the Scripture teaches us in this matter, wherein we must acquiesce, and whereby all experiences on the one side or the other must be tried and regulated.¶

Two things, therefore, I do propose unto myself in the ensuing discourse, concerning both which I shall plainly and briefly endeavor the satisfaction of indifferent and unprejudiced readers. And these are, first, to evince *that there is promised and actually granted a special work of the Spirit of God in the prayers or praises of believers under the New Testament*; secondly, *to declare the nature of that work, wherein it does consist*, or the manner of the operation of the Holy Spirit therein. And if in these things no impression can be made on the minds of men possessed with those mighty prejudices which reject their very proposal and all consideration of them with contempt, yet it may be of use unto them who, being not biased with the undue love or hatred of parties of men, nor elated with high valuations of their own conceptions above those of others, whom they think they have reason if not to hate, yet to scorn, do sincerely desire to live unto God, and to prefer the performance of their duty unto all other considerations, endeavoring to subdue their inclinations and affections thereunto. Nor do I desire more of any reader but that he will grant that he is herein conversant about things which will have an influence into his everlasting account.

2

Zechariah 12:10 Opened
and Vindicated

THE SPECIAL PROMISE of the administration of the Spirit of God unto the end under consideration is that which I shall lay as the foundation of the ensuing discourse. "I will pour upon the house of David, and upon the inhabitants of Jerusalem, the Spirit of grace and of supplications" (Zech. 12:10). The Spirit here promised is the Spirit of God, "the Holy Spirit," with respect unto the special end for which he is promised. And the manner of his administration in the accomplishment of the promise is expressed by ושפכתי, "I will pour out." The same word is used to the same purpose (Ezek. 39:29; Joel 2:28), as are also other words of the same importance, which we render by "pouring out" (as Prov. 1:23; Isa. 32:15; 44:3; 52:15).

EXEGETICAL POINTS

1. Two things have been elsewhere declared concerning this expression, applied unto the communication of the Holy Ghost.[1] (1) That a plentiful dispensation of him unto the end for which he is promised, with respect unto a singular and eminent degree in his operations, is intended therein. The apostle expresses this word, or the accomplishment of what is promised in it, by ἐξέχεεν πλουσίως, "he has richly," or abundantly, "poured out his Spirit" (Titus 3:6). Not, therefore, a mere grant and communication of the Spirit, but a plentiful effusion of him, is intended; which must have some

---

1 *Of Communion with God the Father, Son, and Holy Ghost, Each Person Distinctly, in Love Grace, and Consolation; or, The Saints' Fellowship with the Father, Son, and Holy Ghost Unfolded* (1657), pt. 3, chap. 3.

eminent effects as pledges and tokens thereof. For it is absurd to speak of a "plentiful, abundant effusion," with degrees above what was before granted, and yet there be no certain ways or means whereby it may be evidenced and demonstrated. The Spirit, therefore, is so promised in this place as to produce some notable and peculiar effects of his communication. (2) That this promise is peculiar unto the days of the gospel; I mean, every promise is so where mention is made of pouring out the Spirit on men; which may be evinced by the consideration of every place where this expression is used. But in this place, it is most unquestionable, the immediate effect of it being a looking unto Christ as he was pierced. And it may be yet further observed, that there is a tacit comparison in it with some other time or season, or some other act of God, wherein or whereby he gave his Spirit before, but not in that way, manner, or measure that he now promises to bestow him. Of the whole of these observations, Didymus gives us a brief account: "Now the expression 'pouring forth' indicates a lavish gift of great bounty and abundance. And so, whenever one or two receive the Holy Spirit anywhere [in the Scriptures], 'I will pour forth of my Spirit' is not said. For this is only said when the gift of the Holy Spirit is given in abundance to all nations."[2]

2. Those unto whom he is thus promised are "the house of David, and the inhabitants of Jerusalem," that is, the whole church, expressed in a distribution into the ruling family and the body of the people under their rule. And the family of David, which was then in supreme power among the people in the person of Zerubbabel, is expressly mentioned for three reasons: (1) Because the faithfulness of God in his promises was concerned in the preservation of that family, whereof the Messiah was to spring, Christ himself being thereby, in the rule of the church, typed out in a special manner. (2) Because all the promises in a peculiar manner were first to be fulfilled in the person of Christ, so typed by David and his house. On him the Spirit, under the New Testament, was first to be poured out in all fullness,

---

2   In the text: *Significat autem effusionis verbum, largam, et divitem muneris abundantiam; itaque cum unus quis alicubi, aut duo Spiritum Sanctum accipiunt, non dicitur, 'Effundam de Spiritu meo,' sed tunc, quando in universas gentes munus Spiritus Sancti redundaverit* (De Spir. Sanc. i. 1).—Owen. For the Latin text, see Louis Doutreleau, *Didyme l'Aveugle, traité du Saint-Esprit: Introduction, texte critique, traduction, notes et index*, Sources Chrétiennes 386 (Paris: Les Éditions du Cerf, 1992), 192. For the English translation, see *Works on the Holy Spirit: Athanasius the Great and Didymus the Blind*, trans. Mark DelCogliano, Andrew Radde-Gallwitz, and Lewis Ayres, Popular Patristics 43 (Yonkers, NY: St. Vladimir's Seminary Press, 2011), 159. Dydimus (ca. 313–398) was an Alexandrian theologian and defender of Trinitarianism. His *On the Holy Spirit* is an orthodox defense of the divinity of the third person of the Godhead.

and from him to be communicated unto others. (3) It may be to denote the special gifts and graces that should be communicated unto them who were to be employed in the rule and conduct of the church under him, the king and head thereof. And "the inhabitants of Jerusalem" is a phrase expressive of the whole church, because that was the seat of all their public ordinances of worship (see Ps. 122). Wherefore, the whole spiritual church of God, all believers, are the object of this promise, as represented in the house of David and the inhabitants of Jerusalem.

3. The special qualifications of the promised Spirit are two: for (1) He is to be רוח חן, a "Spirit of grace." חן which the Greek constantly renders χάρις, and we from the Latin *gratia*, "grace," is derived from חנן, as is also the following word, which signifies to "have mercy," or "compassion," to be "gracious," as all the words whereby God's gracious dealings with sinners in the Hebrew do include the signification of pity, compassion, free goodness, and bounty. And it is variously used in the Scripture. Sometimes for the grace and favor of God, as it is the fountain of all gracious and merciful effects toward us (Rom. 1:7; 4:16; 5:2, 15, 20; 6:1; 11:5; 1 Cor. 1:3; and in other places innumerable) and sometimes for the principal effect thereof, or the gracious favor of God whereby he accepts us in Christ (Eph. 2:5; 2 Thess. 1:12), which is the grace the apostle prays for in the behalf of the church (Rom. 16:20; 1 Cor. 16:23). And sometimes it is applied unto the favor of men, and acceptation with them, called the "finding grace" or "favour" in the sight of any (Gen. 39:4, 21; 1 Sam. 2:26; Rom. 15:11; Est. 2:15, 17; 5:2; Luke 2:52; Acts 4:33). And sometimes for the free effectual efficacy of grace in those in whom it is (Acts 14:26; 1 Cor. 15:10; 2 Cor. 12:9). And sometimes for our justification and salvation by the free grace or favor of God in Christ (John 1:17; 1 Pet. 1:13). For the gospel itself, as the instrument of the declaration and communication of the grace of God (2 Cor. 6:1; Eph. 3:2; Col. 1:6; Titus 2:11). For the free donation of the grace and gifts of the Spirit (John 1:16; Eph. 4:7). And many other significations it has, which belong not unto our purpose.

Three things may be intended in this adjunct of grace: [1] A respect of the sovereign cause of his dispensation, which is no other but the mere grace of God. He may be called a "Spirit of grace," because his donation is an effect of grace, without the least respect unto any desert in those unto whom he is given. This reason of the appellation is declared (Titus 3:4–7). The sole cause and reason, in opposition unto our own works or deservings, of the pouring out of the Spirit upon us, is the love and kindness of God in Jesus Christ; whence he may be justly called a "Spirit of grace." [2] Because he is the author of all grace in and unto them on whom he is poured out; so God is called the "God of all grace,"[3] because he is the fountain and author of it. And that the Holy Spirit is the immediate efficient cause of all grace in us has been elsewhere proved, both in general and in the principal instances of regeneration and sanctification, and it shall be yet further confirmed in what does ensue.[4] [3] חן is commonly used for that grace or favor which one has with another: "Let me find grace in thy sight," as in the instances before quoted. And so, the Spirit also may be called a "Spirit of grace," because those on whom he is poured out have grace and favor with God; they are gracious with him, as being "accepted in the Beloved" (Eph. 1:6). Whereas, therefore, all these concur wherever this Spirit is communicated, I know no reason why we may not judge them all here included, though that in the second place be specially intended. The Spirit is promised to work grace and holiness in all on whom he is bestowed.

(2) He is, as thus poured out, a Spirit תחנונים, "of supplications," that is, of prayer for grace and mercy. The word is formed from חנן, as the other, to be gracious or merciful; and, expressing our act toward God, it is prayer for grace—supplication. And the original is never used but to express vocal prayer, either in the assemblies of the people of God or by private persons. "Hearken to the voice of my supplications," is rendered by the apostle Paul ἱκετηρίας (Heb. 5:7), in which place alone in the Scripture that word is used. Originally it signifies a bough or olive branch wrapped about with wool or bays, or something of the like nature, which those carried in their hands and lifted up, who were suppliants unto others for the obtaining of peace or the averting of their displeasure. Hence came the phrase of *velamenta praeferre*, "to hold out such covered branches." So, *Ramos oleae, ac velamenta alia supplicantium porrigentes, orare, ut reciperent sese*—"Holding forth olive-branches, and other covered tokens used by suppliants, they prayed that they might be received" into grace and favor.[5] Which custom Virgil declares in his *Æneas* addressing himself to Evander:

---

3   1 Pet. 5:10.

4   Πνευματολογια, or, A Discourse concerning the Holy Spirit: Wherein an Account Is Given of His Name, Nature, Personality, Dispensation, Operations, and Effects; His Whole Work in the Old and New Creation Is Explained; the Doctrine concerning It Vindicated from Oppositions and Reproaches. The Nature Also and Necessity of Gospel Holiness; the Difference between Grace and Morality, or a Spiritual Life unto God in Evangelical Obedience and a Course of Moral Virtues, Are Stated and Declared (1674), bk. 3.

5   In the text: (Livy, De Bel. Punic., lib. Xxiv. Cap. 30).—Owen. This quote is drawn from Livy's History of Rome, a monumental and influential history of the city and empire, from its mythical founding through the reign of Livy's contemporary, Augustus. For the Latin text and English

Noblest of the sons of Greece, to whom Fortune has willed that I make
my prayer,
and offer boughs decked with fillets[6]

And they called them ἱκετηρίας θαλλοὺς, "branches of supplication," or
prayer. And they constantly called those prayers which they made solemnly
unto their gods, *supplicia* and *supplicationes*: "In that year were many por-
tents, to avert which the senate decreed supplications for two days."[7] A form
of which kind of prayer we have in Cato: "Father Mars, I pray and beseech
you so that calamities . . ."[8]

Some render תחנונים by "miserationes" or "lamentationes," and interpret it
of men's bemoaning themselves in their prayers for grace and mercy, which in
the issue varies not from the sense insisted on. But whereas it is derived from
חנן, which signifies to be "merciful" or "gracious," and expresses an act of ours
toward God, it can properly signify nothing but supplications for mercy and
grace, nor is it otherwise used in the Scripture (see Job 41:3; Prov. 18:23; Dan.
9:3; Jer. 31:9; 2 Chron. 6:21; Jer. 3:21; Pss. 28:2, 6; 31:22; 116:1; 130:2; 140:6;
143:1; Dan. 9:18, 23; Ps. 86:6), which are all the places, besides this, where
the word is used; in all which it denotes deprecation of evil and supplication
for grace, constantly in the plural number, to denote the earnestness of men.

תחנונים, therefore, are properly supplications for grace and mercy, for freedom and deliverance from evil, put by a synecdoche[9] for all sorts of prayer
whatever. We may, therefore, inquire in what sense the Holy Spirit of God is
called a "Spirit of supplications," or what is the reason of this attribution unto

---

translation, see Livy, *History of Rome*, vol. 6, *Books 23–25*, trans. Frank Gardner Moore, Loeb
Classical Library 355 (Cambridge, MA: Harvard University Press, 1940), 272–73.

6 In the text: *Optime Grajugenûm, cui me fortuna precari, Et vittâ comptos voluit praetendere
ramos* (Virg. Aen. viii. 127).—Owen. These lines come from Virgil's *Aeneid*, a first-century BC
epic poem that addresses the founding of Rome. For the Latin text and English translation,
see Virgil, *Aeneid: Books 7–12. Appendix Vergiliana*, trans. H. Rushton Fairclough, rev. G. P.
Goold, Loeb Classical Library 64 (Cambridge, MA: Harvard University Press, 1918), 68–69.

7 In the text: *Eo anno prodigia multa fuerunt: quorum averruncandorum caussa supplicationes in
biduum senatus decrevit* (Liv., lib. x. cap. 23).—Owen. For the Latin text and English translation,
see Livy, *History of Rome*, vol. 4, *Books 8–10*, trans. B. O. Foster, Loeb Classical Library 191
(Cambridge, MA: Harvard University Press, 1926), 442–43.

8 In the text: *De Re Rustica*, cap. xiii, *Mars pater te precor quæsoque ut calamitates.*—Owen. Cato
(234–149 BC) was a Roman soldier and statesmen. Of his many influential writings, his *On
Agriculture*, the earliest surviving work in Latin prose, from which the quoted prayer comes,
is all that survives. The quotation is actually drawn from chap. 141. For Latin text and English
translation, see Cato and Varro, *On Agriculture*, trans. W. D. Hooper and Harrison Boyd Ash,
Loeb Classical Library 283 (Cambridge, MA: Harvard University Press, 1934), 120–23.

9 I.e., a figure of speech in which part of a whole is named as a substitute for the whole.

him. And he must be so either formally or efficiently, either because he is so in himself or unto us. If in the former way, then he is a Spirit who himself prays, and, according to the import of those Hebraisms, abounds in that duty. As a "man of wickedness" (Isa. 55:7), or a "man of blood," is a man wholly given to wickedness and violence, so, on the other hand, a "Spirit of supplication" should be a Spirit abounding in prayer for mercy and the diverting of evil, as the word imports. Now, the Holy Ghost cannot be thus a Spirit of supplication, neither for himself nor us. No imagination of any such thing can be admitted with respect unto himself without the highest blasphemy. Nor can he in his own person make supplications for us. For besides that any such interposition in heaven on our behalf is in the Scripture wholly confined unto the priestly office of Christ and his intercession, all prayer, whether oral or interpretative only, is the act of a nature inferior unto that which is prayed unto. This the Spirit of God has not, he has no nature inferior unto that which is divine. We cannot, therefore, suppose him to be formally a Spirit of supplication, unless we deny his deity. He is so, therefore, efficiently with respect unto us, and as such he is promised unto us. Our inquiry, therefore, in general, is how or in what sense he is so. And there are but two ways conceivable whereby this may be affirmed of him. First, by working gracious inclinations and dispositions in us unto this duty. Second, by giving a gracious ability for the discharge of it in a due manner. These, therefore, must belong unto and do comprise his efficiency as a Spirit of supplication.

THE EFFICIENCY OF THE SPIRIT OF SUPPLICATION

Both of them are included in that of the apostle, "The Spirit itself maketh intercession for us" (Rom. 8:26). Those who can put any other sense on this promise may do well to express it. Every one consistent with the analogy of faith[10] shall be admitted, so that we do not judge the words to be void of sense and to have nothing in them. To deny the Spirit of God to be a Spirit of supplication in and unto believers is to reject the testimony of God himself.

By the ways mentioned we affirm that he is so, nor can any other way be assigned.

---

10 The "analogy of faith" is a general sense of the meaning of Scripture, constructed from the clear or unambiguous passages, used as the basis for interpreting difficult texts. For more on the analogy of faith, see Andrew S. Ballitch, *The Gloss and the Text: William Perkins on Interpreting Scripture with Scripture*, Studies in Historical and Systematic Theology (Bellingham, WA: Lexham, 2020), 66–68; Richard A. Muller, *Dictionary of Latin and Greek Theological Terms: Drawn Principally from Protestant Scholastic Theology* (Grand Rapids, MI: Baker, 1985), 33.

1. He is so by working gracious inclinations and dispositions in us unto this duty. It is he who prepares, disposes, and inclines the hearts of believers unto the exercise thereof with delight and spiritual complacency. And where this is not, no prayer is acceptable unto God. He delights not in those cries which an unwilling mind is pressed or forced unto by earthly desires, distress, or misery (James 4:3). Of ourselves, naturally, we are averse from any converse and intercourse with God, as being alienated from living unto him by the ignorance and vanity of our minds.

And there is a secret alienation still working in us from all duties of immediate communion with him. It is he alone who works us unto that frame wherein we pray continually, as it is required of us; our hearts being kept ready and prepared for this duty on all occasions and opportunities, being in the meantime acted and steered under the conduct and influence of those graces which are to be exercised therein. This some call the "grace of prayer" that is given us by the Holy Ghost, as I suppose improperly, though I will not contend about it. For prayer absolutely and formally is not a peculiar grace distinct from all other graces that are exercised in it, but it is the way and manner whereby we are to exercise all other graces of faith, love, delight, fear, reverence, self-abasement, and the like, unto certain special ends. And I know no grace of prayer distinct or different from the exercise of these graces. It is, therefore, a holy commanded way of the exercise of other graces, but not a peculiar grace itself. Only, where any person is singularly disposed and devoted unto this duty, we may, if we please, though improperly, say that he is eminent in the grace of prayer. And I do suppose that this part of his work will not be denied by any, no, not that it is intended in the promise. If any are minded to stand at such a distance from other things which are ascribed unto him, or have such an abhorrency of allowing him part or interest in our supplications as that we may in any sense be said to pray in the Holy Ghost, that they will not admit of so much as the work of his grace, and that wrought in believers by virtue of this promise, they will manage an opposition unto his other actings at too dear a rate to be gainers by it.

2. He is so by giving an ability for prayer, or communicating a gift unto the minds of men, enabling them profitably unto themselves and others to exercise all his graces in that special way of prayer. It will be granted afterward that there may be a gift of prayer used where there is no grace in exercise, nor perhaps any to be exercised; that is, as some improperly express it, "the gift of prayer," where the grace of prayer is not. But in declaring how the Spirit is a Spirit of supplication, we must take in the consideration of both. He both disposes us to pray, that is, to the exercise of grace in that special way, and

enables us thereunto. And where this ability is wholly and absolutely wanting, or where it is rejected or despised, although he may act and exercise those very graces which are to be exercised in prayer, and whose exercise in that way is commonly called the "grace of prayer," yet this work of his belongs unto the general head of sanctification, wherein he preserves, excites, and acts all our graces, and not unto this special work of prayer, nor is he a Spirit of supplication therein. He is, therefore, only a Spirit of supplication, properly, as he communicates a gift or ability unto persons to exercise all his graces in the way and duty of prayer. This is that which he is here promised for, and promised to be poured out, for that is to be given in an abundant and plentiful manner. Wherever he is bestowed in the accomplishment of this promise, he both disposes the hearts of men to pray and enables them so to do. This ability, indeed, he communicates in great variety, as to the degrees of it and usefulness unto others in its exercise, but he does it unto everyone so far as is necessary unto his own spiritual concerns, or the discharge of his duty toward God and all others. But whereas this assertion contains the substance of what we plead for, the further confirmation of it must be the principal subject of the ensuing discourse.

That this is the sense of the place, and the mind of the Holy Ghost in the words, needs no other demonstration but that it is expressive of their proper signification, neither can any other sense tolerably be affixed on them. To deny the Holy Spirit to be denominated a Spirit of supplication, because he inclines, disposes, and enables them to pray unto whom he is promised, and on whom he is bestowed as such, is to use a little too much liberty in sacred things.

OBJECTIONS ANSWERED

A learned man of late, out of hatred unto the Spirit of prayer, or prayer as his gift, has endeavored to deprive the church of God of the whole benefit and comfort of this promise.[11] For he contends that it belongs not unto the Christian church, but unto the Jews only. Had he said it belonged unto the

11 In the text: (Amyrald. Praefat. in Psal.).—Owen. This is a reference to the preface to Moïse Amyraut, *Paraphrasis in psalmos Davidis una cum annotationibus et argumentis* (Saumur: Desbordes, 1662). No modern edition exists. Moïse Amyraut (1596–1664) was a French Huguenot known for modifying theology regarding the nature of Christ's atonement into a view that took his name, Amyraldianism. Often called hypothetical universalism, this perspective understands the atonement as intended by God for all human beings, though its effectiveness for salvation depends on faith, a free gift of God given only to these whom God elected from eternity. See Brian G. Armstrong, *Calvinism and the Amyraut Heresy: Protestant Scholasticism and Humanism in Seventeenth-Century France* (Madison, WI: University of Wisconsin Press,

Jews in the first place who should be converted unto Christ, he had not gone so wide from the truth nor from the sense of other expositors, though he had said more than he could prove. But to suppose that any grace, any mercy, any privilege by Jesus Christ, is promised unto the Jews, wherein Gentile believers shall be no sharers, that they should not partake of the same kind, whoever has the prerogative as to degrees, is fond and impious. For if they also are children of Abraham, if the blessing of faithful Abraham do come upon them also, if it is through them that he is the heir of the world, his spiritual seed inhabiting it by right in all places, then unto them do all the promises belong that are made unto him and his seed. And whereas most of the exceeding great and precious promises of the Old Testament are made to Jacob and Israel, to Jerusalem and Zion, it is but saying that they are all confined unto the Jews, and so at once to despoil the church of God of all right and title to them, which impious folly and sacrilege has been by some attempted. But whereas all the promises belong unto the same covenant, with all the grace contained in them and exhibited by them, whoever is interested by faith in that covenant is so in all the promises of God that belong thereunto, and has an equal right unto them with those unto whom they were first given.¶

To suppose, now that the Jews are rejected for their unbelief, that the promises of God made unto them while they stood by faith are ceased and of no use, is to overthrow the covenant of Abraham, and, indeed, the whole truth of the New Testament. But the apostle assures us that "all the promises of God in Christ are yea, and in him Amen, unto the glory of God by us"; that is, in their accomplishment in us and toward us (2 Cor. 1:20). So, also, he positively affirms that all believers have received those promises which originally were made unto Israel (2 Cor. 6:16–18; 7:1). And not only so, but he declares also that the promises which were made of old unto particular persons on special occasions, as to the grace, power, and love contained in them and intended by them, do yet belong unto all individual believers, and are applicable by them unto all their special occasions (Heb. 13:5–6). And their right unto or interest in all the promises of God is that which those who are concerned in the obedience of faith would not forgo for all that this world can supply them with. This, therefore, is only a particular instance of the work and effect of the Spirit, as he is in general promised in the covenant. And, as we have declared, the promises of him as a Spirit of grace and holiness in the covenant belong unto the believers of the Gentiles also. If they

---

1969); Jonathan D. Moore, *English Hypothetical Universalism: John Preston and the Softening of Reformed Theology* (Grand Rapids, MI: Eerdmans, 2007).

do not, they have neither share nor interest in Christ, which is a better plea for the Jew than this peculiar instance will afford. But this promise is only a special declaration of what in one case this Spirit shall do, who is promised as a Spirit of grace and holiness in the covenant. And, therefore, the author of the evasion, suspecting that the fraud and sacrilege of it would be detected, betakes himself to other subterfuges,[12] which we shall afterward meet with, so far as we are concerned.

It may be more soberly objected, that the Spirit of grace and supplication was given unto believers under the Old Testament; and, therefore, if there be no more in it, if some extraordinary gift be not here intended, how comes it to be made a special promise with respect unto the times of the New Testament? It may, therefore, be supposed that not the ordinary grace or gift of prayer, which believers, and especially the officers of the church, do receive, but some extraordinary gift bestowed on the apostles and first converts to the church, is here intended. So, the prophecy concerning the effusion of the Spirit on all sorts of persons (Joel 2), is interpreted by Peter, and applied unto the sending of the Holy Ghost in miraculous gifts on the day of Pentecost (Acts 2).

First answer: I have elsewhere already in general obviated[13] this objection by showing the prodigious folly of that imagination, that the dispensation of the Spirit is confined unto the first times of the gospel, whereof this objection is a branch, as enmity unto the matter treated of is the occasion of the whole.[14] Second, we nowhere find grace and prayer, the things here promised, to be reckoned among the extraordinary gifts of the Spirit under the New Testament. Prayer, indeed, in an unknown tongue was so; but prayer itself was not so, no more than grace, which if it were, the whole present church is graceless. Third, the promise in Joel had express respect unto the extraordinary gifts of prophecy and visions, and therefore had its principal accomplishment on the day of Pentecost. This promise is quite of another nature. Fourth, that which is necessary for and the duty of all believers, and that always, is not an extraordinary gift, bestowed on a few for a season. Now, if there are any who think that grace and prayer are not necessary unto all believers, or that they may have abilities, and exercise them, without any aid of the Holy Spirit, I will not at present contend with them; for this is not a place to plead with those by whom the principles of the Christian faith are denied. Divine commands are the rule of our duty, not man's imaginations. Fifth, if this be not a special promise of the New Testament, because the matter of it, or grace

---

12 I.e., deceptions.
13 I.e., anticipated; prevented.
14 Πνευματολογια, or, A Discourse concerning the Holy Spirit.

promised, was in some degree and measure enjoyed under the Old, then is there no promise made with respect unto that season; for the saints under the Old Testament were really made partakers of all the same graces with those under the New. Wherefore, sixth, two things are intended in the promise with respect unto the times of the gospel. First, an ampliation[15] and enlargement of this grace or favor, as unto the subjects of it extensively. It was under the Old Testament confined unto a few, but now it shall be communicated unto many, and diffused all the world over. It shall be so poured out as to be shed abroad, and imparted thereby unto many. That which before was but as the watering of a garden by a special hand is now as the clouds pouring themselves forth on the whole face of the earth. Second, an increase of the degrees of spiritual abilities for the performance of it (Titus 3:5–6). There is now a rich communication of the Spirit of grace and prayer granted unto believers in comparison of what was enjoyed under the Old Testament. This the very nature of the dispensation of the gospel, wherein we receive from Jesus Christ "grace for grace,"[16] does evince and confirm. I suppose it needless to prove that, as unto all spiritual supplies of grace, there is brought in an abundant administration of it by Jesus Christ; the whole Scripture testifying unto it.

There were, indeed, under the Old Testament, prayers to and praises of God dictated by a Spirit of prophecy, and received by immediate divine revelation, containing mysteries for the instruction of the church in all ages. These prayers were not suggested unto them by the aid of the Spirit as a Spirit of supplication, but dictated in and to them by the Spirit as a Spirit of prophecy. Nor did they themselves comprehend the mind of the Holy Spirit in them fully, but inquired diligently thereinto, as into other prophecies given out by the Spirit of Christ which was in them (1 Pet. 1:10–12). An instance whereof we may have in Psalm 22. A prayer it is with thanksgiving from first to last. Now, although David, unto whom it was given by inspiration, might find in his own condition things that had some low and mean resemblance of what was intended in the words suggested unto him by the Holy Spirit, as he was a type of Christ, yet the depth of the mysteries contained therein, the principal scope and design of the Holy Ghost, was in a great measure concealed from him, and much more from others. Only it was given out unto the church by immediate inspiration, that believers might search and diligently inquire into what was signified and foretold therein, that so thereby they might be gradually led into the knowledge of the mysteries of God according as he was

---

15 I.e., amplification.
16 John 1:16.

pleased graciously to communicate of his saving light unto them. But withal it was revealed unto David and the other prophets, that in these things they did not minister unto themselves, but unto us, as having mysteries in them which they could not, which they were not, to comprehend. But as this gift is ceased under the New Testament, after the finishing of the canon of the Scripture, nor is it by any pretended unto, so was it confined of old unto a very few inspired persons, and belongs not unto our present inquiry; for we speak only of those things which are common unto all believers, and herein a preference must in all things be given unto those under the New Testament.

If, therefore, it could be proved, which I know it cannot be, that the generality of the church under the Old Testament made use of any forms of prayers, as mere forms of prayer, without any other end, use, or mystical instruction, all which concurred in their prophetical composures, for the sole end of prayer, yet would it not, whatever any pretend or plead, therefore follow that believers under the New Testament may do the same, much less that they may be obliged always so to do. For there is now a more plentiful and rich effusion of the Spirit of grace and supplication upon them than was upon those of old. And as our duty is to be regulated by God's commands, so God's commands are suited unto the dispensation of his grace. For persons under the New Testament, who are commanded to pray, not to make use constantly in their so doing of the gifts, aids, and assistances of the Spirit, which are peculiarly dispensed and communicated therein, on pretense of what was done under the Old, is to reject the grace of the gospel, and to make themselves guilty of the highest ingratitude. Wherefore, although we may and ought to bear with them who, having not received anything of this promised grace and assistance, nor believing there is any such thing, do plead for the use of forms of prayer to be composed by some and read by others or themselves, and that only, in the discharge of this duty; yet such as have been made partakers of this grace, and who own it their duty constantly to use and improve the promised aids of the Spirit of God, will be careful not to admit of any such principles or practice as would plainly annihilate the promise.

Thus much, then, we may suppose ourselves to have obtained in the consideration of this testimony, *that God has promised under the New Testament to give unto believers, in a plentiful manner or measure, the Spirit of grace and of supplications, or his own Holy Spirit, enabling them to pray according to his mind and will.* The way and manner of his work therein shall be afterward declared. And it may suffice to oppose, in general, this one promise unto the open reproaches and bold contempts that are by many cast on the Spirit of prayer, whose framers, unless they can blot this text out of the Scripture, will fail at last in their design. We shall not, therefore, need to plead any other testimony to the same purpose in the way of promises. Only we may observe, that this being expressly assigned as a part of the gracious work of the Holy Spirit, as promised under the New Testament, there is no one promise to that purpose wherein this grace is not included; therefore, the known multiplication of them adds strength unto our argument.

Galatians 4:6 Opened and Vindicated

THE NEXT GENERAL EVIDENCE given unto the truth under consideration is the account of the accomplishment of this promise under the New Testament, where also the nature of the operation of the Holy Spirit herein is in general expressed. And this is Galatians 4:6: "Because ye are sons, God hath sent forth the Spirit of his Son into your hearts, crying, 'Abba Father.'" An account, as was said, is here given of the accomplishment of the promise before explained. And sundry things may be considered in the words.

EXEGETICAL POINTS

1. The subjects on whom he is bestowed, and in whom he works, are believers, or those who by the Spirit of adoption are made the children of God. We *receive the adoption of sons, and because we are sons, he sends his Spirit into our hearts*. And this privilege of adoption we obtain by faith in Christ Jesus: "As many as received him, to them gave he power to become the sons of God, even to them that believe on his name" (John 1:12). Secondly, there is an especial appellation or description of the Spirit as promised and given unto this purpose. He is the "Spirit of the Son." That the original ground and reason hereof is his eternal relation to the Son, as proceeding from him, has been elsewhere evinced.[1] But there is something more particular here intended. He is called the "Spirit of the Son" with respect unto his communication to believers. There is, therefore, included herein that special regard unto Jesus Christ the Son of God which is in the work mentioned, as it is an evangelical mercy and privilege. He is, therefore,

---

1 *Πνευματολογια, or, A Discourse concerning the Holy Spirit*, bk. 1, chap. 2.

called the "Spirit of the Son," not only because of his eternal procession from him, but (1) because he was in the first place given unto him, as the head of the church, for the unction, consecration, and sanctification of his human nature. Here he laid the foundation, and gave an example of what he was to do in and toward all his members. (2) It is immediately from and by him that he is communicated unto us, and that two ways: [1] Authoritatively, by virtue of the covenant between the Father and him, whereon, upon his accomplishment of the work of the mediation in a state of humiliation, according to it, he received the promise of the Spirit, that is, power and authority to bestow him on whom he would, for all the ends of that mediation (Acts 2:33; 5:32). [2] Formally, in that all the graces of the Spirit are derived unto us from him, as the head of the church, as the spring of all spiritual life, in whom they were all treasured and laid up unto that purpose (Col. 2:19; Eph. 4:16; Col. 3:1–4).

2. The work of this Spirit in general, as bestowed on believers, is partly included, partly expressed, in these words. In general, which is included, he enables them to behave themselves suitably unto that state and condition whereinto they are taken upon their faith in Christ Jesus. They are made children of God by adoption, and it is meet they be taught to carry themselves as becomes that new relation. "Because ye are sons, he hath given you the Spirit of his Son," without which they cannot walk before him as becomes sons. He teaches them to bear and behave themselves no longer as foreigners and strangers, nor as servants only, but as "children" and "heirs of God" (Rom. 8:15[–17]). He endows them with a frame and disposition of heart unto holy, filial obedience; for as he takes away the distance, making them to be nigh who were aliens and far from God, so he removes that fear, dread, and bondage, which they are kept in who are under the power of the law: "God hath not given us the spirit of fear, but of power, and of love, and of a sound mind" (2 Tim. 1:7). Not "the spirit of fear," or a "spirit of bondage unto fear" (as Rom. 8:15), that is, in and by the efficacy of the law, filling our minds with dread and such considerations of God as will keep us at a distance from him. But he is in the sons, on whom he is bestowed, a Spirit of power, strengthening and enabling them unto all duties of obedience.¶

This "Spirit of power"[2] is that whereby we are enabled to obedience, which the apostle gives thanks for, χάριν ἔχω τῷ ἐνδυναμουντί[3] με Χριστῷ, "To Christ that enableth me" (1 Tim. 1:12), that is, by his Spirit of power.

---

2 In the text: πνεῦμα δυνάμεως.—Owen.

3 *Novum Testamentum Graece* reads, ἐνδυναμώσαντί. *Novum Testamentum Graece*, ed. B. Aland et al., 28th rev. ed. (Stuttgart: Deutsche Bibelgesellschaft, 2012).

For without the Spirit of adoption we have not the least strength or power to behave ourselves as sons in the family of God. And he is also, as thus bestowed, a Spirit of love, who works in us that love unto God and that delight in him which becomes children toward their heavenly Father. This is the first genuine consequent of this relation. There may be many duties performed unto God where there is no true love to him, at least no love unto him as a Father in Christ, which alone is genuine and accepted. And, lastly, he is also a Spirit σωφρονισμοῦ, "of a modest, grave, and sober mind." Even children are apt to wax wanton, and curious, and proud in their Father's house; but the Spirit enables them to behave themselves with that sobriety, modesty, and humility, which becomes the family of God. And in these three things, spiritual power, love, and sobriety of mind, consists the whole deportment of the children of God in his family. This is the state and condition of those who, by the effectual working of the Spirit of adoption, are delivered from the "spirit of bondage unto fear," which the apostle discourses of (Rom. 8:15).

Those who are under the power of that spirit, or that efficacious working of the Spirit by the law, cannot, by virtue of any aids or assistance, make their addresses unto him by prayer in a due manner. For although the means whereby they are brought into this state be the Spirit of God acting upon their souls and consciences by the law, yet formally, as they are in the state of nature, the spirit whereby they are acted is the unclean spirit of the world, or the influence of him who rules in the children of disobedience. The law that they obey is the "law of the members" mentioned by the apostle (Rom. 7). The works which they perform are the unfruitful works of darkness, and the fruits of these unfruitful works are sin and death. Being under this bondage, they have no power to approach unto God, and their bondage tending unto fear, they can have no delight in an access unto him. Whatever other provisions or preparations such persons may have for this duty, they can never perform it unto the glory of God, or so as to find acceptance with him. With those who are delivered from this state, all things are otherwise. The Spirit whereby they are acted is the Spirit of God, the Spirit of adoption, of power, love, and a sound mind. The law which they are under obedience unto is the holy law of God, as written in the fleshy tables of their hearts. The effects of it are faith and love, with all other graces of the Spirit, whereof they receive the fruits in peace, with joy unspeakable and full of glory.

3. An instance is given of his effectually working these things in the adopted sons of God, in the duty of prayer crying, "Abba, Father." The object of the special duty intended is "God, even the Father" (Eph. 2:18). "Abba ὁ πατήρ," Abba is

the Syriac or Chaldee name for Father, then in common use among the Jews, and Πατήρ was the same name among the Greeks or Gentiles. So that the common interest of Jews and Gentiles in this privilege may be intended, or rather, a holy boldness and intimate confidence of love is designed in the reduplication of the name. The Jews have a saying in the Babylonian Talmud, in the Treatise of Blessings, "Servants and handmaids," that is, bond servants, "do not call on such a one Abba or Ymma."[4] Freedom of state, with a right unto adoption, whereof they are incapable, is required unto this liberty and confidence. God gives unto his adopted sons רוח נדיבה[5] , "a free Spirit" (Ps. 51:12), a Spirit of gracious, filial ingenuity. This is that Spirit which cries "Abba." That is the word whereby those who were adopted did first salute their fathers, to testify their affection and obedience. For "abba" signifies not only "father," but "my father"; for אבי , "my father," in the Hebrew, is rendered by the Chaldee paraphrast only אבא , "abba." See Genesis 19:34, and elsewhere constantly. To this purpose speaks Chrysostom: "Being willing to show the ingenuity," that is in this duty, "he useth also the language of the Hebrews, and says not only 'Father,' but 'Abba, Father,' which is a word proper unto them who are highly ingenuous."[6]

And this he effects two ways. First, by the excitation of graces and gracious affections in their souls in this duty, especially those of faith, love, and delight. Second, by enabling them to exercise those graces and express those affections in vocal prayer. For κράζον denotes not only crying, but an earnestness of mind expressed in vocal prayer. It is praying "in a loud voice,"[7] as it is said of our Savior (Matt. 27:50). For the whole of our duty in our supplications is expressed herein. Now, we are not concerned, or do not at present inquire, what course they take, what means they employ, or what helps they use in prayer, who are not as yet partakers of this privilege of adoption. It is only

---

4　In the text: אותם וחשפחות אין העבדים ולא אמא פלונית לא אבא פלוני.—Owen. For the Hebrew text and English translation, see Koren Talmud Bavli, noé ed., vol. 1, Berakhot (Jerusalem: Koren Publishers, 2012), Berakhot 16b:15.

5　Biblia Hebraica Stuttgartensia reads, נְדִיבָה. Biblia Hebraica Stuttgartensia, ed. Karl Elliger and Wilhelm Rudolph (Stuttgart: Deutsche Bibelgesellschaft, 1983).

6　In the text: Βουλόμενος δεῖξαι γνησιότητα, καὶ τῇ τῶν Ἑβραίων ἐχρήσατο γλώσσῃ οὐ γὰρ εἶπε μόνον ὁ πατήρ, ἀλλ' αββᾶ ὁ πατήρ, ὅπερ τῶν παίδων μάλιστά ἐστι τῶν γνησίων πρὸς πατέρα ῥῆμα.—Owen. The English translation is Owen's. For the Greek text, see Joannis Chrysostomi, Homiliae in epistolam secundum ad Ephesios, ed. J. P. Migne, Patrologia Graeca 62 (Paris: Migne, 1862). For an English translation, see John Chrysostom, Commentary on the Epistle to the Galatians, and Homilies on the Epistle to the Ephesians, trans. William John Copeland (London: John Henry Parker, J. G. F. and J. Rivington, 1840). John Chrysostom (ca. 347–407), was Archbishop of Constantinople remembered primarily for his preaching. He was one of the church fathers most cited in the Reformed tradition.

7　In the text: ἐν φωνῇ μεγάλῃ.—Owen.

those who are so, whom the Spirit of God assists in this duty. And the only question is, What such persons are to do in compliance with his assistance, or what it is that they obtain thereby?

And we may compare the different expressions used by the apostle in this matter, whereby the general nature of the work of the Spirit herein will further appear. In this place he says, "God hath sent forth into our hearts," τὸ πνεῦμα τοῦ υἱοῦ κράζον, "the Spirit of his Son, crying, Abba, Father" (Rom. 8:15). He says we have received τὸ πνεῦμα υἱοθεσίας ἐν ᾧ κράζομεν, "the Spirit of adoption," the Spirit of the Son, given us because we are sons, "whereby," or in whom, "we cry, Abba, Father."[8] His acting in us, and our acting by him, are expressed by the same word. And the inquiry here is, how, in the same duty, he is said to cry in us, and we are said to cry in him. And there can be no reason hereof but only because the same work is both his and ours in divers respects. As it is an act of grace and spiritual power it is his, or it is wrought in us by him alone. As it is a duty performed by us, by virtue of his assistance, it is ours; by him we cry, "Abba, Father." And to deny his actings in our duties is to overthrow the gospel. And it is prayer formally considered, and as comprising the gift of it, with its outward exercise, which is intended. The mere excitation of the graces of faith, love, trust, delight, desire, self-abasement, and the like animating principles of prayer, cannot be expressed by crying, though it be included in it. Their actual exercise in prayer, formally considered, is that which is ascribed unto the Spirit of God. And they seem to deal somewhat severely with the church of God and all believers who will not allow that the work here expressly assigned unto the Spirit of adoption, or of the Son, is sufficient for its end, or the discharge of this duty, either in private or in the assemblies of the church. There is no more required unto prayer either way but our crying, "Abba, Father," that is, the making our requests known unto him as our Father in Christ, with supplications and thanksgivings, according as our state and occasions do require. And is not the aid of the Spirit of God sufficient to enable us hereunto? It was so of old, and that unto all believers, according as they were called unto this duty, with respect unto their persons, families, or the church of God. If it be not so now, it is either because God will not now communicate his Spirit unto his children or sons, according to the promise of the gospel, or because, indeed, this grace and gift of his is by men despised, neglected, and lost. And the former cannot be asserted on any safe grounds whatever; the latter it is our interest to consider.

8   Owen is combining concepts and quoting Greek from both Rom. 8:15 and Gal. 4:6.

CONCLUSION

This twofold testimony, concerning the promise of the communication of the Holy Spirit or a Spirit of supplication unto believers under the New Testament, and the accomplishment of it, does sufficiently evince our general assertion, that there is a peculiar work or special gracious operation of the Holy Ghost in the prayers of believers enabling them thereunto. For we intend no more hereby but that as they do receive him by virtue of that promise, which the world cannot do, in order unto his gracious efficiency in the duty of supplication, so he does actually incline, dispose, and enable them to cry "Abba, Father," or to call upon God in prayer as their Father by Jesus Christ. To deny this, therefore, is to rise up in contradiction unto the express testimony of God himself, and by our unbelief to make him a liar. And had we nothing further to plead in this cause, this would be abundantly sufficient to reprove the petulant[9] folly of them by whom this work of the Holy Ghost, and the duty of believers thereon to pray in the Spirit, if we may use the despised and blasphemed expressions of the Scripture, is scorned and derided.

For as to the ability of prayer which is thus received, some there are who know no more of it, as exercised in a way of duty, but the outside, shell, and appearance of it; and that not from their own experience, but from what they observed in others. Of these there are not a few who confidently affirm that it is wholly a work of fancy, invention, memory, and wit, accompanied with some boldness and elocution, unjustly fathered on the Spirit of God, who is no way concerned therein. And it may be they do persuade many, no better skilled in these things than themselves, that so it is indeed. Howbeit, those who have any experience of the real aids and assistances of the Spirit of God in this work and duty, any faith in the express testimonies given by God himself hereunto, cannot but despise such fabulous imaginations. You may as soon persuade them that the sun does not give light, nor the fire heat, that they see not with their eyes, nor hear with their ears, as that the Spirit of God does not enable them to pray, or assist them in their supplications. And there might some probability be given unto these pretenses, and unto the total exclusion of the Holy Ghost from any concern herein, if those concerning whom and their duties they thus judge were generally persons known to excel others in those natural endowments and acquired abilities whereunto this faculty of prayer is ascribed. But will this be allowed by them who make use of this pretense, namely, that those who are thus able to pray, as they pretend, by virtue of a spiritual gift, are persons excelling in fancy,

9 I.e., insolent or rude.

memory, wit, invention, and elocution? It is known that they will admit of no such thing; but in all other instances they must be represented as dull, stupid, ignorant, unlearned, and brutish. Only in prayer they have the advantage of those natural endowments.¶

These things are hardly consistent with common ingenuity. For is it not strange that those who are so contemptible with respect unto natural and acquired endowments in all other things, whether of science or of prudence, should yet in this one duty or work of prayer so improve them as to outgo the imitation of them by whom they are despised? For as they do not, as they will not, pray as they do, so their own hearts tell them they cannot, which is the true reason why they so despitefully oppose this praying in the Spirit, whatever pride or passion pretends to the contrary. But things of this nature will again occur unto us, and therefore shall not be here further insisted on.¶

Having, therefore, proved that God has promised a plentiful dispensation of his Spirit unto believers under the New Testament, to enable them to pray according unto his mind, and that, in general, this promise is accomplished in and toward all the children of God, it remains, in the second place, as to what we have proposed, that we declare what is the work of the Holy Ghost in them unto this end and purpose, or how he is unto us a Spirit of prayer or supplication.

4

The Nature of Prayer

Romans 8:26 Opened and Vindicated

PRAYER AT PRESENT I take to be a gift, ability, or spiritual faculty of exercising faith, love, reverence, fear, delight, and other graces, in a way of vocal requests, supplications, and praises unto God: "In everything . . . let your requests be made known unto God" (Phil. 4:6).

This gift and ability I affirm to be bestowed, and this work by virtue thereof to be wrought in us, by the Holy Ghost, in the accomplishment of the promise insisted on, so crying "Abba, Father," in them that do believe. And this is that which we are to give an account of, wherein we shall assert nothing but what the Scripture plainly goes before us in, and what the experience of believers, duly exercised in duties of obedience, does confirm. And in the issue of our endeavor we shall leave it unto the judgment of God and his church, whether they are ecstatic, enthusiastic, unaccountable raptures that we plead for, or a real gracious effect and work of the Holy Spirit of God.

THE MATTER OF PRAYER

The first thing we ascribe unto the Spirit herein is, that he supplies and furnishes the mind with a due comprehension of the matter of prayer, or what ought, both in general and as unto all our particular occasions, to be prayed for. Without this, I suppose it will be granted that, no man can pray as he ought. For how can any man pray that knows not what to pray for? Where there is not a comprehension hereof, the very nature and being of prayer is destroyed. And herein the testimony of the apostle is express: "Likewise the Spirit also helpeth our infirmities, for we know not what we should pray for as we ought, but the Spirit itself maketh intercession for us with groanings which cannot be uttered" (Rom. 8:26).

It is that expression only which at present I urge, "We know not what we should pray for as we ought." This is generally supposed to be otherwise, namely, that men know well enough what they ought to pray for, only they are wicked and careless, and will not pray for what they know they ought so to do. I shall make no excuse or apology for the wickedness and carelessness of men, which, without doubt, are abominable. But yet I must abide by the truth asserted by the apostle, which I shall further evidence immediately, namely, that without the special aid and assistance of the Holy Spirit no man knows what to pray for as he ought.

But yet there is another relief in this matter, and so no need of any work of the Holy Ghost therein. And we shall be accounted impudent if we ascribe anything unto him whereof there is the least colorable pretense that it may be otherwise effected or provided for. So great an unwillingness is there to allow him either place, work, or office in the Christian religion or the practice of it. Wherefore, it is pretended that although men do not of themselves know what to pray for, yet this defect may be supplied in a prescript form of words, prepared on purpose to teach and confine men unto what they are to pray for.

We may, therefore, dismiss the Holy Spirit and his assistance as unto this concern of prayer; for the due matter of it may be so set down and fixed on ink and paper that the meanest capacity cannot miss of his duty therein. This, therefore, is that which is to be tried in our ensuing discourse, namely, that whereas it is plainly affirmed that "we know not" of ourselves "what we should pray for as we ought," which I judge to be universally true as unto all persons, as well those who prescribe prayers as those unto whom they are prescribed, and that the Holy Spirit helps and relieves us herein, whether we may or ought to relinquish and neglect his assistance, and so to rely only on such supplies as are invented or used unto that end for which he is promised; that is, plainly, whether the word of God is to be trusted unto in this matter or not.

It is true, that whatever we ought to pray for is declared in the Scripture, yea, and summarily comprised in the Lord's Prayer. But it is one thing to have what we ought to pray for in the book, another thing to have it in our minds and hearts, without which it will never be unto us the due matter of prayer. It is out of the "abundance of the heart" that the mouth must speak in this matter (Matt. 12:34). There is, therefore, in us a threefold defect with respect unto the matter of prayer, which is supplied by the Holy Spirit, and can be so no other way nor by any other means; and therein is he unto us a Spirit of supplication according to the promise.

For first, we know not our own wants, second, we know not the supplies of them that are expressed in the promises of God, and third, we know not the end whereunto what we pray for is to be directed, which I add unto the former. Without the knowledge and understanding of all these, no man can pray as he ought; and we can no way know them but by the aid and assistance of the Spirit of grace. And if these things be manifest, it will be evident how in this first instance we are enabled to pray by the Holy Ghost.

OUR WANTS

First, our wants, as they are to be the matter of prayer, may be referred unto three heads, and none of them of ourselves do we know aright, so as to make them the due subject of our supplications, and of some of them we know nothing at all.

1. This first consists in our outward straits, pressures, and difficulties, which we desire to be delivered from, with all other temporal things wherein we are concerned. In those things, it should seem wondrously clear that of ourselves we know what to pray for. But the truth is, whatever our sense may be of them and our natural desires about them, yet how and when, under what conditions and limitations, with what frame of heart and spirit, what submission unto the pleasure of God, they are to be made the matter of our prayers, we know not. Therefore, does God call the prayers of most about them "howling," and not a crying unto him with the heart (Hos. 7:14). There is, indeed, a voice of nature crying in its distress unto the God of nature, but that is not the duty of evangelical prayer which we inquire after; and men ofttimes most miss it when they think themselves most ready and prepared. To know our temporal wants so as to make them the matter of prayer according to the mind of God requires more wisdom than of ourselves we are furnished with. For "who knoweth what is good for man in this life, all the days of his vain life which he spendeth as a shadow?" (Eccl. 6:12). And ofttimes believers are never more at a loss than how to pray aright about temporal things. No man is in pain or distress, or under any wants, whose continuance would be destructive to his being, but he may, yes, he ought to make deliverance from them the matter of his prayer. So in that case he knows in some measure, or in general, what he ought to pray for, without any peculiar spiritual illumination. But yet the circumstances of those things, and wherein their respect unto the glory of God and the supreme end or chiefest good of the persons

concerned does stand, with regard whereunto they can alone be made the matter of prayer acceptable unto God in Christ, are that which of themselves they cannot understand, but have need of an interest in that promise made to the church, that "they shall be all taught of God."[1] And this is so much more in such things as belong only unto the conveniences of this life, whereof no man of himself knows what is good for him or useful unto him.

2. We have internal wants that are discerned in the light of a natural conscience; such is the guilt of sin, whereof that accuses, sins against natural light and the plain outward letter of the law. These things we know somewhat of without any special aid of the Holy Spirit (Rom. 2:14–15), and desires of deliverance are inseparable from them. But we may observe here two things. (1) That the knowledge which we have hereof of ourselves is so dark and confused as that we are no way able thereby to manage our wants in prayer aright unto God. A natural conscience, awakened and excited by afflictions or other providential visitations, will discover itself in unfeigned and severe reflections of guilt upon the soul. But until the Spirit does convince of sin, all things are in such disorder and confusion in the mind that no man knows how to make his address unto God about it in a due manner. And there is more required, to treat aright with God about the guilt of sin, than a mere sense of it. So far as men can proceed under that sole conduct and guidance, the heathens went in dealing with their supposed gods, without a due respect unto the propitiation made by the blood of Christ. Yea, prayer about the guilt of sin, discerned in the light of a natural conscience, is but an "abomination." Besides, (2) we all know how small a portion of the concern of believers does lie in those things which fall under the light and determination of a natural conscience. For,

3. The things about which believers do and ought to treat principally and deal with God, in their supplications, are the inward spiritual frames and dispositions of their souls, with the actings of grace and sin in them. Hereon David was not satisfied with the confession of his origin and all known actual sins (Ps. 51:1–5), nor yet with an acknowledgment that "none knoweth his own wanderings," from whence he desires cleansing from "unknown sins" (Ps. 19:12). But, moreover, he begs of God to undertake the inward search of his heart, to find out what was amiss or right in him (Ps. 139:23–24), as knowing that God principally required "truth in the inward parts" (Ps. 51:6). Such is the carrying on of the work of sanctification in the whole spirit and soul (1 Thess. 5:23).

---

1   John 6:45.

The inward sanctification of all our faculties is what we want and pray for. Supplies of grace from God unto this purpose, with a sense of the power, guilt, violence, and deceit of sin, in its inward actings in the mind and affections, with other things innumerable thereunto belonging, make up the principal matter of prayer as formally supplication.

Add hereunto that unto the matter of prayer, taken largely for the whole duty so called, everything wherein we have intercourse with God in faith and love does belong. The acknowledgment of the whole mystery of his wisdom, grace, and love in Christ Jesus, with all the fruits, effects, and benefits which there we do receive, all the workings and actings of our souls toward him, with their faculties and affections, in brief, every thing and every conception of our minds wherein our spiritual access unto the throne of grace does consist, or which does belong thereunto, with all occasions and emergencies of spiritual life, are in like manner comprised herein. And that we can have such an acquaintance with these things as to manage them acceptably in our supplications, without the grace of spiritual illumination from the Holy Ghost, few are so ignorant or profane as to assert. Some, I confess, seem to be strangers unto these things, which yet renders them not of the less weight or moment.

But hence it comes to pass that the prayers of believers about them, especially their confessions of what sense they have of the power and guilt of the inward actings of sin, have been by some exceedingly traduced and reproached. For whereas they cannot out of their ignorance understand such things, out of their pride, heightened by sensuality of life, they despise and contemn[2] them.

The Promises of God: The Measure of Prayer

Secondly, the matter of prayer may be considered with respect unto the promises of God. These are the measure of prayer, and contain the matter of it. What God has promised, all that he has promised, and nothing else, are we to pray for. For "secret things belong unto the Lord our God"[3] alone, but the declaration of his will and grace belongs unto us, and is our rule. Wherefore, there is nothing that we really do or may stand in need of but God has promised the supply of it, in such a way and under such limitations as may make it good and useful unto us. And there is nothing that God has promised but we stand in need of it, or are some way or other concerned in

---

2   I.e., treat or regard with contempt.
3   Deut. 29:29.

it as members of the mystical body of Christ. Wherefore, "we know not what we should pray for as we ought," unless we know or understand the goodness, grace, kindness, and mercy that is prepared and proposed in the promises of God. For how should we, seeing we are to pray for all that God has promised, and for nothing but what God has promised, and as he has promised it? The inquiry, therefore, that remains is, whether we of ourselves, without the special assistance of the Holy Spirit, do understand these things or not. The apostle tells us that the "things of God," spiritual things, "knoweth no man, but the Spirit of God," and that we must receive the Spirit which is of God to know the things that are freely given to us of God (1 Cor. 2:11–12), which are the grace, mercy, love, and kindness of the promises (2 Cor. 7:1). To say that of ourselves we can perceive, understand, and comprehend these things, without the special assistance of the Holy Ghost, is to overthrow the whole gospel and the grace of our Lord Jesus Christ, as has been elsewhere demonstrated.[4]

But it may be, it will be said, there is more stir than needs made in this matter. God help poor sinners, if all this be required unto their prayers. Certainly men may pray at a cheaper rate, and with much less trouble, or very few will continue long in that duty. For some can see no necessity of thus understanding the grace and mercy that is in the promises unto prayer, and suppose that men know well enough what to pray for without it.

But those who so speak neither know what it is to pray, nor, it seems, are willing to learn. For we are to pray in faith (Rom. 10:14), and faith respects God's promises (Heb. 4:1; Rom. 4). If, therefore, we understand not what God has promised, we cannot pray at all. It is marvelous what thoughts such persons have of God and themselves, who, without a due comprehension of their own wants, and without an understanding of God's promises, wherein all their supplies are laid up, do "say their prayers," as they call it, continually. And indeed, in the poverty, or rather misery, of devised aids of prayer, this is not the least pernicious effect or consequent, that they keep men off from searching the promises of God, whereby they might know what to pray for. Let the matter of prayer be so prescribed unto men as that they shall never need either to search their own hearts or God's promises about it, and this whole work is dispatched out of the way. But then is the soul prepared aright for this duty, and then only, when it understands its own condition, the supplies of grace provided in the promises, the suitableness of those supplies unto its wants, and the means of its conveyance unto us by Jesus Christ. That all this we have by the Spirit, and not otherwise, shall be immediately declared.

---

4 E.g., Πνευματολογια, or, A Discourse concerning the Holy Spirit, bk. 3.

The End of Prayer

Thirdly, unto the matter of prayer, I join the end we aim at in the things we pray for, and which we direct them unto. And herein, also, are we in ourselves at a loss; and men may lose all the benefit of their prayers by proposing undue ends unto themselves in the things they pray for. Our Savior says, "Ask, and ye shall receive";[5] but the apostle James affirms of some, "Ye ask, and receive not, because ye ask amiss, that ye may consume it on your pleasures" (James 4:3). To pray for anything, and not expressly unto the end whereunto of God it is designed, is to ask amiss, and to no purpose. And yet, whatever confidence we may have of our own wisdom and integrity, if we are left unto ourselves, without the special guidance of the Spirit of God, our aims will never be suited unto the will of God. The ways and means whereby we may fail, and do so in this kind, when not under the actual conduct of the Spirit of God, that is, when our own natural and distempered affections do immix[6] themselves in our supplications, are innumerable. And there is nothing so excellent in itself, so useful unto us, so acceptable unto God, in the matter of prayer, but it may be vitiated, corrupted, and prayer itself rendered vain, by an application of it unto false or mistaken ends. And what is the work of the Spirit to guide us herein we shall see in its proper place.

5   Matt. 7:7.
6   I.e., mix thoroughly.

The Work of the Holy Spirit as to the Matter of Prayer

THESE THINGS ARE CONSIDERABLE as to the matter of prayer; and with respect unto them, of ourselves we know not what we should pray for, nor how, nor when. And the first work of the Spirit of God, as a Spirit of supplication in believers, is to give them an understanding of all their wants, and of the supplies of grace and mercy in the promises, causing a sense of them to dwell and abide on their minds, as that, according unto their measure, they are continually furnished with the matter of prayer, without which men never pray, and by which, in some sense, they pray always. For,

SUPPLY OF THE MATTER

He alone does, and he alone is able to give us such an understanding of our own wants as that we may be able to make our thoughts about them known unto God in prayer and supplication. And what is said concerning our wants is so likewise with respect unto the whole matter of prayer, whereby we give glory to God, either in requests or prayers. And this I shall manifest in some instances, whereunto others may be reduced.

1. The principal matter of our prayers concerns faith and unbelief. So, the apostles prayed in a particular manner, "Lord, increase our faith";[1] and so the poor man prayed in his distress, "Lord, help thou mine unbelief."[2] I cannot think that they ever pray aright who never pray for the pardon of unbelief,

---

1 Luke 17:5.
2 Mark 9:24.

for the removal of it, and for the increase of faith. If unbelief be the greatest of sins, and if faith be the greatest of the gifts of God, we are not Christians if these things are not one principal part of the matter of our prayers. Unto this end we must be convinced of the nature and guilt of unbelief, as also of the nature and use of faith; nor without that conviction do we either know our own chiefest wants, or what to pray for as we ought. And that this is the special work of the Holy Ghost our Savior expressly declares, "He will convince the world of sin, because they believe not on me" (John 16:8–9). I do and must deny that anyone is or can be convinced of the nature and guilt of that unbelief, either in the whole or in the remainders of it, which the gospel condemns, and which is the great condemning sin under the gospel, without a special work of the Holy Ghost on his mind and soul. For unbelief, as it respects Jesus Christ, not believing in him, or not believing in him as we ought, is a sin against the gospel, and it is by the gospel alone that we may be convinced of it, and that as it is the ministration of the Spirit.¶

Wherefore, neither the light of a natural conscience nor the law will convince anyone of the guilt of unbelief with respect unto Jesus Christ, nor instruct them in the nature of faith in him. No innate notions of our minds, no doctrines of the law, will reach hereunto. And to think to teach men to pray, or to help them out in praying, without a sense of unbelief, or the remainders of it, in its guilt and power, the nature of faith, with its necessity, use, and efficacy, is to say unto the naked and the hungry, "Be ye warmed and filled,"[3] and not give them those things that are needed for the body. This, therefore, belongs unto the work of the Spirit as a Spirit of supplication. And let men tear and tire themselves night and day with a multitude of prayers, if a work of the Spirit of God in teaching the nature and guilt of unbelief, and the nature, efficacy, and use of faith in Christ Jesus, go not with it, all will be lost and perish.¶

And yet it is marvelous to consider how little mention of these things occurs in most of those compositions which have been published to be used as forms of prayer. They are generally omitted in such endeavors, as if they were things wherein Christians were very little concerned. The gospel positively and frequently determines the present acceptance of men with God or their disobedience, with their future salvation and condemnation, according unto their faith or unbelief. For their obedience or disobedience are infallible consequents thereon. Now, if things that are of the greatest importance unto us, and whereon all other things wherein our spiritual estate is concerned do

3   James 2:16.

depend, be not a part of the subject matter of our daily prayer, I know not what deserves so to be.

2. The matter of our prayer respects the depravation of our nature, and our wants on that account. The darkness and ignorance that is in our understandings, our unacquaintedness with heavenly things, and alienation from the life of God thereby, the secret workings of the lusts of the mind under the shade and covert[4] of this darkness, the stubbornness, obstinacy, and perverseness of our wills by nature, with their reluctancies unto and dislike of things spiritual, with innumerable latent guiles from there arising, all keeping the soul from a due conformity unto the holiness of God, are things which believers have a special regard unto in their confessions and supplications. They know this to be their duty, and find by experience that the greatest concern between God and their souls, as to sin and holiness, does lie in these things. And they are never more jealous over themselves than when they find their hearts least affected with them. And to give over treating with God about them, for mercy in their pardon, for grace in their removal, and the daily renovation of the image of God in them thereby, is to renounce all religion and all designs of living unto God.

Wherefore, without a knowledge, a sense, a due comprehension of these things, no man can pray as he ought, because he is unacquainted with the matter of prayer, and knows not what to pray for. But this knowledge we cannot attain of ourselves. Nature is so corrupted as not to understand its own depravation. Hence some absolutely deny this corruption of it, so taking away all necessity of laboring after its cure and the renovation of the image of God in us. And hereby they overthrow the prayers of all believers, which the ancient church continually pressed the Pelagians with. Without a sense of these things, I must profess I understand not how any man can pray. And this knowledge, as was said, we have not of ourselves. Nature is blind, and cannot see them; it is proud, and will not own them; stupid, and is senseless of them. It is the work of the Spirit of God alone to give us a due conviction of, a spiritual insight into, and a sense of the concern of, these things. This I have elsewhere so fully proved as not here again to insist on it.[5]

It is not easy to conjecture how men pray, or what they pray about, who know not the plague of their own hearts. Yea, this ignorance, want of light into, or conviction of, the depravation of their nature, and the remainders thereof even in those that are renewed, with the fruits, consequents, and

---

4   I.e., thicket in which game can hide.
5   Πνευματολογια, or, A Discourse concerning the Holy Spirit, bk. 3.

effects thereof, are the principal cause of men's barrenness in this duty, so that they can seldom go beyond what is prescribed unto them. And they can, therefore, also satisfy themselves with a set or frame of well-composed words, wherein they might easily discern that their own condition and concern are not at all expressed if they were acquainted with them. I do not fix measures unto other men, nor give bounds unto their understandings; only I shall take leave to profess, for my own part, that I cannot conceive or apprehend how any man does or can know what to pray for as he ought, in the whole compass and course of that duty, who has no spiritual illumination, enabling him to discern in some measure the corruption of his nature and the internal evils of his heart. If men judge the faculties of their souls to be undepraved, their minds free from vanity, their hearts from guile and deceit, their wills from perverseness and carnality, I wonder not on what grounds they despise the prayers of others, but should do so to find real humiliation and fervency in their own.

Hereunto I may add the irregularity and disorder of our affections. These, I confess, are discernible in the light of nature, and the rectifying of them, or an attempt for it, was the principal end of the old philosophy. But the chief respect that on this principle it had unto them is as they disquiet the mind, or break forth into outward expressions, whereby men are defiled, or dishonored, or distressed. So far natural light will go, and thereby, in the working of their consciences, as far as I know, men may be put to pray about them. But the chief depravation of the affections lies in their aversation[6] unto things spiritual and heavenly.

They are, indeed, sometimes ready of themselves to like things spiritual under false notions of them, and divine worship under superstitious ornaments and meretricious[7] dresses, in which respect they are the spring and life of all that devotion which is in the Church of Rome. But take heavenly and spiritual things in themselves, with respect unto their proper ends, and there is in all our affections, as corrupted, a dislike of them and aversation unto them, which variously act themselves, and influence our souls unto vanities and disorders in all holy duties. And no man knows what it is to pray who is not exercised in supplications for mortifying, changing, and renewing of these affections as spiritually irregular. And yet is it the Spirit of God alone which discovers these things unto us, and gives us a sense of our concern in them. I say, the spiritual irregularity of our affections, and their aversation from

---

6   I.e., turning away; alienation.
7   I.e., pretentious; gaudy; having the nature of prostitution.

spiritual things, is discernible in no light but that of supernatural illumination. For if without that, spiritual things themselves cannot be discerned, as the apostle assures us they cannot (1 Cor. 2), it is impossible that the disorder of our affections with respect unto them should be so. If we know not an object in the true nature of it, we cannot know the actings of our minds toward it. Wherefore, although there be in our affections an innate, universal aversation from spiritual things, seeing by nature we are wholly alienated from the life of God, yet can it not be discerned by us in any light but that which discovers these spiritual things themselves unto us. Nor can any man be made sensible of the evil and guilt of that disorder who has not a love also implanted in his heart unto those things which it finds obstructed thereby. Wherefore, the mortification of these affections, and their renovation with respect unto things spiritual and heavenly, being no small part of the matter of the prayers of believers, as being a special part of their duty, they have no otherwise an acquaintance with them or sense of them but as they receive them by light and conviction from the Spirit of God. And those who are destitute hereof must needs be strangers unto the life and power of the duty of prayer itself.

As it is with respect unto sin, so it is with respect unto God and Christ, and the covenant, grace, holiness, and privileges. We have no spiritual conceptions about them, no right understanding of them, no insight into them, but what is given us by the Spirit of God. And without an acquaintance with these things, what are our prayers, or what do they signify? Men without them may say on to the world's end without giving anything of glory unto God, or obtaining of any advantage unto their own souls.

And this I place as the first part of the work of the Spirit of supplication in believers, enabling them to pray according to the mind of God, which of themselves they know not how to do, as is afterward in the place of the apostle insisted on. When this is done, when a right apprehension of sin and grace, and of our concern in them, is fixed on our minds, then have we in some measure the matter of prayer always in readiness, which words and expressions will easily follow, though the aid of the Holy Spirit be necessary thereunto also, as we shall afterward declare.

And hence it is, that the duty performed with respect unto this part of the aid and assistance of the Spirit of God is of late by some, as was said, vilified and reproached. Formerly their exceptions lay all of them against some expressions or weakness of some persons in conceived prayer, which they liked. But now scorn is poured out upon the matter of prayer itself, especially the humble and deep confessions of sin, which, on the discoveries before mentioned, are made in the supplications of ministers and others. The things themselves are traduced as absurd, foolish, and irrational, as all spiritual things are unto some sorts of men. Neither do I see how this disagreement is capable of any reconciliation. For they who have no light to discern those respects of sin and grace which we have mentioned cannot but think it uncouth to have them continually made the matter of men's prayers. And those, on the other hand, who have received a light into them and acquaintance with them by the Spirit of God are troubled at nothing more than that they cannot sufficiently abase themselves under a sense of them, nor in any words fully express that impression on their minds which is put on them by the Holy Ghost, nor clothe their desires after grace and mercy with words sufficiently significant and emphatic. And therefore, this difference is irreconcilable by any but the Spirit of God himself. While it does abide, those who have respect only unto what is discernible in the light of nature, or of a natural conscience, in their prayers will keep themselves unto general expressions and outward things, in words prepared unto that purpose by themselves or others, do we what we can to the contrary. For men will not be led beyond their own light, neither is it meet they should. And those who do receive the supplies of the Spirit in this matter will in their prayers be principally conversant about the spiritual, internal concerns of their souls in sin and grace, let others despise them and reproach them while they please. And it is in vain much to contend about these things, which are regulated not by arguments but by principles. Men will invincibly adhere unto the capacity of their light. Nothing can put an end to this difference but a more plentiful effusion of the Spirit from above, which, according unto the promise, we wait for.

SUPPLY OF THE MEASURE

Secondly, we know not what to pray for as we ought, but the Holy Ghost acquaints us with the grace and mercy which are prepared in the promises of God for our relief. That the knowledge hereof is necessary, to enable us to direct our prayers unto God in a due manner, I declared before, and I suppose it will not be denied. For, what do we pray for? What do we take a prospect and design of in our supplications? What is it we desire to be made partakers of? Praying only by saying or repeating so many words of prayer, whose sense and meaning those who make use of them perhaps understand not, as in the Papacy, or so as to rest in the saying or repetition of them without a special design of obtaining some thing or things which we make known in our supplications, is unworthy [of] the disciples of Christ, indeed of rational creatures. "Deal thus with thy governor, will he be pleased with thee, or accept thy person?" (as Mal. 1:8). Neither ruler, nor friend, nor neighbor, would accept it at our hands, if we should constantly make solemn addresses unto them without any special design. We must pray with our understanding, that is, understand what we pray for. And these things are no other but what God has promised, which if we are not regulated by in our supplications, we ask amiss.¶

It is, therefore, indispensably necessary unto prayer that we should know what God has promised, or that we should have an understanding of the grace and mercy of the promises. God knows our wants, what is good for us, what is useful to us, what is necessary to bring us unto the enjoyment of himself, infinitely better than we do ourselves; yea, we know nothing of these things but what he is pleased to teach us. These are the things which he has "prepared for us," as the apostle speaks (1 Cor. 2:9). And what he has so prepared he declares in the promises of the covenant, for they are the declaration of the grace and good pleasure which he has purposed in himself. And hence believers may learn what is good for them, and what is wanting unto them in the promises, more clearly and certainly than by any other means whatever. From them, therefore, do we learn what to pray for as we ought. And this is another reason why men are so barren in their supplications, they know not what to pray for, but are forced to betake themselves unto a confused repetition of the same requests, namely, their ignorance of the promises of God and the grace exhibited in them. Our inquiry, therefore, is, by what way or means we come to an acquaintance with these promises, which all believers have in some measure, some more full and distinct than others, but all in a useful sufficiency. And this, we say, is by the Spirit of God, without whose aid and assistance we can neither understand them nor what is contained in them.

I do confess that some, by frequent reading of the Scripture, by only the help of a faithful memory, may be able to express in their prayers the promises of God, without any spiritual acquaintance with the grace of them, whereby they administer unto others, and not unto themselves. But this remembrance of words or expressions belongs not unto the special work of the Holy Ghost in supplying the hearts and minds of believers with the matter of prayer. But this is that which he does herein: he opens their eyes, he gives an understanding, he enlightens their minds, so that they shall perceive the things that are of God prepared for them, and that are contained in the promises of the gospel; and represents them therein in their beauty, glory, suitableness, and desirableness unto their souls. He makes them to see Christ in them, and all the fruits of his mediation in them, all the effect of the grace and love of God in them, the excellency of mercy and pardon, of grace and holiness, of a new heart, with principles, dispositions, inclinations, and actings, all as they are proposed in the truth and faithfulness of God. Now, when the mind and heart is continually filled with an understanding and due apprehension of these things, it is always furnished with the matter of prayer and praise unto God, which persons make use of according as they have actual assistance and utterance given unto them. And whereas this Holy Spirit together with the knowledge of them does also implant a love unto them upon the minds of believers, they are not only hereby directed what to pray for, but are excited and stirred up to seek after the enjoyment of them with ardent affections and earnest endeavors, which is to pray. And although, among those on whose hearts these things are not implanted, some may, as was before observed, make an appearance of it, by expressing in prayer the words of the promises of God retained in their memories, yet for the most part they are not able themselves to pray in any tolerable useful manner, and do either wonder at or despise those that are so enabled.

But it may be said, that where there is any defect herein, it may be easily supplied. For if men are not acquainted with the promises of God themselves in the manner before described, and so know not what they ought to pray for, others, who have the understanding of them, may compose prayers for their use, according to their apprehensions of the mind of God in them, which they may read, and so have the matter of prayer always in a readiness.

I answer—1. I do not know that anyone has a command or promise of assistance to make or compose prayers to be said or read by others as their prayers; and therefore, I expect no great matter from what anyone shall do in that kind. The Spirit of grace and supplication is promised, as I have proved, to enable us to pray, not to enable us to make or compose prayers for others.

2. It savors of some unacquaintance with the promises of God and the duty of prayer, to imagine that the matter of them, so as to suit the various conditions of believers, can be pent up in any one form of man's devising. Much of what we are to pray about may be in general and doctrinally comprised in a form of words, as they are in the Lord's Prayer, which gives directions in and a boundary unto our requests. But that the things themselves should be prepared and suited unto the condition and wants of them that are to pray is a fond imagination.

3. There is a vast difference between an objective proposal of good things to be prayed for unto the consideration of them that are to pray, which men may do, and the implanting an acquaintance with them and love unto them upon the mind and heart, which is the work of the Holy Ghost.

4. When things are so prepared and cast into a form of prayer, those by whom such forms are used do no more understand them than if they had never been cast into any such form, unless the Spirit of God give them an understanding of them, which the form itself is no sanctified means unto. And where that is done, there is no need of it.

5. It is the work of the Holy Spirit to give unto believers such a comprehension of promised grace and mercy as that they may constantly apply their minds unto that or those things in a special manner which are suited unto their present daily wants and occasions, with the frame and dispositions of their souls and spirit. This is that which gives spiritual beauty and order unto the duty of prayer, namely, the suiting of wants and supplies, of a thankful disposition and praises, of love and admiration, unto the excellencies of God in Christ, all by the wisdom of the Holy Ghost. But when a person is made to pray by his directory for things, though good in themselves, yet not suited unto his present state, frame, inclination, wants, and desires, there is a spiritual confusion and disorder, and nothing else.

Again, what we have spoken concerning the promises must also be applied unto all the precepts or commands of God. These in like manner are the matter of our prayers, both as to confession and supplication. And without a right understanding of them, we can perform no part of this duty as we ought. This is evident in their apprehension who, repeating the words of the decalogue, do subjoin their acknowledgments of a want of mercy, with respect unto the transgression of them, I suppose, and their desires to have their hearts inclined to keep the law. But the law with all the commands of God are spiritual and inward, with whose true sense and importance, in their extent and latitude, we cannot have a useful acquaintance but by the enlightening, instructing efficacy of the grace of the Spirit. And where this is, the mind is greatly supplied with the true matter of prayer. For when the soul has learned the spirituality and holiness of the law, its extent unto the inward frame and disposition of our hearts, as well as unto outward actions, and its requiring absolute holiness, rectitude, and conformity unto God, at all times and in all things, then does it see and learn its own discrepancy from it and coming short of it, even then when as to outward acts and duties it is unblamable. And hence do proceed those confessions of sin, in the best and most holy believers, which they who understand not these things do deride and scorn. By this means, therefore, does the Holy Spirit help us to pray, by supplying us with the due and proper matter of supplications, even by acquainting us and affecting our hearts with the spirituality of the command, and our coming short thereof in our dispositions and frequent inordinate actings of our minds and affections. He who is instructed herein will on all occasions be prepared with a fullness of matter for confession and humiliation, as also with a sense of that grace and mercy which we stand in need of with respect unto the obedience required of us.

SUPPLY OF THE PROPER END TO PRAY FOR

Thirdly, he alone guides and directs believers to pray or ask for anything in order unto right and proper ends. For there is nothing so excellent in itself, so useful unto us, so acceptable unto God, as the matter of prayer, but it may be vitiated, corrupted, and prayer itself be rendered vain, by an application of it unto false or mistaken ends. And that in this case we are relieved by the Holy Ghost, is plain in the text under consideration. For helping our infirmities and teaching us what to pray for as we ought, he "maketh intercession for us according to God," that is, his mind or his will (Rom. 8:27). This is well explained by Origen on the place:

And he is like a teacher who accepts a student who is both a raw recruit and completely ignorant of the alphabet. In order to be able to teach and instruct him, he is forced to stoop down to the elementary attempts of the student and he himself first pronounces the name of each letter so the student learns by repeating. And in a way, the teacher himself becomes like the beginning student, saying and practicing the things that the beginner needs to say and practice. In this way as well then, when the Holy Spirit sees that our spirit is being harassed by the struggles of the flesh and does not know what or how it ought to pray, like the teacher, first says the prayer that our spirit, if it longs to be a pupil of the Holy Spirit, should imitate. He offers groanings by which our spirit may be taught to groan in order to re-propitiate God with itself.[8]

8   In the text: *Velut si magister suscipiens ad rudimenta discipulum, et ignorantem penitus literas, ut eum docere possit et instituere, necesse habet inclinare se ad discipuli rudimenta, et ipse prius dicere nomen literae, ut respondendo discipulus discat, et sit quodammodo magister incipienti discipulo similis, ea loquens et ea meditans, quae incipiens loqui debeat ac meditari; ita et Sanctus Spiritus, ubi oppugnationibus carnis perturbari nostrum spiritum viderit, et nescientem quid orare debeat secundum quod oportet, ipse velut magister orationem praemittit, quam noster spiritus (si tamen discipulus esse Sanctus Spiritus desiderat) prosequatur, ipse gemitus offert quibus noster spiritus discat ingemiscere, ut repropitiet sibi Deum.*—Owen. For a critical Latin edition, see C. P. Hammond Bammel, *Der Römerbriefkommentar des Origenes: Kritische Ausgabe der Übersetzung Rufins,* Buch 7–10 (Freiburg im Breisgau: Herder, 1990), comment on Rom. 8:26–27. For the English translation, see Origen, *Fathers of the Church: Commentary on the Epistle to the Romans, Books 6–10,* trans. Thomas P. Scheck (Washington, DC: Catholic University of America Press,

To the same purpose speaks Damascen[9] and Augustine in sundry places, collected by Bede,[10] in his comment on this. He does it in us and by us, or enables us so to do. For the Spirit himself without us has no office to be performed immediately toward God, nor any nature inferior unto the divine wherein he might intercede. The whole of any such work with respect unto us is incumbent on Christ; he alone in his own person performs what is to be done with God for us. What the Spirit does, he does in and by us. He therefore directs and enables us to make supplications according to the mind of God. And herein God is said to know the mind of the Spirit, that is, his end and design in the matter of his requests. This God knows, that is, approves of and accepts. So, it is the Spirit of God who directs us as to the design and end of our prayers, that they may find acceptance with God.

But yet there may be, and I believe there is, more in that expression, "God knoweth the mind of the Spirit" (Rom. 8:27). For he works such high, holy, spiritual desires and designs in the minds of believers in their supplications as God alone knows and understands in their full extent and latitude. That of ourselves we are apt to fail and mistake has been declared from James 4:3.

I shall not here insist on particulars, but only mention two general ends of prayer which the Holy Spirit keeps the minds of believers unto in all their requests, where he has furnished them with the matter of them according to the mind of God. For he does not only make intercession in them, according unto the mind of God, with respect unto the matter of their requests, but also with respect unto the end which they aim at, that it may be accepted with him. He guides them, therefore, to design,

---

2002), 81. Origen of Alexandria (ca. 185–ca. 253) was an Alexandrian theologian, philosopher, apologist, text critic, exegete, preacher, and ascetic, and one of the greatest minds of the patristic period. His commentary on Romans is the oldest extant commentary on Romans, which, originally written in Greek, survives through the Latin translation of Tyrranius Rufinus (ca. 344–411).

9   In the text: (lib. iv. chap. 3).—Owen. The citation is likely a reference to one of the editions of John of Damascus's complete works circulating at the time of Owen's writing. John of Damascus (ca. 675–749) was a great systematizer of the Eastern church's belief. John of Damascus does comment on Romans 8:26–27 in line with the quoted Origen passage in bk. 4, chap. 22 of *Orthodox Faith*. See *Saint John of Damascus: Writings*, ed. Roy Joseph Deferrari, trans. Frederic H. Chase Jr., Fathers of the Church 37 (Washington, DC: Catholic University of America Press, 1958), 389. For the Greek text, see *Sancti Joannis Damasceni opera omnia quae extant*, ed. J. P. Migne, Patrologia Graeca 94 (Paris: Migne, 1864).

10 Venerable Bede (ca. 673–735) was an English Benedictine monk, perhaps most well known for his *Ecclesiastical History of the English People*, making him one of the first historians of Christian Europe. Here Owen is alluding to Bede's collection of Augustine's comments on Romans, *Collectio Bedae presbyteri ex opusculis sancti Augustini in epistulas Pauli apostoli* (unprinted). For English translation, see *Bede the Venerable: Excerpts from the Works of Saint Augustine on the Letters of the Blessed Apostle Paul*, trans. David Hurst (Kalamazoo, MI: Cistercian, 1999).

1. That all the success of their petitions and prayers may have an imme-diate tendency unto the glory of God. It is he alone who enables them to subordinate all their desires unto God's glory. Without his special aid and assistance we should aim at self only and ultimately in all we do. Our own profit, ease, satisfaction, mercies, peace, and deliverance would be the end whereunto we should direct all our supplications, whereby they would be all vitiated and become abominable.

2. He keeps them unto this also, that the issue of their supplications may be the improvement of holiness in them, and thereby their conformity unto God, with their nearer access unto him. Where these ends are not, the matter of prayer may be good and according to the word of God, and yet our prayers an abomination. We may pray for mercy and grace, and the best promised fruits of the love of God, and yet for want of these ends find no acceptance in our supplications. To keep us unto them is his work, because it consists in casting out all self ends and aims, bringing all natural desires unto a subor-dination unto God, which he works in us if he works in us anything at all.¶

And this is the first part of the work of the Spirit toward believers as a Spirit of grace and supplication. He furnishes and fills their minds with the matter of prayer, teaching them thereby what to pray for as they ought. And where this is not wrought in some measure and degree, there is no praying according to the mind of God.

6

The Due Manner of Prayer, Wherein It Does Consist

THE HOLY SPIRIT HAVING GIVEN the mind a due apprehension of the things we ought to pray for, or furnished it with the matter of prayer, he moreover works a due sense and valuation of them, with desires after them, upon the will and affections, wherein the due manner of it does consist. These things are separable. The mind may have light to discern the things that are to be prayed for, and yet the will and affections be dead unto them or unconcerned in them. And there may be a gift of prayer founded hereon, in whose exercise the soul does not spiritually act toward God, for light is the matter of all common gifts. And by virtue of a perishing illumination, a man may attain a gift in prayer which may be of use unto the edification of others. For the manifestation of the Spirit is given unto every man to profit with. In the meantime, it is with him that so prays not much otherwise than it was with him of old who prayed in an unknown tongue; his spirit prays, but his understanding is unfruitful. He prays by virtue of the light and gift that he has received, but his own soul is not benefited nor improved thereby. Only sometimes God makes use of men's own gifts to convey grace into their own souls. But prayer, properly so called, is the obedient acting of the whole soul toward God.

CONFORMING THE WILL AND AFFECTIONS

Wherefore, where the Holy Spirit completes his work in us as a Spirit of grace and supplication, he works on the will and affections to act obedientially toward God in and about the matter of their prayers. Thus, when he is poured out as a Spirit of supplication, he fills them unto whom he is communicated with mourning and godly sorrow, to be exercised in their prayers as the matter does require (Zech. 12:10). He does not only enable them to pray, but works affections in them suitable unto what they pray about. And in this work of the Spirit lies the fountain of that inexpressible fervency and delight, of those enlarged laborings of mind and desires, which are in the prayers of believers, especially when they are under the power of more than ordinary influences from him. For these things proceed from the work of the Spirit on their wills and affections, stirring them up and carrying them forth unto God, in and by the matter of their prayers, in such a manner as no vehement working of natural affections can reach unto. And therefore is the Spirit said to "make intercession for us with groanings which cannot be uttered," ὑπερε-ντυγχάνει[1] (Rom. 8:26–27). As he had before expressed his work in general by συναντιλαμβάνεται,[2] which intends a help by working, carrying us on in our undertaking in this duty beyond our own strength, for he helps us on under our infirmities or weaknesses, so his special acting is here declared by ὑπερεντυγχάνει, that is, an additional interposition, like that of an advocate for his client, pleading that in his case which he of himself is not able to do.¶

Once this word is used in the service of a contrary design. Speaking of the prayer of Elijah, the apostle says, ὡς ἐντυγχάνει τῷ θεῷ κατὰ τοῦ Ἰσραήλ, "How he maketh intercession to God against Israel" (Rom. 11:2), as בשׁר, which is constantly used in the Old Testament for "to declare good tidings, tidings of peace," is once applied in a contrary signification unto tidings of evil and destruction (1 Sam. 4:17). The man that brought the news of the destruction of the army of the Israelites and the taking of the ark by the Philistines is called המבשר.[3] But the proper use of this word is to intercede for grace and favor. And this he does "with groanings that cannot be uttered."[4] We ourselves are said στενάζειν, "to groan" (Rom. 8:23), that is, humbly, mournfully, and earnestly to desire. And here the Spirit is said to intercede for us with groans, which can be nothing but his working in us and acting by us that frame of heart and those fervent, laboring desires, which are so expressed, and these with such depth of intension and laboring of mind as cannot be uttered. And this he does by the work now mentioned.

Having truly affected the whole soul, enlightened the mind in the perception of the truth, beauty, and excellency of spiritual things, engaged the will

---

1 Gk. "to make intercession."
2 Gk. "to help," "come to the aid of," or "be of assistance to."
3 Heb. "messenger."
4 In the text: στεναγμοῖς ἀλαλήτοις.—Owen. Rom. 8:26.

in the choice of them and prevalent love unto them, excited the affections to delight in them and unto desires after them, there is in the actual discharge of this duty of prayer, wrought in the soul by the power and efficacy of his grace, such an inward laboring of heart and spirit, such a holy, supernatural desire and endeavor after a union with the things prayed for in the enjoyment of them, as no words can utter or expressly declare, that is, fully and completely, which is the sense of the place.

To avoid the force of this testimony, some, one at least,[5] would have this intercession of the Spirit to be the intercession of the Spirit in Christ for us now at the right hand of God, so that no work of the Spirit itself in believers is intended. Such irrational evasions will men sometimes make use of to escape the convincing power of light and truth. For this is such a description of the intercession of Christ at the right hand of God as will scarcely be reconciled unto the analogy of faith. That it is not a humble, oral supplication, but a blessed representation of his oblation, whereby the efficacy of it is continued and applied unto all the particular occasions of the church or believers, I have elsewhere declared, and it is the common faith of Christians.[6] But here it should be reported as the laboring of the Spirit in him with unutterable groans, the highest expression of a humble, burdened, solicitous[7] endeavor. Nothing is more unsuited unto the present glorious condition of the mediator. It is true that in the days of his flesh he prayed with strong crying and tears, in a humble deprecation of evil (Heb. 5:7). But a humble prostration and praying with unutterable groans is altogether inconsistent with his present state of glory, his fullness of power, and right to dispense all the grace and mercy of the kingdom of God. Besides, this exposition is as adverse to the context as anything that could be invented. It is said that we receive the "Spirit of adoption, whereby we cry, Abba, Father" (Rom. 8:15), which Spirit God "sends forth into our hearts" (Gal. 4:6). And the blessed work of this Spirit in us is further described (Rom. 8:16–17). And thereon (Rom. 8:23), having received the firstfruits of this Spirit, we are said to groan within ourselves; to which it is added, that of ourselves not knowing what we ought to pray for, αὐτὸ τὸ πνεῦμα, "that very Spirit," so given unto us, so received by us, so working in us, "maketh intercession for us with groanings which cannot be uttered."[8] Wherefore, without offering violence unto the context, there is no place for

---

5   Owen may be referring to Cressy here, but that is not certain.
6   Owen may be referring to *The Doctrine of the Saints' Perseverance Explained and Confirmed* (1654), chap. 8.
7   I.e., meticulous; careful.
8   Rom. 8:26.

the introduction of the intercession of Christ in heaven, especially under such an expression as is contrary to the nature of it. It is mentioned afterward by the apostle, in its proper place, as a consequent and fruit of his death and resurrection (Rom. 8:34). And there he is said simply ἐντυγχάνειν[9] but the Spirit here is said ὑπερεντυγχάνειν, which implies an additional supply unto what is in ourselves.

Yet, to give countenance unto this uncouth exposition, a force is put upon the beginning of both the verses, 26–27. For whereas ἀσθένεια does constantly in the Scripture denote any kind of infirmity or weakness, spiritual or corporeal, it is said here to be taken in the latter sense, for diseases with troubles and dangers, which latter it nowhere signifies. For so the meaning should be, that in such conditions we know not what to pray for, whether wealth, or health, or peace, or the like, but Christ intercedes for us. And this must be the sense of συναντιλαμβάνεται ταῖς ἀσθενείαις ἡμων,[10] which yet in the text does plainly denote a help and assistance given unto our weaknesses, that is, unto us who are weak, in the discharge of the duty of prayer, as both the words themselves and the ensuing reasons of them do evince. Wherefore, neither the grammatical sense of the words, nor the context, nor the analogy of faith, will admit of this new and uncouth exposition.

In like manner, if it be inquired why it is said "that he who searcheth the hearts knoweth what is the mind of the Spirit," which plainly refers to some great and secret work of the Spirit in the heart of man, if the intercession of Christ be intended, nothing is offered but this paraphrase, "And then God, that, by being a searcher of hearts, knoweth our wants exactly, understands also the desire and intention of the Spirit of Christ" (Rom. 8:27). But these things are ἀπροσδιόνυσα,[11] and have no dependence the one on the other. Nor was there any need of the mentioning the searching of our hearts, to introduce the approbation of the intercession of Christ. But to return.

That is wrought in the hearts of believers in their duty which is pervious[12] to none but him that searches the heart. This frame in all our supplications we ought to aim at, especially in time of distress, troubles, and temptations, such as was the season here especially intended, when commonly we are most sensible of our own infirmities. And wherein we come short hereof in some measure, it is from our unbelief, or carelessness and negligence, which God abhors. I do acknowledge that there may be, that there will be, more

9 Gk. "to appeal."
10 Gk. "helps our infirmities."
11 Gk. "impertinent; irrelevant."
12 I.e., permeable.

earnestness and intension of mind, and of our natural spirit therein, in this duty, at one time than another, according as outward occasions or other motives do excite them or stir them up. So, our Savior in his agony prayed more earnestly than usual, not with a higher exercise of grace, which always acted itself in him in perfection, but with a greater vehemency in the working of his natural faculties. So, it may be with us at special seasons; but yet we are always to endeavor after the same aids of the Spirit, the same actings of grace in every particular duty of this kind.

DELIGHT IN GOD AS THE OBJECT OF PRAYER

The Holy Spirit gives the soul of a believer a delight in God as the object of prayer. I shall not insist on his exciting, moving, and acting all other graces that are required in the exercise of this duty, as faith, love, reverence, fear, trust, submission, waiting, hope, and the like. I have proved elsewhere that the exercise of them all, in all duties, and of all other graces in like manner, is from him, and shall not therefore here again confirm the same truth.[13] But this delight in God as the object of prayer has a peculiar consideration in this matter. For without it ordinarily the duty is not accepted with God, and is a barren, burdensome task unto them by whom it is performed. Now, this delight in God as the object of prayer is, for the substance of it, included in that description of prayer given us by the apostle—namely, that it is "crying Abba, Father."[14] Herein a filial, holy delight in God is included, such as children have in their parents in their most affectionate addresses unto them, as has been declared. And we are to inquire wherein this delight in God as the object of prayer does consist, or what is required thereunto. And there is in it,

1. A sight or prospect of God as on a throne of grace. A prospect, I say, not by carnal imagination, but spiritual illumination. "By faith we see him who is invisible" (Heb. 11:27). For it is the "evidence of things not seen"[15] making its proper object evident and present unto them that do believe. Such a sight of God on a throne of grace is necessary unto this delight. Under this consideration he is the proper object of all our addresses unto him in our supplications: "Let us come boldly unto the throne of grace, that we may obtain mercy, and find grace to help in time of need" (Heb. 4:16). The duty of prayer is described by the subject matter of it, namely, "mercy" and "grace," and by the only object of it, "God on a throne of grace."

13 Owen is likely referring to *Πνευματολογια, or, A Discourse concerning the Holy Spirit*.
14 Gal. 4:6.
15 Heb. 11:1.

And this "throne of grace" is further represented unto us by the place where it is erected or set up, and that is in the holiest or most holy place. For in our coming unto God as on that throne, we have "boldness to enter into the holiest by the blood of Jesus" (Heb. 10:19). And hereby the apostle shows that in the expression he has respect or alludes unto the mercy seat upon the ark, covered with the cherubims, which had a representation of a throne. And because of God's special manifestation of himself thereon, it was called his throne. And it was a representation of Jesus Christ, as I have showed elsewhere.

God, therefore, on a throne of grace is God as in a readiness through Jesus Christ to dispense grace and mercy to suppliant sinners. When God comes to execute judgment, his throne is otherwise represented (Dan. 7:9–10). And when sinners take a view in their minds of God as he is in himself, and as he will be unto all out of Christ, it ingenerates[16] nothing but dread and terror in them, with foolish contrivances to avoid him or his displeasure (Isa. 33:14; Mic. 6:6–7; Rev. 6:16–17). All these places and others testify that when sinners do engage into serious thoughts and conceptions of the nature of God, and what entertainment they shall meet with from him, all their apprehensions issue in dread and terror. This is not a frame wherein they can cry, "Abba, Father." If they are delivered from this fear and bondage, it is by that which is worse, namely, carnal boldness and presumption, whose rise lies in the highest contempt of God and his holiness. When men give up themselves to the customary performance of this duty, or rather "saying of their prayers," I know not out of what conviction that so they must do, without a due consideration of God and the regard that he has unto them, they do but provoke him to his face in taking his name in vain; nor, however they satisfy themselves in what they do, have they any delight in God in their approaches unto him.

Wherefore, there is required hereunto a prospect of God, by faith, as on a "throne of grace," as exalted in Christ to show mercy unto sinners. So is he represented: "Therefore will the Lord wait, that he may be gracious, and therefore will he be exalted, that he may have mercy" (Isa. 30:18). Without this we cannot draw nigh to him, or call upon him with delight, as becomes children, crying, "Abba, Father." And by whom is this discovery made unto us? Is this a fruit of our own fancy and imagination? So, it may be with some, to their ruin. But it is the work of the Spirit, who alone, in and through Christ, reveals God unto us, and enables us to discern him in a due manner. Hence our apostle prays for the Ephesians "that the God of our Lord Jesus Christ, the

---

16   I.e., generates or produces.

Father of glory, would give unto them the Spirit of wisdom and revelation in the knowledge of him, that the eyes of their understanding being enlightened, they might know what is the hope of his calling, and what the riches of the glory of his inheritance in the saints" (Eph. 1:17–18). All the acquaintance which we have with God, in a way of grace, is from the revelation made in us by his Spirit (Col. 2:1–2). By him does God say unto us that "fury is not in him," and that if we lay hold on his arm, that we may have peace, we shall have peace (Isa. 27:4–5).

2. Unto this delight is required a sense of God's relation unto us as a Father. By that name, and under that consideration, has the Lord Christ taught us to address ourselves unto him in all our supplications. And although we may use other titles and appellations in our speaking to him, even such as he has given himself in the Scripture, or those which are analogous thereunto, yet this consideration principally influences our souls and minds, that God is not ashamed to be called our Father, that "the Lord Almighty hath said that he will be a Father unto us, and that we shall be his sons and daughters" (2 Cor. 6:18). Wherefore, as a Father is he the ultimate object of all evangelical worship, of all our prayers. So is it expressed in that holy and divine description of it given by the apostle, "Through Christ we have access by one Spirit unto the Father" (Eph. 2:18). No tongue can express, no mind can reach, the heavenly placidness and soul-satisfying delight which are intimated in these words. To come to God as a Father, through Christ, by the help and assistance of the Holy Spirit, revealing him as a Father unto us, and enabling us to go to him as a Father, how full of sweetness and satisfaction is it! Without a due apprehension of God in this relation, no man can pray as he ought. And hereof we have no sense, herewith we have no acquaintance, but by the Holy Ghost. For we do not consider God in a general manner, as he may be said to be a Father unto the whole creation, but in a special, distinguishing relation, as he makes us his children by adoption. And as it is "the Spirit that beareth witness with our spirit that we are thus the children of God" (Rom. 8:16), giving us the highest and utmost assurance of our estate of sonship in this world; so being the Spirit of adoption, it is by him alone that we have any acquaintance with our interest in that privilege.

Some may apprehend that these things belong but little, and that very remotely, unto the duty of prayer, and the assistance we receive by the Spirit therein. But the truth is, those who are so minded, on consideration, know neither what it is to pray nor what does belong thereunto. There is nothing more essential unto this duty than that, in the performance of it, we address ourselves unto God under the notion of a Father, that is, the Father of our

Lord Jesus Christ, and in him our Father also. Without this we cannot have that holy delight in this duty which is required in us, and the want whereof ordinarily ruins our design in it. And this we can have no spiritual, satisfactory sense of but what we receive by and from the Spirit of God.

3. There belongs thereunto that boldness which we have in our access into the holy place, or unto the throne of grace: "Having therefore boldness to enter into the holiest by the blood of Jesus, let us draw near with a true heart in full assurance of faith" (Heb. 10:19, 22). Where there is on men a "spirit of fear unto bondage," they can never have any delight in their approaches unto God. And this is removed by the Spirit of grace and supplication: "Ye have not received the spirit of bondage again to fear; but ye have received the Spirit of adoption, whereby we cry, 'Abba, Father'" (Rom. 8:15). These things are opposed, and the one is only removed and taken away by the other. And where the "spirit of bondage unto fear" abides, there we cannot cry, "Abba, Father," or pray in a due manner. But "where the Spirit of the Lord is, there is liberty" (2 Cor. 3:17). And this, as we render the word, consists in two things: first, *In orandi libertate*;[17] second, *In exauditionis fiducia*.[18]¶

(1) There is in it an enlarged liberty and freedom of speech in prayer unto God. So the word signifies. Παρρησία is as much as πανρησία, a freedom to speak all that is to be spoken, a confidence that countenances men in the freedom of speech, according to the exigency of their state, condition, and cause. So the word is commonly used (Eph. 6:19). Where there is servile fear and dread, the heart is straitened, bound up, knows not what it may, what it may not, utter, and is pained about the issue of all it thinks or speaks; or it cannot pray at all beyond what is prescribed unto it to say, as it were, whether it will or no. But where this Spirit of liberty and boldness is, the heart is enlarged with a true, genuine openness and readiness to express all its concerns unto God as a child unto its father. I do not say that those who have this aid of the Spirit have always this liberty in exercise, or equally so. The exercise of it may be variously impeded, by temptations, spiritual indispositions, desertions, and by our own negligence in stirring up the grace of God. But believers have it always in the root and principle, even all that have received the Spirit of adoption, and are ordinarily assisted in the use of it. Hereby are they enabled to comply with the blessed advice of the apostle, "Be careful for nothing; but in every thing by prayer and supplication with thanksgiving let your requests be made known unto God" (Phil. 4:6). The whole of our concerns in this world is to be com-

---

17 Lat. "in freedom of prayer."
18 Lat. "in confidence of acceptance."

mitted unto God in prayer, so that we should not retain any dividing cares in our own minds about them. And herein the apostle would have us to use a holy freedom and boldness in speaking unto God on all occasions, as one who concerns himself in them; hide nothing from God, which we do what lies in us when we present it not unto him in our prayers, but use a full, plain-hearted, open liberty with him: "In every thing let your requests be made known unto God." He is ready to hear all that you have to offer unto him or plead before him. And in so doing, the "peace of God, which passeth all understanding, shall keep your hearts and minds through Jesus Christ" (Phil. 4:7), which is ordinarily the condition of those who are found in diligent obedience unto this command.

(2) There is also in it a confidence of acceptance, or being heard in prayer; that is, that God is well pleased with their duties, accepting both them and their persons in Jesus Christ. Without this we can have no delight in prayer, or in God as the object of it, which vitiates the whole duty. When Adam thought there was no acceptance with God for him, he had no confidence of access unto him, but, as the first effect of folly that ensued on the entrance of sin, went to hide himself. And all those who have no ground of spiritual confidence for acceptance with Christ do in their prayers but endeavor to hide themselves from God by the duty which they perform. They cast a mist about them, to obscure themselves from the sight of their own convictions, wherein alone they suppose that God sees them also. But in such a frame there is neither delight, nor enlargement, nor liberty, nor indeed prayer itself.

Now, this confidence or boldness, which is given unto believers in their prayers by the Holy Ghost, respects not the answer of every particular request, especially in their own understanding of it; but it consists in a holy persuasion that God is well pleased with their duties, accepts their persons, and delights in their approaches unto his throne. Such persons are not terrified with apprehensions that God will say unto them, "What have ye to do to take my name into your mouths, or to what purpose are the multitude of your supplications? When ye make many prayers, I will not hear."[19] "Will he," says Job, "plead against me with his great power? No, but he would put strength in me" (Job 23:6). Yea, they are assured that the more they are with God, the more constantly they abide with him, the better is their acceptance. For as they are commanded to pray always and not to faint, so they have a sufficient warranty from the encouragement and call of Christ to be frequent in their spiritual addresses to him. So, he speaks to his church, "O my dove, let me see thy countenance, let me hear thy voice; for sweet is thy voice, and thy countenance is comely" (Song 2:14).

---

19 This seems to be a combination of Psalm 50:16 and Isaiah 1:15.

And herein also is comprised a due apprehension of the goodness and power of God, whereby he is, in all conditions, ready to receive them and able to relieve them. The voice of sinners by nature, let presumption and superstition pretend what they please to the contrary, is, that God is austere, and not capable of condescension or compassion. And the proper acting of unbelief lies in limiting the Most Holy, saying, "Can God do this or that thing, which the supplies of our necessities do call for? Are they possible with God?" So long as either of these works in us with any kind of prevalency, it is impossible we should have any delight in calling upon God. But we are freed from them by the Holy Ghost, in the representation he makes of the engaged goodness and power of God in the promises of the covenant, which gives us boldness in his presence.

It is the work of the Holy Spirit in prayer to keep the souls of believers intent upon Jesus Christ, as the only way and means of acceptance with God. This is the fundamental direction for prayer now under the gospel. We are now to ask in his name; which was not done expressly under the Old Testament. Through him we act faith on God in all our supplications. By him we have an access unto the Father. We enter into the holiest through the new and living way that he has consecrated for us. The various respect which faith has unto Jesus Christ as mediator in all our prayers is a matter worthy a particular inquiry, but is not of our present consideration, wherein we declare the work of the Spirit alone. And this is a part of it, that he keeps our souls intent upon Christ, according unto what is required of us, as he is the way of our approach unto God, the means of our admittance, and the cause of our acceptance with him. And where faith is not actually exercised unto this purpose, all prayer is vain and unprofitable. And whether our duty herein be answered with a few words, wherein his name is expressed with little spiritual regard unto him, is worth our inquiry.

To enable us hereunto is the work of the Holy Ghost. He it is that glorifies Jesus Christ in the hearts of believers (John 16:14). And this he does when he enables them to act faith on him in a due manner. So speaks the apostle expressly: "Through him we have access by one Spirit unto the Father" (Eph. 2:18). It is through Jesus alone that we have our access unto God, and that by faith in him. So we have our access unto him for our persons in justification: "By whom we have access by faith into this grace wherein we stand" (Rom. 5:2). And by him we have our actual access unto him in our supplications when we draw nigh to the throne of grace. But this is by the Spirit. It is he who enables us hereunto, by keeping our minds spiritually intent on him in all our addresses unto God. This is a genuine effect of the Spirit as he is the "Spirit of the Son," under which consideration in a special manner he is bestowed on us to enable us to pray (Gal. 4:6). And hereof believers have a refreshing experience in themselves. Nor does anything leave a better savor or relish on their souls than when they have had their hearts and minds kept close, in the exercise of faith, on Christ the mediator in their prayers.

CONCLUSION

I might yet insist on more instances in the declaration of the work of the Holy Ghost in believers, as he is a Spirit of grace and supplication. But my design is not to declare what may be spoken, but to speak what ought not to be omitted. Many other things, therefore, might be added, but these will suffice to give an express understanding of this work unto them who have any spiritual experience of it, and those who have not will not be satisfied with volumes to the same purpose.

Yet something may be here added to free our passage from any just exceptions. For, it may be, some will think that these things are not pertinent unto our present purpose, which is to discover the nature of the duty of prayer, and the assistance which we receive by the Spirit of God therein. Now, this is only in the words that we use unto God in our prayers, and not in that spiritual delight and confidence which have been spoken unto, which, with other graces, if they may be so esteemed, are of another consideration. Answer 1: It may be that some think so, and also it may be, and is very likely, that some who will be talking about these things are utterly ignorant what it is to pray in the Spirit, and the whole nature of this duty. Not knowing, therefore, the thing, they hate the very name of it; as indeed it cannot but be uncouth unto all who are no way interested in the grace and privilege intended by it. The objections of such persons are but as the strokes of blind men, whatever strength and violence be in them, they always miss the mark. Such are the fierce arguings of the most against this duty; they are full of fury and violence, but never touch the matter intended. Answer 2: My design is so to discover the nature of praying in the Spirit in general as that therewith I may declare what is a furtherance thereunto and what is a hindrance thereof. For if there be any such ways of praying, which men use or oblige themselves unto, which do not comply with, or are not suited to promote, or are unconcerned in, or do not express those workings of the Holy Ghost which are so directly assigned unto him in the prayers of believers, they are all nothing but means of quenching the Spirit, of disappointing the work of his grace, and rendering the prayers themselves so used, and as such, unacceptable with God. And apparent it is, at least, that most of the ways and modes of prayer used in the Papacy are inconsistent with, and exclusive of, the whole work of the Spirit of supplication.

The Nature of Prayer in General, with Respect unto Forms of Prayer and Vocal Prayer

Ephesians 6:18 Opened and Vindicated

THE DUTY I AM ENDEAVORING to express is that enjoined in Ephesians 6:18: "Praying always with all prayer and supplication in the Spirit, and watching thereunto with all perseverance and supplication for all saints." Some have made bold to advance a fond imagination, as what will not enmity unto the holy ways of God put men upon? That "praying in the Spirit" intends only praying by virtue of an extraordinary and miraculous gift. But the use of it is here enjoined unto all believers, none excepted, men and women, who yet, I suppose, had not all and every one of them that extraordinary, miraculous gift which they fancy to be intended in that expression. And the performance of this duty is enjoined them, in the manner prescribed, ἐν παντὶ καιρῷ—"always," say we, "in every season," that is, such just and due seasons of prayer as duty and our occasions call for. But the apostle expressly confines the exercise of extraordinary gifts unto some certain seasons, when, under some circumstances, they may be needful or useful unto edification (1 Cor. 14). There is, therefore, "a praying in the Spirit," which is the constant duty of all believers, and it is a great reproach unto the profession of Christianity where that name itself is a matter of contempt. If there be anything in it that is foolish, conceited, fanatical, the holy apostle must answer for it, yea, he by whom he was inspired. But if this be the expression of God himself of that duty which he requires of us, I would not willingly be among the number of them by whom it is derided, let their pretenses be what they please. Besides, in the text, all believers are said thus "to pray in the Spirit at all seasons," διὰ πάσης προσευχῆς καὶ δεήσεως, and ἐν πάσῃ προσευχῇ καὶ δεήσει, "with all prayer and supplication"; that is, with all manner of prayer, according as our own occasions and necessities do require. A man, certainly, by virtue of this rule, can scarce judge himself obliged to confine his performance of this duty unto a prescript form of words. For a variety in our prayers, commensurate unto the various occasions of ourselves and of the church of God, being here enjoined us, how we can comply therewith in the constant use of any one form I know not; those who do are left unto their liberty. And this we are obliged unto, εἰς αὐτὸ τοῦτο ἀγρυπνοῦντες, "diligently watching unto this very end,"[1] that our prayers may be suited unto our occasions. He who can divide this text, or cut it out into a garment to clothe set forms of prayer with, will discover an admirable dexterity in the using and disposal of a text of Scripture.

But yet neither do I conclude from hence that all such forms are unlawful; only, that another way of praying is here enjoined us is, I suppose, unquestionable unto all impartial searchers after truth. And, doubtless, they are not to be blamed who endeavor a compliance therewith. And if persons are able, in the daily, constant reading of any book whatever, merely of a human composition, to rise up in answer to this duty of "praying always with all manner of prayer and supplication in the Spirit," or the exercise of the aid and assistance received from him, and his holy acting of them as a Spirit of grace and supplication, endeavoring, laboring, and watching thereunto, I shall say no more but that they have attained what I cannot understand.

The sole inquiry remaining is, how they are enabled to pray in whose minds the Holy Ghost does thus work as a Spirit of grace and supplication. And I do say, in answer thereunto, that those who are thus affected by him do never want a gracious ability of making their addresses unto God in vocal prayer, so far as is needful unto them in their circumstances, callings, states, and conditions. And this is that which is called the gift of prayer. I speak of ordinary cases; for there may be such interpositions of temptations and desertions as that the soul, being overwhelmed with them, may for the present be able only to "mourn as a dove," or to "chatter as a crane," that is, not to express the sense of their minds clearly and distinctly, but only as it were to mourn and groan before the Lord in brokenness of spirit and expressions. But this also is sufficient for their acceptance in that condition. And hereof there are few believers but at one time or other they

1 Eph. 6:18.

have more or less experience. And as for those whose devotion discharges itself in a formal course of the same words, as it must needs be in the Papacy, wherein for the most part they understand not the signification of the words which they make use of, they are strangers unto the true nature of prayer, at least unto the work of the Spirit therein. And such supplications as are not variously influenced by the variety of the spiritual conditions of them that make them, according to the variety of our spiritual exercises, are like one constant tone or noise, which has no harmony nor music in it.

I say, therefore, first, that the things insisted on are in some degree and measure necessary unto all acceptable prayer. The Scripture assigns them thereunto, and believers find them so by their own experience. For we discourse not about prayer as it is the working of nature in its straits and difficulties toward the God of nature, expressing thereby its dependence on him, with an acknowledgment of his power, in which sense all flesh, in one way or other, under one notion or other, come to God; nor yet upon those cries which legal convictions will wrest from them that fall under their power; but we treat only of prayer as it is required of believers under the gospel, as they have an "access through Christ by one Spirit unto the Father."[2]

And, second, that those in whom this work is wrought by the Holy Spirit in any degree do not, in ordinary cases, want an ability to express themselves in this duty, so far as is needful for them. It is acknowledged that an ability herein will be greatly increased and improved by exercise, and that not only because the exercise of all moral faculties is the genuine way of their strengthening and improvement, but principally because it is instituted, appointed, and commanded of God unto that end. God has designed the exercise of grace for the means of its growth, and gives his blessing in answer to his institution. But the nature of the thing itself requires a performance of the duty suitably unto the condition of him that is called unto it. And if men grow not up unto further degrees in that ability by exercise in the duty itself, by stirring up the gifts and graces of God in them, it is their sin and folly.

And hence it follows, third, that although set forms of prayer may be lawful unto some, as is pretended, yet are they necessary unto none, that is, unto no true believers, as unto acceptable, evangelical prayer. But whoever is made partaker of the work of the Spirit of God herein, which he does infallibly effect in everyone who through him is enabled to cry, "Abba, Father," as every child of God is, he will be able to pray according to the mind and will of God, if he neglect not the aid and assistance offered unto him for

2   Eph. 2:18.

that purpose. Wherefore, to plead for the necessity of forms of prayer unto believers, beyond what may be doctrinal or instructive in them, is a fruit of inclination unto parties, or of ignorance, or of the want of a due attendance unto their own experience.

Of what use forms of prayer may be unto those that are not regenerate, and have not, therefore, received the Spirit of adoption, belongs not directly unto our disquisition. Yet I must say that I understand not clearly the advantage of them unto them, unless a contrivance to relieve them in that condition, without a due endeavor after a deliverance from it, may be so esteemed. For these persons are of two sorts,

1. Such as are openly under the power of sin, their minds being not effectually influenced by any convictions. These seldom pray, unless it be under dangers, fears, troubles, pains, or other distresses. When they are smitten they will cry, even to the Lord they will cry, and not else. And their design is to treat about their special occasions, and the present sense which they have thereof. And how can any man conceive that they should be supplied with forms of prayer expressing their sense, conceptions, and affections, in their particular cases? And how ridiculously they may mistake themselves in reading those prayers which are no way suited unto their condition, is easily supposed. A form to such persons may prove little better than a charm, and their minds be diverted by it from such a performance of duty as the light of nature would direct to. Jonah's mariners in the storm "cried every one unto his god," and called on him also to do so too (Jonah 1:5–6). The substance of their prayer was, that God would "think upon them, that they might not perish." And men in such condition, if not diverted by this pretended relief, which indeed is none, will not want words to express their minds, so far as there is anything of prayer in what they do; and beyond that, whatever words they are supplied with, they are of no use or advantage unto them. And it is possible when they are left to work naturally toward God, however unskilled and rude their expressions may be, a deep sense may be left upon their minds, with a reverence of God, and remembrance of their own error, which may be of use to them. But the bounding and directing of the workings of natural religion by a form of words, perhaps little suited unto their occasions and not at all to their affections, tends only to stifle the operation of an awakened conscience, and to give them up unto their former security.

2. Others there are, such as by education and the power of convictions from the word, by one means or other, are so far brought under a sense of the authority of God and their own duty as conscientiously, according unto their light, to attend unto prayer, as unto other duties also. Now, the case

of these men will be more fully determined afterward, when the whole use
of the forms of prayer will be spoken unto. For the present I shall only say,
that I cannot believe, until further conviction, that anyone whose duty it is
to pray is not able to express his requests and petitions in words, so far as
he is affected with the matter of them in his mind; and what he does by any
advantage beyond that belongs not to prayer. Men may, by sloth and other
vicious distempers of mind, especially by a negligence in getting their hearts
and consciences duly affected with the matter and object of prayer, keep themselves under a real or supposed disability in this matter. But whereas prayer
in this sort of persons is an effect of common illumination and grace, which
are also from the Spirit of God, if persons do really and sincerely endeavor
a due sense of what they pray for and about, he will not be wanting to help
them to express themselves so far as is necessary for them, either privately
or in their families. But those who will never enter the water but with flags
or bladders under them will scarce ever learn to swim. And it cannot be
denied but that the constant and unvaried use of set forms of prayer may
become a great occasion of quenching the Spirit, and hindering all progress
or growth in gifts or graces. When everyone has done what he can, it is his
best, and will be accepted of him, it being according unto what he has, before
that which is none of his.

8

The Duty of External Prayer
by Virtue of a Spiritual Gift
Explained and Vindicated

WHAT WE HAVE HITHERTO discoursed concerning the work of the Spirit of grace and supplication enabling believers to pray, or to cry "Abba, Father," belongs principally unto the internal, spiritual nature of the duty, and the exercise of grace therein, wherein we have occasionally only diverted unto the consideration of the interest of words, and the use of set forms, either freely or imposed. And, indeed, what has been evinced from Scripture testimony herein does upon the matter render all further dispute about these things needless. For if the things mentioned be required unto all acceptable prayer, and if they are truly effected in the minds of all believers by the Holy Ghost, it is evident how little use there remains of such pretended aids.

But, moreover, prayer falls under another consideration, namely, as to its external performance, and as the duty is discharged by anyone in lesser or greater societies, wherein upon his words and expressions do depend their conjunction with him, their communion in the duty, and consequently their edification in the whole. This is the will of God, that in assemblies of his appointment, as churches and families, and occasional meetings of two or three or more in the name of Christ, one should pray in the name of himself and the rest that join with him. Thus are ministers enabled to pray in church assemblies, as other Christians in occasional meetings of the disciples of Christ in his name, parents in their families, and, in secret, every believer for himself.

111

There is a *spiritual ability given unto men by the Holy Ghost, whereby they are enabled to express the matter of prayer, as taught and revealed in the manner before described, in words fitted and suited to lead on their own minds and the minds of others unto a holy communion in the duty, to the honor of God and their own edification.* I do not confine the use of this ability unto assemblies; everyone may, and usually is to make use of it, according to the measure which he has received, for himself also. For if a man have not an ability to pray for himself in private and alone, he can have none to pray in public and societies. Wherefore, take prayer as vocal, without which adjunct it is not complete, and this ability belongs to the nature and essence of it. And this also is from the Spirit of God.

This is that which meets with such contradiction and opposition from many, and which has other things set up in competition with it, yea, to the exclusion of it, even from families and closets also. What they are we shall afterward examine. And judged it is by some, not only to be separable from the work of the Spirit of prayer, but no way to belong thereunto. A fruit, they say, it is of wit, fancy, memory, elocution, volubility and readiness of speech, namely, in them in whom on other accounts they will acknowledge none of these things to be, at least in no considerable degree! Some while since, indeed, they defended themselves against any esteem of this ability, by crying out that all those who thus prayed by the Spirit, as they call it, did but babble and talk nonsense. But those who have any sobriety and modesty are convinced that the generality of those who do pray according to the ability received do use words of truth and soberness in the exercise thereof. And it is but a sorry relief that any can find in caviling[1] at some expressions, which, perhaps good and wholesome in themselves, yet suit not their palates; or if they are such as may seem to miss of due order and decency, yet is not their failure to be compared with the extravagances, considering the nature of the duty, of some in supposed quaint and elegant expressions used in this duty. But herein they take themselves unto this countenance, that this ability is the effect of the natural endowments before mentioned only, which they think to be set off by a boldness and confidence but a little beneath an intolerable impudence. Thus, it seems, is it with all who desire to pray as God enables them, that is, according to his mind and will, if anything in the light of nature, the common voice of mankind, examples of Scripture, express testimonies and commands, are able to declare what is so. I shall, therefore, make way unto the declaration and confirmation of the truth asserted by the ensuing observations.

---

1   I.e., raising frivolous objections.

UNPRESCRIBED WORDS

1. *Every man is to pray or call upon God, according as he is able*, with respect unto his own condition, relations, occasions, and duties. Certainly, there is not a man in the world who has not forfeited all his reason and understanding unto atheism, or utterly buried all their operations under the fury of brutish affections, but he is convinced that it is his duty to pray to the deity he owns, in words of his own, as well as he is able. For this, and none other, is the genuine and natural notion of prayer. This is implanted in the heart of mankind, which they need not be taught nor directed unto. The artificial help of constant forms is an arbitrary invention. And I would hope that there are but few in the world, especially of those who are called Christians, but that at one time or other do so pray. And those who, for the most part, do take themselves to other reliefs, as unto the reading of prayers, composed unto some good end and purpose, though not absolutely to their occasions, as to the present state of their minds and the things they would pray for, which is absolutely impossible, cannot, as I conceive, but sometimes be conscious to themselves not only of the weakness of what they do, but of their neglect of the duty which they profess to perform. And as for such who, by the prevalency of ignorance, the power of prejudice, and infatuation of superstition, are diverted from the dictates of nature and light of Scripture directions to say a *pater-noster*, it may be an *ave* or a *credo*,[2] for their prayer, intending it for this or that end, the benefit, it may be, of this or that person, or the obtaining of what is no way mentioned or included in what they utter, there is nothing of prayer in it, but a mere taking the name of God in vain, with the horrible profanation[3] of a holy ordinance.

Persons tied up unto such rules and forms never pray in their lives, but in their occasional ejaculations, which break from them almost by surprisal.[4] And there has not been any one more effectual means of bringing unholiness, with an ungodly course of conversation, into the Christian world, than this one of teaching men to satisfy themselves in this duty by their saying, reading, or repetition of the words of other men, which, it may be, they understand not, and certainly are not in a due manner affected with. For it is this duty whereby our whole course is principally influenced. And, let men say what they will, our conversation in walking before God, which

---

2   *Pater-noster*: "our Father"; *Ave*: "hail"; *Credo*: "I believe." These are three abbreviated references to Roman Catholic prayers: the Lord's Prayer, *Ave Maria* ("Hail, Mary"), and the Apostles' Creed.

3   I.e., the act of treating something sacred with abuse, irreverence, or contempt; desecration.

4   I.e., state of being surprised.

principally regards the frame and disposition of our hearts, is influenced and regulated by our attendance unto and performance of this duty. He whose prayers are hypocritical is a hypocrite in his whole course; and he who is but negligent in them is equally negligent in all other duties. Now, whereas our whole obedience unto God ought to be our "reasonable service" (Rom. 12:1), how can it be expected that it should be so when the foundation of it is laid in such an irrational supposition, that men should not pray themselves what they are able, but read the forms of others instead thereof, which they do not understand?

2. All the *examples* we have in the Scripture of the prayers of the holy men of old, either under the Old Testament or the New, were all of them the in expressing the gracious conceptions of their minds, wrought in them by the Holy Ghost in the way and manner before described. I call it their own ability, in opposition to all outward aids and assistances from others, or an antecedaneous[5] prescription of a form of words unto themselves. Not one instance can be given to the contrary. Sometimes it is said they "spread forth their hands," sometimes that they "lifted up their voices," sometimes that they "fell upon their knees and cried," sometimes that they "poured out their hearts"[6] when overwhelmed, all according to present occasions and circumstances. The solemn benediction of the priests, instituted of God, like the present forms in the administration of the sacraments, were of another consideration, as shall be showed. And as for those who, by immediate inspiration, gave out and wrote discourses in the form of prayers, which were in part mystical and in part prophetical, we have before given an account concerning them. Some plead, indeed, that the church of the Jews, under the second temple, had sundry forms of prayers in use among them, even at the time when our Savior was conversant in the temple and their synagogues. But they pretend and plead what they cannot prove, and I challenge any learned man to give but a tolerable evidence unto the assertion. For what is found to that purpose among the Talmudists[7] is mixed with such ridiculous fables, as the first, suiting the number of their prayers to the number of the bones in the back of a man, as fully defeats its own evidence.

3. The *commands* which are given us to pray thus according unto our own abilities are no more nor less than all the commands we have in the Scripture to pray at all. Not one of them has any regard or respect unto outward forms, aids, or helps of prayer. And the manner of prayer itself is so described,

5   I.e., antecedent; preceding in time.
6   Isa. 1:15; 24:14; Acts 7:60; Ps. 62:8.
7   I.e., scholars and adherents of the Jewish Talmud.

limited, and determined, as that no other kind of prayer can be intended. For whereas we are commanded to pray in the Spirit, to pray earnestly and fervently, with the mind and understanding, continually, with all manner of prayer and supplication, to make our requests known unto God, so as not to take care ourselves about our present concerns, to pour out our hearts unto God, to cry, "Abba, Father," by the Spirit, and the like—I do not understand how these things are suited unto any kind of prayer, but only that which is from the ability which men have received for the entire discharge of that duty. For there are evidently intimated in these precepts and directions, such various occasional workings of our minds and spirits, such actings of gracious affections, as will not comply with a constant use of a prescribed form of words.

4. When we speak of men's own ability in this matter, we do include therein the conscientious, diligent use of *all means* which God has appointed for the communication of this ability unto them, or to help them in the due use, exercise, and improvement of it. Such means there are, and such are they to attend unto.

As (1) the diligent searching of our own hearts, in their frames, dispositions, inclinations, and actings, that we may be in some measure acquainted with their state and condition toward God. Indeed, the heart of man is absolutely unsearchable unto any but God himself, that is, as unto a complete and perfect knowledge of it. Hence David prays that God would "search and try him," and lead and conduct him by his grace according unto what he found in him, and not leave him wholly to act or be acted according unto his own apprehensions of himself (Ps. 139:23–24). But yet where we do in sincerity inquire into them, by the help of that spiritual light which we have received, we may discern so much of them as to guide us aright in this and all other duties. If this be neglected, if men live in the dark unto themselves, or satisfy themselves only with an acquaintance with those things which an accusing conscience will not suffer them to be utterly ignorant of, they will never know either how to pray or what to pray for in a due manner. And the want of a due discharge of this duty, which we ought continually to be exercised in, especially on the account of that unspeakable variety of spiritual changes which we are subject unto, is a cause of that barrenness in prayer which is found among the most, as we have observed. He that would abound in all manner of supplication, which is enjoined us, who would have his prayers to be proper, useful, fervent, must be diligent in the search and consideration of his own heart, with all its dispositions and inclinations, and the secret guilt which it does variously contract.

(2) Constant, diligent reading of the Scriptures is another duty that this ability greatly depends upon. From the precepts of God therein may we learn our own wants, and from his promises the relief which he has provided for them. And these things, as has been showed, supply us with the matter of prayer. Moreover, we learn from this what words and expressions are meet and proper to be used in our accesses unto God. No words nor expressions in themselves or their signification are meet or acceptable herein, but from their analogy unto those in the Scripture, which are of God's own teaching and direction. And where men are much conversant in the word, they will be ready for and furnished with meet expressions of their desires to God always. This is one means whereby they may come so to be; and other helps of the like nature might be insisted on.

5. There is a use herein of the *natural abilities* of invention, memory, and elocution. Why should not men use in the service and worship of God what God has given them, that they may be able to serve and worship him? Yea, it sets off the use and excellency of this spiritual gift, that in the exercise of it we use and act our natural endowments and abilities, as spiritualized by grace, which, in the way, set up in competition with it, cannot be done. The more the soul is engaged in its faculties and powers, the more intent it is in and unto the duty.

Nor do I deny but that this gift may be varied in degrees and divers circumstances according unto these abilities, though it have a being of its own distinct from them. Even in extraordinary gifts, as in the receiving and giving out of immediate revelations from God, there was a variety in outward modes and circumstances which followed the diversity and variety of the natural abilities and qualifications of them who were employed in that work. Much more may this difference both be and appear in the exercise of ordinary gifts, which do not so absolutely influence and regulate the faculties of the mind as the other.

And this difference we find by experience among them who are endowed with this spiritual ability. All men who have the gift of prayer do not pray alike, as to the matter of their prayers, or the manner of their praying; but some do greatly excel others, some in one thing, some in another. And this does in part proceed from that difference that is between them in the natural abilities of invention, judgment, memory, elocution, especially as they are improved by exercise in this duty. But yet neither is this absolutely so, nor does the difference in this matter which we observe in constant experience depend solely hereon. For if it did, then those who, having received this spiritual ability, do excel others in those natural endowments, would also constantly excel them in the exercise of the gift itself, which is not so, as is known to all who have observed anything in this matter. But the exercise of these abilities in prayer depends on the special assistance of the Spirit of God. And, for the most part, the gift, as the scion[8] engrafted or inoculated, turns the nature of those abilities into itself, and modifies them according unto its own efficacy and virtue, and is not itself changed by them. Evidently, that which makes any such difference in the discharge of this duty as wherein the edification of others is concerned, is the frequent conscientious exercise of the gift received, without which, into whatever stock of natural abilities it may be planted, it will neither thrive nor flourish.

6. *Spiritual gifts* are of two sorts: (1) Such as are distinct from all other abilities, having their whole foundation, nature, and power in themselves. Such were the extraordinary gifts of miracles, healing, tongues, and the like. These were entire in themselves, not built upon or adjoined unto any other gifts or graces whatever. (2) Such as were adjuncts of, or annexed unto, any other gifts or graces, without which they could have neither place nor use, as the gift of utterance depends on wisdom and knowledge. For utterance without knowledge, or that which is anything but the way of expressing sound knowledge unto the benefit of others, is folly and babbling. And of this latter sort is the gift of prayer, as under our present consideration, with respect unto the interest of words in that duty. And this we affirm to be a peculiar gift of the Holy Ghost, and shall now further prove it so to be. For,

THE SPIRIT'S GIFT OF PRAYER

1. It is an inseparable *adjunct* of that work of the Spirit which we have described, and is therefore from him who is the author of it. For he who is the author of anything as to its being is the author of all its inseparable adjuncts. That the work of enabling us to pray is the work of the Spirit has been proved; and it is an immeasurable boldness for any to deny it, and yet pretend themselves to be Christians. And he is not the author of any one part of this work, but of the whole, all that whereby we cry, "Abba, Father." Hereunto the expression of the desires of our souls, in words suited unto the acting of our own graces and the edification of others, does inseparably belong. When we are commanded to pray, if our necessity, condition, edification, with the advantage and benefit of others, do require the use of words in prayer, then are we so to pray. For instance, when a minister is commanded to pray in the church or congregation, so as to go before the flock in the discharge of

8 I.e., a young shoot or twig of a plant.

that duty, he is to use words in prayer. Yet are we not in such cases required to pray any otherwise than as the Spirit is promised to enable us to pray, and so as that we may still be said to pray in the Holy Ghost. So, therefore, to pray falls under the command and promise, and is a gift of the Holy Spirit.

And the nature of the thing itself, that is, the duty of prayer, does manifest it. For all that the Spirit of God works in our hearts with respect unto this duty is in order unto the expression of it, for what he does is to enable us to pray. And if he gives not that expression, all that he does besides may be lost as to its principal end and use. And, indeed, all that he does in us where this is wanting, or that in fixed meditation, which in some particular cases is equivalent thereunto, rises not beyond that frame which David expresses by his keeping silence, whereby he declares an estate of trouble, wherein yet he was not freely brought over to deal with God about it, as he did afterward by prayer, and found relief therein.

That which with any pretense of reason can be objected hereunto, namely, that not any part only, but the whole duty of prayer as we are commanded to pray, is an effect in us of the Holy Spirit as a Spirit of grace and supplication, or that the grace of prayer and the gift of prayer, as some distinguish, are inseparable, consists in two unsound consequents, which, as is supposed, will therefore ensue. As first, that everyone who has the grace of prayer, as it is called, or in whom the Holy Spirit works the gracious disposition before described, has also the gift of prayer, seeing these things are inseparable. And second, that everyone who has the gift of prayer, or who has an ability to pray with utterance unto the edification of others, has also the grace of prayer, or the actings of saving grace in prayer, which is the thing intended. But these things, it will be said, are manifestly otherwise, and contrary to all experience.

Answer (1) For the first of these inferences, I grant it follows from the premises, and therefore affirm that it is most true, under the ensuing limitations.

[1] We do not speak of what is called the grace of prayer in its habit or principle, but in its actual exercise. In the first respect, it is in all that are sanctified, even in those infants that are so from the womb. It does not hence follow that they must also have the gift of prayer, which respects only grace in its exercise. And thus, our meaning is, that all those in whom the Spirit of God does graciously act faith, love, delight, desire, in a way of prayer unto God, have an ability from him to express themselves in vocal prayer.

[2] It is required hereunto that such persons be found in a way of duty, and so meet to receive the influential assistance of the Holy Spirit. Whoever will use or have the benefit of any spiritual gift must himself, in a way of duty, stir up, by constant and frequent exercise, the ability wherein it does consist:

"Stir up the gift of God which is in thee" (2 Tim. 1:6). And where this duty is neglected, which neglect must be accounted for, it is no wonder if any persons who may have, as they speak, the "grace of prayer," should not yet have the gift or faculty to express their minds and desires in prayer by words of their own. Some think there is no such ability in any, and therefore never look after it in themselves, but despise whatever they hear spoken unto that purpose. What assistance such persons may have in their prayers from the Spirit of grace I know not; but it is not likely they should have much of his aid or help in that wherein they despise him. And some are so accustomed unto and so deceived by pretended helps in prayer, as making use of or reading prayers by others composed for them, that they never attempt to pray for themselves, but always think they cannot do that which, indeed, they will not. As if a child being bred up among none but such impotent persons as go on crutches, as he grows up should refuse to try his own strength, and resolve himself to make use of crutches also. Good instruction, or some sudden surprise with fear, removing his prejudice, he will cast away this needless help, and make use of his strength. Some gracious persons brought up where forms of prayer are in general use may have a spiritual ability of their own to pray, but neither know it nor ever try it, through a compliance with the principles of their education, yea, so as to think it impossible for them to pray any otherwise. But when instruction frees them from this prejudice, or some sudden surprise with fear or affliction casts them into an entrance of the exercise of their own ability in this kind, their former aids and helps quickly grow into disuse with them.

[3] The ability which we ascribe unto all who have the gracious assistance of the Spirit in prayer is not absolute, but suited unto their occasions, conditions, duties, callings, and the like. We do not say that everyone who has received the Spirit of grace and supplication must necessarily have a gift enabling him to pray as becomes a minister in the congregation, or any person on the like solemn occasion; no, nor yet it may be to pray in a family, or in the company of many, if he be not in his condition of life called thereunto. But everyone has this ability according to his necessity, condition of life, and calling. He that is only a private person has so, and he who is the ruler of the family has so, and he that is a minister of the congregation has so also. And as God enlarges men's occasions and calls, so he will enlarge their abilities, provided they do what is their duty to that end and purpose; for the slothful, the negligent, the fearful, those that are under the power of prejudices, will have no share in this mercy. This, therefore, is the sum of what we affirm in this particular: every adult person who has received, and is able to exercise,

grace in prayer, any saving grace, without which prayer itself is an abomination, if he neglect not the improvement of the spiritual aids communicated unto him, does so far partake of this gift of the Holy Spirit as to enable him to pray according as his own occasions and duty do require. He who wants mercy for the pardon of sin, or supplies of grace for the sanctification of his person, and the like, if he be sensible of his wants, and have gracious desires after their supply wrought in his heart, will be enabled to ask them of God in an acceptable manner, if he be not woefully and sinfully wanting unto himself and his own duty.

(2) As to the second inference, namely, that if this ability be inseparable from the gracious assistance of the Spirit of prayer, then whosoever has this gift and ability, he has in the exercise of it that gracious assistance, or he has received the Spirit of grace, and has saving graces acted in him, I answer, [1] it does not follow on what we have asserted. For although wherever is the grace of prayer there is the gift also in its measure, yet it follows not that where the gift is, there must be the grace also. For the gift is for the grace's sake, and not on the contrary. Grace cannot be acted without the gift, but the gift may without the grace. [2] We shall assent that this gift does grow in another soil, and has not its root in itself. It follows on and arises from one distinct part of the work of the Holy Spirit as a Spirit of supplication, from which it is inseparable. And this is his work on the mind, in acquainting it with the things that are to be prayed for, which he does both in the inward convictions of men's own souls, and in the declaration made thereof in the Scripture. Now, this may in some be only a common work of illumination, which the gift of vocal prayer may flow from and accompany, when the Spirit of grace and supplication works no further in them. Wherefore, it is acknowledged that men in whom the Spirit of grace did never reside nor savingly operate may have the gift of utterance in prayer unto their own and others' edification. For they have the gift of illumination, which is its foundation, and from which it is inseparable. Where this spiritual illumination is not granted in some measure, no abilities, no industry, can attain the gift of utterance in prayer unto edification. For spiritual light is the matter of all spiritual gifts, which in all their variety are but the various exercise of it. And to suppose a man to have a gift of prayer without it, is to suppose him to have a gift to pray for he knows not what; which real or pretended enthusiasm[9] we abhor. Wherefore, wherever is this gift of illumination and conviction, there is such

---

9   I.e., an extrabiblical, external, immediate revelation received after the close of the biblical canon.

a foundation of the gift of prayer as that it is not ordinarily absent in some measure, where due use and exercise are observed.

Add unto what has been spoken that the duty of prayer ordinarily is not complete unless it be expressed in words. It is called "pleading with God," "filling our mouths with arguments," "crying unto him," and "causing him to hear our voice";[10] which things are so expressed, not that they are any way needful unto God, but unto us. And whereas it may be said that all this may be done in prayer by internal meditation, where no use is made of the voice or of words, as it is said of Hannah that "she spake in her heart, but her voice was not heard" (1 Sam. 1:13), I grant in some cases it may be so, where the circumstances of the duty do not require it should be otherwise, or where the vehemency of affections, which causes men to cry out and roar, will permit it so to be. But withal I say, that in this prayer by meditation, the things and matter of prayer are to be formed in the mind into that sense and those sentences which may be expressed; and the mind can conceive no more in this way of prayer than it can express. So of Hannah it is said, when she prayed in her heart, and, as she said herself, "out of the abundance of her meditation" (1 Sam. 1:16), that "her lips moved," though "her voice was not heard"; she not only framed the sense of her supplications into petitions, but tacitly expressed them to herself. And the obligation of any person unto prescribed forms is as destructive of prayer by inward meditation as it is of prayer conceived and expressed; for it takes away the liberty and prevents the ability of framing petitions, or any other parts of prayer, in the mind according to the sense which the party praying has of them. Wherefore, if this expression of prayer in words do necessarily belong unto the duty itself, it is an effect of the Holy Spirit, or he is not the Spirit of supplication unto us.

2. *Utterance* is a peculiar gift of the Holy Ghost: so it is mentioned (1 Cor. 1:5; 2 Cor. 8:7; Eph. 6:19; Col. 4:3). And hereof there are two parts, or there are two duties to be discharged by virtue of it. (1) An ability to speak unto men in the name of God in the preaching of the word. (2) An ability to speak unto God for ourselves, or in the name and on the behalf of others. And there is the same reason of utterance in both these duties. And in each of them it is equally a peculiar gift of the Spirit of God (1 Cor. 1:5; 2 Cor. 8:7; Eph. 6:19; Col. 4:3). The word used in these places is λόγος, "speech," which is well rendered "utterance," that is, παῤῥσία ἐν τῷ ἀποφθέγγεσθαι, *facultas et libertas dicendi*, an "ability and liberty to speak" out the things we have conceived. Λογος ἐν ἀνοίξει τοῦ στόματος ἐν παῤῥησία, "Utterance

10   2 Cor. 12:8; Job 23:4; Ps. 31:22; Ps. 116:1.

in the opening of the mouth with boldness," or rather freedom of speech (Eph. 6:19). This in sacred things, in praying and preaching, is the gift of the Holy Spirit; and as such, are we enjoined to pray for it that it may be given unto us or others, as the edification of the church does require. And although this gift may by some be despised, yet the whole edification of the church depends upon it; yea, the foundation of the church was laid in it, as it was an extraordinary gift (Acts 2:4), and its superstructure is carried on by it. For it is the sole means of public or solemn intercourse between God and the church. It is so if there be such a thing as the Holy Ghost, if there be such things as spiritual gifts. The matter of them is spiritual light, and the manner of their exercise is utterance.

This gift or ability, as all others of the like nature, may be considered either as to the habit or as to the external exercise of it. And those who have received it in the habit have yet experience of great variety in the exercise, which in natural and moral habits, where the same preparations precede, does not usually appear. For as the Spirit of grace is free, and acts arbitrarily with respect unto the persons unto whom he communicates the gift himself, for "he divideth to every man as he will,"[11] so he acts also as he pleases in the exercise of those gifts and graces which he does bestow. Hence believers do sometimes find a greater evidence of his gracious working in them in prayer, or of his assistance to pray, as also enlargement in utterance, than at other times; for in both he breathes and acts as he pleases. These things are not their own, nor absolutely in their own power; nor will either the habitual grace they have received enable them to pray graciously, nor their gift of utterance unto edification, without his actual excitation of that grace and his assistance in the exercise of that gift. Both the conceiving and utterance of our desires in an acceptable manner are from him, and so are all spiritual enlargements in this duty. Vocal prayer, whether private or public, whereof we speak, is the uttering of our desires and requests unto God, called "the making of our requests known unto him" (Phil. 4:6). This utterance is a gift of the Holy Ghost, so also is prayer as to the manner of the performance of it, by words in supplication. And if anyone say he cannot so pray suitably unto his own occasions, he does only say that he is a stranger to this gift of the Holy Ghost, and if anyone will not, by him it is despised. And if these things are denied by any because they understand them not, we cannot help it.

3. *It is the Holy Spirit that enables men to discharge and perform every duty that is required of them in a due manner, so that without his enabling of us*

---

11   1 Cor. 12:11.

we can do nothing as we should. As this has been sufficiently confirmed in other discourses on this subject,[12] so we will not always contend with them by whom such fundamental principles of Christianity are denied or called into question. And he does so with respect unto all sorts of duties, whether such as are required of us by virtue of special office and calling, or on the more general account of a holy conversation according to the will of God. And vocal prayer is a duty under both these considerations. For,

(1) It is the duty of the ministers of the gospel by virtue of special office. Supplications, prayers, intercessions, and giving of thanks are to be made in the assemblies of the church (1 Tim. 2:1). Herein it is the office and duty of ministers to go before the congregation, and to be as the mouth of the church unto God. The nature of the office and the due discharge of it, with what is necessary unto the religious worship of public assemblies, manifest it so to be. The apostles, as their example, "gave themselves continually to prayer, and to the ministry of the Word" (Acts 6:4). It is therefore the gift of the Holy Ghost whereby these are enabled so to do. For of themselves they are not able to do anything. This is one of those "good gifts" which are "from above, and come down from the Father of lights" (James 1:17). And these gifts do they receive "for the perfecting of the saints, for the work of the ministry, for the edifying of the body of Christ" (Eph. 4:12). Utterance, therefore, in praying and preaching, is in them the gift of the Holy Ghost with respect unto their office. And that such a gift as those who are utterly destitute of it cannot discharge their office unto the edification of the church.

Let men pretend what they please, if a spiritual ability in praying and preaching belong not necessarily unto the office of the ministry, no man can tell what does so, or what the office signifies in the church. For no other ordinance can be administered without the word and prayer, nor any part of rule itself in a due manner. And to deny these to be gifts of the Holy Ghost is to deny the continuance of his dispensation unto and in the church, which at once overthrows the whole truth of the gospel, and the sole foundation that the ministry of it is built upon.

(2) The like may be spoken with respect unto duties to be performed by virtue of our general vocation. Such are the duties of parents and masters of families. I know not how far any are gone in ways of profaneness, but hope none are carried unto such a length as to deny it to be the duty of such persons to pray with their families as well as for them. The families that call not on the name of the Lord are under his curse. And if this be their duty,

---

12 *Πνευματολογια, or, A Discourse concerning the Holy Spirit.*

the performance of it must be by the aid of the Spirit of God, by virtue of the general rule we proceed upon.

4. *The benefit, profit, advantage, and edification of particular persons, of families, but especially of the church in its assemblies, in and by the use and exercise of this gift, are such and so great as that it is impious not to ascribe it to the operation of the Holy Spirit.* Men are not of themselves, without his special aid, authors or causers of the principal spiritual benefit and advantage which the church receives in the world. If they are so, or may be so, what need is there of him or his work for the preservation and edification of the church? But that it has this blessed effect and fruit, we plead the experience of all who desire to walk before God in sincerity, and leave the determination of the question unto the judgment of God himself. Nor will we at present refuse in our plea a consideration of the different conditions, as to a holy conversation, between them who constantly, in their life and at their death, give this testimony, and theirs by whom it is opposed and denied. We are none of us to be ashamed of the gospel of Christ, nor of any effect of his grace. It must therefore be said, that the experience which believers of all sorts have of the spiritual benefit and advantage of this ability, both in themselves and others, is not to be moved or shaken by the cavils or reproaches of such as dare profess themselves to be strangers thereunto.

5. The event of things may be pleaded in evidence of the same truth. For were not the ability of praying a gift of him who divides to everyone according unto his own will, there would not be that difference, as to the participation of it among those who all pretend unto the faith of the same truth, as there is openly and visibly in the world. And if it were a matter purely of men's natural abilities, it were impossible that so many, whose concern it is in the highest degree to be interested in it, should be such strangers to it, so unacquainted with it, and so unable for it. They say, indeed, it is but the mere improvement of natural abilities, with confidence and exercise. Let it be supposed for once that some of them at least have confidence competent unto such a work, and let them try what success mere exercise will furnish them with. In the meantime, I deny that, without that illumination of the mind, which is a peculiar gift of the Holy Ghost, the ability of prayer treated of is attainable by any. And it will be a hard thing to persuade persons of any ordinary consideration that the difference which they do or may discover between men as to this gift and ability proceeds merely from the difference of their natural and acquired abilities, wherein, as it is strenuously pretended, the advantage is commonly on that side which is most defective herein.

Some, perhaps, may say that they know there is nothing in this faculty but the exercise of natural endowments, with boldness and elocution, and that because they themselves were expert in it, and found nothing else therein, on which ground they have left it for that which is better. But, for evident reasons, we will not be bound to stand unto the testimony of those men, although they shall not here be pleaded. In the meantime, we know that "from him which has not is taken away that which he had."[13] And it is no wonder if persons endowed sometimes with a gift of prayer proportionable unto their light and illumination, improving neither the one nor the other as they ought, have lost both their light and gift also.

And thus, suitably unto my design and purpose, I have given a delineation of the work of the Holy Ghost as a Spirit of grace and supplication, promised unto and bestowed on all believers, enabling them to cry, "Abba, Father."

---

13 Matt. 13:12.

Duties Inferred from the Preceding Discourse

THE ISSUE OF ALL INQUIRIES in these things, is how we may improve them unto obedience in the life of God. For if we know them, happy are we if we do them, and not otherwise. And our practice herein may be reduced unto these two heads. First, due and constant returning of glory unto God on the account of his grace in that free gift of his, whose nature we have inquired into. Second, a constant attendance unto the duty which we are graciously enabled unto thereby. And,

GLORY TO GOD

1. We ought continually to bless God and give glory to him for this great privilege of the Spirit of grace and supplication granted unto the church. This is the principal means on their part of all holy intercourse with God, and of giving glory unto him. How does the world, which is destitute of this fruit of divine bounty, grope in the dark and wander after vain imaginations, while it knows not how to manage its convictions, nor how at all to deal with God about its concerns? That world which cannot receive the Spirit of grace and truth can never have ought[1] to do with God in a due manner. There are [those] by whom this gift of God is despised, is reviled, is blasphemed; and under the shades of many pretenses do they hide themselves from the light in their so doing. But they know not what they do, nor by what spirit they are acted. Our duty it is to pray that God would pour forth his Spirit even

---

1 I.e., anything whatsoever.

on them also, who will quickly cause them to look on him whom they have pierced, and mourn.

And it appears two ways how great a mercy it is to enjoy and improve this privilege. (1) In that both the psalmist and the prophet pray directly, in a spirit of prophecy, and without limitation, that God would "pour out his fury on the families that call not on his name" (Ps. 79:6; Jer. 10:25). And, (2) in that the whole work of faith in obedience is denominated from this duty of prayer, for so it is said, that "whosoever shall call upon the name of the Lord shall be saved" (Rom. 10:13). For invocation or prayer, in the power of the Spirit of grace and supplication, is an infallible evidence and fruit of saving faith and obedience, and therefore is the promise of salvation so eminently annexed unto it, or it is placed by a synecdoche for the whole worship of God and obedience of faith. And it were endless to declare the benefits that the church of God, and everyone that belongs thereunto, has thereby. No heart can conceive that treasury of mercies which lies in this one privilege, in having liberty and ability to approach unto God at all times, according unto his mind and will. This is the relief, the refuge, the weapons, and assured refreshment of the church in all conditions.

2. It is a matter of praise and glory to God, in a special manner, that he has granted an ampliation of this privilege under the gospel. The Spirit is now poured forth from above, and enlarged in his dispensation, both intensively and extensively. Those on whom he is bestowed do receive him in a larger measure than they did formerly under the Old Testament. Thence is that liberty and boldness in their access unto the throne of grace, and their crying "Abba, Father," which the apostle reckons among the great privileges of the dispensation of the Spirit of Christ, which they of old were not partakers of. If the difference between the Old Testament state and the New lay only in the outward letter and the rule thereof, it would not be so easily discerned on which side the advantage lay; especially, methinks, it should not be so by them who seem really to prefer the pomp of legal worship before the plainness and simplicity of the gospel. But he who understands what it is not to "receive the spirit of bondage to fear," but to "receive the Spirit of adoption, whereby we cry, 'Abba, Father,'"[2] and what it is to serve God in the newness of the Spirit, and not in the oldness of the letter, understands their difference well enough.¶

And I cannot but admire that some will make use of arguments, or a pretense of them, for such helps and forms of prayer as seem not compliant

2   Rom. 8:15.

with the work of the Spirit of supplication before described from the Old Testament, and the practice of the church of the Jews before the time of our Savior, though indeed they can prove nothing from these. For do they not acknowledge that there is a more plentiful effusion of the Spirit on the church under the New Testament than under the Old? To deny it is to take away the principal difference between the law and the gospel. And is not the performance of duties to be regulated according to the supplies of grace? If we should suppose that the people, being then carnal, and obliged to the observation of carnal ordinances, did in this particular stand in need of forms of prayer, which indeed they did not, of those which were merely so and only so, nor had, that we know of, any use of them, does it follow that therefore believers under the New Testament, who have unquestionably a larger portion of the Spirit of grace and supplication poured on them, should either stand in need of them or be obliged unto them? And it is in vain to pretend a different dispensation of the Spirit unto them and us, where different fruits and effects are not acknowledged. He that has been under the power of the law, and has been set free by the law of the Spirit of life in Christ Jesus, knows the difference and will be thankful for the grace that is in it.

Again, it is extensively enlarged, in that it is now communicated unto multitudes, whereas of old it was confined unto a few. Then the dews of it only watered the land of Canaan, and the posterity of Abraham according to the flesh; now the showers of it are poured down on all nations, even on all that in every place call on the name of Jesus Christ our Lord, both theirs and ours. In every assembly of Mount Zion through the world, called according to the mind of Christ, prayers and supplications are offered unto God through the effectual working of the Spirit of grace and supplication, unless he be despised. And this is done in the accomplishment of that great promise, "'From the rising of the sun to the going down of the same, my name shall be great among the Gentiles, and in every place incense shall be offered unto my name, and a pure offering; for my name shall be great among the heathen,' saith the Lord of hosts" (Mal. 1:11). Prayer and praises in the assemblies of the saints is the pure offering and that sacrifice which God promises shall be offered unto him. And this oblation is not to be kindled without the eternal fire of the Spirit of grace. No sacrifice was to be offered of old but with fire taken from the altar. Be it what it would, if it were offered with strange fire, it was an abomination; hence they were all called אִשִּׁים, the "firings" of the Lord. And this was in a resemblance of the Holy Ghost. Whence Christ is said to offer himself to God through the eternal Spirit. And so must we do our prayers. In the fruits and effects of his works lies all the glory and beauty of our assemblies and worship. Take them away, and they are contemptible, dead, and carnal. And he carries this work into the families of them that do believe. Every family apart is enabled to pray and serve God in the Spirit; and such as are not do live in darkness all their days. He is the same to believers all the world over, in their closets or their prisons. They have all, wherever they are, an "access by one Spirit unto the Father" (Eph. 2:18). And for this enlargement of grace God justly expects a revenue of glory from us.

DILIGENT USE

1. It is assuredly our duty to make use of the gift of the Spirit, as that which is purchased for us by Christ, and is of inestimable advantage unto our souls. There are two ways whereby men may be guilty of the neglect of this heavenly favor. (1) They are so when the gift itself is not valued nor sought after, nor endeavored to be attained. And this is done under various pretenses. Some imagine that it is no gift of the Spirit, and so despise it; others think that either by them it is not attainable, or that if it be attained it will not answer the labor in it and diligence about it which it does require, and therefore take up with another way and means, which they know to be more easy, and hope to be as useful. By many the whole duty is despised, and consequently all assistance in the performance of it is so also. None of these do I speak unto at present. But, (2) we are guilty of this neglect when we do not constantly and diligently, on all occasions, make use of it for the end for which it is given us, yea, abound in the exercise of it. Have you an ability to pray always freely given you by the Holy Ghost? Why do you not pray always, in private, in families, according to all occasions and opportunities administered? Of what concern unto the glory of God, and in our living unto him, prayer is, will be owned by all. It is that only single duty wherein every grace is acted, every sin opposed, every good thing obtained, and the whole of our obedience in every instance of it is concerned. What difficulties lie in the way of its due performance, what discouragements rise up against it, how unable we are of ourselves in a due manner to discharge it, what aversation there is in corrupted nature unto it, what distractions and weariness are apt to befall us under it, are generally known also unto them who are any way exercised in these things. Yet does the blessedness of our present and future condition much depend thereon. To relieve us against all these things, to help our infirmities, to give us freedom, liberty, and confidence in our approaches to the throne of grace, to enable us as children to cry, "Abba, Father," with delight and complacency, is this gift of the Spirit of grace and supplication given unto us by Jesus Christ.

Who can express how great a folly and sin it is not to be found in the constant exercise of it? Can we by any means more grieve this Holy Spirit and endamage[3] our own souls? Has God given unto us the Spirit of grace and supplication, and shall we be remiss, careless, and negligent in prayer? Is not this the worst way whereby we may quench the Spirit, which we are so cautioned against? Can we go from day to day in the neglect of opportunities, occasions, and just seasons of prayer? How shall we answer for the contempt of this gracious aid offered us by Jesus Christ? Do others go from day to day in a neglect of this duty in their closets and families? Blame them not, or at least they are not worthy of so much blame as we. They know not how to pray, they have no ability for it. But for those to walk in a neglect hereof who have received this gift of the Holy Ghost enabling them thereunto, making it easy unto them and pleasant unto the inner man, how great an aggravation is it of their sin!¶

Shall others at the tinkling of a bell rise and run unto prayers to be said or sung, wherein they can have no spiritual interest, only to pacify their consciences, and comply with the prejudices of their education, and shall we be found in the neglect of that spiritual aid which is graciously afforded unto us? How will the blind devotion and superstition of multitudes, with their diligence and pains therein, rise up in judgment against such negligent persons? We may see in the Papacy how, upon the ringing of a bell, or the lifting up of any ensign of superstition, they will some of them rise at midnight, others in their houses, yea, in the streets, fall on their knees unto their devotions. Having lost the conduct of the Spirit of God, and his gracious guidance unto the performance of duty in its proper seasons, they have invented ways of their own to keep up a frequency in this duty after their manner, which they are true and punctual unto. And shall they who have received that Spirit which the world cannot receive be treacherous and disobedient unto his motions, or what he constantly inclines and enables them unto? Besides all other disadvantages which will accrue hereby unto our souls, who can express the horrible ingratitude of such a sin? I press it the more, and that unto all sorts of prayer, in private, in families, in assemblies for that end, because the temptations and dangers of the days wherein we live do particularly and eminently call for it. If we would talk less and pray more about them, things would be better than they are in the world; at least, we should be better enabled to bear them, and undergo our portion in them with the more satisfaction. To be negligent herein at such a season is a sad token of such a security as foreruns destruction.

3   I.e., damage.

2. Have any received this gift of the Holy Ghost? Let them know that it is their duty to cherish it, to stir it up and improve it. It is freely bestowed, but it is carefully to be preserved. It is a gospel talent given to be traded with, and thereby to be increased. There are various degrees and measures of this gift in those that do receive it. But whatever measure anyone has, from the greatest to the least, he is obliged to cherish, preserve, and improve. We do not assert such a gift of prayer as should render our diligence therein unnecessary, or the exercise of our natural abilities useless. Yea, the end of this gift is to enable us to the diligent exercise of the faculties of our souls in prayer in a due manner. And, therefore, as it is our duty to use it, so it is to improve it. And it is one reason against the restraint of forms, because there is in them too little exercise of the faculties of our minds in the worship of God. Therefore, this being our duty, it may be inquired by what way or means we may stir up this grace and gift of God, so at least as that if, through any weakness or infirmity of mind, we thrive not much in the outward part of it, yet that we decay not nor lose what we have received. The gifts of the Holy Ghost are the fire that kindles all our sacrifices to God. Now, although that fire of old on the altar first came down from heaven, or "forth from the Lord" (Lev. 9:24), yet after it was once there placed it was always to be kept alive with care and diligence; for otherwise it would have been extinguished as any other fire (Lev. 6:12–13). Hence the apostle warns Timothy, ἀναζωπυρεῖν τὸ χάρισμα, to excite and "quicken the fire of his gift" (2 Tim. 1:6), by blowing off the ashes and adding fuel unto it. Now, there are many things that are useful and helpful unto this end, as,

(1) A constant *consideration and observation of ourselves*, our own hearts, with our spiritual state and condition. From this are the matters of our requests or petitions in prayer to be taken (Ps. 16:7). And as our state in general, by reason of the depths and deceitfulness of our hearts, with our darkness in spiritual things, is such as will find us matter of continual search and examination all the days of our lives, as is expressed in those prayers (Ps. 19:12; 139:23–24), so we are subject unto various changes and alterations in our spiritual frames and actings every day, as also unto temptations of all sorts. About these things, according as our occasions and necessities do require, are we to deal with God in our supplications (Phil. 4:6). How shall we be in a readiness hereunto, prepared with the proper matter of prayer, if we neglect a constant and diligent observation of ourselves herein, or the state of our own souls? This being the food of the gift, where it is neglected the gift itself will decay. If men consider only a form of things in a course, they will quickly come to a form of words.

To assist us in this search and examination of ourselves, to give light into our state and wants, to make us sensible thereof, is part of the work of the Spirit as a Spirit of grace and supplication; and if we neglect our duty toward him herein, how can we expect that he should continue his aid unto us, as to the outward part of the duty? Wherefore, let a man speak in prayer with the tongues of men and angels, to the highest satisfaction, and, it may be, good edification of others, yet if he be negligent, if he be not wise and watchful, in this duty of considering the state, actings, and temptations of his own soul, he has but a perishing, decaying outside and shell of this gift of the Spirit. And those by whom this self-search and judgment is attended unto shall ordinarily thrive in the power and life of this duty. By this means may we know the beginnings and entrances of temptation, the deceitful actings of indwelling sin, the risings of particular corruptions, with the occasions yielding them advantages and power, the supplies of grace which we daily receive, and ways of deliverance. And as he who prays without a due consideration of these things prays at random, fighting uncertainly as one beating the air, so he whose heart is filled with a sense of them will have always in a readiness the due matter of prayer, and will be able to fill his mouth with pleas and arguments whereby the gift itself will be cherished and strengthened.

(2) Constant searching of the Scripture unto the same purpose is another subservient duty unto this of prayer itself. That is the glass wherein we may take the best view of ourselves, because it at once represents both what we are and what we ought to be; what we are in ourselves, and what we are by the grace of God; what are our frames, actions, and ways, and what is their defect in the sight of God. And a higher instruction what to pray for, or how to pray, cannot be given us (Ps. 19:7–9). Some imagine that to "search the Scriptures,"[4] from there to take forms of speech or expressions accommodated unto all the parts of prayer, and to set them in order, or retain them in memory, is a great help to prayer. Whatever it be, it is not that which I intend at present. It is most true, if a man be mighty in the Scriptures, singularly conversant and exercised in them, abounding in their senses and expressions, and have the help of a faithful memory withal, it may exceedingly further and assist him in the exercise of this gift unto the edification of others. But this collection of phrases, speeches, and expressions, where perhaps the mind is barren in the sense of the Scripture, I know not of what use it is. That which I press for is a diligent search into the Scriptures as to the things revealed in them. For therein are our wants in all their circumstances and consequents discovered

4   John 5:39.

and represented unto us, and so are the supplies of grace and mercy which God has provided for us. The former with authority, to make us sensible of them, and the latter with that evidence of grace and faithfulness as to encourage us to make our requests for them. The word is the instrument whereby the Holy Spirit reveals unto us our wants, when we know not what to ask, and so enables us to make intercessions according to the mind of God (Rom. 8:26–27). Yea, who is it who almost at any time reading the Scripture, with a due reverence of God, and subjection of conscience unto him, has not some particular matter of prayer or praise effectually suggested unto him? And Christians would find no small advantage, on many accounts not here to be insisted upon, if they would frequently, if not constantly, turn what they read into prayer or praise unto God, whereby the instructions unto faith and obedience would be more confirmed in their minds, and their hearts be more engaged into their practice. An example hereof we have (Ps. 119), wherein all considerations of God's will and our duty are turned into petitions.

(3) A due meditation on God's glorious excellencies tends greatly to the cherishing of this gracious gift of the Holy Spirit. There is no example that we have of prayer in the Scripture but the entrance into it consists in expressions of the name, and most commonly of some of the glorious titles of God, whereunto the remembrance of some mighty acts of his power is usually added. And the nature of the thing requires it should be so; for besides that God has revealed his name unto us for this very purpose, that we might call upon him by the name which he owns and takes to himself, it is necessary we should by some external description determine our minds unto him to whom we make our addresses, seeing we cannot conceive any image or idea of him therein. Now, the end hereof is twofold. [1] To ingenerate in us that reverence and godly fear which is required of all that draw nigh to this infinitely holy God (Lev. 10:3; Heb. 12:28). The most signal encouragement unto boldness in prayer, and an access to God thereby, is in Hebrews 10:19–22, with chapter 4:16. Into the holy place we may go with boldness, and unto the throne of grace. And it is a throne of grace that God in Christ is represented unto us upon. But yet it is a throne still whereon majesty and glory do reside, and God is always to be considered by us as on a throne. [2] Faith and confidence are excited and acted unto a due frame thereby. For prayer is our betaking ourselves unto God as our shield, our rock, and our reward (Prov. 18:10). Wherefore, a due previous consideration of those holy properties of his nature which may encourage us so to do, and assure us in our so doing, is necessary. And this being so great a part of prayer, the great foundation of supplication and praise, frequent meditation on these holy excellencies of the

divine nature must needs be an excellent preparation for the whole duty, by filling the heart with a sense of those things which the mouth is to express, and making ready those graces for their exercise which is required therein.

(4) Meditation on the mediation and intercession of Christ, for our encouragement, is of the same importance and tendency. To this end spiritually is he proposed unto us as abiding in the discharge of his priestly office (Heb. 4:15–16; 10:19–22). And this is not only an encouragement unto and in our supplications, but a means to increase and strengthen the grace and gift of prayer itself. For the mind is thereby made ready to exercise itself about the effectual interposition of the Lord Christ at the throne of grace in our behalf, which has a principal place and consideration in the prayers of all believers. And hereby, principally, may we try our faith of what race and kind it is, whether truly evangelical or no. Some relate or talk that the eagle tries the eyes of her young ones by turning them to the sun, which if they cannot look steadily on, she rejects them as spurious.[5] We may truly try our faith by immediate intuitions of the Sun of Righteousness. Direct faith to act itself immediately and directly on the incarnation of Christ and his mediation, and if it be not of the right kind and race it will turn its eye aside unto anything else. God's essential properties, his precepts and promises, it can bear a fixed consideration of; but it cannot fix itself on the person and mediation of Christ with steadiness and satisfaction. There is, indeed, much profession of Christ in the world, but little faith in him.

(5) Frequency in exercise is the immediate way and means of the increase of this gift and its improvement. All spiritual gifts are bestowed on men to be employed and exercised: for "the manifestation of the Spirit is given to everyone to profit withal" (1 Cor. 12:7). God both requires that his talents be traded with, that his gifts be employed and exercised, and will also call us to an account of the discharge of the trust committed unto us in them (1 Pet. 4:10–11). Wherefore, the exercise of this and of the like gifts tend unto their improvement on a double account.¶

For [1] whereas they reside in the mind after the manner and nature of a habit or a faculty, it is natural that they should be increased and strengthened by exercise, as all habits are by a multiplication of acts proceeding from them. So also by desuetude[6] they will weaken, decay, and in the issue be utterly lost and perish. So is it with many as to the gift of prayer. They were known to

---

5   This idea originates with Pliny the Elder (AD 23–79). For the Latin text and an English translation, see Pliny, *Natural History,* vol. 3, *Books 8–11*, trans. H. Rackham, Loeb Classical Library 353 (Cambridge, MA: Harvard University Press, 1940), 298–99.

6   I.e., discontinuance from use or exercise; disuse.

have received it in some good measure of usefulness unto their own edification and that of others. But upon a neglect of the use and exercise of it in
public and private, which seldom goes alone without some secret or open
enormities, they have lost all their ability, and cannot open their mouths on
any occasion in prayer beyond what is prescribed unto them or composed
for them. But the just hand of God is also in this matter, depriving them of
what they had, for their abominable neglect of his grace and bounty therein.¶

[2] The increase will be added unto, by virtue of God's blessing on his own
appointment. For having bestowed these gifts for that end, where persons
are faithful in the discharge of the trust committed unto them, he will graciously add unto them in what they have. This is the eternal law concerning
the dispensation of evangelical gifts, "Unto everyone that hath shall be given,
and he shall have abundance; but from him that hath not shall be taken
away even that which he hath" (Matt. 25:29). It is not the mere having or
not having of them that is intended, but the using or not using of what we
have received, as is plain in the context. Now, I do not say that a man may
or ought to exercise himself in prayer merely with this design, that he may
preserve and improve his gift. It may, indeed, in some cases be lawful for a
man to have respect hereunto, but not only. As where a master of a family has
anyone in his family who is able to discharge that duty and can attend unto
it, yet he will find it his wisdom not to omit his own performance of it, unless
he be contented that his gift, as to the use of his family, should wither and
decay. But all that I plead is, that he who conscientiously, with respect unto
all the ends of prayer, does abound in the exercise of this gift, shall assuredly
thrive and grow in it, or at least preserve it in answer unto the measure of
the gift of Christ. For I do not propose these things as though every man in
the diligent use of them may constantly grow and thrive in that part of the
gift which consists in utterance and expression. For there is a "measure of
the gift of Christ" assigned unto everyone, whose bounds he shall not pass
(Eph. 4:7). But in these paths and ways the gift which they have received will
be preserved, kept thrifty and flourishing, and from the least beginnings of
a participation of it, they will be carried on unto their own proper measure,
which is sufficient for them.

(6) Constant fervency and intension of mind and spirit in this duty works
directly toward the same end. Men may multiply prayers as to the outward
work in them, and yet not have the least spiritual advantage by them. If they
are dull, dead, and slothful in them, if under the power of customariness
and formality, what issue can they expect? Fervency and intension of mind
quickens and enlarges the faculties, and leaves vigorous impressions upon

them of the things treated about in our supplications. The whole soul is cast into the mold of the matter of our prayers, and is thereby prepared and made ready for continual fresh spiritual engagements about them. And this fervency we intend consists not in the vehemency or loudness of words, but in the intension of the mind; for the earnestness or vehemency of the voice is allowable only in two cases: first, when the edification of the congregation does require it, which being numerous cannot hear what is spoken unless a man lift up his voice; second, when the vehemency of affections will bear no restraint (Ps. 22:1; Heb. 5:7).⁊

Now, as all these are means whereby the gift of prayer may be cherished, preserved, and improved, so are they all of them the ways whereby grace acts itself in prayer, and have, therefore, an equal respect unto the whole work of the Spirit of supplication in us.

3. Our duty it is to use this gift of prayer unto the ends for which it is freely bestowed on us. And it is given, first, with respect unto themselves who do receive it, and, second, with respect unto the benefit and advantage of others. And (1) with respect unto them that receive it, its end is, and it is a blessed means and help, to stir up, excite, quicken, and act all those graces of the Spirit whereby they have communion with God in this duty. Such are faith, love, delight, joy, and the like. For [1] under the conduct of this gift, the mind and soul are led into the consideration of, and are fixed on, the proper objects of those graces, with the due occasions of their exercise. When men are bound unto a form, they can act grace only by the things that are expressed therein, which, whatever any apprehend, is strait and narrow, compared with the extent of that divine intercourse with God which is needful unto believers in this duty. But in the exercise of this gift there is no concern of faith, or love, or delight, but it is presented unto them, and they are excited unto a due exercise about them. Unto this end, therefore, is it to be used; namely, as a means to stir up and act those graces and holy affections in whose working and exercise the life and efficacy of prayer does consist. [2] Although the exercise of the gift itself ought to be nothing but the way of those graces acting themselves toward God in this duty, for words are supplied only to clothe and express gracious desires, and when they wholly exceed them they are of no advantage, yet as by virtue of the gift the mind is able to comprehend and manage the things about which those graces and gracious desires are to be exercised, so in the use of expressions they are quickened and engaged therein. For as when a man has heard of a miserable object, he is moved with compassion toward it, but when he comes to behold it "his own eye affecteth his heart," as the prophet speaks (Lam. 3:51), whereby his compassion is actually moved and

increased; so, although a man has a comprehension in his mind of the things of prayer, and is affected with them, yet his own words also will affect his heart, and by reflection stir up and inflame spiritual affections. So do many, even in private, find advantage in the use of their own gift, beyond what they can attain in mere mental prayer; which must be spoken unto afterward.

Again, (2) this gift respects others, and is to be used unto that end. For as it is appointed of God to be exercised in societies, families, church assemblies, and occasionally for the good of any, so it is designed for their edification and profit. For there is in it an ability of expressing the wants, desires, and prayers of others also. And as this discharge of the duty is in a peculiar manner incumbent on ministers of the gospel, as also on masters of families and others, as they are occasionally called thereunto, so they are to attend unto a fourfold direction therein.

[1] Unto their own experience. If such persons are believers themselves, they have experience in their own souls of all the general concerns of those in the same condition. As sin works in one, so it does in another; as grace is effectual in one, so it is in another; as he that prays longs for mercy and grace, so do they that join with him. Of the same kind with his hatred of sin, his love to Christ, his laboring after holiness and conformity to the will of God, are also those in other believers. And hence it is that persons "praying in the Spirit"[7] according to their own experience are oftentimes supposed by everyone in the congregation rather to pray over their condition than their own. And so, it will be while the same corruption in kind, and the same grace in kind, with the same kind of operations, are in them all. But this extends not itself unto particular sins and temptations, which are left unto everyone to deal about between God and their own souls.

[2] Unto Scripture light. This is that which lively expresses the spiritual state and condition of all sorts of persons, namely, both of those that are unregenerate, and of those which are converted unto God. Whatever that expresses concerning either sort may safely be pleaded with God on their behalf. And hence may abundant matter of prayer be taken for all occasions. Especially may it be so in a peculiar manner from that holy summary of the church's desires to God given us in the Lord's Prayer. All we can duly apprehend, spiritually understand, and draw out of that mine and heavenly treasury of prayer, may be safely used in the name and behalf of the whole church of God. But without understanding of the things intended, the use of the words profits not.

---

7   Eph. 6:18.

[3] Unto an observation of their ways and walking, with whatever overt discovery they make of their condition and temptations. He who is constantly to be the mouth of others to God is not to pray at random, as though all persons and conditions were alike unto him. None prays for others constantly, by virtue of special duty, but he is called also to watch over them and observe their ways. In so doing he may know that of their state which may be a great direction unto his supplications with them and for them. Yea, without this no man can ever discharge this duty aright in the behalf of others, so as they may find their particular concerns therein. And if a minister be obliged to consider the ways, light, knowledge, and walking of his flock, in his preaching unto them, that what he teaches may be suited unto their edification, he is no less bound unto the same consideration in his prayers also with them and for them, if he intend to pray unto their use and profit. The like may be said of others in their capacity. The wisdom and caution which are to be used herein I may not here insist upon.

[4] Unto the account which they receive from themselves concerning their wants, their state and condition. This, in some cases, persons are obliged to give unto those whose duty it is to help them by their prayers (James 5:16). And if this duty were more attended unto, the minds of many might receive inconceivable relief thereby.

4. Let us take heed, first, that this gift be not solitary or alone and, second, that it be not solitarily acted at any time. (1) When it is solitary, that is, where the gift of prayer is in the mind, but no grace to exercise in prayer in the heart, it is at best but a part of that form of godliness which men may have, and deny the power thereof, and is, therefore, consistent with all sorts of secret lusts and abominations. And it were easy to demonstrate that whatever advantage others may have by this gift in them who are destitute of saving grace, yet themselves are many ways worsted by it. For hence are they lifted up with spiritual pride, which is the ordinary consequent of all unsanctified light, and hereby do they countenance themselves against the reflections of their consciences on the guilt of other sins, resting and pleasing themselves in their own performances. But, to the best observation that I have been able to make, of all spiritual gifts which may be communicated for a time unto unsanctified minds, this does soonest decay and wither. Whether it be that God takes it away judicially from them, or that themselves are not able to bear the exercise of it, because it is diametrically opposite unto the lusts wherein they indulge themselves, for the most part it quickly and visibly decays, especially in such as with whom the continuance of it, by reason of open sins and apostasy, might be a matter of danger or scandal unto others.

(2) Let it not be acted solitarily. Persons in whom is a principle of spiritual life and grace, who are endowed with those graces of the Spirit which ought to be acted in all our supplications, may yet, even in the use and exercise of this gift, neglect to stir them up and act them. And there is no greater evidence of a weak, sickly, spiritual constitution, than often to be surprised into this miscarriage. Now, this is so when men in their prayers engage only their light, invention, memory, and elocution, without special actings of faith and delight in God. And he who watches his soul and its actings may easily discern when he is sinfully negligent in this matter, or when outward circumstances and occasions have made him more to attend unto the gift than unto the grace in prayer; for which he will be humbled.

And these few things I thought meet to add concerning the due use and improvement of this gift of the Spirit of God.

Of Mental Prayer as Pretended Unto
by Some in the Church of Rome

HAVING DESCRIBED or given an account of the gift of prayer, and the use of it in the church of God, and the nature of the work of the Spirit therein, it will be necessary to consider briefly what is by some set up in competition with it, as a more excellent way in this part of divine worship. And, in the first place, mental prayer, as described by some devout persons of the Church of Rome, is preferred above it. They call it "pure spiritual prayer, or a quiet repose of contemplation; that which excludes all images of the fancy, and in time all perceptible actuations of the understanding, and is exercised in signal elevations of the will, without any force at all, yet with admirable efficacy." And to dispose a soul for such prayer, there is previously required "an entire calmness and even death of the passions, a perfect purity in the spiritual affections of the will, and an entire abstraction from all creatures."[1]

THE NECESSITY OF THE INTELLECT

1. The truth is, I am so fixed in a dislike of that mere outside, formal course of reading or singing prayers which is in use in the Roman church, which though, in Mr. Cressy's esteem, it have a show of a very civil conversation with God, yet is it indeed accompanied with the highest contempt of his infinite purity and all divine excellencies, and do so much more abhor that magical incantation which many among them use, in the repetition

---

1 In the text: (Cressy, Church Hist. pref. parag. 42–43).—Owen. This is a reference to Cressy's *The Church-History of Brittany, or England, from the Beginning of Christianity to the Norman Conquest* (Rouen, 1668), specifically paras. 42–43 of the preface.

of words which they understand not, or of applying what they repeat to another end than what the words signify—as saying so many prayers for such an end or purpose, whereof it may be there is not one word of mention in the prayers themselves—that I must approve of any search after a real internal intercourse of soul with God in this duty. But herein men must be careful of two things: (1) That they assert not what they can fancy, but what indeed, in some measure, they have an experience of. For men to conjecture what others do experience, for they can do no more, and thence to form rules or examples of duty, is dangerous always, and may be pernicious unto those who shall follow such instructions. And herein this author fails, and gives nothing but his own fancies of others' pretended experience. (2) That what they pretend unto an experience of be confirmable by Scripture rule or example. For if it be not so, we are directed unto the conduct of all extravagant imaginations in everyone who will pretend unto spiritual experience.⁋

Attend unto these rules, and I will grant in prayer all the ways whereby the soul, or the faculties of it, can rationally act itself toward God in a holy and spiritual manner. But if you extend it unto such kind of actings as our nature is not capable of, at least in this world, it is the open fruit of a deceived fancy, and makes all that is tendered from the same hand to be justly suspected. And such is that instance of this prayer, that it is *in the will and its affections without any actings of the mind or understanding.* For although I grant that the adhesion of the will and affections unto God by love, delight, complacency, rest and satisfaction, in prayer, belongs to the improvement of this duty, yet to imagine that they are not guided, directed, acted by the understanding, in the contemplation of God's goodness, beauty, grace, and other divine excellencies, is to render our worship and devotion brutish or irrational, whereas it is, and ought to be, our reasonable service.

And that this very description here given us of prayer is a mere effect of fancy and imagination, and not that which the author of it was led unto by the conduct of spiritual light and experience, is evident from hence, that it is borrowed from those contemplative philosophers who, after the preaching of the gospel in the world, endeavored to refine and advance heathenism into a compliance with it, at least is fancied in imitation of what they ascribe unto a perfect mind. One of them, and his expressions in one place, may suffice for an instance. For after many other ascriptions unto a soul that has attained union with the chiefest good, [Plotinus] adds, "A mind thus risen up is no way moved, no anger, no desire of anything is in it," a perfect rest of the affections; "nay, neither reason nor understanding," are acted, "nor, if I may say so, itself; but being ecstasied[2] and filled with God, it comes into a quiet, still, immovable repose and state, no way declining," by any sensible actings, "from its own essence, nor exercising any reflex act upon itself, is wholly at rest, as having attained a perfect state," or to this purpose, with much more to the same.[3] And as it is easy to find the substance of our author's notion in these words, so the reader may see it more at large declared in that last chapter of his *Ennead*. And all his companions in design about that time speak to the same purpose.

THE NECESSITY OF WORDS

2. The spiritual intense fixation of the mind, by contemplation on God in Christ, until the soul be as it were swallowed up in admiration and delight, and being brought unto an utter loss, through the infiniteness of those excellencies which it does admire and adore, it returns again into its own abasements, out of a sense of its infinite distance from what it would absolutely and eternally embrace, and, withal, the inexpressible rest and satisfaction which the will and affections receive in their approaches unto the eternal fountain of goodness, are things to be aimed at in prayer, and which, through the riches of divine condescension, are frequently enjoyed. The soul is hereby raised and ravished, not into ecstasies or unaccountable raptures, not acted into motions above the power of its own understanding and will, but in all the faculties and affections of it, through the effectual workings of the Spirit of grace and the lively impressions of divine love, with intimations of the relations and kindness of God, is filled with rest, in joy unspeakable and full of glory. And these spiritual acts of communion with God, whereof I may say with Bernard, "how rare the time and how brief the stay,"[4] may be enjoyed

---

2   I.e., experience of a trance state in which intense absorption (as in religious ideation) is accompanied by loss of sense perception and voluntary control.

3   In the text: Οὐ γάρ τι ἐκινεῖτο παρ' αὐτῷ, οὐ θυμός, οὐκ ἐπιθυμία ἄλλου παρῆν αὐτῷ, ἀναβεβηκότι' ἀλλ' οὐ δὲ λόγος, οὐ δέ τις νόησις οὐ δ' ὅλως αὐτός, εἰ δεῖ καὶ τοῦτο λέγειν ἀλλ' ὥσπερ ἁρπασθεὶς ἢ ἐνθουσιάσας ἡσυχῇ ἐν ἐρήμῳ καταστάσει γεγένηται ἀτρεμεῖ, τῇ αὐτοῦ οὐσίᾳ οὐδαμοῦ ἀποκλίνων, οὐδὲ περὶ αὐτὸν στρεφόμενος, ἑστὼς πάντη καὶ οἷον στάσις γενόμενος (Plotinus, Ennead. vi., lib. 9, cap. 10).—Owen. The English translation is Owen's. This is a reference to vol. 6, bk. 9, chap. 10 of Plotinus's (204/5–270) *Ennead*. However, the quotation actually comes from chap. 11. Plotinus was the first and greatest of the Neoplatonic philosophers. For the Greek text and an English translation, see Plotinus, *Ennead VI.6–9*, trans. A. H. Armstrong, Loeb Classical Library 468 (Cambridge, MA: Harvard University Press, 1988), 340–43.

4   In the text: *Rara hora, brevis mora.*—Owen. Bernard of Clairvaux (1090–1153) was a reformer of monasticism and one read with great appreciation by many of the Protestant Reformers.

in mental or vocal prayer indifferently. But as the description here given of mental, spiritual prayer has no countenance given it from the Scriptures, yea, those things are spoken of it which are expressly contrary thereunto, as perfect purity and the like, and as it cannot be confirmed by the rational experience of any, so it no way takes off from the necessity and usefulness of vocal prayer, whereunto it is opposed. For still the use of words is necessary in this duty, from the nature of the duty itself, the command of God, and the edification of the church.¶

And it is fallen out unhappily, as to the exaltation of the conceived excellency of this mental prayer, that our Lord Jesus Christ not only instructed his disciples to pray by the use of words, but did so himself, and that constantly, so far as we know (Matt. 26:39, 42). Yea, when he was most intense and engaged in this duty, instead of this pretended still prayer of contemplation, he prayed μετὰ κραυγῆς ἰσχυρᾶς, "with a strong outcry" (Heb. 5:7), which is called the "voice of his roaring" (Ps. 22:1). And all the reproaches which this author casts on fervent, earnest, vocal prayer, namely, that it is a tedious, loud, impetuous, and an uncivil conversation with God, a mere artificial slight and facility, may with equal truth be cast on the outward manner of the praying of our Lord Jesus Christ, which was ofttimes long, sometimes loud and vehement. And unto the example of their Lord and Master we may add that of the prophets and apostles, who mention nothing of this pretended elevation, but constantly made use of and desired God to hear their voices, their cry, their words, in their supplication, the words of many of them being accordingly recorded.¶

Wherefore, words proper, suggested by the Spirit of God, and taken either directly or analogically out of the Scripture, do help the mind and enlarge it with supplications. "Sometimes we may rouse ourselves sharply toward devotion."[5] The use of such words, being first led unto by the desires of the

---

This quotation comes from his sermons on the Song of Solomon. For a Latin critical edition, see *Sancti Bernardi opera,* vol. 1, *Sermones super cantica canticorum 1–35,* ed. Jean Leclercq, C. H. Talbot, and Henri Rochais (Rome: Editiones Cistercienses, 1957), 148. For the English translation, see Bernard of Clairvaux, *Sermons on the Song of Songs,* vol. 2, trans. Kilian Walsh, Cistercian Fathers 7 (Kalamazoo, MI: Cistercian, 1976), 23.15.

5   In the text: *Interdum voce nos ipsos ad devotionem et acrius incitamus* (August. Epist. cxxi. ad Probam).—Owen. This is likely a quotation from and reference to the sixteenth-century edition of Augustine's collected works prepared by theological scholars at the University of Louvain, given that the citation can be found in authors contemporary with Owen. It is also possible that it is, in fact, a loose paraphrase, rather than a quotation, from chap. 9 of Augustine's letter to Proba, a wealthy Roman widow, explaining the Lord's Prayer. This letter is indexed as letter 130 in modern editions of Augustine's works. For a Latin critical edition, see Augustinus, *Epistulae ci–cxxxix,* ed. K. D. Daur, Corpus Christianorum: Series Latina 31B (Turnhout, BE:

mind, may and does lead the mind on to express its further desires also, and increases those which are so expressed. It is from God's institution and blessing that the mind and will of praying do lead unto the words of prayer, and the words of prayer do lead on the mind and will, enlarging them in desires and supplications. And without this aid many would oftentimes be straitened in acting their thoughts and affections toward God, or distracted in them, or diverted from them. And we have experience that an obedient, sanctified persistency in the use of gracious words in prayer has prevailed against violent temptations and injections of Satan, which the mind in its silent contemplations was not able to grapple with. And holy affections are thus also excited hereby. The very words and expressions which the mind chooses to declare its thoughts, conceptions, and desires about heavenly things, do reflect upon the affections, increasing and exciting them. Not only the things themselves fixed on do affect the heart, but the words of wisdom and sobriety whereby they are expressed do so also. There is a recoiling of efficacy, if I may so speak, in deep impressions on the affections, from the words that are made use of to express those affections by. But we treat of prayer principally as it is to be performed in families, societies, assemblies, congregations, where this mental prayer would do well to promote the edification which is attainable in the silent meetings of the Quakers.[6]

And because this kind of prayer, as it is called, is not only recommended unto us, but preferred before all other ways and methods of prayer, and chosen as an instance to set off the devotion of the Church of Rome, to invite others thereunto, I shall a little more particularly inquire into it. And I must needs say, that, on the best view I can take, or examination of it, it seems to be a matter altogether useless, uncertain, an effect of and entertainment for vain curiosity, whereby men intrude themselves into those things which they have not seen, being vainly puffed up by their own fleshly mind. For to call over what was before intimated in things that are practical in religion, no man can understand anything whereof he can have no experience. Nothing is rejected by virtue of this rule, whereof some men, through their own default, have no experience; but everything is so justly, whereof no man in the discharge of his duty can attain any experience. He that speaks of such things unto others, if any such there might be belonging unto our condition in this world, must needs be a barbarian unto them in what he speaks. And whereas also he

Brepols, 2009). For modern English translation, see Saint Augustine, *Letters,* vol. 2, *83–130,* trans. Sister Wilfred Parsons, Fathers of the Church 18 (Washington, DC: Catholic University of America Press, 1953), 390.

6   See the introduction on the Quakers in vol. 7.

speaks of that wherein his own reason and understanding have no interest, he must be so also unto himself. For no man can by the use of reason, however advanced by spiritual light, understand such actings of the souls of other men or his own as wherein there is no exercise of reason or understanding, such as these raptures are pretended to consist in. So whereas one of them says, "the lowest part of my breath touches the lowest part of the being of God,"[7] it had certainly been better for him to have kept his apprehensions or fancy to himself, than to express himself in words which in their own proper sense are blasphemous, and whose best defensative[8] is that they are unintelligible.⁋

And if it be not unlawful, it is doubtless inexpedient, for anyone, in things of religion, to utter what it is impossible for anybody else to understand, with this only plea, that they do not indeed understand it themselves, it being what they enjoyed without any acts or actings of their own understanding. To allow such pretenses is the ready way to introduce Babel into the church, and expose religion to scorn. Some pretending unto such raptures among ourselves I have known, wherein for a while they stirred up the admiration of weak and credulous[9] persons; but through a little observation of what they did, spoke, and pretended unto, with an examination of all by the unerring rule, they quickly came into contempt.⁋

All I intend at present is, that whatever be in this pretense, it is altogether useless unto edification, and therefore ought the declaration of it to be of no regard in the church of God. If the apostle would not allow the use of words, though miraculously suggested unto them that used them, without an immediate interpretation of their signification, what would he have said of such words and things as are capable of no interpretation, so as that any man living should understand them? For those by whom at present they are so extolled and commended unto us do themselves discourse at random, as blind men talk of colors, for they pretend not to have any experience of these things themselves. And it is somewhat an uncouth way of procedure to enhance the value of the communion of their church, and to invite others unto it, by declaring that there are some among them who enjoyed such spiritual ecstasies as could neither by themselves nor any others be understood. For nothing can be so wherein or whereabout there is no exercise of reason or understanding. Wherefore, the old question, "*cui bono?*"[10] will discharge this pretense from being of any value or esteem in religion with considerate men.

---

7   In the text: *Fundus animae meae tangit fundum essentiae Dei.*—Owen.
8   I.e., defense or protection.
9   I.e., overly ready to believe things.
10 Lat. "Who stands to gain?"

Again, as the whole of this kind of prayer is useless as to the benefit and edification of the church or any member of it, so it is impossible there should ever be any certainty about the raptures wherein it is pretended to consist, but they must everlastingly be the subject of contention and dispute. For who shall assure me that the persons pretending unto these duties or enjoyments are not mere pretenders? Any man that lives, if he has a mind unto it, may say such things, or use such expressions concerning himself. If a man, indeed, shall pretend and declare that he does or enjoys such things as are expressed in the word of God as the duty or privilege of any, and thereon are acknowledged by all to be things in themselves true and real, and likewise attainable by believers, he is ordinarily, so far as I know, to be believed in his profession, unless he can be convicted of falsehood by anything inconsistent with such duties or enjoyments. Nor do I know of any great evil in our credulity herein, should we happen to be deceived in or by the person so professing, seeing he speaks of no more than all acknowledge it their duty to endeavor after. But when anyone shall pretend unto spiritual actings or enjoyments which are neither prescribed nor promised in the Scripture, nor are investigable in the light of reason, no man is upon this mere profession obliged to give credit thereunto; nor can any man tell what evil effects or consequences his so doing may produce. For when men are once taken off from that sure ground of Scripture and their own understandings, putting themselves afloat on the uncertain waters of fancies or conjectures, they know not how they may be tossed, nor whither they may be driven.⁋

If it shall be said that the holiness and honesty of the persons by whom these special privileges are enjoyed are sufficient reason why we should believe them in what they profess, I answer, they would be so in a good measure if they did not pretend unto things repugnant unto reason and unwarranted by the Scripture, which is sufficient to crush the reputation of any man's integrity. Nor can their holiness and honesty be proved to be such as to render them absolutely impregnable against all temptations, which was the preeminence of Christ alone. Neither is there any more strength in this plea but what may be reduced unto this assertion, that there neither are nor ever were any hypocrites in the world undiscoverable unto the eyes of men. For if such there may be, some of these pretenders may be of their number, notwithstanding the appearance of their holiness and honesty. Besides, if the holiness of the best of them were examined by evangelical light and rule, perhaps it would be so far from being a sufficient countenance unto other things as that it would not be able to defend its own reputation. Neither is it want of charity which makes men doubtful and unbelieving in such cases, but godly jealousy and Christian prudence, which require them to take care that they be not deceived or deluded, do not only warrant them to abide on that guard, but make it their necessary duty also. For it is no new thing that pretenses of raptures, ecstasies, revelations, and unaccountable, extraordinary enjoyments of God, should be made use of unto corrupt ends, yea, abused to the worst imaginable. The experience of the church, both under the Old Testament and the New, witnesses hereunto, as the apostle Peter declares (2 Pet. 2:1). For among them of old there were multitudes of false pretenders unto visions, dreams, revelations, and such spiritual ecstasies, some of whom wore a "rough garment to deceive," which went not alone, but accompanied with all such appearing austerities as might beget an opinion of sanctity and integrity in them. And when the body of the people were grown corrupt and superstitious, this sort of men had credit with them above the true prophets of God; yet did they for the most part show themselves to be hypocritical liars. And we are abundantly warned of such spirits under the New Testament, as we are foretold that such there would be, by whom many should be deluded; and all such pretenders unto extraordinary intercourse with God we are commanded to try by the unerring rule of the word, and desire only liberty so to do.

But suppose that those who assert these devotions and enjoyments of God in their own experience are not false pretenders unto what they profess, nor design to deceive, but are persuaded in their own minds of the reality of what they endeavor to declare, yet neither will this give us the least security of their truth. For it is known that there are so many ways, partly natural, partly diabolical, whereby the fancies and imaginations of persons may be so possessed with false images and apprehensions of things, and that with so vehement an efficacy as to give them a confidence of their truth and reality, that no assurance of them can be given by a persuasion of the sincerity of them by whom they are pretended. And there are so many ways whereby men are disposed unto such a frame and actings, or are disposed to be imposed on by such delusions, especially where they are prompted by superstition, and are encouraged doctrinally to an expectation of such imaginations, that it is a far greater wonder that more have not fallen into the same extravagancies than that any have so done. We find by experience that some have had their imaginations so fixed on things evil and noxious by satanical delusions, that they have confessed against themselves things and crimes that have rendered them obnoxious unto capital punishments, whereof they were never really and actually guilty. Wherefore, seeing these acts or duties of devotion are pretended to be such as wherein there is no sensible actuation of the mind or understanding, and so cannot rationally be accounted for, nor rendered perceptible unto the understanding of others, it is not unreasonable to suppose that they are only fond imaginations of deluded fancies, which superstitious, credulous persons have gradually raised themselves unto, or such as they have exposed themselves to be imposed on with by Satan, through a groundless, unwarrantable desire after them or expectation of them.

But whatever there may be in the height of this "contemplative prayer," as it is called, it neither is prayer nor can on any account be so esteemed. That we allow of mental prayer, and all actings of the mind in holy meditations, was before declared. Nor do we deny the usefulness or necessity of those other things, of mortifying the affections and passions, of an entire resignation of the whole soul unto God, with complacency in him, so far as our nature is capable of them in this world. But it is that incomparable excellency of it in the silence of the soul, and the pure adhesion of the will, without any actings of the understanding, that we inquire into. And I say, whatever else there may be herein, yet it has not the nature of prayer, nor is to be so esteemed, though under that name and notion it be recommended unto us. Prayer is a natural duty, the notion and understanding whereof is common unto all mankind. And the concurrent voice of nature deceives not. Whatever, therefore, is not compliant therewith, at least what is contradictory unto it or inconsistent with it, is not to be esteemed prayer.¶

Now, in the common sense of mankind, this duty is that acting of the mind and soul wherein, from an acknowledgment of the sovereign being, self-sufficiency, rule, and dominion of God, with his infinite goodness, wisdom, power, righteousness, and omniscience and omnipresence, with a sense of their own universal dependence on him, his will and pleasure, as to their beings, lives, happiness, and all their concerns, they address their desires with faith and trust unto him, according as their state and condition does require, or ascribe praise and glory unto him for what he is in himself and what he is to them. This is the general notion of prayer, which the reason of mankind centers in; neither can any man conceive of it under any other notion whatever. The gospel directs the performance of this duty in an acceptable manner with respect unto the mediation of Christ, the aids of the Holy Ghost, and the revelation of the spiritual mercies we all do desire; but it changes nothing in the general nature of it. It does not introduce a duty of another kind, and call it by the name of that which is known in the light of nature but is quite another thing.¶

But this general nature of prayer all men universally understand well enough in whom the first innate principles of natural light are not extinguished or woefully depraved. This may be done among some by a long traditional course of an atheistical and brutish conversation. But as large and extensive as are the convictions of men concerning the being and existence of God, so are their apprehensions of the nature of this duty. For the first actings of nature toward a divine Being are in invocation. Jonah's mariners knew every one how to call on his god, when they were in a storm. And where there is not trust or affiance in God acted, whereby men glorify him as God, and where desires or praises are not offered unto him, neither of which can be without express acts of the mind or understanding, there is no prayer, whatever else there may be. Wherefore, this contemplative devotion, wherein, as it is pretended, the soul is ecstasied into an advance of the will and affections above all the actings of the mind or understanding, has no one property of prayer, as the nature of it is manifest in the light of nature and common agreement of mankind. Prayer without an actual acknowledgment of God in all his holy excellencies, and the actings of faith in fear, love, confidence, and gratitude, is a monster in nature, or a by-blow[11] of imagination, which has no existence in *rerum natura*.[12] These persons, therefore, had best find out some other name wherewith to impose this kind of devotion upon our admiration, for from the whole precincts of prayer or invocation on the name of God it is utterly excluded; and what place it may have in any other part of the worship of God, we shall immediately inquire.

But this examination of it by the light of nature will be looked on as most absurd and impertinent. For if we must try all matters of spiritual communion with God, and that in those things which wholly depend on divine, supernatural revelation, by this rule and standard, our measures of them will be false and perverse. And, I say, no doubt they would. Wherefore, we call only that concern of it unto a trial hereby whose true notion is confessedly fixed in the light of nature. Without extending that line beyond its due bounds, we may by it take a just measure of what is prayer and what is not; for therein it cannot deceive nor be deceived. And this is all which at present we engage about. And in the pursuit of the same inquiry we may bring it also unto the Scripture, from which we shall find it as foreign as from the light of nature. For as it is described, so far as anything intelligible may be from thence collected, it exceeds or deviates from whatever is said in the Scripture concerning prayer, even in those places where the grace and privileges of it are most emphatically expressed, and as it is exemplified in the prayers of the Lord Christ himself

---

11   I.e., illegitimate child; bastard.

12   Lat. "nature of things."

and all the saints recorded therein. Wherefore, the light of nature and the Scripture do by common consent exclude it from being prayer in any kind. Prayer, in the Scripture representation of it, is the soul's access and approach unto God by Jesus Christ, through the aids of his Holy Spirit, to make known its requests unto him, with supplication and thanksgiving. And that whereon it is recommended unto us are its external adjuncts, and its internal grace and efficacy. Of the first sort, earnestness, fervency, importunity, constancy, and perseverance, are the principal. No man can attend unto these, or any of them, in a way of duty, but in the exercise of his mind and understanding. Without this, whatever looks like any of them is brutish fury or obstinacy.

And as unto the internal form of it, in that description which is given us of its nature in the Scripture, it consists in the special exercise of faith, love, delight, fear, all the graces of the Spirit, as occasion does require. And in that exercise of these graces, wherein the life and being of prayer does consist, a continual regard is to be had unto the mediation of Christ and the free promises of God, through which means he exhibits himself unto us as a God hearing prayer. These things are both plainly and frequently mentioned in the Scripture, as they are all of them exemplified in the prayers of those holy persons which are recorded therein. But for this contemplative prayer, as it is described by our author and others, there is neither precept for it, nor direction about it, nor motive unto it, nor example of it, in the whole Scripture. And it cannot but seem marvelous, to some at least, that whereas this duty and all its concerns are more insisted on therein than any other Christian duty or privilege whatever, the height and excellency of it, and that in comparison whereof all other kinds of prayer, all the actings of the mind and soul in them, are decried, should not obtain the least intimation therein.

For if we should take a view of all the particular places wherein the nature and excellency of this duty are described, with the grace and privilege wherewith it is accompanied (such as, for instance Eph. 6:18; Phil. 4:6; Heb. 4:16; 10:19–22), there is nothing that is consistent with this contemplative prayer. Neither is there in the prayers of our Lord Jesus Christ, nor of his apostles, nor of any holy men from the beginning of the world, either for themselves or the whole church, anything that gives the least countenance unto it. Nor can any man declare what is or can be the work of the Holy Spirit therein, as he is a Spirit of grace and supplication, nor is any gift of his mentioned in the Scripture capable of the least exercise therein; so that in no sense can it be that "praying in the Holy Ghost" which is prescribed unto us. There is, therefore, no example proposed unto our imitation, no mark set before us, nor any direction given, for the attaining of this pretended excellency and perfection. Whatever is fancied or spoken concerning it, it is utterly foreign to the Scripture, and must owe itself unto the deluded imagination of some few persons.

Besides, the Scripture does not propose unto us any other kind of access unto God under the New Testament, nor any nearer approaches unto him, than what we have in and through the mediation of Christ, and by faith in him. But in this pretense there seems to be such an immediate enjoyment of God in his essence aimed at as is regardless of Christ, and leaves him quite behind. But God will not be all in all immediately unto the church, until the Lord Christ has fully delivered up the mediatory kingdom unto him. And, indeed, the silence concerning Christ in the whole of what is ascribed unto this contemplative prayer, or rather the exclusion of him from any concern in it as mediator, is sufficient with all considerate persons to evince that it has not the least interest in the duty of prayer, name or thing.

Neither does this imagination belong any more unto any other part or exercise of faith in this world; and yet here we universally walk by faith, and not by sight. The whole of what belongs unto it may be reduced unto the two heads of what we do toward God, and what we do enjoy of him therein. And as to the first, all the actings of our souls toward God belong unto our "reasonable service" (Rom. 12:1); more is not required of us in a way of duty. But that is no part of our reasonable service wherein our minds and understandings have no concern. Nor is it any part of our enjoyment of God in this life. For no such thing is anywhere promised unto us, and it is by the promises alone that we are made partakers of the divine nature, or have anything from God communicated unto us. There seems, therefore, to be nothing in the bravery of these affected expressions, but an endeavor to fancy somewhat above the measure of all possible attainments in this life, falling unspeakably beneath those of future glory. A kind of purgatory it is in devotion, somewhat out of this world and not in another, above the earth and beneath heaven, where we may leave it in clouds and darkness.

11

Prescribed Forms of Prayer Examined

THERE ARE ALSO great pleas for the use of prescribed limited forms of prayer, in opposition to that spiritual ability in prayer, which we have described and proved to be a gift of the Holy Ghost. Where these forms are contended for by men with respect unto their own use and practice only, as suitable to their experience, and judged by them a serving of God with the best that they have, I shall not take the least notice of them, nor of any dissent about them; but whereas a persuasion not only of their lawfulness but of their necessity is made use of unto other ends and purposes, wherein the peace and edification of believers are highly concerned, it is necessary we should make some inquiry thereinto. I say, it is only with respect unto such a sense of their nature and necessity of their use as gives occasion or a supposed advantage unto men to oppose, deny, and speak evil of that way of prayer, with its causes and ends, which we have described, that I shall any way consider these forms of prayer, and their use. For I know well enough that I have nothing to do to judge or condemn the persons or duties of men in such acts of religious worship as they choose for their best, and hope for acceptance in, unless they are expressly idolatrous. For unless it be in such cases, or the like, which are plain either in the light of nature or Scripture revelation, it is a silly apprehension, and tending to atheism, that God does not require of all men to regulate their actings toward him according to that sovereign light which he has erected in their own minds.

What the forms intended are, how composed, how used, how in some cases imposed, are things so known to all that we shall not need to speak to them. Prayer is God's institution, and the reading of these forms is that which men have made and set up in the likeness thereof, or in compliance with it. For it is said that the Lord Christ having provided the matter of prayer, and commanded us to pray, it is left unto us or others to compose prayer, as unto the manner of it, as we or they shall see cause. But besides that there is no appearance of truth in the inference, the direct contrary rather ensuing on the proposition laid down, it is built on the supposition that besides the provision of matter of prayer and the command of the duty, the Lord Christ has not moreover promised, does not communicate unto his church, such spiritual aids and assistances as shall enable them, without any other outward pretended helps, to pray according unto the mind of God; which we must not admit if we intend to be Christians. In like manner, he has provided the whole subject matter of preaching, and commanded all his ministers to preach; but it does not hence follow that they may all or any of them make one sermon, to be constantly read in all assemblies of Christians without any variation, unless we shall grant also that he ceases to give gifts unto men for the work of the ministry. Our inquiry, therefore, will be, what place or use they may have therein, or in our duty as performed by virtue thereof; which may be expressed in the ensuing observations.

THE ORIGIN OF PRESCRIBED FORMS

1. The Holy Ghost, as a Spirit of grace and supplication, is nowhere, that I know of, promised unto any to help or assist them in composing prayers for others; and therefore, we have no ground to pray for him or his assistance unto that end in particular, nor foundation to build faith or expectation of receiving him upon. Wherefore, he is not in any special or gracious manner concerned in that work or endeavor. Whether this be a duty that falls under his care as communicating gifts in general for the edification of the church shall be afterward examined. That which we plead at present is, that he is nowhere peculiarly promised for that end, nor have we either command or direction to ask for his assistance therein. If any shall say that he is promised to this purpose where he is so as a Spirit of grace and supplication, I answer, besides what has been already pleaded at large in the explication and vindication of the proper sense of that promise, that he is promised directly to them that are to pray, and not to them that make prayers for others, which themselves will not say is praying. But supposing it a duty in general so to compose prayers for our own use or the use of others, it is lawful and warrantable to pray for the aid and guidance of the Holy Ghost therein, not as unto his peculiar assistance in prayer, not as he is unto believers a Spirit of supplication, but as he is our sanctifier, the author and efficient cause of every gracious work and duty in us.

It may be the prayers composed by some holy men under the Old Testament, by the immediate inspiration of the Holy Ghost, for the use of the church, will be also pretended. But as the inspiration or assistance which they had in their work was a thing quite of another kind than anything that is ordinarily promised, or that any persons can now pretend unto, so whether they were dictated unto them by the Holy Ghost to be used afterward by others as mere forms of prayer, may be yet further inquired into.

The great plea for some of these external aids of prayer is by this one consideration utterly removed out of the way. It is said that some of these prayers were prepared by great and holy men, martyrs, it may be, some of them, for the truth of the gospel and testimony of Jesus. And, indeed, had any men in the world a promise of special assistance by the Spirit of God in such a work, I should not contend but the persons intended were as likely to partake of that assistance as any others in these latter ages. Extraordinary, supernatural inspiration they had not; and the holy apostles, who were always under the influence and conduct of it, never made use of it unto any such purpose as to prescribe forms of prayer, either for the whole church or single persons. Whereas, therefore, there is no such special promise given unto any, this work of composing prayers is foreign unto the duty of prayer, as unto any interest in the gracious assistance which is promised thereunto, however it may be a common duty, and fall under the help and blessing of God in general. So some men, from their acquaintance with the matter of prayer above others, which they attain by spiritual light, knowledge, and experience, and their comprehension of the arguments which the Scripture directs unto to be used and pleaded in our supplications, may set down and express a prayer, that is, the matter and outward form of it, that shall declare the substance of things to be prayed for, much more accommodate to the conditions, wants, and desires of Christians than others can who are not so clearly enlightened as they are, nor have had the experience which they have had. For those prayers, as they are called, which men without such light and experience compose of phrases and expressions gathered up from others, taken out of the Scripture, or invented by themselves, and cast into a contexture[1] and method such as they suppose suited unto prayer in general, be they never so well worded, so quaint and elegant in expression, are so empty and jejune[2] as that they can be of no manner of use unto any, unless to keep them from praying while they live. And of such we have books, good store filled with, easy enough to

1 I.e., the fact or manner of being woven or linked together to form a connected whole.
2 I.e., naive; simplistic; juvenile.

be composed by such as never in their lives prayed according to the mind of God. From the former sort much may be learned, as they doctrinally exhibit the matter and arguments of prayer. But the composition of them for others, to be used as their prayers, is that which no man has any promise of peculiar spiritual assistance in, with respect unto prayer in particular.

2. No man has any promise of the Spirit of grace and supplication to enable him to compose a form or forms of prayer for himself. The Spirit of God helps us to pray, not to make prayers in that sense. Suppose men, as before, in so doing may have his assistance in general, as in other studies and endeavors, yet they have not that special assistance which he gives as a Spirit of grace and supplication, enabling us to cry, "Abba, Father." For men do not compose forms of prayer, however they may use them, by the immediate actings of faith, love, and delight in God, with those other graces which he excites and acts in those supplications which are according to the divine will. Nor is God the immediate object of the actings of the faculties of the souls of men in such a work. Their inventions, memories, judgments, are immediately exercised about their present composition, and there they rest. Wherefore, whereas the exercise of grace immediately on God in Christ, under the formal notion of prayer, is no part of men's work or design when they compose and set down forms for themselves or others, if any so do they are not under a promise of special assistance therein in the manner before declared.

3. As there is no assistance promised unto the composition of such forms, so it is no institution of the law or gospel. Prayer itself is a duty of the law of nature, and being of such singular and indispensable use unto all persons, the commands for it are reiterated in the Scripture beyond those concerning any other particular duty whatever. And if it has respect unto Jesus Christ, with sundry ordinances of the gospel to be performed in his name, it falls under a new divine institution. Hereon are commands given us to pray, to pray continually without ceasing, to pray and faint not, to pray for ourselves, to pray for one another, in our closets, in our families, in the assemblies of the church. But as for this work of making or composing forms of prayers for ourselves, to be used as prayers, there is no command, no institution, no mention in the scriptures of the Old Testament or the New. It is a work of human extract and origin, nor can anything be expected from it but what proceeds from that fountain. A blessing possibly there may be upon it, but not such as issues from the special assistance of the Spirit of God in it, nor from any divine appointment or institution whatever. But the reader must observe that I do not urge these things to prove forms of prayer unlawful to

be used, but only at present declare their nature and origin, with respect unto that work of the Holy Spirit which we have described.

ADVANTAGES OF PRESCRIBED FORMS

4. This being the origin of forms of prayer, the benefit and advantage which is in their use, which alone is pleadable in their behalf, comes next under consideration. And this may be done with respect unto two sorts of persons: (1) Such as have the gift or ability of free prayer bestowed on them, or however have attained it. (2) Such as are mean and low in this ability, and therefore incompetent to perform this duty without that aid and assistance of them. And unto both sorts they are pleaded to be of use and advantage.

(1) It is pleaded that there is so much good and so much advantage in the use of them that it is expedient that those who can pray otherwise unto their own and others' edification yet ought sometimes to use them. What this benefit is has not been distinctly declared, nor do I know nor can I divine wherein it should consist. Sacred things are not to be used merely to show our liberty. And there seems to be herein a neglect of stirring up the gift, if not also the grace of God, in those who have received them. The manifestation of the Spirit is given to everyone to profit with. And to forgo its exercise on any just occasion seems not warrantable. We are bound at all times, in the worship of God, to serve him with the best that we have. And if we have a male in the flock, and do sacrifice that which, in comparison thereof, is a corrupt thing, we are deceivers. Free prayer, unto them who have an ability for it, is more suited to the nature of the duty in the light of nature itself, and to Scripture commands and examples, than the use of any prescribed forms. To omit, therefore, the exercise of a spiritual ability therein, and voluntarily to divert unto the other relief, which yet, in that case at least, is no relief, does not readily present its advantage unto a sober consideration. And the reader may observe that at present I examine not what men or churches may agree upon by common consent, as judging and avowing it best for their own edification, which is a matter of another consideration, but only of the duty of believers as such in their respective stations and conditions.

(2) It is generally supposed that the use of such forms is of singular advantage unto them that are low and mean in their ability to pray of themselves. I propose it thus because I cannot grant that any who sincerely believes that there is a God, is sensible of his own wants and his absolute dependence upon him, is utterly unable to make requests unto him for relief without any help but what is suggested unto him by the working of the natural faculties of his

own soul. What men will willfully neglect is one thing, and what they cannot do, if they seriously apply themselves unto their duty, is another. Neither do I believe that any man who is so far instructed in the knowledge of Christ by the gospel as that he can make use of a composed prayer with understanding, but also that in some measure he is able to call upon God in the name of Christ, with respect unto what he feels in himself and is concerned in; and further no man's prayers are to be extended.¶

I speak, therefore, of those who have the least measure and lowest degree of this ability, seeing none are absolutely uninterested therein. Unto this sort of persons, I know not of what use these forms are, unless it be to keep them low and mean all the days of their lives. For whereas, both in the state of nature and the state of grace, in one whereof every man is supposed to be, there are certain heavenly sparks suited unto each condition, the main duty of all men is to stir them up and increase them. Even in the remainders of lapsed nature there are *coelestes igniculi*,[3] in notices of good and evil, accusations and apologies of conscience. These none will deny but that they ought to be stirred up and increased; which can be no otherwise done but in their sedulous[4] exercise. Nor is there any such effectual way of their exercise as in the soul's application of itself unto God with respect unto them, which is done in prayer only. But as for those whom in this matter we principally regard, that is, professed believers in Jesus Christ, there is none of them but have such principles of spiritual life, and therein of all obedience unto God and communion with him, as, being improved and exercised under those continual supplies of the Spirit which they receive from Christ their head, will enable them to discharge every duty that in every condition or relation is required of them in an acceptable manner. Among these is that of an ability for prayer; and to deny them to have it, supposing them true believers, is expressly to contradict the apostle affirming that "because we are sons, God sends forth the Spirit of his Son into our hearts, whereby we cry, 'Abba, Father.'"[5] But this ability, as I have showed, is no way to be improved but in and by a constant exercise. Now, whether the use of the forms inquired into, which certainly takes men off from the exercise of what ability they have, does not tend directly to keep them still low and mean in their abilities, is not hard to determine.

But suppose those spoken of are not yet real believers, but only such as profess the gospel, not yet sincerely converted unto God, whose duty also it

3   Lat. "heavenly sparks."
4   I.e., dedicated or diligent.
5   Gal. 4:6.

is to pray on all occasions; these have no such principle or ability to improve, and therefore this advantage is not by them to be neglected. I answer, that the matter of all spiritual gifts is spiritual light; according, therefore, to their measure in the light of the knowledge of the gospel, such is their measure in spiritual gifts also. If they have no spiritual light, no insight into the knowledge of the gospel, prayers framed and composed according unto it will be of little use unto them. If they have any such light, it ought to be improved by exercise in this duty, which is of such indispensable necessity unto their souls.

5. But yet the advantage which all sorts of persons may have hereby, in having the matter of prayer prepared for them and suggested unto them, is also insisted on. This they may be much to seek in who yet have sincere desires to pray, and whose affections will comply with what is proposed unto them. And this, indeed, would carry a great appearance of reason with it, but that there are other ways appointed of God unto this end, and which are sufficient thereunto, under the guidance, conduct, and assistance of the blessed Spirit, whose work must be admitted in all parts of this duty, unless we intend to frame prayers that shall be an abomination to the Lord. Such are, men's diligent and sedulous consideration of themselves, their spiritual state and condition, their wants and desires; a diligent consideration of the Scripture, or the doctrine of it in the ministry of the word, whereby they will be both instructed in the whole matter of prayer and convinced of their own concern therein, with all other helps of coming to the knowledge of God and themselves, all which they are to attend unto who intend to pray in a due manner. To furnish men with prayers to be said by them, and so to satisfy their consciences, while they live in the neglect of these things, is to deceive them, and not to help or instruct them. And if they do conscientiously attend unto these things, they will have no need of those other pretended helps. For men to live and converse with the world, not once inquiring into their own ways, or reflecting on their own hearts, unless under some charge of conscience, accompanied with fear or danger, never endeavoring to examine, try, or compare their state and condition with the Scripture, nor scarce considering either their own wants or God's promises, to have a book lie ready for them wherein they may read a prayer, and so suppose they have discharged their duty in that matter, is a course which surely they ought not to be countenanced or encouraged in. Nor is the perpetual rotation of the same words and expressions suited to instruct or carry on men in the knowledge of anything, but rather to divert the mind from the due consideration of the things intended, and, therefore, commonly issues in formality. And where men have words or expressions prepared for them and suggested unto them

that really signify the things wherein they are concerned, yet if the light and knowledge of those principles of truth whence they are derived, and whereinto they are resolved, be not in some measure fixed and abiding in their minds, they cannot be much benefited or edified by their repetition.

6. Experience is pleaded in the same case; and this with me, where persons are evidently conscientious, is of more moment than a hundred notional arguments that cannot be brought to that trial. Some, therefore, say that they have had spiritual advantage, the exercise of grace, and holy intercourse with God, in the use of such forms, and have their affections warmed and their hearts much bettered thereby. And this they take to be a clear evidence and token that they are not disapproved of God; yea, that they are a great advantage, at least unto many, in prayer. Answer: Whether they are approved or disapproved of God, whether they are lawful or unlawful, we do not consider; but only whether they are for spiritual benefit and advantage, for the good of our own souls and the edification of others, as set up in competition with the exercise of the gift before described. And herein I am very unwilling to oppose the experience of anyone who seems to be under the conduct of the least beam of gospel light. Only, I shall desire to propose some few things to their consideration. As,

(1) Whether they understand aright the difference that is between natural devotion occasionally excited, and the due actings of evangelical faith and love, with other graces of the Spirit, in a way directed unto by divine appointment? All men who acknowledge a deity or divine power which they adore, when they address themselves seriously to perform any religious worship thereunto in their own way, be it what it will, will have their affections moved and excited suitably unto the apprehensions they have of what they worship, yea, though in particular it have no existence but in their own imaginations. For these things ensue on the general notion of a divine power, and not on the application of them to such idols as indeed are nothing in the world. There will be in such persons, dread, and reverence, and fear, as there was in some of the heathen, unto an unspeakable horror, when they entered into the temples and merely imaginary presence of their gods, the whole work being begun and finished in their fancies. And sometimes great joys, satisfactions, and delights do ensue on what they do. For as what they so do is suited to the best light they have, and men are apt to have a complacency in their own inventions, as Micah had (Judg. 17:13), and upon inveterate[6] prejudices, which are the guides of most men in religion, their consciences

6   I.e., well-established.

find relief in the discharge of their duty. These things, I say, are found in persons of the highest and most dreadful superstitions in the world, yea, heightened unto inexpressible agitations of mind, in horror on the one side, and raptures or ecstasies on the other. And they are all tempered and qualified according to the mode and way of worship wherein men are engaged; but in themselves they are all of the same nature, that is, natural, or effects and impressions upon nature. So, it is with the Mohammedans, who excel in this devotion; and so it is with idolatrous Christians, who place the excellency and glory of their profession herein. Wherefore, such devotion, such affections, will be excited by religious offices, in all that are sincere in their use, whether they be of divine appointment or no. But the actings of faith and love on God through Christ, according to the gospel, or the tenor of the new covenant, with the effects produced thereby in the heart and affections, are things quite of another kind and nature; and unless men do know how really to distinguish between these things, it is to no purpose to plead spiritual benefit and advantage in the use of such forms, seeing possibly it may be no other but of the same kind with what all false worshipers in the world have, or may have, experience of.

(2) Let them diligently inquire whether the effects on their hearts which they plead do not proceed from a precedent preparation, a good design and upright ends, occasionally excited. Let it be supposed that those who thus make use of and plead for forms of prayer, especially in public, do in a due manner prepare themselves for it by holy meditation, with an endeavor to bring their souls into a holy frame of fear, delight, and reverence of God; let it also be supposed that they have a good end and design in the worship they address themselves unto, namely, the glory of God and their own spiritual advantage—the prayers themselves, though they should be in some things irregular, may give occasion to exercise those acts of grace which they were otherwise prepared for. And I say yet further,

(3) That while these forms of prayer are clothed with the general notions of prayer, that is, are esteemed as such in the minds of them that use them, are accompanied in their use with the motives and ends of prayer, express no matter unlawful to be insisted on in prayer; directing the souls of men to none but lawful objects of divine worship and prayer, the Father, Son, and Holy Spirit; and while men make use of them with the true design of prayer, looking after due assistance unto prayer, I do not judge there is any such evil in them as that God will not communicate his Spirit to any in the use of them, so as that they should have no holy communion with him in and under them. Much less will I say that God never therein regards their

persons or rejects their praying as unlawful. For the persons and duties of men may be accepted with God when they walk and act in sincerity according to their light, though in many things, and those of no small importance, sundry irregularities are found both in what they do and in the manner of doing it. Where persons walk before God in their integrity, and practice nothing contrary to their light and conviction in his worship, God is merciful unto them, although they order not everything according to the rule and measure of the word. So was it with them who came to the passover in the days of Hezekiah; they had not cleansed themselves, but did "eat the passover otherwise than it was written" (2 Chron. 30:18). For whom the good king made the solemn prayer suited to their occasion, "The good Lord pardon everyone that prepareth his heart to seek God, the Lord God of his fathers, though he be not cleansed according to the purification of the sanctuary. And the Lord hearkened unto Hezekiah, and healed the people" (2 Chron. 30:18–20). Here was a duty for the substance of it appointed of God; but in the manner of its performance there was a failure, they did it not according to what was written, which is the sole rule of all religious duties. This God was displeased with, yet graciously passed by the offense, and accepted them whose hearts were upright in what they did. In the meantime, I do yet judge that the use of them is in itself obstructive of all the principal ends of prayer and sacred worship. Where they are alone used, they are opposite to the edification of the church, and where they are imposed to the absolute exclusion of other prayer, are destructive of its liberty, and render a good part of the purchase of Christ of none effect.

LAWFULNESS OF PRESCRIBED FORMS

Things being thus stated, it will be inquired whether the use of such forms of prayer is lawful or no. To this inquiry something shall be returned briefly in way of answer, and an end put unto this discourse. And I say—

1. To compose and write forms of prayer to be directive and doctrinal helps unto others, as to the matter and method to be used in the right discharge of this duty, is lawful, and may in some cases be useful. It were better, it may be, if the same thing were done in another way, suited to give direction in the case, and not cast into the form of a prayer, which is apt to divert the mind from the due consideration of its proper end and use unto that which is not so. But this way of instruction is not to be looked on as unlawful merely for the form and method wherein to it is cast, while its true use only is attended unto.

2. To read, consider, and meditate upon, such written prayers, as to the matter and arguments of prayer expressed in them, composed by persons from their own experience and the light of Scripture directions, or to make use of expressions set down in them, where the hearts of them that read them are really affected, because they find their state and condition, their wants and desires, declared in them, is not unlawful, but may be of good use unto some, though I must acknowledge I never heard any expressing any great benefit which they had received thereby. But it is possible that some may so do. For no such freedom of prayer is asserted as should make it unlawful for men to make use of any proper means the better to enable them to pray, nor is any such ability of prayer granted as to supersede the duty of using means for the increase and furtherance of it.

3. To set up and prescribe the use of such forms universally, in opposition and unto the exclusion of free prayer by the aid of the Spirit of grace, is contrary not only to many divine precepts before insisted on, but to the light of nature itself, requiring every man to pray, and on some occasions necessitating them thereunto. But whatever be the practice of some men, I know not that any such opinion is pleaded for, and so shall not further oppose it.

4. It is not inquired whether forms of prayer, especially as they may be designed unto and used for other ends, and not to be read instead of prayer, have in their composition anything of intrinsical evil in them, for it is granted they have not. But the inquiry is whether in their use as prayers they are not hindrances unto the right discharge of the duty of prayer according to the mind of God, and so may be unlawful in that respect. For I take it as granted that they are nowhere appointed of God for such a use, nowhere commanded so to be used; whence an argument may be formed against their having any interest in divine, acceptable worship, but it is not of our present consideration. For if on the accounts mentioned they appear not contrary unto, or inconsistent with, or are not used in a way exclusive of, that work of the Holy Spirit in prayer which we have described from the Scripture, nor are reducible unto any divine prohibition, while I may enjoy my own liberty I shall not contend with any about them. Nor shall I now engage into the examination of the arguments that are pleaded on their behalf, which some have greatly multiplied, as I suppose, not much to the advantage of their cause. For in things of religious practice, one testimony of Scripture rightly explained and applied, with the experience of believers thereon, is of more weight and value than a thousand dubious reasonings, which cannot be evidently resolved into those principles. Wherefore some few additional considerations shall put an issue unto this discourse.

CONCLUSION

1. Some observe that there are forms of prayer composed and prescribed to be used both in the Old Testament and the New. Such, they say, was the form of blessing prescribed unto the priests on solemn occasions (Num. 6:22–26), and the psalms of David, as also the Lord's Prayer in the New Testament. (1) If this be so, it proves that forms of prayer are not intrinsically evil, which is granted, yet may the use of them be unnecessary. (2) The argument will not hold, so far as it is usually extended at least: God himself has prescribed some forms of prayer, to be used by some persons on some occasions; therefore, men may invent, yea, and prescribe those that shall be for common and constant use. He who forbade all images, or all use of them, in sacred things, appointed the making of the cherubims in the tabernacle and temple. (3) The argument from the practice in use under the Old Testament in this matter, if any could from there be taken, when the people were carnal and tied up unto carnal ordinances, unto the duty and practice of believers under the New Testament and a more plentiful effusion of the Spirit, has been before disproved.[7] (4) The words prescribed unto the priests were not a prayer properly, but an authoritative benediction, and an instituted sign of God's blessing the people; for so it is added in the explication of that ordinance, "They shall put my name upon the children of Israel; and I will bless them" (Num. 6:27). (5) David's psalms were given out by immediate inspiration, and were most of them mystical and prophetical, appointed to be used in the church, as all other Scriptures, only some of them in a certain manner, namely, of singing, and that manner also was determined by divine appointment. (6) That any form of prayer is appointed in the New Testament, to be used as a form, is neither granted nor can be proved. (7) Give us prayers composed by divine inspiration, with a command for their use, with the time, manner, and form of their usage, which, these instances prove to be lawful, if they prove anything in this case, and there will be no contest about them. (8) All and every one of the precedents or examples which we have in the whole Scripture of the prayers of any of the people of God, men or women, being all accommodated to their present occasions, and uttered in the freedom of their own spirits, do all give testimony unto free prayer, if not against the use of forms in that duty.

2. Moreover, it seems that when anyone prays, his prayer is a form unto all that join with him, whether in families or church assemblies; which some lay great weight upon, though I am not able to discern the force of it in this case. For (1) the question is solely about him that prays, and his discharge of duty

---

7   Πνευματολογια, or, *A Discourse concerning the Holy Spirit*, bk. 2, chaps. 1–2.

according to the mind of God, and not concerning them who join with him. (2) The conjunction of others with him that prays according to his ability is an express command of God. (3) Those who so join are at liberty, when it is their duty, to pray themselves. (4) That which is not a form in itself is not a form to any; for there is more required to make it so than merely that the words and expressions are not of their own present invention. It is to them the benefit of a gift, bestowed for their edification in its present exercise, according to the mind of God. That only is a form of prayer unto any which he himself uses as a form; for its nature depends on its use. (5) The argument is incogent: God has commanded some to pray according to the ability they have received, and others to join with them therein, therefore, it is lawful to invent forms of prayer for ourselves or others, to be used as prayers by them or us.

3. That which those who pretend unto moderation in this matter plead, is that prayer itself is a commanded duty; but praying by or with a prescribed form is only an outward manner and circumstance of it, which is indifferent, and may or may not be used, as we see occasion. And might a general rule to this purpose be duly established, it would be of huge importance. But (1) it is an easy thing to invent and prescribe such outward forms and manner of outward worship as shall leave nothing of the duty prescribed but the empty name. (2) Praying before an image, or worshiping God or Christ by an image, is but an outward mode of worship, yet such as renders the whole idolatrous. (3) Any outward mode of worship, the attendance whereunto or the observance whereof is prejudicial unto the due performance of the duty whereunto it is annexed, is inexpedient; and what there is hereof in the present instance must be judged from the preceding discourse.

TWO DISCOURSES CONCERNING THE HOLY SPIRIT AND HIS WORK

The One,
of the Spirit as a Comforter.
The Other,
as He Is the Author of Spiritual Gifts.

In the former discourse these particulars are distinctly handled:

By the Late Reverend John Owen, D.D.

———

London, Printed for William Marshall
at the Bible in Newgate-street,
where you may be supplied with
most of Dr. Owen's works:
1693

The Holy Spirit as a Comforter
Contents

Preface

THAT THERE ARE SUNDRY great and eminent promises, referring to New Testament times, concerning the pouring out of the Spirit, none who is acquainted with the Scriptures and believes them can doubt. By the performance of them a church has been begotten and maintained in the world through all ages since the ascension of Christ, sometimes with greater light and spiritual luster, and sometimes with less. It has been one of the glories of the Protestant Reformation that it has been accompanied with a very conspicuous and remarkable effusion of the Spirit; and, indeed, thereby there has from heaven a seal been set and a witness borne unto that great work of God. In this invaluable blessing, we in this nation have had a rich and plentiful share, insomuch that it seems Satan and his ministers have been tormented and exasperated thereby; and so it is come to pass that there have some risen up among us who have manifested themselves to be not only despisers in heart, but virulent reproachers of the operations of the Spirit. God, who knows how to bring good out of evil, did, for holy and blessed ends of his own, suffer those horrid blasphemies to be particularly vented.

On this occasion it was that this great, and learned, and holy person, the author of these discourses, took up thoughts of writing concerning the blessed Spirit and his whole economy, as I understood from himself sundry years ago, discoursing with him concerning some books, then newly published, full of contumely[1] and contempt of the Holy Spirit and his operations. For as it was with Paul at Athens when he saw the city wholly given to idolatry, so was Dr. Owen's spirit stirred in him when he read the scoffs and blasphemies cast upon the Holy Spirit and his grace, and gifts, and aids, in some late writers.

---

1 I.e., harsh treatment; contempt.

Had not Pelagius[2] vented his corrupt opinions concerning the grace of God, it is like the church had never had the learned and excellent writings of Augustine[3] in defense thereof. It appears from Bradwardine that the revival of Pelagianism in his days stirred up his zealous and pious spirit to write that profound and elaborate book of his, *De causa Dei*.[4] Arminius[5] and the Jesuists,[6] endeavoring to plant the same weed again, produced the scholastic writings of Twisse[7] and Ames,[8] not to mention foreign divines, for which we in this generation have abundant cause of enlarged thankfulness unto the Father of lights. The occasion which the Holy Ghost laid hold on to carry forth Paul to write his epistle to the Galatians, wherein the doctrine of justification by faith is so fully cleared, was the bringing in among them of "another gospel"[9] by corrupt teachers, after which many in those churches were soon drawn away. The obstinate adherence of many among the Jews to the Mosaic rites and observances, and the inclination of others to apostatize from the New Testament worship and ordinances, was in like manner the occasion of the epistle to the Hebrews. The light which shines and is held out in these epistles, the church of Christ could ill have wanted.

2   Pelagius (ca. 354–418) was a heretic who denied original sin and believed that human beings had the free will to achieve perfection without the aid of divine grace.

3   Augustine of Hippo (354–430) was the primary orthodox opponent of Pelagius and the theological giant among the church fathers of the West.

4   Thomas Bradwardine (ca. 1300–1349) was an English polymath, with proficiency in math, physics, and politics, and served briefly as the Archbishop of Canterbury. His *De causa Dei* (1344) upheld a robust Augustinianism as it pertains to divine, sovereign grace and human free will. *De causa Dei* was republished in Latin in England in 1618, the year of the start of the Synod of Dort. See Luca Baschera, "Witnessing to the Calvinism of the English Church: The 1618 Edition of Thomas Bradwardine's *De causa dei adversus pelagium*," in *Bewegung und Beharrung: Aspekte des reformierten Protestantismus, 1520-1650*, ed. Christian Moser and Peter Opitz (Leiden: Brill, 2009), 433–46. For more on Bradwardine and the semi-Pelagians of his day, see Heiko A. Oberman, *Forerunners of the Reformation: The Shape of Late Medieval Thought* (1966; repr., Cambridge: James Clarke, 2002).

5   Jacob Arminius (1560–1609) was a Dutch theologian whose views became the basis for the Remonstrant movement. His criticism of the Belgic Confession (1561) spurred the discussions and conclusions of the Synod of Dort (1618–1619), which reaffirmed Reformed soteriology.

6   The Jesuits, also known as the Society of Jesus, founded by Ignatius of Loyola (ca. 1491–1556) in 1540, were the preeminent Counter-Reformation Roman Catholic religious order. Catholic and Arminianian views were often conflated for polemical purposes by adherents of the Reformed tradition.

7   William Twisse (1578–1648) was a prominent English divine of the early Westminster Assembly. His *Vindiciae gratiae* (1632) was an attack on Jacob Arminius.

8   William Ames (1576–1633) was an active participant in the Synod of Dort (1618–1619) and an opponent of Remonstrant theology.

9   Gal. 1:8.

The like way and working of the wisdom of God is to be seen and adored in stirring up this learned and excellent person to communicate and leave unto the world that light, touching the Spirit and his operations, which he had received by that Spirit from the sacred oracles of truth, the Scriptures.

To what advantage and increase of light it is performed is not for so incompetent a pen to say as writes this. Nevertheless, I doubt not but the discerning reader will observe such excellencies shining out in this and other of this great author's writings, as do greatly commend them to the church of God, and will do so in after ages, however this corrupt and degenerate generation entertain them. They are not the crude, and hasty, and untimely abortions of a self-full, distempered spirit, much less the boilings-over of inward corruption and rottenness put into a fermentation; but the mature, sedate,[10] and seasonable issues of a rich magazine of learning, well digested with great exactness of judgment. There is in them a great light cast and reflected on, as well as derived from, the holy Scriptures, those inexhaustible mines of light in sacred things. They are not filled with vain, impertinent jangling, nor with a noise of multiplied futilous[11] distinctions, nor with novel and uncouth terms foreign to the things of God, as the manner of some writers is *ad nauseam usque*.[12] But there is in them a happy and rare conjunction of firm solidity, enlightening clearness, and heart-searching spiritualness, evidencing themselves all along, and thereby approving and commending his writings to the judgment, conscience, spiritual taste, and experience of all those who have any acquaintance with and relish of the gospel.

On these and such like accounts the writings of this great and learned man, as also his ordinary sermons, if any of them shall be published, as possibly some of them may, will be, while the world stands, an upbraiding and condemning of this generation, whose vitiated[13] and ill-affected eyes could not bear so great a light set up and shining on a candlestick, and which did therefore endeavor to put it under a bushel.

These two discourses, with those formerly published, make up all that Dr. Owen perfected or designed on this subject of the Spirit, as the reader may perceive in the account which himself has given in his prefaces to some of the former pieces, published by himself in his lifetime. Not but that there are some other lucubrations[14] of his on subjects nearly allied unto these, which possibly

---

10 I.e., calm.
11 I.e., futile or trifling.
12 Lat. "all the way to nausea."
13 I.e., impaired.
14 I.e., intensive studies.

may be published hereafter, namely, one entitled, *The Evidences of the Faith of God's Elect*,[15] and perhaps some others. What further he might have had in his thoughts to do is known to him whom he served so industriously and so faithfully in his spirit in the gospel while he was here on earth, and with whom he now enjoys the reward of all his labors and all his sufferings. For certain it is concerning Dr. Owen, that as God gave him very transcendent abilities, so he did therewith give him a boundless enlargedness of heart, and unsatiable desire to do service to Christ and his church, insomuch that he was thereby carried on through great bodily weakness, languishing, and pains, besides manifold other trials and discouragements, to bring forth out of his treasury, like a scribe well instructed unto the kingdom of heaven, many useful and excellent fruits of his studies, much beyond the expectation and hopes of those who saw how often and how long he was near unto the grave.

But while he was thus indefatigably and restlessly laying out for the service of Christ, in this and succeeding generations, those rich talents with which he was furnished, his Lord said unto him, "Well done, thou good and faithful servant, enter thou into the joy of thy Lord."[16] No man ever yet, but Jesus Christ, was able to finish all that was in his heart to do for God. On the removal of such accomplished and useful persons, I have sometimes relieved myself with this thought, that Christ lives in heaven still, and the blessed Spirit, from whom the head and heart of this chosen vessel were so richly replenished, lives still.

Nathaniel Mather[17]

OCTOBER 27, 1692

---

15 This work was published as *Gospel Grounds and Evidences of the Faith of God's Elect Shewing: I. The Nature of True Saving Faith, in Securing of the Spiritual Comfort of Believers in This Life, Is of the Highest Importance, II. The Way Wherein True Faith Doth Evidence Itself in the Soul and Consciences of Believers, unto Their Supportment and Comfort, under All Their Conflicts with Sin, in All Their Tryals and Temptations, III. Faith Will Evidence Itself, by a Diligent, Constant Endeavour to Keep Itself and All Grace in Due Exercise, in All Ordinances of Divine Worship, Private and Publick, IV. A Peculiar Way Whereby True Faith Will Evidence Itself, by Bringing the Soul into a State of Repentance* (1695).

16 Matt. 25:21.

17 Nathaniel Mather (1631–1697) was part of the powerful New England Mather family, serving as an Independent, or Congregationalist, minister largely in the British Isles.

A Discourse on the Holy Spirit
as a Comforter

1

The Holy Ghost the Comforter of the Church by Way of Office

How He Is the Church's Advocate; John 14:16;
1 John 2:1–2; John 16:8–11 Opened

THAT WHICH REMAINS to complete our discourses concerning the dispensation of the Holy Spirit, is the office and work that he has undertaken for the consolation of the church. And,

Three things are to be considered with respect unto this head of the grace of the gospel. First, that the Holy Spirit is the comforter of the church by way of special office. Second, what is in that office, or wherein the discharge of it does consist. Third, what are the effects of it toward believers.

It must be granted that there is some impropriety in that expression, "by the way of office." An office is not simply, nor may it be properly spoken of a divine person, who is absolutely so and nothing else. But the like impropriety is to be found in most of the expressions which we use concerning God, for who can speak of him aright or as he ought? Only, we have a safe rule whereby to express our conceptions, even what he speaks of himself. And he has taught us to learn the work of the Holy Ghost toward us in this matter by ascribing unto him those things which belong unto an office among men.

Four things are required unto the constitution of an office. First, a special trust. Second, a special mission or commission. Third, a special name. Fourth, a special work. All these are required unto an office properly so called; and where they are complied with by a voluntary susception[1] in the person designed thereunto,[2] an office is completely constituted. And we must inquire

---

1 I.e., reception.
2 I.e., in order for this to occur.

how these things in a divine manner do concur in the work of the Holy Spirit as he is the comforter of the church.

THE SPIRIT'S SPECIAL TRUST

First, he is entrusted with this work, and of his own will has taken it on himself. For when our Savior was leaving of the world, and had a full prospect of all the evils, troubles, dejections, and disconsolations which would befall his disciples, and knew full well that if they were left unto themselves they would faint and perish under them, he gives them assurance that the work of their consolation and support was left entrusted and committed unto the Holy Spirit, and that he would both take care about it and perfect it accordingly.

The Lord Christ, when he left this world, was very far from laying aside his love unto and care of his disciples. He has given us the highest assurance that he continues forever the same care, the same love and grace, toward us, which he had and exercised when he laid down his life for us (Heb. 4:14–16; 7:25–26). But inasmuch as there was a double work yet to be performed on our behalf, one toward God and the other in ourselves, he has taken a twofold way for the performance of it. That toward God he was to discharge immediately himself in his human nature; for other mediator between God and man there neither is nor can be any. This he does by his intercession. Hence there was a necessity that, as to his human nature, the "heaven should receive him until the times of the restitution of all things" (as Acts 3:21). There was so both with respect unto himself and us.

1. Three things with respect unto himself made the exaltation of his human nature in heaven to be necessary. For,

(1) It was to be a pledge and token of God's acceptation of him, and approbation of what he had done in the world (John 16:7–8). For what could more declare or evidence the consent and delight of God in what he had done and suffered, than, after he had been so ignominiously[3] treated in the world, to receive him visibly, gloriously, and triumphantly into heaven? He was manifested in the flesh, justified in the Spirit, seen of angels, and, in the issue, received up into glory (1 Tim. 3:16). Herein God set the great seal of heaven unto his work of mediation, and the preaching of the gospel which ensued thereon.[4] And a testimony hereunto was that which filled his enemies with rage and madness (Acts 7:55–58). His resurrection confirmed his doctrine

3 I.e., disgracefully.
4 I.e., as a result.

with undeniable efficacy; but his assumption into heaven testified unto his person with an astonishing glory.

(2) It was necessary with respect unto the human nature itself, that, after all its labors and sufferings, it might be "crowned with glory and honour."[5] He was to "suffer" and "enter into his glory" (Luke 24:26). Some dispute whether Christ in his human nature merited anything for himself or not; but, not to immix[6] ourselves in the niceties of that inquiry, it is unquestionable that the highest glory was due to him upon his accomplishment of the work committed unto him in this world, which he therefore lays claim to accordingly (John 17:4–5). It was so,

(3) With respect unto the glorious administration of his kingdom. For as his kingdom is not of this world, so it is not only over this world, or the whole creation here below; the angels of glory, those principalities and powers above, are subject unto him, and belong unto his dominion (Eph. 1:21; Phil. 2:9–11). Among them, attended with their ready service and obedience unto all his commands, does he exercise the powers of his glorious kingdom. And they would but degrade him from his glory, without the least advantage unto themselves, who would have him forsake his high and glorious throne in heaven to come and reign among them on the earth, unless they suppose themselves more meet[7] attendants on his regal dignity than the angels themselves, who are mighty in strength and glory.

2. The presence of the human nature of Christ in heaven was necessary with respect unto us. The remainder of his work with God on our behalf was to be carried on by intercession (Heb. 7:25–27). And whereas this intercession consists in the virtual representation of his oblation, or of himself as a lamb slain in sacrifice, it could not be done without his continual appearing in the presence of God (Heb. 9:24).

The other part of the work of Christ respects the church, or believers, as its immediate object. So, in particular, does his comforting and supporting of them. This is that work which, in a peculiar manner, is committed and entrusted unto the Holy Spirit, after the departure of the human nature of Christ into heaven.

But two things are to be observed concerning it.¶[8]

1. That whereas this whole work consists in the communication of spiritual light, grace, and joy to the souls of believers, it was no less the immediate work of the Holy Ghost while the Lord Christ was upon the earth than it is now he

---

5   Heb. 2:7.
6   I.e., mix thoroughly.
7   I.e., fitting; proper.
8   The ¶ symbol indicates that a paragraph break has been added to Owen's original text.

is absent in heaven; only, during the time of his conversation here below, in the days of his flesh, his holy disciples looked on him as the only spring and foundation of all their consolation, their only support, guide, and protector, as they had just cause to do. They had yet no insight into the mystery of the dispensation of the Spirit, nor was he yet so given or poured out as to evidence himself and his operation unto their souls. Wherefore they looked on themselves as utterly undone when their Lord and Master began to acquaint them with his leaving of them. No sooner did he tell them of it but "sorrow filled their hearts" (John 16:6). Wherefore he immediately lets them know that this great work of relieving them from all their sorrows and fears, of dispelling their disconsolations, and supporting them under their trouble, was committed to the Holy Ghost, and would by him be performed in so eminent a manner as that his departure from them would be unto their advantage (John 16:7).¶

Wherefore the Holy Spirit did not then first begin really and effectually to be the comforter of believers upon the departure of Christ from his disciples, but he is then first promised so to be, upon a double account. (1) Of the full declaration and manifestation of it. So, things are often said in the Scripture then to be, when they do appear and are made manifest. An eminent instance hereof we have in this case (John 7:38–39). The disciples had hitherto looked for all immediately from Christ in the flesh, the dispensation of the Spirit being hid from them. But now this also was to be manifested unto them. Hence the apostle affirms, that "though we have known Christ after the flesh, yet henceforth know we him no more" (2 Cor. 5:16). That is, so as to look for grace and consolation immediately from him in the flesh, as it is evident the apostles did before they were instructed in this unknown office of the Holy Ghost. (2) Of the full exhibition and eminent communication of him unto this end. This in every kind was reserved for the exaltation of Christ, when he received the promise of the Spirit from the Father, and poured it out upon his disciples.

2. The Lord Christ does not hereby cease to be the comforter of his church. For what he does by his Spirit, he does by himself. He is with us unto the end of the world by his Spirit being with us, and he dwells in us by the Spirit dwelling in us; and whatever else is done by the Spirit is done by him. And it is so upon a threefold account. For,¶

(1) The Lord Christ as mediator is God and man in one person, and the divine nature is to be considered in all his mediatory operations. For he who works them is God, and he works them all as God-man, whence[9] they are

---

9   I.e., where.

the theandric.[10] And this is proposed unto us in the greatest acts of his humiliation, which the divine nature in itself is not formally capable of. So God redeemed the church with his own blood (Acts 20:28). "Inasmuch as he who was in the form of God, and thought it not robbery to be equal with God, humbled himself, and became obedient unto death, the death of the cross" (Phil. 2:6–8). Now, in this respect the Lord Christ and the Holy Spirit are one in nature, essence, will, and power. As he said of the Father, "I and my Father are one" (John 10:30), so it is with the Spirit; he and the Spirit are one. Hence all the works of the Holy Spirit are his also. As his works were the works of the Father, and the works of the Father were his, all the operations of the holy Trinity, as to things external unto their divine subsistence, being undivided. So is the work of the Holy Spirit in the consolation of the church his work also.

(2) Because the Holy Spirit in this condescension unto office acts for Christ and in his name. So, the Son acted for and in the name of the Father, where he everywhere ascribed what he did unto the Father in a peculiar manner. "The word," says he, "which you hear is not mine, but the Father's which sent me" (John 14:24). It is his originally and eminently, because, as spoken by the Lord Christ, he was said by him to speak it. So are those acts of the Spirit whereby he comforts believers the acts of Christ, because the Spirit speaks and acts for him and in his name.

(3) All those things, those acts of light, grace, and mercy, whereby the souls of the disciples of Christ are comforted by the Holy Ghost, are the things of Christ, that is, special fruits of his mediation. So speaks our Savior himself of him and his work: "He shall glorify me; for he shall receive of mine, and shall show it unto you" (John 16:14). All that consolation, peace, and joy, which he communicates unto believers, yea, all that he does in his whole work toward the elect, is but the effectual communication of the fruits of the mediation of Christ unto them. And this is the first thing that constitutes the office of the comforter; this work is committed and entrusted unto him in a special manner, which, in the infinite condescension of his own will, he takes upon himself.

THE SPIRIT'S SPECIAL MISSION

Secondly, it further evinces[11] the nature of an office in that he is said to be sent unto the work. And mission always includes commission. He who is

10 I.e., joint operation between man and God.
11 I.e., provides evidence for.

sent is entrusted and empowered as unto what he is sent about (Ps. 104:30; John 14:26; 15:26; 16:7). The nature of this sending of the Spirit, and how it is spoken of him in general, has been considered before, in our declaration of his general adjuncts, or what is affirmed of him in the Scripture, and may not here again be insisted on.[12] It is now mentioned only as an evidence to prove, that in this work of his toward us, he has taken that on him which has the nature of an office. For that which he is sent to perform is his office, and he will not fail in the discharge of it. And it is in itself a great principle of consolation unto all true believers, an effectual means of their support and refreshment, to consider that not only is the Holy Ghost their comforter, but also that he is sent of the Father and the Son so to be. Nor can there be a more uncontrollable evidence of the care of Jesus Christ over his church, and toward his disciples in all their sorrows and sufferings, than this is, that he sends the Holy Ghost to be their comforter.

THE SPIRIT'S SPECIAL NAME

Thirdly, he has a special name given him, expressing and declaring his office. When the Son of God was to be incarnate and born in the world, he had a special name given unto him: he was called Jesus. Now, although there was in this name a signification of the work he was to do—for he was called Jesus, "because he was to save his people from their sins" (Matt. 1:21)—yet was it also that proper name whereby he was to be distinguished from other persons. So, the Holy Spirit has no other name but that of the Holy Spirit, which, how it is characteristic of the third person in the holy Trinity, has been before declared. But as both the names of Jesus and Christ, though neither of them is the name of an office, as one has dreamed of late, yet have respect unto the work which he had to do and the office which he was to undergo, without which he could not have rightly been so called. So has the Holy Ghost a name given unto him, which is not distinctive with respect unto his personality, but denominative with respect unto his work, and this is ὁ παράκλητος.[13]

---

12 Πνευματολογια, or, A Discourse concerning the Holy Spirit: Wherein an Account Is Given of His Name, Nature, Personality, Dispensation, Operations, and Effects; His Whole Work in the Old and New Creation Is Explained; the Doctrine concerning It Vindicated from Oppositions and Reproaches. The Nature Also and Necessity of Gospel Holiness; the Difference between Grace and Morality, or a Spiritual Life unto God in Evangelical Obedience and a Course of Moral Virtues, Are Stated and Declared (1674), bk. 1, chap. 5.

13 Gk. "comforter," "advocate," or "helper."

This name is used only by the apostle John, and that in his Gospel only, from the mouth of Christ (John 14:16, 26; 15:26; 16:7). And once he uses it himself, applying it unto Christ (1 John 2:1–2), where we render it an "advocate."

The Syriac interpreter retains the name פרהליטא,[14] *Paraclita*; not, as some imagine, from the use of that word before among the Jews, which cannot be proved. Nor is it likely that our Savior made use of a Greek word barbarously corrupted. הַמְנַחֵם was the word he employed to this purpose.[15] But looking on it a proper name of the Spirit with respect unto his office, he would not translate it.

As this word is applied unto Christ, which it is in that one place of 1 John 2:1, it respects his intercession, and gives us light into the nature of it. That it is his intercession which the apostle intends is evident from its relation unto his being our propitiation. For the oblation of Christ on the earth is the foundation of his intercession in heaven. And he does therein undertake our patronage, as our advocate, to plead our cause, and in a special manner to keep off evil from us. For although the intercession of Christ in general respects the procurement of all grace and mercy for us, everything whereby we may be "saved to the uttermost" (Heb. 7:25–26), yet his intercession for us as an advocate respects sin only, and the evil consequents of it. For so is he in this place said to be our advocate, and in this place alone is he said to be so only with respect unto sin: "If any man sin, we have an advocate."[16] Wherefore, his being so does in particular respect that part of his intercession wherein he undertakes our defense and protection when accused of sin. For Satan is ὁ κατήγορος, "the accuser" (Rev. 12:10); and when he accuses believers for sin, Christ is their παράκλητος, their patron and "advocate." For, according unto the duty of a patron or advocate in criminal causes, partly he shows wherein the accusation is false, and aggravated above the truth, or proceeds upon mistakes; partly, that the crimes charged have not that malice in them that is pretended, and principally he pleads his propitiation for them, that so far as they are really guilty, they may be graciously discharged.

For this name, as applied unto the Holy Spirit, some translate it a comforter, some an advocate, and some retain the Greek word *paraclete*. It may be best interpreted from the nature of the work assigned unto him under that name. Some would confine the whole work intended under this name unto his teaching, which he is principally promised for; for the matter and manner of his teaching, what he teaches, and the way how he does it, is, they say, the

14 The correct spelling is פְּרַקְלִיט.
15 Heb. "the comforter."
16 1 John 2:1.

ground of all consolation unto the church. And there may be something in this interpretation of the word, taking "teaching" in a large sense, for all internal, divine, spiritual operations. So are we said to be taught of God when faith is wrought in us, and we are enabled to come unto Christ thereby. And all our consolations are from such internal divine operations. But take "teaching" properly, and we shall see that it is but one distinct act of the work of the Holy Ghost, as here promised, among many.

But the work of a comforter is principally ascribed unto him.¶

1. That he is principally under this name intended as a comforter is evident from the whole context and the occasion of the promise. It was with respect unto the troubles and sorrows of his disciples, with their relief therein, that he is promised under this name by our Savior. "I will not," says he, "leave you orphans" (John 14:18). Though I go away from you, yet I will not leave you in a desolate and disconsolate condition. How shall that be prevented in his absence, who was the life and spring of all their comforts? Says he, "I will pray the Father, and he shall give you ἄλλον παράκλητον" (John 14:16), that is, "another to be your comforter." So he renews again his promise of sending him under this name, because "sorrow had filled their heart" upon the apprehension of his departure (John 16:6–7). Wherefore, he is principally considered as a comforter. And, as we shall see further afterward, this is his principal work, most suited unto his nature, as he is the Spirit of peace, love, and joy. For he who is the eternal, essential love of the Divine Being, as existing in the distinct persons of the Trinity, is most meet to communicate a sense of divine love, with delight and joy, unto the souls of believers. Hereby he sets up the kingdom of God in them, which is "righteousness, and peace, and joy in the Holy Ghost" (Rom. 14:17). And in nothing does he so evidence his presence in the hearts and spirits of any as by the disposal of them unto spiritual love and joy. For "shedding abroad the love of God in our hearts" (as Rom 5:5), he produces a principle and frame of divine love in our souls, and fills us with "joy unspeakable and full of glory."[17] The attribution, therefore, of this name unto him, the comforter, evidences that he performs this work in the way of an office.

2. Neither is the signification of an advocate to be omitted, seeing what he does as such tends also to the consolation of the church. And we must first observe, that the Holy Spirit is not our advocate with God. This belongs alone unto Jesus Christ and is a part of his office. He is said, indeed, to "make intercession for us with groanings that cannot be uttered" (Rom. 8:26), but

---

17   1 Pet. 1:8.

this he does not immediately, or in his own person. He no otherwise "makes intercession for us" but by enabling us to make intercession according to the mind of God. For to make intercession formally is utterly inconsistent with the divine nature and his person, who has no other nature but that which is divine. He is, therefore, incapable of being our advocate with God. The Lord Christ is so alone, and that on the account of his precedent propitiation made for us. But he is an advocate for the church, in, with, and against the world. Such an advocate is one that undertakes the protection and defense of another as to any cause wherein he is engaged. The cause wherein the disciples of Christ are engaged in and against the world is the truth of the gospel, the power and kingdom of their Lord and Master. This they testify unto; this is opposed by the world; and this, under various forms, appearances, and pretenses, is that which they suffer reproaches and persecutions for in every generation. In this cause, the Holy Spirit is their advocate, justifying Jesus Christ and the gospel against the world.

And this he does three ways. (1) By suggesting unto and furnishing the witnesses of Christ with pleas and arguments to the conviction of gainsayers.[18] So, it is promised that he should do:

And ye shall be brought before governors and kings for my sake, for a testimony against them and the Gentiles. But when they deliver you up, take no thought how or what ye shall speak, for it shall be given you in that same hour what ye shall speak. For it is not ye that speak, but the Spirit of your Father which speaketh in you. (Matt. 10:18–20)

They were to be "given up," that is, delivered up as malefactors[19] unto kings and rulers, for their faith in Christ, and the testimony they gave unto him. In this condition, the best of men are apt to be solicitous[20] about their answers, and the plea they are to make in the defense of themselves and their cause. Our Savior, therefore, gives them encouragement, not only from the truth and goodness of their cause, but also from the ability they should have in pleading for it unto the conviction or confusion of their adversaries. And this he tells them should come to pass, not by any power or faculty in themselves, but by the aid and supply they should receive from this advocate, who in them would speak by them. This was that mouth and wisdom which he promised unto them, which all their adversaries should not be able to

18 I.e., those who declare to be untrue or invalid what is true.
19 I.e., those who break the law; felons.
20 I.e., meticulous; careful.

gainsay nor resist (Luke 21:15), a present supply of courage, boldness, and liberty of speech, above and beyond their natural temper and abilities, immediately upon their receiving of the Holy Ghost. And their very enemies saw the effects of it unto their astonishment. Upon the plea they made before the council at Jerusalem, it is said that "when they saw the boldness of Peter and John, and perceived that they were unlearned and ignorant men, they marvelled" (Acts 4:13). They saw their outward condition, that they were poor, and of the meanest of the people, yet carried it with courage and boldness before this great Sanhedrin, with whose authority and unusual appearance in grandeur all persons of that sort were want to be abashed and to tremble at them. They found them ignorant and unlearned in that skill and learning which the world admired, yet plead their cause unto their confusion. They could not, therefore, but discern and acknowledge that there was a divine power present with them, which acted above themselves, their state, their natural or acquired abilities. This was the work of this advocate in them, who had undertaken the defense of their cause. So, when Paul pleaded the same cause before Agrippa and Felix, one of them confessed his conviction, and the other trembled in his judgment seat.

Neither has he been wanting unto the defense of the same cause, in the same manner, in succeeding generations. All the story of the church is filled with instances of persons mean in their outward condition, timorous[21] by nature, and unaccustomed unto dangers, unlearned and low in their natural abilities, who, in the face of rulers and potentates, in the sight of prisons, tortures, fires, provided for their destruction, have pleaded the cause of the gospel with courage and success, unto the astonishment and confusion of their adversaries. Neither shall any disciple of Christ in the same case want the like assistance in some due measure and proportion, who expects it from him in a way of believing, and depends upon it. Examples we have hereof every day in persons acted above their own natural temper and abilities, unto their own admiration. For being conscious unto themselves of their own fears, despondencies, and disabilities, it is a surprise unto them to find how all their fears have disappeared and their minds have been enlarged, when they have been called unto trial for their testimony unto the gospel. We are, in such cases, to make use of any reason, skill, wisdom, or ability of speech which we have, or other honest and advantageous circumstances which present themselves unto us, as the apostle Paul did on all occasions. But our dependence is to be solely on the presence and supplies of our blessed

---

21 I.e., timid; fearful.

advocate, who will not suffer us to be utterly defective in what is necessary unto the defense and justification of our cause.

(2) He is the advocate for Christ, the church, and the gospel, in and by his communication of spiritual gifts, both extraordinary and ordinary, unto them that do believe. For these are things, at least in their effects, visible unto the world. Where men are not utterly blinded by prejudice, love of sin and of the world, they cannot but discern somewhat of a divine power in these supernatural gifts. Wherefore, they openly testify unto the divine approbation of the gospel, and the faith that is in Christ Jesus. So, the apostle confirms the truths that he had preached by this argument, that therewith and thereby, or in the confirmation of it, the Spirit, as unto the communication of gifts, was received (Gal. 3:2). And herein is he the church's advocate, justifying their cause openly and visibly by this dispensation of his power toward them and on their behalf. But because we have treated separately and at large of the nature and use of these spiritual gifts, I shall not here insist on the consideration of them.[22]

(3) By internal efficacy in the dispensation of the word. Herein also is he the advocate of the church against the world, as is declared: "For when he is come, he will reprove the world of sin, and of righteousness, and of judgment. Of sin, because they believe not on me. Of righteousness, because I go to my Father, and ye see me no more. Of judgment, because the prince of this world is judged" (John 16:8–11). That which is ascribed unto him with respect unto the world is expressed by the word ἐλέγξει, "he shall reprove" or convince. Ἐλέγχω in the Scripture is used variously. Sometimes it is to manifest, or bring forth unto light: τὰ δὲ πάντα ἐλεγχόμενα ὑπὸ τοῦ φωτὸς φανεροῦται, "For all things that are reproved," or discovered, "are made manifest by the light" (Eph. 5:13). And it has the same sense in John 3:20. Sometimes it is to rebuke and reprove: τοὺς ἁμαρτάνοντας ἐνώπιον πάντων ἔλεγχε, "Those that sin rebuke before all" (1 Tim. 5:20; so also Rev. 3:19; Titus 1:13). Sometimes it is so to convince, as in that to stop the mouth of an adversary, that he shall have nothing to answer or reply: ὑπὸ τῆς συνειδήσεως ἐλεγχόμενοι, "Being convicted by their own consciences" so as, not having a word to reply, they deserted their cause (John 8:9). So, τοὺς ἀντιλέγοντας ἐλέγχειν, "To convince gainsayers" (Titus 1:9), is explained by ἐπιστομίζειν, "to stop their mouth," namely, by the convincing evidence of truth (Titus 1:11). Ἔλεγχος is an uncontrollable evidence, or an evident argument (Heb. 11:1). Wherefore,

---

22 Owen addresses spiritual gifts occasionally in various writings on the Holy Spirit and the church. It is likely that he is here referring to the next treatise in this volume, *A Discourse of Spiritual Gifts, Being the Second Part of the Work of the Holy Spirit* (1693).

ἐλέγχειν, here is, "by undeniable argument and evidence" so to convince the world, or the adversaries of Christ and the gospel, as that they shall have nothing to reply. This is the work and duty of an advocate, who will absolutely vindicate his client when his cause will bear it.

And the effect hereof is twofold. For all persons, upon such an overpowering conviction, take one of these two ways. [1] They yield unto the truth and embrace it, as finding no ground to stand upon in its refusal. Or, [2] they fly out into desperate rage and madness, as being obstinate in their hatred against the truth, and destitute of all reason to oppose it. An instance of the former way we have in those Jews unto whom Peter preached on the day of Pentecost. Reproving and convincing of them beyond all contradiction, "they were pricked in their heart, and said, 'Men and brethren, what shall we do?'" and therewith came over unto the faith (Acts 2:37, 41). Of the latter we have many instances in the dealing of our Savior with that people; for when he had at any time convinced them, and stopped their mouths as to the cause in hand, they called him Beelzebub, cried out that he had a devil, took up stones to throw at him, and conspired his death with all demonstrations of desperate rage and madness (John 8:48, 59; 10:20, 31, 39). So it was in the case of Stephen, and the testimony he gave unto Christ (Acts 7:54–58); and with Paul (Acts 22:22–23), an instance of bestial rage not to be paralleled in any other case, but in this it has often fallen out in the world. And the same effects this work of the Holy Ghost, as the advocate of the church, ever had, and still has upon the world. Many, being convicted by him in the dispensation of the word, are really humbled and converted unto the faith. So, God adds daily to the church such as shall be saved. But the world in general is enraged by the same work against Christ, the gospel, and those by whom it is dispensed. While the word is preached in a formal manner, the world is well enough contented that it should have a quiet passage among them. But wherever the Holy Ghost puts forth a convincing efficacy in the dispensation of it, the world is enraged by it: which is no less an evidence of the power of their conviction than the other is of a better success.

The subject matter concerning which the Holy Ghost manages his plea by the word against the world, as the advocate of the church, is referred unto the three heads of sin, righteousness, and judgment (John 16:8), the special nature of them being declared (John 16:9–11).

[1] What sin it is in particular that the Holy Spirit shall so plead with the world about, and convince them of, is declared: "Of sin, because they believe not on me" (John 16:9). There are many sins whereof men may be convinced by the light of nature (Rom. 2:14–15), more that they are reproved for by the

letter of the law. And it is the work of the Spirit also in general to make these convictions effectual. But these belong not unto the cause which he has to plead for the church against the world, nor is that such as any can be brought unto conviction about by the light of nature or sentence of the law, but it is the work of the Spirit alone by the gospel. And this, in the first place, is unbelief, particularly not believing in Jesus Christ as the Son of God, the promised Messiah and Savior of the world. This he testified concerning himself, this his works evinced him to be, and this both Moses and the prophets bore witness unto. Hereon he tells the Jews, that if they believed not that he was he, that is, the Son of God, the Messiah and Savior of the world, "they should die in their sins" (John 8:21, 24). But in this unbelief, in this rejection of Christ, the Jews and the rest of the world justified themselves, and not only so, but despised and persecuted them who believed in him. This was the fundamental difference between believers and the world, the head of that cause wherein they were rejected by it as foolish and condemned as impious. And herein was the Holy Ghost their advocate; for he did by such undeniable evidences, arguments, and testimonies, convince the world of the truth and glory of Christ, and of the sin of unbelief, that they were everywhere either converted or enraged thereby. So some of them, upon this conviction, "gladly received the Word, and were baptized" (Acts 2:41). Others, upon the preaching of the same truth by the apostles, "were cut to the heart, and took counsel to slay them" (Acts 5:33). In this work he still continues. And it is an act of the same kind whereby he yet in particular convinces any of the sin of unbelief, which cannot be done but by the effectual internal operation of his power.

[2] He thus convinces the world of righteousness: "Of righteousness, because I go to my Father, and ye see me no more" (John 16:10). Both the personal righteousness of Christ and the righteousness of his office are intended. For concerning both these the church has a contest with the world, and they belong unto that cause wherein the Holy Spirit is their advocate. Christ was looked on by the world as an evildoer, accused to be a glutton, a wine bibber, a seditious person, a seducer, a blasphemer, a malefactor of every kind, whence his disciples were both despised and destroyed for believing in such a one. And it is not to be declared how they were scorned and reproached, and what they suffered on this account. In the meantime, they pleaded and gave testimony unto his righteousness, that he did no sin, neither was guile found in his mouth, that he fulfilled all righteousness, and was the Holy One of God. And herein was the Holy Ghost their advocate, convincing the world principally by this argument, that after all he did and suffered in this world, as the highest evidence imaginable of God's approbation of him and what he

did, he was gone to the Father, or assumed up into glory. The poor blind man whose eyes were opened by him pleaded this as a forcible argument against the Jews, that he was no sinner, in that God heard him so as that he had opened his eyes; whose evidence and conviction they could not bear, but it turned them into rage and madness (John 9:30–34). How much more glorious and effectual must this evidence needs be of his righteousness and holiness, and of God's approbation of him, that after all he did in this world, he went unto his Father, and was taken up into glory. For such is the meaning of these words, "Ye shall see me no more,"[23] that is, "There shall be an end put unto my state of humiliation, and of my converse with you in this world, because I am to enter into my glory." That the Lord Christ then went unto his Father, that he was so gloriously exalted, undeniable testimony was given by the Holy Ghost, unto the conviction of the world. So, this argument is pleaded by Peter (Acts 2:33). This is enough to stop the mouths of all the world in this cause, that he sent the Holy Ghost from the Father to communicate spiritual gifts of all sorts unto his disciples. And there could be no higher evidence of his acceptance, power, and glory with him. And the same testimony he still continues, in the communication of ordinary gifts in the ministry of the gospel.

Respect also may be had, which sense I would not exclude, unto the righteousness of his office. There ever was a great contest about the righteousness of the world. This the Gentiles looked after by the light of nature, and the Jews by the works of the law. In this state the Lord Christ is proposed as the "Lord our righteousness,"[24] as he who was to "bring in," and had brought in, "everlasting righteousness" (Dan. 9:24), being "the end of the law for righteousness to all that believe" (Rom. 10:4). This the Gentiles rejected as folly, Christ crucified was "foolishness" unto them; and to the Jews it was a "stumbling-block,"[25] as that which everted[26] the whole law. And, generally, they all concluded that he could not save himself, and therefore it was not probable that others should be saved by him. But herein also is the Holy Spirit the advocate of the church. For, in the dispensation of the word, he so convinces men of an impossibility for them to attain a righteousness of their own, as that they must either submit to the righteousness of God in Christ or die in their sins.

[3] He convinces the world of judgment, because the prince of this world is judged. Christ himself was judged and condemned by the world. In that

---

23   John 14:19.
24   Jer. 23:6.
25   1 Cor. 1:23.
26   I.e., overthrew or upset.

judgment, Satan, the prince of this world, had the principal hand; for it was affected in the hour and under the power of darkness. And no doubt but he hoped that he had carried his cause when he had prevailed to have the Lord Christ publicly judged and condemned. And this judgment the world sought by all means to justify and make good. But the whole of it is called over again by the Holy Ghost, pleading in the cause and for the faith of the church. And he does it so effectually as that the judgment is turned on Satan himself. Judgment, with unavoidable conviction, passed on all that superstition, idolatry, and wickedness, which he had filled the world with. And whereas he had borne himself, under various marks, shades, and pretenses, to be the god of this world, the supreme ruler over all, and accordingly was worshiped all the world over, he is now by the gospel laid open and manifested to be an accursed apostate, a murderer, and the great enemy of mankind.

Wherefore, taking the name *Paracletus* in this sense for an advocate, it is proper unto the Holy Ghost in some part of his work in and toward the church. And whensoever we are called to bear witness unto Christ and the gospel, we abandon our strength and betray our cause if we do not use all means appointed of God unto that end to engage him in our assistance.

But it is as a comforter that he is chiefly promised unto us, and as such is he expressed unto the church by this name.

THE SPIRIT'S SPECIAL WORK

Fourthly, that he has a peculiar work committed unto him, suitable unto this mission or commission and name, is that which will appear in the declaration of the particulars wherein it does consist. For the present we only assert, in general, that his work it is to support, cherish, relieve, and comfort the church, in all trials and distresses. And this is all that we intend when we say that it is his office so to do.

2

General Adjuncts or Properties
of the Office of a Comforter,
as Exercised by the Holy Spirit

TO EVIDENCE YET FURTHER the nature of this office and work, we may consider and inquire into the general adjuncts of it, as exercised by the Holy Spirit. And they are four.

INFINITE CONDESCENSION

First, infinite condescension. This is among those mysteries of the divine dispensation which we may admire but cannot comprehend; and it is the property of faith alone to act and live upon incomprehensible objects. What reason cannot comprehend it will neglect, as that which it has no concern in nor can have benefit by. Faith is most satisfied and cherished with what is infinite and inconceivable, as resting absolutely in divine revelation. Such is this condescension of the Holy Ghost. He is by nature over all, God blessed forever. And it is a condescension in the divine excellency to concern itself in a particular manner in any creature whatever. God humbles himself to behold the things that are in heaven, and in the earth (Ps. 113:5–6). How much more does he do so in submitting himself unto the discharge of an office in the behalf of poor worms here below.

This, I confess, is most astonishing, and attended with the most incomprehensible rays of divine wisdom and goodness in the condescension of the Son. For he carried the term of it unto the lowest and most abject condition that a rational, intelligent nature is capable of. So is it represented by the apostle

(Phil. 2:6–8). For he not only took our nature into personal union with himself, but became in it, in his outward condition, as a servant, yea, as a worm and no man, a reproach of men, and despised of the people, and became subject to death, the ignominious, shameful death of the cross. Hence this dispensation of God was filled up with infinite wisdom, goodness, and grace. How this exinanition[1] of the Son of God was compensated with the glory that did ensue, we shall rejoice in the contemplation of unto all eternity. And then shall the character of all divine excellencies be more gloriously conspicuous on this condescension of the Son of God than ever they were on the works of the whole creation, when this goodly fabric of heaven and earth was brought, by divine power and wisdom, through darkness and confusion, out of nothing.

The condescension of the Holy Spirit unto his work and office is not, indeed, of the same kind, as to the *terminus ad quem*, or "the object of it." He assumes not our nature, he exposes not himself unto the injuries of an outward state and condition. But yet it is such as is more to be the object of our faith in adoration than of our reason in disquisition. Consider the thing in itself; how one person in the holy Trinity, subsisting in the unity of the same divine nature, should undertake to execute the love and grace of the other persons, and in their names—what do we understand of it? This holy economy, in the distinct and subordinate actings of the divine persons in these external works, is known only unto, is understood only by, themselves. Our wisdom it is to acquiesce[2] in express divine revelation. Nor have they scarcely more dangerously erred by whom these things are denied, than those have done who, by a proud and conceited subtlety of mind, pretend unto a conception of them, which they express in words and terms, as they say, precise and accurate, indeed, foolish and curious, whether of other men's coining or their own finding out. Faith keeps the soul at a holy distance from these infinite depths of the divine wisdom, where it profits more by reverence and holy fear than any can do by their utmost attempt to draw nigh unto that inaccessible light wherein these glories of the divine nature do dwell.

But we may more steadily consider this condescension with respect unto its object: The Holy Spirit thereby becomes a comforter unto us, poor, miserable worms of the earth. And what heart can conceive the glory of this grace? What tongue can express it? Especially will its eminency appear if we consider the ways and means whereby he does so comfort us, and the opposition from us which he meets with therein; whereof we must treat afterward.

---

1   I.e., emptying; exhaustion.
2   I.e., accept, comply, or submit tacitly or passively.

UNSPEAKABLE LOVE

Secondly, unspeakable love accompanies the susception[3] and discharge of this office, and that working by tenderness and compassion. The Holy Spirit is said to be the divine, eternal, mutual love of the Father and the Son. And although I know that much wariness is to be used in the declaration of these mysteries, nor are expressions concerning them to be ventured on not warranted by the letter of the Scripture, yet I judge that this notion does excellently express, if not the distinct manner of subsistence, yet the mutual, internal operation of the persons of the blessed Trinity. For we have no term for, nor notion of, that ineffable[4] complacence[5] and eternal rest which is therein beyond this of love. Hence it is said that "God is love" (1 John 4:8, 16). It does not seem to be an essential property of the nature of God only that the apostle does intend, for it is proposed unto us as a motive unto mutual love among ourselves, and this consists not simply in the habit or affection of love, but in the actings of it in all its fruits and duties: for so is God love, as that the internal actings of the holy persons, which are in and by the Spirit, are all the ineffable actings of love, wherein the nature of the Holy Spirit is expressed unto us. The apostle prays for the presence of the Spirit with the Corinthians under the name of the "God of love and peace" (2 Cor. 13:11).¶

And the communication of the whole love of God unto us is committed unto the Spirit, for the love of God is shed abroad in our hearts by the Holy Ghost which is given unto us (Rom. 5:5). And hence the same apostle distinctly mentions the love of the Spirit, conjoining it with all the effects of the mediation of Christ: "I beseech you, brethren, for the Lord Jesus Christ's sake, and for the love of the Spirit" (Rom. 15:30), I do so on the account of the respect you have unto Christ, and all that he has done for you, which is a motive irresistible unto believers. I do it also for the love of the Spirit; all that love which he acts and communicates unto you. Wherefore, in all the actings of the Holy Ghost toward us, and especially in this of his susception of an office on the behalf of the church, which is the foundation of them all, his love is principally to be considered, and that he chooses this way of acting and working toward us to express his peculiar, personal character, as he is the eternal love of the Father and the Son. And among all his actings toward us, which are all acts of love, this is most conspicuous in those wherein he is a comforter.

Wherefore, because this is of great use unto us, as that which ought to have, and which will have, if duly apprehended, a great influence on our faith and

3   I.e., taking on oneself, reception, assumption.
4   I.e., unspeakable.
5   I.e., satisfaction.

obedience, and is, moreover, the spring of all the consolations we receive by and from him, we shall give a little evidence unto it, namely, that the love of the Spirit is principally to be considered in this office and the discharge of it. For whatever good we receive from anyone, whatever benefit or present relief we have thereby, we can receive no comfort or consolation in it unless we are persuaded that it proceeds from love; and what does so, be it never so small, has refreshment and satisfaction in it unto every ingenuous nature. It is love alone that is the salt of every kindness or benefit, and which takes out of it everything that may be noxious or hurtful. Without an apprehension hereof and satisfaction herein, multiplied beneficial effects produce no internal satisfaction in them that do receive them, nor put any real engagement on their minds (Prov. 23:6–8). It is, therefore, of concern unto us to secure this ground of all our consolation, in the full assurance of faith that there was infinite love in the susception of this office by the Holy Ghost. And it is evident that so it was,

1. From the nature of the work itself; for the consolation or comforting of any who stand in need thereof is an immediate effect of love, with its inseparable properties of pity and compassion. Especially it must be so where no advantage redounds[6] unto the comforter, but the whole of what is done respects entirely the good and relief of them that are comforted. For what other affection of mind can be the principle hereof, from whence it may proceed? Persons may be relieved under oppression by justice, under want by bounty, but to comfort and refresh the minds of any is a peculiar act of sincere love and compassion. So, therefore, must this work of the Holy Ghost be esteemed to be. I do not intend only that his love is eminent and discernible in it, but that it proceeds solely from love. And without a faith hereof we cannot have the benefit of this divine dispensation, nor will any comforts that we receive be firm or stable. But when this is once graciously fixed in our minds, that there is not one drop of comfort or spiritual refreshment administered by the Holy Ghost, but that it proceeds from his infinite love, then are they disposed into that frame which is needed to comply with him in his operations. And, in particular, all the acts wherein the discharge of this office does consist are all of them acts of the highest love, of that which is infinite, as we shall see in the consideration of them.

2. The manner of the performance of this work is so expressed as to evince and expressly demonstrate that it is a work of love. So is it declared where he is promised unto the church for this work: "As one whom his mother

---

6 I.e., overflows.

comforteth, so will I comfort you; and ye shall be comforted in Jerusalem" (Isa. 66:13). He whom his mother comforts is supposed to be in some kind of distress; nor, indeed, is there any, of any kind, that may befall a child, whose mother is kind and tender, but she will be ready to administer unto him all the consolation that she is able. And how, or in what manner, will such a mother discharge this duty, it is better conceived than it can be expressed. We are not, in things natural, able to take in a conception of greater love, care, and tenderness, than is in a tender mother who comforts her children in distress. And hereby does the prophet graphically represent unto our minds the manner whereby the Holy Ghost discharges this office toward us. Neither can a child contract greater guilt, or manifest a more depraved habit of mind, than to be regardless of the affection of a mother endeavoring its consolation. Such children may, indeed, sometimes, through the bitterness of their spirits, by their pains and distempers, be surprised into frowardness,[7] and a present regardlessness of the mother's kindness and compassion, which she knows full well how to bear with. But if they continue to have no sense of it, if it makes no impression upon them, they are of a profligate[8] constitution. And so it may be sometimes with believers; they may, by surprisals[9] into spiritual frowardness, by weakness, by unaccountable despondencies, be regardless of divine influences of consolation.¶

But all these things the great comforter will bear with and overcome.

Thus saith the high and lofty One that inhabiteth eternity, whose name is Holy, "I dwell in the high and holy place, with him also that is of a contrite and humble spirit, to revive the spirit of the humble, and to revive the heart of the contrite ones. For I will not contend forever, neither will I be always wroth: for the spirit should fail before me, and the souls which I have made. For the iniquity of his covetousness was I wroth, and smote him: I hid me, and was wroth, and he went on frowardly in the way of his heart. I have seen his ways, and will heal him: I will lead him also, and restore comforts unto him and to his mourners. I create the fruit of the lips; Peace, peace to him that is far off, and to him that is near," saith the Lord, "and I will heal him." (Isa. 57:15–19)¶

When persons are under sorrows and disconsolations upon the account of pain and sickness, or the like, in a design of comfort toward them, it will

7 I.e., contrariness.
8 I.e., wasteful; licentious.
9 I.e., states of being surprised.

yet be needful sometimes to make use of means and remedies that may be painful and vexatious.[10] And these may be apt to irritate and provoke poor, wayward patients. Yet is not a mother discouraged hereby, but proceeds on in her way until the cure be effected and consolation administered. So does God by his Spirit deal with his church. His design is "to revive the spirit of the humble, and to revive the heart of the contrite ones" (Isa. 57:15). And he gives this reason of it, namely, that if he should not act in infinite love and condescension toward them, but deal with them after their deservings, they would utterly be consumed, "the spirit would fail before him, and the souls which he had made" (Isa. 57:16). However, in the pursuit of this work, he must use some sharp remedies, that were needful for the curing of their distempers and for their spiritual recovery. Because of their iniquity, "the iniquity of their covetousness," which was the principal disease they labored under, "he was wroth and smote them, and hid his face from them," because his so doing was necessary to their cure (Isa. 57:17). And how do they behave themselves under this dealing of God with them? They grow peevish[11] and froward under his hand, choosing rather to continue in their disease than to be thus healed by him: "They went on frowardly in the way of their hearts" (Isa. 57:17). How, therefore, does this holy comforter now deal with them? Does he give them up unto their frowardness? Does he leave and forsake them under their distemper? No; a tender mother will not so deal with her children. He manages his work with such infinite love, tenderness, and compassion, as that he will overcome all their frowardness, and ceases not until he has effectually administered consolation unto them: "I have seen," says he, all these "his ways," all his frowardness and miscarriages, and yet, says he, "I will heal him"; I will not for all this be diverted from my work and the pursuit of my design; before I have done, I will lead him into a right frame, "and restore comforts unto him." And that there may be no failure herein, I will do it by a creating act of power (Isa. 57:18). "I create the fruit of the lips; Peace, peace" (Isa. 57:19).¶

This is the method of the Holy Ghost in administering consolation unto the church, by openly evidencing that love and compassion from whence it does proceed. And without this method should no one soul be ever spiritually refreshed under its dejections. For we are apt to behave ourselves frowardly, more or less, under the work of the Holy Ghost toward us. Infinite love and compassion alone, working by patience and long-suffering, can carry it on

10   I.e., stressful.
11   I.e., obstinate; quarrelsome.

unto perfection. But if we are not only froward under particular occasions, temptations, and surprisals, clouding our present view of the Holy Spirit in his work, but are also habitually careless and negligent about it, and do never labor to come into satisfaction in it, but always indulge unto the peevishness and frowardness of unbelief, it argues a most depraved, unthankful frame of heart, wherein the soul of God cannot be well pleased.

3. It is an evidence that his work proceeds from and is wholly managed in love, in that we are cautioned not to grieve him (Eph. 4:30). And a double evidence of the greatness of his love is herein tendered unto us in that caution. (1) In that those alone are subject to be grieved by us who act in love toward us. If we comply not with the will and rule of others, they may be provoked, vexed, instigated unto wrath against us; but those alone who love us are grieved at our miscarriages. A severe schoolmaster may be more provoked with the fault of his scholar than the father is, but the father is grieved with it when the other is not. Whereas, therefore, the Holy Spirit is not subject or liable unto the affection of grief as it is a passion in us, we are cautioned not to grieve him, namely, to teach us with what love and compassion, with what tenderness and holy delight, he performs his work in us and toward us. (2) It is so in that he has undertaken the work of comforting them who are so apt and prone to grieve him, as for the most part we are. The great work of the Lord Christ was to die for us. But that which puts an eminence on his love is, that he died for us while we were yet his enemies, sinners, and ungodly (Rom. 5:6–10). And as the work of the Holy Ghost is to comfort us, so a luster is put upon it by this, that he comforts those who are very prone to grieve himself. For although, it may be, we will not, through a peculiar affection, hurt, molest, or grieve them again by whom we are grieved, yet who is it that will set himself to comfort those that grieve him, and that when so they do? But even herein the Holy Ghost commends his love unto us, that even while we grieve him, by his consolations he recovers us from those ways wherewith[12] he is grieved.

This, therefore, is to be fixed as an important principle in this part of the mystery of God, that the principal foundation of the susception of this office of a comforter by the Holy Spirit is his own peculiar and ineffable love. For both the efficacy of our consolation and the life of our obedience do depend hereon. For when we know that every acting of the Spirit of God toward us, every gracious impression from him on our understandings, wills, or affections, are all of them in pursuit of that infinite peculiar love from whence

---

12 I.e., by which.

it was that he took upon him the office of a comforter, they cannot but all of them influence our hearts with spiritual refreshment. And when faith is defective in this matter, so that it does not exercise itself in the consideration of this love of the Holy Ghost, we shall never arrive unto solid, abiding, strong consolation. And as for those by whom all these things are despised and derided, it is no strait unto me whether I should renounce the gospel or reject them from an interest in Christianity, for the approbation of both is inconsistent. Moreover, it is evident how great a motive hence arises unto cheerful, watchful, universal obedience. For all the actings of sin or unbelief in us are, in the first place, reactions unto those of the Holy Ghost in us and upon us. By them is he resisted in his persuasions, quenched in his motions, and himself grieved. If there be any holy ingenuity in us, it will excite a vigilant diligence not to be overtaken with such wickednesses against unspeakable love. He will walk both safely and fruitfully whose soul is kept under a sense of the love of the Holy Spirit herein.

INFINITE POWER

Thirdly, infinite power is also needful unto, and accordingly evident in, the discharge of this office. This we have fixed, that the Holy Ghost is, and ever was, the comforter of the church. Whatever, therefore, is spoken thereof belongs peculiarly unto him. And it is expressed as proceeding from and accompanied with infinite power, as also the consideration of persons and things declares it necessary that so it should be. Thus, we have the church's complaint in a deep disconsolation: "My way is hid from the Lord, and my judgment is passed over from my God" (Isa. 40:27). It is not so much her affliction and miseries, as an apprehension that God regards her not therein, which causes her dejection. And when this is added unto any pressing trouble, whether internal or external, it does fully constitute a state of spiritual disconsolation. For when faith can take a prospect of the love, care, and concern of God in us and our condition, however grievous things may be at present unto us, yet can we not be comfortless. And what is it that, in the consolation which God intends his church, he would have them to consider in himself, as an assured ground of relief and refreshment? This he declares himself in the following verses: "Hast thou not known? Hast thou not heard, that the everlasting God, the Lord, the Creator of the ends of the earth, fainteth not, neither is weary?" etc. (Isa. 40:28–31). The church seems not at all to doubt of his power, but of his love, care, and faithfulness toward her. But it is his infinite power that he chooses first to satisfy her in, as that which all his actings toward her were founded in and resolved into, without a due consideration whereof all that otherwise could be expected would not yield her relief. And this being fixed on their minds, he next proposes unto them his infinite understanding and wisdom: "There is no searching of his understanding."[13] Conceive aright of his infinite power, and then leave things unto his sovereign, unsearchable wisdom for the management of them, as to ways, degrees, times, and seasons. An apprehension of want of love and care in God toward them was that which immediately caused their disconsolation; but the ground of it was in their unbelief of his infinite power and wisdom.

Wherefore, in the work of the Holy Ghost for the comforting of the church, his infinite power is peculiarly to be considered. So the apostle proposes it unto the weakest believers for their supportment[14], and as that which should assure them of the victory in their conflict, that "greater is he that is in them than he that is in the world" (1 John 4:4). That Holy Spirit which is bestowed on them and dwells in them is greater, more able and powerful, than Satan, that attempts their ruin in and by the world, seeing he is of power omnipotent. Thoughts of our disconsolation arise from the impressions that Satan makes upon our minds and consciences, by sin, temptation, and persecution. For we find not in ourselves such an ability of resistance as from whence we may have an assurance of a conquest. This, says the apostle, you are to expect from the power of the Holy Spirit, which is infinitely above whatever Satan has to make opposition unto you, or to bring any disconsolation on you. This will cast out all that fear which has torment accompanying of it. And however this may be disregarded by them who are filled with an apprehension of their own self-sufficiency, as unto all the ends of their living and obedience unto God, as likewise that they have a never-failing spring of rational considerations about them, able to administer all necessary relief and comfort at all times; yet those who are really sensible of their own condition and that of other believers, if they understand what it is to be comforted with the consolations of God, and how remote they are from those delusions which men embrace under the name of their rational considerations, will grant that the faith of infinite power is requisite unto any solid spiritual comfort. For,

1. Who can declare the dejections, sorrows, fears, despondencies, and discouragements that believers are obnoxious unto, in the great variety of their natures, causes, effects, and occasions? What relief can be suited unto them but what is an emanation from infinite power? Yea, such is the

13 Isa. 40:28.
14 I.e., support.

spiritual frame and constitution of their souls, as that they will ofttimes reject all means of comfort that are not communicated by an almighty efficacy. Hence God "creates the fruit of the lips, 'Peace, peace'" (Isa. 57:19), produces peace in the souls of men by a creating act of his power, and directs us, in the place before mentioned, to look for it only from the infinite excellency of his nature. None, therefore, was meet for this work of being the church's comforter but the Spirit of God alone. He only, by his almighty power, can remove all their fears, and support them under all their dejections, in all that variety wherewith they are attempted[15] and exercised. Nothing but omnipotence itself is suited to obviate[16] those innumerable disconsolations that we are obnoxious unto. And those whose souls are pressed in earnest with them, and are driven from all the reliefs which not only carnal security and stoutheartedness in adversity do offer, but also from all those lawful diversions which the world can administer, will understand that true consolation is an act of the exceeding greatness of the power of God, and without which it will not be wrought.

2. The means and causes of their disconsolation direct unto the same spring of their comfort. Whatever the power of hell, of sin, and the world, separately or in conjunction, can effect, it is all levelled against the peace and comfort of believers. Of how great force and efficacy they are in their attempts to disturb and ruin them, by what various ways and means they work unto that end, would require great enlargement of discourse to declare. And yet when we have used our utmost diligence in an inquiry after them, we shall come short of a full investigation of them, yea, it may be, of what many individual persons find in their own experience. Wherefore, with respect unto one cause and principle of disconsolation, God declares that it is he who comforts his people:

> I, even I, am he that comforteth you: who art thou, that thou shouldest be afraid of a man that shall die, and of the son of man which shall be made as grass? And forgettest the Lord thy maker, that has stretched forth the heavens, and laid the foundations of the earth? And hast feared continually every day because of the fury of the oppressor, as if he were ready to destroy? And where is the fury of the oppressor? The captive exile hasteneth that he may be loosed, and that he should not die in the pit, nor that his bread should fail. But I am the Lord thy God, that divided the sea, whose waves roared: The Lord of hosts is his name.[17]

15   I.e., tempted.
16   I.e., anticipate and prevent; make unnecessary.
17   Isa. 51:12–15.

He sees it necessary to declare his infinite power, and to express in sundry instances the effects thereof.

Wherefore, if we take a view of what is the state and condition of the church in itself and in the world, how weak is the faith of most believers! How great their fears! How many their discouragements! As also with how great temptations, calamities, oppositions, persecutions, they are exercised! How vigorously and sharply these things are set on upon their spirits, according unto all advantages, inward and outward, that their spiritual adversaries can lay hold upon! It will be manifest how necessary it was that their consolation should be entrusted with him with whom infinite power does always dwell. And if our own inward or outward peace seem to abate of the necessity of this consideration, it may not be amiss, by the exercise of faith herein, to lay in provision for the future, seeing we know not what may befall us in the world. And should we live to see the church in storms, as who knows but we may, our principal support will be, that our comforter is of almighty power, wonderful in counsel, and excellent in operation.

UNCHANGEABLE DISPENSATION

Fourthly, this dispensation of the Spirit is unchangeable. Unto whomsoever he is given as a comforter, he abides with them forever. This our Savior expressly declares in the first promise he made of sending him as a comforter, in a peculiar manner: "I will pray the Father, and he shall give you another comforter, that he may abide with you forever" (John 14:16). The moment of this promise lies in his unchangeable continuance with the church. There was, indeed, a present occasion rendering necessary this declaration of the unchangeableness of his abode. For in all this discourse our Savior was preparing the hearts of his disciples for his departure from them, which was now at hand. And whereas he lays the whole of the relief which in that case he would afford unto them upon his sending of the Holy Ghost, he takes care not only to prevent an objection which might arise in their minds about this dispensation of the Spirit, but also in so doing to secure the faith and consolation of the church in all ages. For as he himself, who had been their immediate, visible comforter during the whole time of his ministry among them, was now departing from them, and that so as that the heaven was to receive him until the times of restitution of all things, they might be apt to fear that this comforter who was now promised unto them might continue also only for a season, whereby they should be reduced unto a new loss and sorrow. To assure their minds herein, our Lord Jesus Christ lets them know that this other comforter should not only always continue with them, unto the end of their lives, work, and ministry, but abide with the church absolutely unto the consummation of all things. He is now given in an eternal and unchangeable covenant (Isa. 59:21), and he can no more depart from the church than the everlasting sure covenant of God can be abolished.

But it may be objected by such as really inquire into the promises of Christ, and after their accomplishment, for the establishment of their faith, whence it is, that if the comforter abide always with the church, so great a number of believers do in all ages spend, it may be, the greatest part of their lives in troubles and disconsolation, having no experience of the presence of the Holy Ghost with them as a comforter. But this objection is not of force to weaken our faith as unto the accomplishment of this promise. For,

1. There is in the promise itself a supposition of troubles and disconsolations thereon to befall the church in all ages. For with respect unto them it is that the comforter is promised to be sent. And they do but dream who fancy such a state of the church in this world as wherein it should be accompanied with such an assurance of all inward and outward satisfaction as scarce to stand in need of this office or work of the Holy Ghost. Yea, the promise of his abiding with us forever as a comforter is an infallible prediction that believers in all ages shall meet with troubles, sorrows, and disconsolation.

2. The accomplishment of Christ's promise does not depend as to its truth upon our experience, at least not on what men sensibly feel in themselves under their distresses, much less on what they express with some mixture of unbelief. So we observed before, from that place of the prophet concerning the church, that "her way was hidden from the Lord, and her judgment passed over from her God" (Isa. 40:27). As she complained also, "The Lord hath forsaken me, and my Lord hath forgotten me" (Isa. 49:14). But yet in both places God convinces her of her mistake, and that indeed her complaint was but a fruit of unbelief. And so, it is usual in great distresses, when persons are so swallowed up with sorrow or overwhelmed with anguish that they are not sensible of the work of the Holy Ghost in their consolation.

3. He is a comforter unto all believers at all times, and on all occasions wherein they really stand in need of spiritual consolation. But yet if we intend to have experience of his work herein, to have the advantage of it or benefit by it, there are sundry things required of ourselves in a way of duty. If we are negligent herein, it is no wonder if we are at a loss for those comforts which he is willing to administer. Unless we understand aright the nature of spiritual consolations, and value them both as sufficient and satisfactory, we are not likely to enjoy them, at least not to be made sensible of them.

Many under their troubles suppose there is no comfort but in their removal, and know not of any relief in their sorrows but in the taking away of their cause. At best, they value any outward relief before internal supports and refreshments. Such persons can never receive the consolation of the Holy Spirit unto any refreshing experience. To look for all our comforts from him, to value those things wherein his consolations do consist above all earthly enjoyments, to wait upon him in the use of all means for the receiving of his influences of love and grace, to be fervent in prayer for his presence with us and the manifestation of his grace, are required in all those toward whom he discharges this office. And while we are found in these ways of holy obedience and dependence, we shall find him a comforter, and that forever.

These things are observable in the office of the Holy Ghost, in general, as he is the comforter of the church, and the manner of his discharge thereof. What is further considerable unto the guidance of our faith, and the participation of consolation with respect hereunto, will be evident in the declaration of the particulars that belong thereunto.

3

Unto Whom the Holy Spirit Is Promised and Given as a Comforter; or the Object of His Acting in This Office

WE HAVE CONSIDERED the promise of Christ to send the Holy Spirit to be the comforter of the church, and unto that end to abide with them forever. The nature also of that office and work, in general, which hereon he undertakes and discharges, with the properties of them, have been declared. Our next inquiry is, unto whom this promise is made, and toward whom it is infallibly fulfilled. How and unto what ends, in what order, as unto his effects and operations, the Holy Spirit is promised unto any persons and received by them, has been already declared in our former discourses.[1] We shall, therefore, here only declare in particular whom he is promised unto and received by as a comforter. And this is to all, and only unto, believers; those who are actually so. All his operations required unto the making of them so to be are antecedent hereunto. For the promise of him unto this end, wherever it is recorded, is made directly unto them, and unto them it is confined. Immediately it was given unto the apostles, but it was not given unto them as apostles, but as believers and disciples of Christ, with a particular respect unto the difficulties and causes of disconsolation which they were under or should meet with upon the account of their being so. See the promises unto this purpose expressly (John 14:16–17, 26; 15:26; 16:7–8). And it is declared withal that the world, which in that place is opposed unto them that do believe, cannot receive him (John 14:17). Other effectual

---

1 In addition to the treatises in this as well as the preceding volume, see Πνευματολογια, or, *A Discourse concerning the Holy Spirit.*

operations he has upon the world, for their conviction and the conversion of many of them. But as a Spirit of consolation he is neither promised unto them nor can they receive him, until other gracious acts of his have passed on their souls. Besides, we shall see that all his actings and effects as a comforter are confined unto them that believe, and do all suppose saving faith as antecedent unto them.

And this is the great fundamental privilege of true believers, whereby, through the grace of our Lord Jesus Christ, they are exalted above all other persons in this world. And this will the more evidently appear when we shall consider those special operations, acts, and effects, whereby consolation is administered unto them. That the life of man is the subject of innumerable troubles is made evident and uncontrollable by catholic[2] experience. That man is born to trouble as the sparks fly upward, has been the constant acknowledgment of all that have been wise in all ages. And those who have designed to drown the sense of them in security and sensuality of life have been ever looked on as greatly exorbitant from the principles of nature and dictates of reason, voluntarily degenerating into the condition of creatures brutish and irrational. Others, who will not forego the privilege of their being, have always made it a principal inquiry how or whence they might take and receive relief and comfort for their support against their unavoidable troubles, sorrows, and disconsolation. Yea, it is natural and necessary unto all men so to do.¶

All men cannot but seek after rest and peace, not only out of choice but instinct of nature, trouble and sorrow being diametrically contrary unto it in its being, and tending unto its dissolution. Wherefore, they all naturally seek for consolation. Hence the best and most useful part of the old philosophy[3] consisted in the prescription of the ways and means of comforting and supporting the minds of men against things noxious and grievous to nature, with the sorrows which ensue thereon. And the topics they had found out unto this purpose were not to be despised where men are destitute of spiritual light and supernatural revelation. Neither did the wisdom or reason of man ever arise unto anything more useful in this world than to discover any rational considerations that might allay the sorrows or relieve the minds of them that are disconsolate. For things that are really grievous unto the generality of mankind do outweigh all the real satisfaction which this life and world can afford. And to place either satisfaction or relief in the pursuit of sensual lusts is brutish. But yet what did all the

---

2   I.e., universal.
3   "Old philosophy" is a reference to the classical Greek philosophies.

springs and wellheads of rational and philosophical consolation rise unto? What refreshment did their streams afford? The utmost they attained unto was but to confirm and make obstinate the minds of men in a fancy, an opinion, or persuasion, contrary unto what they felt and had experience of. For what they contended for was but this, that the consideration of the common lot of mankind, the unavoidableness of grieving accidents, the shortness of human life, the true exercise of reason upon more noble objects, with others of the like nature, should satisfy men that the things which they endured were not evil or grievous.¶

But what does all this amount unto in comparison of this privilege of believers, of this provision made for them in all their disconsolations, by him in whom they do believe? This is a relief that never entered into the heart of man to think of or conceive. Nor can it be understood by any but those by whom it is enjoyed. For the world, as our Savior testifies, neither knows this Spirit nor can receive him. And, therefore, what is spoken of him and this work of his is looked on as a fancy or the shadow of a dream. And although the Sun of Righteousness be risen in this matter, and shines on all that dwell in the land of Goshen, yet those that abide still in Egypt make use only of their lanterns. But those who are really partakers of this privilege do know in some measure what they do enjoy, although they are not able to comprehend it in its excellency, nor value it in a due manner. For how can the heart of man, or our poor weak understandings, fully conceive this glorious mystery of sending the Holy Ghost to be our comforter? Only they receive it by faith, and have experience of it in its effects.¶

There is, in my judgment, an unspeakable privilege of those who are believers, antecedent unto their believing, as they are elect, namely, that Christ died in their stead alone. But this is like the wells which Isaac's servants dug, that the Philistines strove about as those which belonged unto them, which, though fresh, useful springs in themselves, caused them to be called Esek and Sitnah, (that is, contention and hatred). Mighty strivings there are to break down the enclosure of this privilege, and lay it common unto all the world, which is, indeed, waste and useless. For it is contended that the Lord Christ died equally for all and everyone of mankind, for believers and unbelievers, for those that are saved and those that are damned. And to this purpose many pretenses are pleaded to show how the most of them for whom Christ died have no real benefit by his death, nor is anything required in them to evidence that they have an interest therein. But this privilege we now treat of is like the well Rehoboth. Isaac kept it unto himself, and the Philistines strove not about it. None contend that the Spirit is a comforter unto any but believers. Therefore is it by the world despised and reproached, because they have no interest in it, nor have the least pretense to strive about it. Did believers, therefore, duly consider how they are advanced hereby, through the love and care of Jesus Christ, into an inexpressible dignity above the residue of mankind, they would more rejoice in it than in all that this world can supply them with. But we must proceed.

It appears, from what has been discoursed, that this is not the first saving work of the Holy Spirit on the souls of men. Regeneration and habitual sanctification do always precede it. He comforts none but those whom he has before sanctified. Nor are any other but such capable of his consolations. There is nothing in them that can discern his acting, or value what he does of this kind. And this is the true reason why the whole work of the Holy Spirit as a comforter, wherein consists the accomplishment of the most glorious promise that ever Christ made to his church, and the greatest evidence of his continued care thereof, is so neglected, yea, despised, among the generality of professed Christians, a great evidence of the apostatized state of Christianity. They can have no concern in any work of his but in its proper order. If men be not first sanctified by him, they can never be comforted by him. And they will themselves prefer in their troubles any natural reliefs before the best and highest of his consolations. For however they may be proposed unto them, however they may be instructed in the nature, ways, and means of them, yet they belong not unto them, and why should they value that which is not theirs? The world cannot receive him. He works on the world for conviction (John 16:8), and on the elect for conversion (John 3:8). But none can receive him as a comforter but believers. Therefore is this whole work of the Holy Spirit little taken notice of by the most, and despised by many. Yet is it nevertheless glorious in itself, being fully declared in the Scripture, nor the less useful to the church, being testified unto by the experience of them that truly believe.

That which remains for the full declaration of this office and work of the Holy Ghost, is the consideration of those acts of his which belong properly thereunto, and of those privileges whereof believers are made partakers thereby. And whereas many blessed mysteries of evangelical truth are contained herein, they would require much time and diligence in their explanation. But as to the most of them, according unto the measure of light and experience which I have attained, I have prevented myself the handling of them in this place. For I have spoken already unto most of them in two other discourses, the one concerning the perseverance of true believers, and the other of our communion with God, and of the Holy Spirit in particular.[4] As, therefore, I shall be sparing in the repetition of what is already in them proposed unto public view, so it is not much that I shall add thereunto. Yet what is necessary unto our present design must not be wholly omitted, especially seeing I find that further light and evidence may be added unto our former endeavors in this kind.

---

4   *The Doctrine of the Saints' Perseverance Explained and Confirmed* (1654), and *Of Communion with God the Father, Son, and Holy Ghost, Each Person Distinctly, in Love Grace, and Consolation; or, The Saints' Fellowship with the Father, Son, and Holy Ghost Unfolded* (1657).

4

Inhabitation of the Spirit
the First Thing Promised

THE FIRST THING which the comforter is promised for unto believers is that he should dwell in them, which is their great fundamental privilege, and whereon all others do depend. This, therefore, must in the first place be inquired into.

The inhabitation of the Spirit in believers is among those things which we ought, as to the nature or being of it, firmly to believe, but as to the manner of it cannot fully conceive. Nor can this be the least impeachment of its truth unto any who assent unto the gospel, wherein we have sundry things proposed as objects of our faith which our reason cannot comprehend. We shall, therefore, assert no more in this matter but what the Scripture directly and expressly goes before us in. And where we have the express letter of the Scripture for our warrant we are eternally safe, while we affix no sense thereunto that is absolutely repugnant unto reason or contrary unto more plain testimonies in other places. Wherefore, to make plain what we intend herein, the ensuing observations must be premised.

DISTINCTIONS: WHAT THE INHABITATION
OF THE SPIRIT IS NOT

First, this personal inhabitation of the Holy Spirit in believers is distinct and different from his essential omnipresence, whereby he is in all things. Omnipresence is essential; inhabitation is personal. Omnipresence is a necessary property of his nature, and so not of him as a distinct person in the Trinity, but as God essentially, one and the same in being and substance with the Father and the Son. To be everywhere, to fill all things, to be present with them or indistant from them, always equally existing in the power of an infinite being, is an inseparable property of the divine nature as such. But this inhabitation is personal, or what belongs unto him distinctly as the Holy Ghost. Besides, it is voluntary, and that which might not have been, whence it is the subject of a free promise of God, and wholly depends on a free act of the will of the Holy Spirit himself.

Secondly, it is not a presence by virtue of a metonymical denomination, or an expression of the cause for the effect, that is intended. The meaning of this promise, "The Spirit shall dwell in you,"[1] is not, he shall work graciously in you, for this he can without any special presence. Being essentially everywhere, he can work where and how he pleases without any special presence. But it is the Spirit himself that is promised, and his presence in a special manner, and a special manner of that presence; he shall be in you, and dwell in you, as we shall see. The only inquiry in this matter is, whether the Holy Spirit himself be promised unto believers, or only his grace, which we shall immediately inquire into.

Thirdly, the dwelling of the person of the Holy Spirit in the persons of believers, of what nature soever it be, does not effect a personal union between them. That which we call a personal union is the union of divers natures in the same person, and there can be but one person by virtue of this union. Such is the hypostatical union in the person of the Son of God. It was our nature he assumed, and not the person of any. And it was impossible he should so assume any more but in one individual instance; for if he could have assumed another individual being of our nature, then it must differ personally from that which he did assume, for there is nothing that differs one man from another but a distinct personal subsistence of each. And it implies the highest contradiction that the Son of God could be hypostatically united unto more than one; for if they are more than one, they must be more persons than one; and many persons cannot be hypostatically united, for that is to be one person, and no more. There may be a manifold union, mystical and moral, of divers, of many persons, but a personal union there cannot be of anything but of distinct natures. And as the Son of God could not assume many persons, so supposing that human nature which he did unite to himself to have been a person, that is, to have had a distinct subsistence of its own antecedent unto its union, and there could have been no personal union between it and the Son of God. For the Son of God was a distinct person, and if the human nature

[1] John 14:17.

had been so too, there would have been two persons still, and so no personal union. Nor can it be said that although the human nature of Christ was a person in itself, yet it ceased so to be upon its union with the divine, and so two persons were conjoined and compounded into one. For if ever human nature has in any instance a personal subsistence of its own, it cannot be separated from it without the destruction and annihilation of the individual. For to suppose otherwise is to make it to continue what it was and not what it was; for it is what it is, distinct from all other individuals, by virtue of its personality. Wherefore, upon this inhabitation of the Spirit, whereinsoever it does consist, there is no personal union ensuing between him and believers, nor is it possible that any such thing should be. For he and they are distinct persons, and must eternally abide so while their natures are distinct. It is only the assumption of our nature into union with the Son of God antecedent unto any individual personal subsistence of its own that can constitute such a union.

Fourthly, the union and relation that ensues on this inhabitation of the Spirit is not immediate between him and believers, but between them and Jesus Christ. For he is sent to dwell in them by Christ, in his name, as his Spirit, to supply his room in love and grace toward them, making use of his things in all his effects and operations unto his glory. Hence, I say, is the union of believers with Christ by the Spirit, and not with the Spirit himself. For this Holy Spirit dwelling in the human nature of Christ, manifesting and acting himself in all fullness therein, as has been declared, being sent by him to dwell in like manner and act in a limited measure in all believers, there is a mystical union thence arising between them, whereof the Spirit is the bond and vital principle.

THE MANNER OF THE SPIRIT'S INHABITATION

On these considerations, I say, it is the person of the Holy Ghost that is promised unto believers, and not only the effects of his grace and power; and his person it is that always dwells in them. And as this, on the one hand, is an argument of his infinite condescension in complying with this part of his office and work, to be sent by the Father and Son to dwell in believers, so it is an evident demonstration of his eternal deity, that the one and self-same person should at the same time inhabit so many thousands of distinct persons as are or were at any time of believers in the world, which is fondness[2] to imagine concerning anyone that is not absolutely infinite. And, therefore, that which some oppose as unmeet for him, and beneath his glory, namely,

---

2   I.e., foolishness.

this his inhabitation in the saints of God, is a most illustrious and incontrollable demonstration of his eternal glory. For none but he who is absolutely immense in his nature and omnipresence can be so present with and indistant from all believers in the world; and none but he whose person, by virtue of his nature, is infinite, can personally, equally inhabit in them all. An infinite nature and person is required hereunto. And in the consideration of the incomprehensibility thereof are we to acquiesce as to the manner of his inhabitation, which we cannot conceive.

1. There are very many promises in the Old Testament that God would thus give the Holy Spirit in and by virtue of the new covenant (Ezek. 36:27; Isa. 59:21; Prov. 1:23). And in every place God calls this promised Spirit, and as promised, his Spirit, "My Spirit"; which precisely denotes the person of the Spirit himself. It is generally apprehended, I confess, that in these promises the Holy Spirit is intended only as unto his gracious effects and operations, but not as to any personal inhabitation. And I should not much contend upon these promises only, although in some of them his person, as promised, be expressly distinguished from all his gracious effects. But the exposition which is given of them in their accomplishment under the New Testament will not allow us so to judge of them. For,

2. We are directed to pray for the Holy Spirit, and assured that God will give him unto them that ask of him in a due manner (Luke 11:13). If these words must be expounded metonymically,[3] and not properly, it must be because either (1) they agree not in the letter with other testimonies of Scripture. Or (2) contain some sense absurd and unreasonable. Or (3) that which is contrary unto the experience of them that believe. The first cannot be said, for other testimonies innumerable concur with it. Nor the second, as we shall show. And as for the third, it is that whose contrary we prove. What is it that believers intend in that request? I suppose I may say that there is no one petition wherein they are more intense and earnest, nor which they more frequently insist upon. As David prayed that "God would not take his Holy Spirit from him" (Ps. 51:11), so do they that God would bestow him on them. For this they do, and ought to do, even after they have received him. His continuance with him, his evidencing and manifestation of himself in and to them, are the design of their continual supplications for him. Is it merely external operations of the Spirit in grace that they desire herein? Do they not always pray for his ineffable presence and inhabitation? Will any thoughts of grace or mercy relieve or satisfy them if once they apprehend

---

3   I.e., using the name of one thing for another because an attribute of it is associated with it.

that the Holy Spirit is not in them or does not dwell with them? Although they are not able to form any conception in their minds of the manner of his presence and residence in them, yet is it that which they pray for, and without the apprehension whereof by faith they can have neither peace nor consolation. The promise hereof being confined unto believers, those that are truly and really so, as we showed before, it is their experience whereby its accomplishment is to be judged, and not the presumption of such by whom both the Spirit himself and his whole work is despised.

3. And this inhabitation is that which principally our Lord Jesus Christ directs his disciples to expect in the promise of him: "He dwelleth with you, and shall be in you" (John 14:17). He does so who is the "Comforter, the Spirit of truth"; or, as it is emphatically expressed, "He the Spirit of truth" (John 16:13). He is promised unto and he inhabits them that do believe. So, it is expressly affirmed toward all that are partakers of this promise: "Ye are not in the flesh, but in the Spirit, if so be that the Spirit of God dwells in you" (Rom. 8:9). "If the Spirit of him that raised up Jesus from the dead dwelleth in you" (Rom. 8:11). "The Holy Spirit dwelleth in us" (2 Tim. 1:14). "Greater is he that is in you, than he that is in the world" (1 John 4:4). And many other express testimonies there are unto the same purpose. And whereas the subject of these promises and propositions is the Holy Ghost himself, the person of the Holy Ghost, and that so expressed as not to leave any pretense for anything else, and not his person, to be intended; and whereas nothing is ascribed unto him that is unreasonable, inconvenient unto him in the discharge of his office, or inconsistent with any of his divine perfections, but rather what is every way suitable unto his work, and evidently demonstrative of his divine nature and subsistence, it is both irrational and unsuitable unto the economy of divine grace to wrest these expressions unto a lower, meaner, figurative signification. And I am persuaded that it is contrary to the faith of the catholic church of true believers so to do. For however some of them may not have exercised their minds about the manner of the abode of the Holy Spirit with the church, and some of them, when they hear of his personal indwelling, wherein they have not been duly instructed, do fear, it may be, that indeed that cannot be which they cannot comprehend, and that some evil consequences may ensue upon the admittance of it, although they cannot say what they are, yet it is with them all even an article of faith that the "Holy Ghost dwelleth in the church,"[4] that is, in them that truly believe, and herein have they an

4 1 Cor. 3:16.

apprehension of such a personal presence of his as they cannot conceive. This, therefore, being so expressly, so frequently affirmed in the Scripture, and the comfort of the church, which depends thereon, being singular and eminent, it is unto me an important article of evangelical truth.

4. Although all the principal actings of the Holy Spirit in us and toward us as a comforter do depend on this head, or flow from this spring of his inhabitation, yet, in the confirmation of its truth, I shall here name one or two by which itself is evidenced and its benefits unto the church declared.

(1) This is the spring of his gracious operations in us. So our Savior himself declares: "The water that I shall give him shall be in him a well of water springing up into everlasting life" (John 4:14). The water here promised is the Holy Spirit, called the "gift of God" (John 4:10). This is evident from that parallel place (John 7:38–39), where this living water is plainly declared to be the Holy Ghost. And this water which is given unto any is to be in him, and there to abide, which is but a metaphorical expression for the inhabitation of the Spirit. For it is to be in him as a well, as a living fountain, which cannot be spoken of any gracious habit whatever.[5] No quality in our minds can be a spring of living water. Besides, all gracious habits are effects of the operation of the Holy Spirit, and therefore, they are not the well itself, but belong unto the springing of it up in living waters. So is the Spirit in his indwelling distinguished from all his evangelical operations of grace, as the well is distinct from the streams that flow from it. And as it is natural and easy for a spring of living water to bubble up and put forth refreshing streams, so it belongs unto the consolation of believers to know how easy it is unto the Holy Spirit, how ready he is, on the account of his gracious inhabitation, to carry on and perfect the work of grace, holiness, and sanctification in them. And what instruction they may take for their own deportment toward him may be afterward spoken unto. So in many other places is his presence with us, which we have proved to be by the way of gracious inhabitation, proposed as the cause and spring of all his gracious operations, and so distinct from them. So the Holy Ghost that is given us, "sheds abroad the love of God in our hearts" (Rom. 5:5). The Spirit of God that dwells in us, "shall quicken our mortal bodies" (Rom. 8:12).[6] "He beareth witness

---

5   "Habit" or *habitus* is a technical term in medieval and post-Reformation scholasticism carrying the idea of individual constitution or predisposition. For a detailed discussion, see Nicolas Faucher and Magali Roques, eds., *The Ontology, Psychology and Axiology of Habits (Habitus) in Medieval Philosophy*, Historical-Analytical Studies on Nature, Mind and Action 7 (Cham: Springer, 2019).

6   The correct reference for this quotation is Rom. 8:11.

with our spirit, that we are the sons of God" (Rom. 8:16), which places have been elsewhere explained and vindicated.[7]

(2) This is the hidden spring and cause of that inexpressible distance and difference that is between believers and the rest of the world. Our apostle tells us that the "life" of believers is "hid with Christ in God" (Col. 3:3). A blessed life they have while they are here, dead to the world, and as dead in the world. A life that will issue in eternal glory. But no such thing appears, no luster of it is cast abroad into the eyes of men. "True," says the apostle, "for it is 'hid with Christ in God.'" It is so both in its causes, nature, operations, and means of preservation. But by this hidden life it is that they are differenced from the perishing world. And it will not be denied, as I suppose, that this difference is real and great. For those who believe do enjoy the special love and favor of God, whereas those who do not are under the curse, and "the wrath of God abideth on them."[8] They are alive unto God, but these are dead in trespasses and sins. And if men will not believe that there is so inexpressible a difference between them in this world, they will be forced to confess it at the last day, when the decretory sentences of, "Come, ye blessed," and "Go, ye cursed,"[9] shall be openly denounced. But, for the most part, there is no visible cause in the eyes of the world of this inexpressible and eternal difference between these two sorts of persons. For besides that, for the most part, the world does judge amiss of all that believers are and do, and does rather, through an inbred enmity, working by wicked and foolish surmises, suppose them to be the worst than absolutely the best of men. There is not, for the most part, such a visible, manifest difference in outward actions and duties, on which alone a judgment may be passed in man's day, as to be a just foundation of believing so unspeakable a difference between their persons as is spoken of. There is a difference in their works, which indeed ought to be far greater than it is, and so a greater testimony is given to the righteousness of God (1 John 3:12). There is yet a greater difference in internal, habitual grace, whereby the minds of believers are transformed initially into the image of God (Titus 1:15). But these things will not bear the weight of this inconceivable distance. Principally, therefore, it depends hereon, namely, the inhabitation of the Spirit in them that believe. The great difference between the two houses that Solomon built, was that God dwelt in the one, and he himself in the other. Though any two houses, as unto their outward fabric,

[7] See *Of Communion with God the Father, Son, and Holy Ghost*, pt. 3, "Of Communion with the Holy Ghost."

[8] John 3:36.

[9] Matt. 25:34–46.

make the same appearance, yet if the king dwell in the one and a robber in the other, the one may be a palace and the other a den. It is this inhabitation of the Spirit whereon all the privileges of believers do immediately depend, and all the advantages which they have above the men of the world. And the difference which is made hereby or ensues hereon is so inconceivably great, as that a sufficient reason may thence be given of all the excellent things which are spoken of them who are partakers of it.

5

Particular Actings of the Holy Spirit as a Comforter

How He Is an Unction

THE SPECIAL ACTINGS of the Holy Spirit toward believers as their comforter, with the privileges and advantages which by them they are made partakers of, have been severally spoken unto by many, and I have also in other discourses had occasion to treat concerning some of them.[1] I shall, therefore, be the more brief in the present discourse of them, and, waiving things commonly known and received, shall endeavor to state right conceptions of them, and to add further light unto what has been already received.

THE SPIRIT'S ANOINTING

The first of this sort which we shall mention, because, as I think, the first in order of nature, is the unction or anointing which believers have by him. So are they said to be "anointed" (2 Cor. 1:21). "Ye have τὸ χρίσμα," an unction, an unguent,[2] "from the Holy One" (1 John 2:20). "The anointing which ye have received abideth in you. And the same anointing teacheth you of all things" (1 John 2:27). What this χρίσμα is which we do receive, and wherein this anointing does consist, we must, in the first place, inquire. For a distinct comprehension and knowledge of that which is so great a privilege, and of so much use unto us, is our duty and advantage. It is the more so, because by the

---

1 See, e.g., *Of Communion with God the Father, Son, and Holy Ghost*, pt. 3, "Of Communion with the Holy Ghost," and *Πνευματολογια, or, A Discourse concerning the Holy Spirit*.

2 I.e., oil for anointing.

222 THE HOLY SPIRIT AS A COMFORTER

most these things are neglected. That is an empty sound unto them which has in itself the fullness of the blessing of the gospel of Christ. Some things there are which pretend unto this unction, or which some would have it to consist in, that we must remove out of our way to render the truth more evident.

First, some think that by this unction the doctrine of the gospel, or the truth itself, is intended. This Episcopius[3] pleads for in his exposition of the place. That doctrine of the gospel which they had received was that which would preserve them from the seducers which in that place of the apostle (1 John 2:20), believers are warned to beware of. But neither the context nor the text will admit of this interpretation. For (1) the thing itself in question was the doctrine of the gospel. This the seducers pretended to be on their side, which the apostle denies. Now, although the doctrine itself was that whereby this difference was to be determined, yet is not the doctrine itself, but the advantage they had for the right understanding of it, that which is proposed for their relief and comfort. (2) This unction is said to abide in them who have received it, whereas we are said to abide in the doctrine or the truth, and not that in us properly. (3) This unction is said to teach us all things, but the doctrine of the truth is that which we are taught, and there must be a difference between that which teaches and that which is taught thereby. (4) Whereas, in all other places of the Scripture, either the Holy Ghost himself or some special operation of his is hereby intended, there is no reason nor pretense of any to be taken from the words or context why another signification should be here imposed on that expression. (5) For the reason which he adds, that there is no mention in any other place of Scripture of any peculiar internal act or work toward any persons, in their teaching or reception of the truth, it is so extremely remote from the truth, and is so directly opposite unto express testimonies almost innumerable, that I wonder how any man could be so forgetful as to affirm it. Let the reader satisfy himself in what has been discoursed on the head of spiritual illumination.

Secondly, the testimony given by the Holy Ghost unto the truth of the gospel imparted unto them, is the exposition of this unction in the paraphrase of another. This testimony was by his miraculous operations, at his first effusion on the apostles. But neither can this be the mind of the Holy Ghost herein; for this unction which believers had is the same with their being anointed of God (2 Cor. 1:21), and that was a privilege whereof they were all personally made partakers. So, also, is that which is here mentioned, namely,

---

3 Simon Episcopius (1583–1643) was an eminent Dutch Remonstrant theologian known for the systematization of Arminianism.

that which was in them, which abode with them, and taught them. Neither is this a tolerable exposition of these words, "Ye have an unction from the Holy One, abiding in you, teaching of you"; that is, you have heard of the miraculous operations of the Holy Ghost, in the confirmation of the gospel, giving testimony unto the truth.

Thirdly, it is to no purpose to examine the pretenses of some of the Romanists, that respect is had herein to the chrism[4] or unguent that they use in baptism, confirmation, and in their fictitious sacraments of order and extreme unction.[5] For besides that all their unctions are inventions of their own, no institution of Christ, nor of any efficacy unto the ends for which this unction is granted unto believers, the more sober of their expositors take no notice of them on this occasion. Those who would know what respect they have thereunto may find it in the commentaries of à Lapide[6] on this place.

These apprehensions being removed, as no way suiting the mind of the Holy Ghost, nor expressing the privilege intended, nor the advantage which we have thereby, we shall follow the conduct of the Scripture in the investigation of the true nature of it. And to this end we may observe,

1. That all persons and things that were dedicated or consecrated unto God under the Old Testament were anointed with material oil. So were the kings of the people of God, so were priests and prophets. In like manner, the sanctuary, the altar, and all the holy utensils of divine worship, were anointed. And it is confessed that among all the rest of the Mosaical institutions, those also concerning unction were typical and figurative of what was to come.

2. That all these types had their first, proper, and full signification and accomplishment in the person of Jesus Christ. And because every person and thing that was made holy to God was so anointed, he who was to be the Most Holy, the only spring and cause of holiness in and unto others, had his name and denomination from this. Both Messiah in the Old Testament, and Christ in the New, are as much as the Anointed One. For he was not only in his person typified in the anointed kings, priests, and prophets, but also, in his mediation, by the tabernacle, sanctuary, altar, and temple. Hence his unction is expressed in these words, למשה קדש קדשים, "To anoint the Holy

---

4 "Chrism" is the oil mixture consecrated and applied at baptism and in other rites of the Roman Catholic Church.
5 "Extreme Unction" is also referred to as "last rites" or "anointing the sick." It is intended to be the final anointing of the Roman Catholic sacramental system in the final hours of the Christian's life.
6 Cornelius à Lapide (1567–1637) was a Flemish Jesuit who wrote commentaries on every book in the Catholic canon except Job and Psalms.

of Holies," who was prefigured by all the holy anointed ones before (Dan. 9:24). This became his name as he was the hope of the church under the Old Testament, the Messiah; and the immediate object of the faith of the saints under the New, the Christ. Here, therefore, in the first place, we must inquire into the nature of this unction, that of believers being an emanation from thence, and to be interpreted by analogy thereunto. For, as it is usually expressed by way of allusion, it is as the oil, which, being poured on the head of Aaron, went down to the skirts of his garments.[7]

3. That the Lord Christ was anointed, and how, is declared: "The Spirit of the Lord God is upon me, because the Lord hath anointed me" (Isa. 61:1). His unction consisted principally in the communication of the Spirit unto him. For he proves that the Spirit of the Lord was upon him, because he was anointed. And this gives us a general rule, that the anointing with material oil under the Old Testament did prefigure and represent the effusion of the Spirit under the New, which now answers all the ends of those typical institutions. Hence the gospel, in opposition unto them all, in the letter, outwardly, visibly, and materially, is called the "ministration of the Spirit" (2 Cor. 3:6, 8). So is the unction of Christ expressed: "The Spirit of the Lord shall rest upon him, the Spirit of wisdom and understanding, the Spirit of counsel and might, the Spirit of knowledge and of the fear of the Lord" (Isa. 11:2).

4. Whereas the unction of Christ did consist in the full communication of the Spirit unto him, not by measure, in all his graces and gifts, needful unto his human nature or his work, though it be essentially one entire work, yet was it carried on by several degrees and distinctions of time. For (1) he was anointed by the Spirit in his incarnation in the womb (Luke 1:35), the nature of which work we have at large before explained.[8] (2) He was so at his baptism and entrance into his public ministry, when he was anointed to preach the gospel, as Isaiah 61:1. "The Spirit of God descended like a dove, and lighted upon him" (Matt. 3:16). The first part of his unction more peculiarly respected a fullness of the grace, the latter of the gifts of the Spirit. (3) He was peculiarly anointed unto his death and sacrifice in that divine act of his whereby he sanctified himself thereunto (John 17:19), which has also been before declared.[9] (4) He was so at his ascension, when he received of the Father the promise of the Spirit, pouring him forth on his disciples (Acts 2:33). And in this latter instance he was anointed with the oil of gladness, which includes his glorious exaltation also. For this was absolutely peculiar

<hr>

7   Owen is alluding to passages such as Exod. 29:7, 21; Lev. 8:12; and Ps. 133:2.
8   Πνευματολογια, or, A Discourse concerning the Holy Spirit, bk. 2, chap. 3.
9   Salus Electorum, Sanguis Jesu; or, The Death of Death in the Death of Christ (1647), bk. 2, chap. 3.

unto him, whence he is said to be so anointed above his fellows. For although in some other parts of this anointing, he has them who partake of them, by and from him, in their measure, yet in this of receiving the Spirit with a power of communicating him unto others, herein he is singular, nor was ever any other person sharer with him therein in the least degree. See the exposition on Hebrews 1:8–9.[10] Now, although there be an inconceivable difference and distance between the unction of Christ and that of believers, yet is his the only rule of the interpretation of theirs, as to the kind thereof. And,

5. Believers have their unction immediately from Christ. So is it in the text: "Ye have an unction from the Holy One." So is he called, "These things saith he that is holy" (Acts 3:14; Rev. 3:7). He himself was anointed as the "Most Holy" (Dan. 9:24). And it is his Spirit which believers do receive (Eph. 3:16; Phil. 1:19). It is said that he who anoints us is God (2 Cor. 1:21). And I do take God there personally for the Father, as the same name is in the verse foregoing: "All the promises of God in him," that is, in Christ, "are yea, and in him, Amen." Wherefore, the Father is the original, supreme cause of our anointing, but the Lord Christ, the Holy One is the immediate efficient cause thereof. This himself expresses when he affirms that he will send the Spirit from the Father. The supreme donation is from the Father; the immediate collation,[11] from the Son.

6. It is therefore manifest that the anointing of believers consists in the communication of the Holy Spirit unto them from and by Jesus Christ. It is not the Spirit that does anoint us, but he is the unction wherewith we are anointed by the Holy One. This the analogy unto the unction of Christ makes undeniable; for as he was anointed so are they, in the same kind of unction, though in a degree inferior unto him. For they have nothing but a measure and portion from his fullness, as he pleases (Eph. 4:7). Our unction, therefore, is the communication of the Holy Spirit, and nothing else. He is that unction which is given unto us and abides with us. But this communication of the Spirit is general and respects all his operations. It does not yet appear wherein the special nature of it does consist, and whence this communication of him is thus expressed by an unction. And this can be no otherwise learned but from the effects ascribed unto him as he is an unction, and the relation with the resemblance that is therein unto the unction of Christ. It is, therefore, some particular grace and privilege which is intended in this unction (2 Cor. 1:21). It is mentioned only neutrally, without the ascription

10 John Owen, *An Exposition of the First Two Chapters of the Epistle of Paul the Apostle unto the Hebrews* (London: Nathaniel Ponder, 1668), 104–15.

11 I.e., institution; placing in proper order.

of any effects unto it, so that therein we cannot learn its special nature. But there are two effects elsewhere ascribed unto it. The first is teaching, with a saving, permanent knowledge of the truth thereby produced in our minds. This is fully expressed: "You have an unction from the Holy One, and you know all things" (1 John 2:20, 27), that is, all those things of the fundamental, essential truths of the gospel, all you need to know that you may obey God truly and be saved infallibly. This you have by this unction. For this anointing which you have received abides in you and teaches you all things. And we may observe, that it is spoken of in a special manner with respect unto our permanency and establishment in the truth against prevalent seducers and seductions; so it is joined with establishing in that other place (2 Cor. 1:21).

Wherefore, in the first place, this anointing with the Holy Ghost is the communication of him unto us with respect unto that gracious work of his in the spiritual, saving illumination of our minds, teaching us to know the truth, and to adhere firmly unto it in love and obedience. This is that which is peculiarly ascribed unto it; and we have no way to know the nature of it but by its effects.

The anointing, then, of believers with the Spirit consists in the collation of him upon them to this end, that he may graciously instruct them in the truths of the gospel by the saving illumination of their minds, causing their souls firmly to cleave unto them with joy and delight, and transforming them in the whole inward man into the image and likeness of it. Hence it is called the "anointing of our eyes with eye-salve" that we may see (Rev. 3:18). So does it answer that unction of the Lord Christ with the Spirit, which made him "quick of understanding in the fear of the Lord" (Isa. 11:3). Let these things, therefore, be fixed in the first place, namely, that the χρίσμα, the unction which believers receive from the Holy One, is the Spirit himself; and that his first, peculiar, special effect as an unction, is his teaching of us the truths and mysteries of the gospel by saving illumination, in the manner before described.

Hereunto also is referred what is said of believers being made "kings and priests" (Rev. 1:6). For there is an allusion therein unto the anointing of those sorts of persons under the Old Testament. Whatever was typical therein was fully accomplished in the unction of Christ unto his office, wherein he was the sovereign king, priest, and prophet of the church. Wherefore, by a participation in his unction, they are said to be made "kings and priests," or "a royal priesthood," as it is (1 Pet. 2:9), and this participation of his unction consists in the communication of the same Spirit unto them wherewith he was anointed. Whereas, therefore, these titles denote the dignity of believers in their special relation unto God, by this unction they are peculiarly dedicated and consecrated unto him.

It is manifest, therefore, first, that this unction we receive from the Holy One is the Holy Spirit, which he has promised unto all that believe in him; and then that we have these two things by virtue thereof: (1) Spiritual instruction, by saving illumination in the mind of God and the mysteries of the gospel; (2) A special dedication unto God, in the way of a spiritual privilege.

BENEFITS OF THE SPIRIT'S ANOINTING

What remains, is to inquire first, what benefit or advantage we have by this unction; second, how this belongs unto our consolation, seeing the Holy Spirit is thus bestowed on us as he is promised to be the comforter of the church.

1. As unto the first head, it is hereon that our stability in believing does depend. For it is pleaded unto this purpose in a peculiar manner by the apostle (1 John 2:20, 27). It was the "unction from the Holy One" which then kept believers from being carried from the faith by the craft of seducers. Hereby he makes men, according unto their measure, of quick understanding in the fear of the Lord. Nor will anything else give assurance in this case. Temptations may come as a storm or tempest, which will quickly drive men from their greatest fleshly confidences. Hence oftentimes those who are forward enough to say, though all men should forsake the truth, yet would not they so do, are the forwardest upon trials so to do. Neither will men's skill, cunning, or disputing abilities secure them from being, at one time or other, inveigled[12] with fair pretenses, or entangled with the cunning sleights of them who lie in wait to deceive. Nor will the best defenses of flesh and blood stand firmly and unshaken against powerful allurements on the one hand, and fierce persecutions on the other, the present artillery of the patrons and promoters of apostasy. None of these things does the apostle prescribe or recommend unto believers as an effectual means of their preservation, when a trial of their stability in the truth shall befall them. But this unction he assures them will not fail, neither shall they fail, because of it.

And to this end we may consider (1) the nature of the teaching which we have by this anointing; "The anointing teacheth you." It is not merely an external doctrinal instruction, but an internal effectual operation of the Holy Ghost. Herein does God give unto us the Spirit of wisdom and revelation in the knowledge of him, the eyes of our understanding being enlightened, that

12 I.e., enticed.

we may know what is the hope of his calling (Eph. 1:17–18). He makes use, indeed, of the outward means of instruction by the word, and teaches nothing but what is revealed therein. But he gives us an understanding that we may know him that is true, and opens our eyes that we may clearly and spiritually see the wondrous things that are in his law. And there are no teachings like unto his. None so abiding, none so effectual. When spiritual things, through this anointing, are discovered in a spiritual manner, then do they take up an immovable possession in the minds of men. As God will destroy every oppressing yoke because of the anointing of Christ (Isa. 10:27), so will he break every snare of seduction by the anointing of Christians. So, it is promised that under the gospel, "wisdom and knowledge shall be the stability of the times" (Isa. 33:6). Nothing will give stability in all seasons but the wisdom and knowledge which are the effects of this teaching, when God gives us the Spirit of wisdom and revelation in the knowledge of him.

(2) What it is that it teaches, and that is all things; the same anointing teaches you of all things. So was the promise that he should "teach us all things," and "bring all things to our remembrance" that Christ has said unto us (John 14:26), and "guide us into all truth" (John 16:13). It is not all things absolutely that are intended, for they are restrained unto those of one certain kind, even the things which Christ had spoken, that is, such as belonged unto the kingdom of God. Neither are they all of them absolutely intended, especially as to the degrees of the knowledge of them. For in this life we know but in part and see all things darkly as in a glass. But it is all things, and all truth, with respect unto the end of this promise and teaching. In the promise, the whole life of faith, with joy and consolation thereon, is the end designed. All things necessary thereunto this unction teaches us. And in the other place of the apostle, it respects the great fundamental truths of the gospel, which the seducers opposed, from whose seduction this unction does secure believers. Wherefore, it teaches all that are made partakers of it all that truth, all those things, all that Christ has spoken, that are necessary unto these ends, that they may live unto God in the consolation of faith and be delivered from all attempts to draw them into error.

The degrees of this knowledge, which are exceedingly various, both with respect unto the clearness and evidence of conception and the extent of the things known, depend on the various measures whereby the Spirit acts, according unto his own will, and the different use of the external means of knowledge which we do enjoy. But what is necessary unto the ends mentioned, none shall come short of who enjoy this anointing. And where its teachings are complied with in a way of duty, where we obstruct them not by prejudices and sloth, where we give up ourselves unto their directive efficacy in a diligent, impartial attendance unto the word, whereby alone we are to be taught, we shall not fail of that knowledge in the whole counsel of God, and all the parts of it, which he will accept and bless. And this gives stability unto believers when trials and temptations about the truth do befall them; and the want hereof, in the uncured darkness of their minds, and ignorance of the doctrine of the gospel, is that which betrays multitudes into a defection from it in seasons of temptation and persecution.

(3) It so teaches as to give withal an approbation of and love unto the things that are taught. These are the next principle and cause of practice, or the doing of the things that we know, which is the only cement of all the means of our security, rendering them firm and stable. The mind may discern spiritual truths, but if the will and affections be not wrought over to love them and delight in them, we shall never conform ourselves unto them in the diligent exercise and practice of what they do require. And what we may do on the solitary efficacy of light and conviction, without the adherence of love and delight, will neither be acceptable unto God, nor shall we be permanent or stable therein. All other means in the world, without the love and practice of the truth, will be insufficient unto our preservation in the saving profession of it. And this is the characteristic note of the teaching by this unction. It gives and communicates with it the love of that truth wherein we are instructed, and delight in obedience unto what it does require. Where these are not, however raised our minds may be, or enlarged our understandings in the apprehension of objective truths, whatever sublime notions or subtle conceptions about them we may have, though we could master and manage all the speculations and niceties of the schools, in their most pretended accuracy of expression, yet as to the power and benefit of religion, we should be but as sounding brass and tinkling cymbals. But when this Holy Spirit does, in and by his teaching, breathe into our hearts a holy, divine love unto and complacency in the things we are taught; when he enables us to taste how gracious the Lord is in them, rendering them sweeter unto us than the honey or the honeycomb; when he makes them our delight and joy, exciting and quickening the practical principles of our minds unto a compliance with them in holy obedience, then have we that unction from the Holy One which will both sanctify and secure our souls unto the end.

And hereby may we know whether we have ourselves received of this anointing. Some would fain[13] put it off unto what was peculiar unto the times

---

13   I.e., gladly.

of the apostles, and would suppose another kind of believers in those days than any that are now in the world, or need to be; though what our Savior prayed for them, even for the apostles themselves, as to the Spirit of grace and consolation, he prayed also for all them who should believe on him through their word unto the end of the world. But take away the promise of the Spirit, and the privileges thereon depending, from Christians, and in truth they cease so to be. Some neglect it as if it were an empty expression, and either wholly insignificant, or at best intending somewhat wherein they need not much concern themselves; and whatever it be, they doubt not but to secure the pretended ends of it, in their preservation from seduction, by their own skill and resolution. On such pretenses are all the mysteries of the gospel by many despised, and a religion is formed wherein the Spirit of Christ has no concern. But these things are otherwise stated in the minds of the true disciples of Christ. They know and own of how great importance it is to have a share in this unction; how much their conformity unto Christ, their participation of him, and the evidence of their union with him, how much their stability in profession, their joy in believing, their love and delight in obedience, with their dignity in the sight of God and all his holy angels, do depend thereon. Neither do we look upon it as a thing obscure or unintelligible, that which no man can know whether he has or not. For if it were so, a thing so thin, aerial, and imperceptible, as that no spiritual sense or experience could be had of it, the apostle would not have referred all sorts and degrees of believers, fathers, young men, and little children unto it for their relief and encouragement in the times of danger. Wherefore, it evidences itself in the way and manner of its acting, operation, and teaching, as before declared. And as by those instances they satisfy themselves as unto what experience they have of it, so it is their duty to pray continually for its increase and further manifestation of its power in them. Yea, it is their duty to labor that their prayers for it may be both fervent and effectual. For the more express and eminent the teachings of this anointing in them are, the more fresh and plentiful is their unction, the more will their holiness and consolation abound.

And whereas this is that by which, as it immediately proceeds from the Holy Spirit, they have their peculiar dedication unto God, being made kings and priests unto him, they are highly concerned to secure their interest therein. For it may be they are so far from being exalted, promoted, and dignified in the world by their profession, as that they are made thereby the scorn of men and the outcasts of the people. Those, indeed, whose kingdom and priesthood, their dignity and honor in Christianity, their approximation unto God and Christ in a peculiar manner, consist in secular titles, honor, power, and grandeur, as it is in the Papacy, may content themselves with their chrism, or the greasy unction of their outward, ceremonious consecration, without much inquiry after or concern in this spiritual anointing. But those who get little or nothing in this world, that is, of the world, by their profession, but labor, pain, travail of soul and body, with scorns, reproaches, and persecutions, had need look after that which gives them a dignity and honor in the sight of God, and which brings in satisfaction and peace unto their own souls; and this is done by that anointing alone, whereby they are made kings and priests unto God, having honor before him, and a free, sacred access unto him.

2. I shall only add, that whereas we ascribe this anointing in a peculiar manner unto the Holy Ghost as the comforter of the church, we may easily discern wherein the consolation which we receive by it does consist. For who can express that satisfaction, refreshment, and joy, which the mind is possessed with in those spiritual, effectual teachings, which give it a clear apprehension of saving truth in its own nature and beauty, and enlarge the heart with love unto it and delight in it? It is true, that the greatest part of believers are ofttimes either at such a loss as unto a clear apprehension of their own spiritual state, or so unskilled in making a right judgment of the causes and means of divine consolations, or so confused in their own experiences, or so negligent in their inquiries into these things, or so disordered by temptations, as that they receive not a refreshing sense of those comforts and joys which are really inseparable from this anointing. But still it is in itself that spring from whence their secret refreshments and supportments do arise. And there is none of them but, upon guidance and instruction, are able to conceive how their chiefest joys and comforts, even those whereby they are supported in and against all their troubles, are resolved into that spiritual understanding which they have into the mysteries of the will, love, and grace of God in Christ, with that ineffable complacency and satisfaction which they find in them, whereby their wills are engaged into an unconquerable constancy in their choice. And there is no small consolation in a due apprehension of that spiritual dignity which ensues hereon. For when they meet with the greatest troubles and the most contemptuous scorns in this world, a due apprehension of their acceptance with God, as being made kings and priests unto him, yields them a refreshment which the world knows nothing of, and which themselves are not able to express.

6

The Spirit a Seal, and How

SECONDLY, ANOTHER EFFECT of the Holy Spirit as the comforter of the church is, that by him believers are sealed: "He who anointed us is God, who hath also sealed us" (2 Cor. 1:21–22). And how this is done the same apostle declares, "In whom also after that ye believed, ye were sealed with that Holy Spirit of promise" (Eph. 1:13). And, "Grieve not the Holy Spirit of God, whereby ye are sealed unto the day of redemption" (Eph. 4:30). In the first place, it is expressly said that we are sealed with the Spirit; whereby the Spirit himself is expressed as this seal, and not any of his special operations, as he is also directly said himself to be the "earnest of our inheritance." In the latter, the words are, ἐν ᾧ ἐσφραγίσθητε, "In whom," in and by the receiving of whom, "ye are sealed." Wherefore, no special act of the Spirit, but only a special effect of his communication unto us, seems to be intended hereby.

The common exposition of this sealing is taken from the nature and use of sealing among men, the sum whereof is this: Sealing may be considered as a natural or moral action, that is, either with respect unto the act of it as an act, or with respect unto its use and end. In the first way, it is the communication of the character or image that is on the seal unto the thing that is sealed, or that the impression of the seal is set unto. In answer hereunto, the sealing of the Spirit should consist in the communication of his own spiritual nature and likeness unto the souls of believers; so, this sealing should materially be the same with our sanctification. The end and use of sealing among men is twofold. (1) To give security unto the performance of deeds, grants, promises, testaments, and wills, or the like engaging significations of our minds. And in answer hereunto, we may be said to be sealed, when the promises of God are confirmed and established unto our souls, and we are secured of them by the Holy Ghost. But the truth is, this were to seal the promises of God, and not believers. But it is persons, and not promises, that are said to be sealed. (2) It is for the safekeeping or preservation of that which a seal is set upon. So, things precious and highly valuable are sealed up, that they may be kept safe and inviolable. So, on the other hand, when Job expressed his apprehension that God would keep an everlasting remembrance of his sin, that it should not be lost or out of the way, he says, "his transgression was sealed up in a bag" (Job 14:17). And so, it is that power which the Holy Ghost puts forth in the preservation of believers which is intended; and in this respect, they are said to be "sealed unto the day of redemption."[1]

These things have been spoken unto and enlarged on by many, so that there is no need again to insist upon them. And what is commonly delivered unto this purpose is good and useful in the substance of it, and I have on several occasions long since myself made use of them.[2] But upon renewed thoughts and consideration, I cannot fully acquiesce in them. For (1) I am not satisfied that there is such an allusion herein unto the use of sealing among men as is pretended. And if there be, it will fall out, as we see it has done, that, there being so many considerations of seals and sealing, it will be hard to determine on any one in particular which is principally intended. And if you take in more, as the manner of the most is to take in all they can think of, it will be unavoidable that acts and effects of various kinds will be assigned unto the Holy Ghost under the term of sealing, and so we shall never come to know what is that one determinate act and privilege which is intended therein. (2) All things which are usually assigned as those wherein this sealing does consist are acts or effects of the Holy Ghost upon us whereby he seals us, whereas it is not said that the Holy Spirit seals us, but that we are sealed with him; he is God's seal unto us.

All our spiritual privileges, as they are immediately communicated unto us by Christ, so they consist wholly in a participation of that head, spring, and fullness of them which is in him. And as they proceed from our union with him, so their principal end is conformity unto him. And in him, in whom all things are conspicuous, we may learn the nature of those things which, in lesser measure and much darkness in ourselves, we are made partakers of. So do we learn our unction in his. So must we inquire into the nature of our being sealed by the Spirit in his sealing also. For as it is said that "he who hath sealed us is God" (2 Cor. 1:21–22), so of him it is said emphatically, "For him

---

1 Eph. 4:30.
2 *Of Communion with God the Father, Son, and Holy Ghost*, pt. 2, chap. 5; pt. 3, chap. 7.

hath God the Father sealed" (John 6:27). And if we can learn aright how God the Father sealed Christ, we shall learn how we are sealed in a participation of the same privilege.

THE SPIRIT'S SEALING OF CHRIST

I confess there are a variety of apprehensions concerning the act of God whereby Christ was sealed, or what it is that is intended thereby. Maldonate,[3] on the place, reckons up ten several expositions of the words among the fathers, and yet embraces no one of them. It is not suited unto my design to examine or refute the expositions of others, whereof a large and plain field does here open itself unto us. I shall only give an account of what I conceive to be the mind of the Holy Ghost in that expression. And we may observe,

First, that this is not spoken of Christ with respect unto his divine nature. He is, indeed, said to be the character of the person of the Father in his divine person as the Son, because there are in him, communicated unto him from the Father, all the essential properties of the divine nature, as the thing sealed receives the character or image of the seal. But this communication is by eternal generation, and not by sealing. But it is an external, transient act of God the Father on the human nature, with respect unto the discharge of his office. For it is given as the reason why he should be complied with and believed on in that work: "Labour for that bread which the Son of man shall give unto you; for him hath God the Father sealed."[4] It is the ground whereon he persuades them to faith and obedience unto himself.

Secondly, it is not spoken of him with a special respect unto his kingly office, as some conceive. For this sealing of Christ they would have to be his designation of God unto his kingdom, in opposition unto what is affirmed (John 6:15), that the people designed to come and make him a king by force. For that is only an occasional expression of the sense of the people, the principal subject treated on is of a nobler nature. But whereas the people did flock after him, on the account of a temporal benefit received by him, in that they were fed, filled, and satisfied with the loaves which he had miraculously increased (John 6:26), he takes occasion from thence to propose unto them the spiritual mercies that he had to tender unto them. And this he does, in answer unto the bread that they had eaten, under the name of meat, and bread enduring to everlasting life, which he would give unto them. Under

---

3 Juan Maldonato (1533–1583) was a Spanish Jesuit theologian and exegete, among the most learned of his day.
4 John 6:27.

this name and notion of meat he did comprise all the spiritual nourishment, in his doctrine, person, mediation, and grace, that he had prepared for them. But on what grounds should they look for these things from him? How might it appear that he was authorized and enabled thereunto? In answer unto that inquiry he gives this account of himself, "For him hath God the Father sealed," namely, unto this end.

Thirdly, wherefore the sealing of God unto this end and purpose must have two properties and two ends also annexed unto it. (1) There is in it a communication of authority and ability. For the inquiry is, how he could give them that meat which endures unto everlasting life, as afterward they ask expressly, "How can this man give us his flesh to eat?" (John 6:52). To this it is answered, that God the Father had sealed him; that is, he it was who was enabled of God the Father to give and dispense the spiritual food of the souls of men. This, therefore, is evidently included in this sealing. (2) It must have evidence in it also; that is, somewhat whereby it may be evinced that he was thus authorized and enabled by God the Father. For whatever authority or ability anyone may have unto any end, none is obliged to make application unto him for it, or depend upon him therein, unless it be evidenced that he has that authority and ability. This the Jews immediately inquired after. "What sign," say they, "dost thou then, that we may see and believe thee? What dost thou work?" (John 6:30). How shall it be demonstrated unto us that you are authorized and enabled to give us the spiritual food of our souls? This also belonged unto his sealing; for therein there was such an express representation of divine power communicated unto him as evidently manifested that he was appointed of God unto this work. These two properties, therefore, must be found in this sealing of the Lord Christ with respect unto the end here mentioned, namely, that he might be the *promus condus*, or "principal dispenser" of the spiritual food of the souls of men.

Fourthly, it being God's seal, it must also have two ends designed in it. (1) God's owning of him to be his. Him has God the Father sealed, unto this end, that all may know and take notice of his owning and approbation of him. He would have him not looked on as one among the rest of them that dispensed spiritual things, but as him whom he had singled out and peculiarly marked for himself. And therefore, this he publicly and gloriously testified at the entrance, and again a little before the finishing, of his ministry; for upon his baptism there came "a voice from heaven, saying, 'This is my beloved Son, in whom I am well pleased'" (Matt. 3:17), which was nothing but a public declaration that this was he whom God had sealed, and so owned in a peculiar manner. And this testimony was afterward renewed again, at his transfiguration on the mount: "Behold a voice out of the cloud, which said, 'This is my beloved Son, in whom I am well pleased; hear ye him'" (Matt. 17:5); this is he whom I have sealed. And this testimony is pleaded by the apostle Peter as that whereinto their faith in him, as the sealed one of God, was resolved (2 Pet. 1:17–18). (2) To manifest that God would take care of him, and preserve him in his work unto the end (Isa. 42).

Fifthly, wherefore, this sealing of the Son is the communication of the Holy Spirit in all fullness unto him, authorizing him unto, and acting his divine power in, all the acts and duties of his office, so as to evidence the presence of God with him, and his approbation of him, as the only person that was to distribute the spiritual food of their souls unto men. For the Holy Spirit, by his powerful operations in him and by him, did evince and manifest that he was called and appointed of God to this work, owned by him and accepted with him, which was God's sealing of him. Hence the sin of them who despised this seal of God was unpardonable. For God neither will nor can give greater testimony unto his approbation of any person than by the great seal of his Spirit, and this was given unto Christ in all the fullness of it. He was "declared to be the Son of God, according to the Spirit of holiness" (Rom. 1:4) and justified in the Spirit, or by his power evidencing that God was with him (1 Tim. 3:16). Thus did God seal the head of the church with the Holy Spirit; and thus, undoubtedly, may we best learn how the members are sealed with the same Spirit, seeing we have all our measures out of his fullness, and our conformity unto him is the design of all gracious communications unto us.

THE SPIRIT'S SEALING OF BELIEVERS

Sixthly, wherefore, God's sealing of believers with the Holy Spirit is his gracious communication of the Holy Ghost unto them, so to act his divine power in them as to enable them unto all the duties of their holy calling, evidencing them to be accepted with him both unto themselves and others, and asserting their preservation unto eternal salvation. The effects of this sealing are gracious operations of the Holy Spirit in and upon believers; but the sealing itself is the communication of the Spirit unto them. They are sealed with the Spirit. And further to evidence the nature of it, with the truth of our declaration of this privilege, we may observe,

1. That when any persons are so effectually called as to become true believers, they are brought into many new relations, as to God himself, as his children; unto Jesus Christ, as his members; unto all saints and angels in the families of God above and below; and are called to many new works, duties,

and uses, which before they knew nothing of. They are brought into a new world, erected by the new creation, and which way soever they look or turn themselves, they say, "Old things are passed away, behold, all things are become new." So, it is with everyone that is made a new creature in Christ Jesus (2 Cor. 5:17). In this state and condition, wherein a man has new principles put within him, new relations contracted about him, new duties presented unto him, and a new deportment in all things required of him, how shall he be able to behave himself aright, and answer the condition and holy station wherein he is placed? This no man can do of himself, for who is sufficient for these things? Wherefore,

2. In this state God owns them, and communicates unto them his Holy Spirit, to fit them for their relations, to enable them unto their duties, to act their new principles, and every way to discharge the work they are called unto, even as their head, the Lord Christ, was unto his. God does not now give unto them the spirit of fear, but of power, and of love, and of a sound mind (2 Tim. 1:7). And hereby does God seal them. For,

(1) Hereby he gives his testimony unto them that they are his, owned by him, accepted with him, his sons or children, which is his seal. For if they were not so, he would never have given his Holy Spirit unto them. And herein consists the greatest testimony that God does give, and the only seal that he does set, unto any in this world. That this is God's testimony and seal, the apostle Peter proves (Acts 15:8–9). For on the debate of that question, whether God approved and accepted of the humble believers, although they observed not the rites of Moses, he confirms that he did with this argument: "God," says he, "which knoweth the hearts, bare them witness." How did he do it? How did he set his seal to them as his? Says he, "By giving them the Holy Ghost, even as he did unto us." Hereby God gives testimony unto them. And lest any should suppose that it was only the gifts and miraculous operations of the Holy Ghost which he had respect unto, so as that this sealing of God should consist therein alone, he adds, that his gracious operations also were no less an effect of this witness which God gave unto them: "And put no difference between us and them, purifying their hearts by faith." This, therefore, is that whereby God gives his testimony unto believers, namely, when he seals them with his Spirit, or by the communication of the Holy Spirit unto them. And this he does in two respects. For,

(2) This is that whereby he gives believers assurance of their relation unto him, of their interest in him, and of his love and favor to them. It has been generally conceived that this sealing with the Spirit is that which gives assurance unto believers; and so indeed it does, although the way whereby it does

it has not been rightly apprehended. And, therefore, none have been able to declare the special nature of that act of the Spirit whereby he seals us, from whence such assurance should ensue. But it is indeed not any act of the Spirit in us that is the ground of our assurance, but the communication of the Spirit unto us. This the apostle plainly testifies. "Hereby we know that he abideth in us, by the Spirit which he hath given us" (1 John 3:24). That God abides in us and we in him is the subject matter of our assurance. "This we know," says the apostle; which expresses the highest assurance we are capable of in this world. And how do we know it? Even "by the Spirit which he hath given us." But, it may be, the sense of these words may be, that the Spirit which God gives us does, by some special work of his, effect this assurance in us; and so, it is not his being given unto us, but some special work of his in us, that is the ground of our assurance, and consequently our sealing. I do not deny such a special work of the Spirit as shall be afterward declared, but I judge that it is the communication of the Spirit himself unto us that is here intended. For so the apostle declares his sense to be, "Hereby know we that we dwell in God, and he in us, because he has given us of his Spirit" (1 John 4:13). This is the great evidence, the great ground of assurance, which we have that God has taken us into a near and dear relation unto himself, because he has given us of his Spirit, that great and heavenly gift which he will impart unto no others. And, indeed, on this one hinge depends the whole case of that assurance which believers are capable of. If the Spirit of God dwell in us, we are his; but "if any man have not the Spirit of Christ, he is none of his" (Rom. 8:9). Hereon alone depends the determination of our special relation unto God. By this, therefore, does God seal believers, and therein gives them assurance of his love. And this is to be the sole rule of your self-examination whether you are sealed of God or no.

(3) Hereby God evidences them unto the world, which is another end of sealing. He marks them so hereby for his own as that the world cannot but in general take notice of them. For where God sets this seal in the communication of his Spirit, it will so operate and produce such effects as shall fall under the observation of the world. As it did in the Lord Christ, so also will it do in believers according unto their measure. And there are two ways whereby God's sealing does evidence them unto the world. The one is by the effectual operation of the Spirit, communicated unto them both in gifts and graces. Though the world is blinded with prejudices, and under the power of a prevalent enmity against spiritual things, yet it cannot but discover what a change is made in the most of those whom God thus seals, and how, by the gifts and graces of the Spirit, which they hate, they are different from other

men. And this is that which keeps up the difference and enmity that is in the world between the seeds. For God's sealing of believers with his Spirit evidences his special acceptance of them, which fills the hearts of them who are acted with the spirit of Cain with hatred and revenge. Hence many think that the respect which God had unto the sacrifice of Abel was testified by some visible sign, which Cain also might take notice of. And that there was an ἐμπυρισμός, "the kindling of his sacrifice by fire from heaven," which was the type and resemblance of the Holy Ghost, as has been showed. All other causes of difference are capable of a composition, but this about the seal of God can never be composed. And that which follows from hence is, that those who are thus sealed with the Spirit of God cannot but separate themselves from the most of the world, whereby it is more evidenced unto whom they do belong.

(4) Hereby God seals believers unto the day of redemption or everlasting salvation. For the Spirit thus given unto them is, as we have showed already, to abide with them forever, as a "well of water in them, springing up into everlasting life" (John 4:14; 7:38).

This, therefore, is that seal which God grants unto believers, even his Holy Spirit, for the ends mentioned, which, according unto their measure, and for this work and end, answers that great seal of heaven which God gave unto the Son, by the communication of the Spirit unto him in all its divine fullness, authorizing and enabling him unto his whole work, and evidencing him to be called of God thereunto.

7

The Spirit an Earnest, and How

THIRDLY, AGAIN, the Holy Spirit, as thus communicated unto us, is said to be an "earnest."[1] Ἀῤῥαβών, the word in the original, is nowhere used in the New Testament but in this matter alone (2 Cor. 1:22; 5:5; Eph. 1:14). The Latin translator renders this word by *pignus*, "a pledge." But he is corrected therein by Jerome on Ephesians 1. "The Latin word *pignus*," says he, "has been used to translate the Greek *arrhabon*. But *pignus* does not signify precisely that which *arrhabon* does. For an *arrhabon* is given for a future purchase, as if it were some proof and obligation. Security, on the other hand, that is ἐνέχορον, is pledged for a loan so that when the loan has been repaid the security owed to the borrower is returned by the creditor."[2] And this reason is generally admitted by expositors. For a pledge is that which is committed to and left in the hand of another, to secure him that the money which is borrowed thereon shall be repaid, and then the pledge is to be received back again. Hence it is necessary that a pledge be more in value than the money received, because it is taken in security for repayment. But an earnest is a part only of what is to be given or paid, or some lesser thing that is given to secure somewhat that is more or

---

1   Modern English translations render this variously: e.g., "deposit" (NIV), "guarantee" (ESV), and "down payment" (CSB).

2   In the text: *Pignus*, says he, *Latinus interpres pro arrhabone posuit. Non id ipsum autem arrhabo quod pignus sonat. Arrhabo enim futurae emptioni quasi quoddam testimonium, et obligamentum datur. Pignus vero, hoc est ἐνέχορον pro mutua pecunia apponitur, ut quum illa reddita fuerit, reddenti debitum pignus a creditore reddatur.*—Owen. For the Latin text, see Hieronymus, *Commentariorum in epistolam Ephesios*, ed. J. P. Migne, Patrologia Latina 26 (Paris: Migne, 1845), 457. For the English translation, see Ronald E. Heine, *The Commentaries of Origen and Jerome on St Paul's Epistle to the Ephesians*, Oxford Early Christian Studies (Oxford: Oxford University Press, 2002), 104. Saint Jerome (ca. 347–420) is most well known for his translation of the Latin Vulgate, but he was also a prolific commentator.

241

greater in the same or another kind. And this difference must be admitted if we are obliged to the precise signification and common use of pledges and earnests among men, which we must inquire into. The word is supposed to be derived from the Hebrew עָרַב;[3] and the Latins make use of it also, *arrhabon* and *arrha*. It is sometimes used in other authors, as Plutarch in *Galba*: "That worthy minister, however, had won the protection of Vinius betimes, by means of large advances."[4] He prepossessed[5] Obinius with great sums of money, as an earnest of what he would do afterward. Hesychius[6] explains it by πρόδομα, "a gift beforehand." As to what I apprehend to be the mind of the Holy Ghost in this expression, I shall declare it in the ensuing observations.

First, it is not any act or work of the Holy Spirit on us or in us that is called his being an "earnest." It is he himself who is this earnest. This is expressed in every place where there is mention made of it: δοὺς τὸν ἀρραβῶνα τοῦ πνεύματος, "The earnest of the Spirit" (2 Cor. 1:22)—that earnest which is the Spirit, or the Spirit as an earnest, as Augustine reads the words, *Arrhabona Spiritum*. "Who hath also given unto us the earnest of the Spirit" (2 Cor. 5:5). The giving of this earnest is constantly assigned to be the act of God the Father, who, according to the promise of Christ, would send the comforter unto the church. And in the other place (Eph. 1:14), it is expressly said that the Holy Spirit is the "earnest of our inheritance." Everywhere the article is of the masculine gender, ὅς ἐστιν ἀρραβών and πνεῦμα, "the Spirit," is of the neuter. Some would have it to refer unto Christ (Eph. 1:12). But as it is not unusual in Scripture that the subjunctive article and relative should agree in gender with the following substantive, as ὅς here does with ἀρραβών; so the Scripture, speaking of the Holy Ghost, though πνεῦμα be of the neuter gender, yet having respect unto the thing, that is, the person of the Spirit, it subjoins the pronoun of the masculine gender unto it (John 14:26). Wherefore, the Spirit himself is the earnest, as given unto us from the Father by the Son. And this act of God is expressed by giving or putting him into our hearts (2 Cor. 1:22). How he does this has been before declared, both in general and with respect in particular to his inhabitation. The meaning,

---

3   The Hebrew word is עֵרָבוֹן.

4   In the text: Ἐφθάκει προειληφὼς ἀρραβῶσι μεγάλοις τὸν Ὀβίνιον.—Owen. For the Greek text and English translation, see Plutarch, *Lives*, vol. 11, *Aratus. Artaxerxes. Galba. Otho. General Index*, trans. Bernadotte Perrin, Loeb Classical Library 103 (Cambridge, MA: Harvard University Press, 1926), 240–41. Plutarch (d. 120) was a Greek biographer whose *Lives of the Noble Greeks and Romans* includes a narrative of the life of the Roman emperor Galba, from which this quotation is drawn.

5   I.e., convinced, persuaded.

6   Probably Hesychius of Alexandria, a fifth- or sixth-century Greek grammarian, who compiled a lexicon called *Alphabetical Collection of All Words*.

therefore, of the words is, that God gives unto us his Holy Spirit to dwell in us, and to abide with us, as an earnest of our future inheritance.

Secondly, it is indifferent whether we use the name of an earnest or a pledge in this matter, and although I choose to retain that of an earnest, from the most usual acceptation of the word, yet I do it not upon the reason alleged for it, which is taken from the special nature and use of an earnest in the dealings of men. For it is the end only of an earnest whereon the Holy Ghost is so called, which is the same with that of a pledge, and we are not to force the similitude or allusion any further. For precisely among men, an earnest is the confirmation of a bargain and contract made on equal terms between buyers and sellers or exchangers. But there is no such contract between God and us. It is true, there is a supposition of an antecedent covenant, but not as a bargain or contract between God and us. The covenant of God, as it respects the dispensation of the Spirit, is a mere free, gratuitous promise; and the stipulation of obedience on our part is consequential thereunto. Again; he that gives an earnest in a contract or bargain does not principally aim at his own obligation to pay such or such a sum of money, or somewhat equivalent thereunto, though he do that also; but his principal design is to secure unto himself that which he has bargained for, that it may be delivered up unto him at the time appointed. But there is nothing of this nature in the earnest of the Spirit, wherein God intends our assurance only, and not his own. And sundry other things there are wherein the comparison will not hold nor is to be urged, because they are not intended.

The general end of an earnest or a pledge is all that is alluded unto; and this is, to give security of somewhat that is future or to come. And this may be done in a way of free bounty as well as upon the strictest contract. As if a man have a poor friend or relation, he may, of his own accord, give unto him a sum of money, and bid him take it as a pledge or earnest of what he will yet do for him. So does God, in a way of sovereign grace and bounty, give his Holy Spirit unto believers, and withal lets them know that it is with a design to give them yet much more in his appointed season. And here is he said to be an earnest. Other things that are observed, from the nature and use of an earnest in civil contracts and bargains between men, belong not hereunto, though many things are occasionally spoken and discoursed from them of good use unto edification.

Thirdly, in two of the places wherein mention is made of this matter, the Spirit is said to be an earnest, but wherein, or unto what end, is not expressed (2 Cor. 1:22; 5:5). The third place affirms him to be an "earnest of our inheritance" (Eph. 1:14). What that is, and how he is so, may be briefly declared. And,

1. We have already manifested that all our participation of the Holy Spirit, in any kind, is upon the account of Jesus Christ, and we do receive him immediately as the Spirit of Christ; for "to as many as receive Christ, the Father gives power to become the sons of God" (John 1:12). "And because we are sons, he sends forth the Spirit of his Son into our hearts" (Gal. 4:6). And as we receive the Spirit from him, and as his Spirit, so he is given unto us to make us conformable unto him, and to give us a participation of his gifts, graces, and privileges.

2. Christ himself, in his own person, is the "heir of all things." So he was appointed of God (Heb. 1:2), and therefore the whole inheritance is absolutely his. What this inheritance is, what is the glory and power that is contained therein, I have at large declared in the exposition of that place.[7]

3. Man by his sin had universally forfeited his whole right unto all the ends of his creation, both on the earth below and in heaven above. Death and hell were become all that the whole race of mankind had either right or title unto. But yet all the glorious things that God had provided were not to be cast away; an heir was to be provided for them. Abraham when he was old and rich had no child, and complained that his steward, a servant, was to be his heir (Gen. 15:2–4), but God lets him know that he would provide another heir for him of his own seed. When man had lost his right unto the whole inheritance of heaven and earth, God did not so take the forfeiture as to seize it all into the hands of justice and destroy it. But he invested the whole inheritance in his Son, making him the heir of all. This he was meet for, as being God's eternal Son by nature; and hereof the donation was free, gratuitous, and absolute. And this grant was confirmed unto him by his unction with the fullness of the Spirit. But,

4. This inheritance, as to our interest therein, lay under a forfeiture; and as unto us it must be redeemed and purchased, or we can never be made

---

7   Owen is here referring to his *Exercitations on the Epistle to the Hebrews Also concerning the Messiah Wherein the Promises concerning Him to Be a Spiritual Redeemer of Mankind Are Explained and Vindicated, His Coming and Accomplishment of His Work according to the Promises Is Proved and Confirmed, the Person, or Who He Is, Is Declared, the Whole Oeconomy of the Mosaical Law, Rites, Worship, and Sacrifice Is Explained: And in All the Doctrine of the Person, Office, and Work of the Messiah Is Opened, the Nature and Demerit of the First Sin Is Unfolded, the Opinions and Traditions of the Antient and Modern Jews Are Examined, Their Objections against the Lord Christ and the Gospel Are Answered, the Time of the Coming of the Messiah Is Stated, and the Great Fundamental Truths of the Gospel Vindicated: With an Exposition and Discourses on the Two First Chapters of the Said Epistle to the Hebrews* (1668).

partakers of it. Wherefore, the Lord Christ, who had a right in his own person unto the whole inheritance by the free grant and donation of the Father, yet was to redeem it from under the forfeiture, and purchase the possession of it for us. Hence is it called the purchased possession. How this purchase was made, what made it necessary, by what means it was effected, are declared in the doctrine of our redemption by Christ, the price which he paid, and the purchase that he made thereby. And hereon, the whole inheritance is vested in the Lord Christ, not only as unto his own person and his right unto the whole, but he became the great trustee for the whole church and had their interest in this inheritance committed unto him also. No man, therefore, can have a right unto this inheritance, or to any part of it, not unto the least share of God's creation here below, as a part of the rescued or purchased inheritance, but by virtue of an interest in Christ and union with him. Wherefore,

Fourthly, the way whereby we come to have an interest in Christ, and thereby a right unto the inheritance, is by the participation of the Spirit of Christ, as the apostle fully declares (Rom. 8:14–17). For it is by the Spirit of adoption, the Spirit of the Son, that we are made children. Now, says the apostle, "If we are children, then heirs, heirs of God, and joint heirs with Christ." Children are heirs unto their father. And those who are children of God are heirs of that inheritance which God has provided for his children, "heirs of God." And all the good things of grace and glory which believers are made partakers of in this world or that which is to come are called their "inheritance," because they are the effects of free, gratuitous adoption. They are not things that themselves have purchased, bargained for, earned, or merited, but an inheritance depending on and following solely upon their free, gratuitous adoption. But how can they become "heirs of God," seeing God has absolutely appointed the Son alone to be "heir of all things" (Heb. 1:2)? He was the heir, unto whom the whole inheritance belonged. Why, says the apostle, by the participation of the Spirit of Christ, we are made joint heirs with Christ. The whole inheritance, as unto his own personal right, was entirely his by the free donation of the Father, all power in heaven and earth being given unto him. But if he will take others into a joint right with him, he must purchase it for them, which he did accordingly.

Fifthly, thus it is manifest how the Holy Spirit becomes the earnest of our inheritance. For by him, that is, by the communication of him unto us, we are made joint heirs with Christ, which gives us our right and title, whereby our names are, as it were, inserted into the assured conveyance of the great and full inheritance of grace and glory. In the giving of his Spirit unto us, God making of us coheirs with Christ, we have the greatest and most assured earnest and pledge of our future inheritance. And he is to be thus an earnest until or unto the redemption of the purchased possession. For after that a man has a good and firm title unto an inheritance settled in him, it may be a long time before he can be admitted into an actual possession of it, and many difficulties he may have in the meantime to conflict with. And it is so in this case. The earnest of the Spirit given unto us, whereby we become coheirs with Christ, whose Spirit we are made partakers of, secures the title of the inheritance in and unto our whole persons. But before we can come unto the full possession of it, not only have we many spiritual trials and temptations to conflict with in our souls, but our bodies also are liable unto death and corruption. Wherefore, whatever firstfruits we may enjoy, yet can we not enter into the actual possession of the whole inheritance, until not only our souls are delivered from all sins and temptations, but our bodies also are rescued out of the dust of the grave. This is the full "redemption of the purchased possession," whence it is signally called the "redemption of the body" (Rom. 8:23).

Thus as the Lord Christ himself was made heir of all things by that communication of the Spirit unto him whereby he was anointed unto his office, so the participation of the same Spirit from him and by him makes us coheirs with him; and so he is an earnest given us of God of the future inheritance. It belongs not unto my present purpose to declare the nature of that inheritance whereof the Holy Spirit is the earnest. In brief, it is the highest participation with Christ in that glory and honor that our natures are capable of.

And in like manner we are said to receive ἀπαρχὴν τοῦ Πνεύματος (Rom. 8:23); that is, the Spirit himself as the firstfruits of our spiritual and eternal redemption. God had appointed that the firstfruits, which are called רשׁית[8] and בכורים,[9] should be a חרומה,[10] an offering unto himself. Hereunto ἀπαρχή answers, and is taken generally for that which is first in any kind (Rom. 16:5; 1 Cor. 15:20; James 1:18; Rev. 14:4). And the firstfruits of the Spirit must be either what he first works in us, or all his fruits in us with respect unto the full harvest that is to come, or the Spirit himself as the beginning and pledge of future glory. And the latter of these is intended in this place. For the apostle discourses about the liberty of the whole creation from that state of bondage whereunto all things were subjected by sin. With respect hereunto, he says that believers themselves having not as yet obtained a full deliverance, as he had expressed it (Rom. 7:24), do groan after its

8   Heb. "finest."
9   Heb. "the firstfruits."
10 Heb. "contribution."

perfect accomplishment. But yet, says he, we have the beginning of it, the firstfruits of it, in the communication of the Spirit unto us: for "where the Spirit of the Lord is, there is liberty" (2 Cor. 3:17). For although we are not capable of the full and perfect estate of the liberty provided for the children of God while we are in this world, conflicting with the remainders of sin, pressed and exercised with temptations, our bodies also being subject unto death and corruption, yet where the Spirit of the Lord is, where we have that firstfruit of the fullness of our redemption, there is liberty in the real beginning of it, and assured consolation, because it shall be consummated in the appointed season.

CONCLUSION

These are some of the spiritual benefits and privileges which believers enjoy by a participation of the Holy Ghost as the promised comforter of the church. These things he is unto them, and as unto all other things belonging unto their consolation, he works them in them, which we must in the next place inquire into. Only something we may take notice of from what we have already insisted on. As (1) that all evangelical privileges whereof believers are made partakers in this world do center in the person of the Holy Spirit. He is the great promise that Christ has made unto his disciples, the great legacy which he has bequeathed unto them. The grant made unto him by the Father, when he had done all his will, and fulfilled all righteousness, and exalted the glory of his holiness, wisdom, and grace, was this of the Holy Spirit, to be communicated by him unto the church. This he received of the Father as the complement of his reward; wherein he saw of the travail of his soul and was satisfied. This Spirit he now gives unto believers, and no tongue can express the benefits which they receive thereby. Therein are they anointed and sealed; therein do they receive the earnest and firstfruits of immortality and glory; in a word, therein are they taken into a participation with Christ himself in all his honor and glory. Hereby is their condition rendered honorable, safe, comfortable, and the whole inheritance is unchangeably secured unto them. In this one privilege, therefore, of receiving the Spirit, are all others enwrapped. For (2) no one way, or thing, or similitude, can express or represent the greatness of this privilege. It is anointing, it is sealing, it is an earnest and firstfruit, everything whereby the love of God and the blessed security of our condition may be expressed or intimated unto us. For what greater pledge can we have of the love and favor of God? What greater dignities can we be made partakers of? What greater assurance of a future blessed condition, than that God has given us of his Holy Spirit? And (3) hence also is it manifest how abundantly willing he is that the heirs of promise should receive strong consolation in all their distresses, when they flee for refuge unto the hope that is set before them.

A DISCOURSE
OF
SPIRITUAL GIFTS

Being the Second Part of the
Work of the Holy Spirit.

In which these particulars are distinctly
handled in the following chapters:

By the Late Reverend John Owen, D.D.

———

London, Printed for William Marshall
at the Bible in Newgate Street:
1693

A Discourse of Spiritual Gifts
Contents

1

Spiritual Gifts, Their Names
and Significations

THE SECOND PART of the dispensation of the Spirit in order unto the perfecting of the new creation, or the edification of the church, consists in his
communication of spiritual gifts unto the members of it, according as their
places and stations therein do require. By his work of saving grace, which in
other discourses we have given a large account of, he makes all the elect living
stones; and by his communication of spiritual gifts, he fashions and builds
those stones into a temple for the living God to dwell in. He spiritually unites
them into one mystical body, under the Lord Christ as a head of influence,
by faith and love; and he unites them into an organic body, under the Lord
Christ as a head of rule, by gifts and spiritual abilities. Their nature is made
one and the same by grace, their use is various by gifts. Everyone is a part of
the body of Christ, of the essence of it, by the same quickening, animating
Spirit of grace; but one is an eye, another a hand, another a foot, in the body,
by virtue of peculiar gifts: for "unto everyone of us is given grace according
to the measure of the gift of Christ" (Eph. 4:7).

These gifts are not saving, sanctifying graces; those were not so in themselves which made the most glorious and astonishing appearance in the world,
and which were most eminently useful in the foundation of the church and
propagation of the gospel, such as were those that were extraordinary and
miraculous. There is something of the divine nature in the least grace, that
is not in the most glorious gift, which is only so. It will therefore be part of
our work to show wherein the essential difference between these gifts and
sanctifying graces does consist; as also, what is their nature and use must be
inquired into. For although they are not grace, yet they are that without which

the church cannot subsist in the world, nor can believers be useful unto one another and the rest of mankind, unto the glory of Christ, as they ought to be. They are the "powers of the world to come,"[1] those effectual operations of the power of Christ whereby his kingdom was erected and is preserved.

And hereby is the church's state under the New Testament different from that under the Old. There is, indeed, a great difference between their ordinances and ours; theirs being suited unto the dark apprehensions which they had of spiritual things, ours accommodated unto the clearer light of the gospel, more plainly and expressly representing heavenly things unto us (Heb. 10:1). But our ordinances with their spirit would be carnal also. The principal difference lies in the administration of the Spirit for the due performance of gospel worship by virtue of these gifts, bestowed on men for that very end. Hence the whole of evangelical worship is called the "ministration of the Spirit," and therefore said to be "glorious" (2 Cor. 3:8). And where they are neglected, I see not the advantage of the outward worship and ordinances of the gospel above those of the law. For although their institutions are accommodated unto that administration of grace and truth which came by Jesus Christ, yet they must lose their whole glory, force, and efficacy, if they be not dispensed and the duties of them performed by virtue of these spiritual gifts. And, therefore, no sort of men by whom they are neglected do or can content themselves with the pure and unmixed gospel institutions in these things, but do rest principally in the outward part of divine service, in things of their own finding out. For as gospel gifts are useless without attending unto gospel institutions, so gospel institutions are found to be fruitless and unsatisfactory without the attaining and exercising of gospel gifts.

Be it so, therefore, that these gifts we intend are not in themselves saving graces, yet are they not to be despised. For they are, as we shall show, the powers of the world to come, by means whereof the kingdom of Christ is preserved, carried on, and propagated in the world. And although they are not grace, yet are they the great means whereby all grace is ingenerated[2] and exercised. And although the spiritual life of the church does not consist in them, yet the order and edification of the church depend wholly on them. And therefore are they so frequently mentioned in the Scripture as the great privilege of the New Testament, directions being multiplied in the writings of the apostles about their nature and proper use. And we are commanded earnestly to desire and labor after them, especially those which are most useful and subservient unto

---

1   Heb. 6:5.
2   I.e., generated or produced.

edification (1 Cor. 12:31). And as the neglect of internal saving grace, wherein the power of godliness does consist, has been the bane of Christian profession as to obedience, issuing in that form of it which is consistent with all manner of lusts, so the neglect of these gifts has been the ruin of the same profession as to worship and order, which has thereon[3] issued in fond superstition.

The great and signal promise of the communication of these gifts is recorded, "Thou hast ascended on high, thou hast led captivity captive, thou hast received gifts for men" (Ps. 68:18). For these words are applied by the apostle unto that communication of spiritual gifts from Christ whereby the church was founded and edified (Eph. 4:8). And whereas it is foretold in the psalm that Christ should receive gifts, that is, to give them unto men, as that expression is expounded by the apostle—so he did this by receiving of the Spirit, the proper cause and immediate author of them all, as Peter declares: "Therefore being by the right hand of God exalted, and having received of the Father the promise of the Holy Ghost, he hath shed forth this, which ye now see and hear" (Acts 2:33), speaking of the miraculous gifts conferred on the apostles at the day of Pentecost. For these gifts are from Christ, not as God absolutely, but as mediator, in which capacity he received all from the Father in a way of free donation. Thus, therefore, he received the Spirit as the author of all spiritual gifts. And whereas all the powers of the world to come consisted in them, and the whole work of the building and propagation of the church depended on them, the apostles, after all the instructions they had received from Christ, while he conversed with them in the days of his flesh, and also after his resurrection, were commanded not to go about the great work which they had received commission for until they had received power by the coming of the Holy Ghost upon them in the communication of those gifts (Acts 1:4, 8). And as they neither might nor could do anything in their peculiar work, as to the laying of the foundation of the Christian church, until they had actually received those extraordinary gifts which gave them power so to do, so if those who undertake, in any place, degree, or office, to carry on the edification of the church, do not receive those more ordinary gifts which are continued unto that end, they have neither right to undertake that work, nor power to perform it in a due manner.

The things which we are to inquire into concerning these gifts are, (1) their name; (2) their nature in general, and therein how they agree with and differ from saving graces; (3) their distinction; (4) the particular nature of them; and, (5) their use in the church of God.

---

3   I.e., as a result.

The general name of those spiritual endowments which we intend is δόματα; so the apostle renders מַתָּנוֹת, from Psalm 68:18, *dona*, "gifts" (Eph. 4:8). That is, they are free and undeserved effects of divine bounty. In the minds of men on whom they are bestowed they are spiritual powers and endowments with respect unto a certain end. But as to their original and principal cause, they are free, undeserved gifts. Hence the Holy Spirit, as the author of them, and with respect unto them, is called δωρεὰ τοῦ θεοῦ, "The gift of God" (John 4:10). And the effect itself is also termed δωρεὰ τοῦ ἁγίου πνεύματος, "The gift of the Holy Ghost" (Acts 10:45); "The gift of God" (Acts 8:20); "The gift of the grace of God" (Eph. 3:7); "The gift of Christ" (Eph. 4:7); "The heavenly gift" (Heb. 6:4)—all expressing the freedom of their communication on the part of the Father, Son, and Spirit. And in like manner, on the same account, are they called χαρίσματα, that is, "gracious largesses," gifts proceeding from mere bounty. And therefore, saving graces are also expressed by the same name in general, because they also are freely and undeservedly communicated unto us (Rom. 11:28).[4] But those gifts are frequently and almost constantly so expressed (Rom. 12:6; 1 Cor. 1:7; 7:7; 12:4, 9, 28, 30; 2 Tim. 1:6; 1 Pet. 4:10). And it is absolute freedom in the bestower of them that is principally intended in this name. Hence, he has left his name as a curse unto all posterity who thought this free gift of God might be purchased with money (Acts 8:20). A pageantry of which crime the apostate ages of the church erected, in applying the name of that sin to the purchase of benefices and dignities, while the gift of God was equally despised on all hands. And, indeed, this was that whereby in all ages, countenance was given unto apostasy and defection from the power and truth of the gospel. The names of spiritual things were still retained but applied to outward forms and ceremonies, which thereby were substituted insensibly into their room, to the ruin of the gospel in the minds of men. But as these gifts were not any of them to be bought, no more are they absolutely to be attained by the natural abilities and industry of any, whereby an image of them is attempted to be set up by some, but deformed and useless. They will do those things in the church by their own abilities which can never be acceptably discharged but by virtue of those free gifts which they despise; whereof we must speak more afterward. Now, the full signification of these words in our sense is peculiar unto the New Testament; for although in other authors they are used for a gift or free grant, yet they never denote the endowments or abilities of the minds of men who do receive them, which is their principal sense in the Scripture.

With respect unto their special nature they are called πνευματικὰ, sometimes absolutely, περὶ δὲ τῶν πνευματικῶν, "But concerning spirituals"

---

4   The correct reference is Rom. 11:29.

(1 Cor. 12:1), that is, "spiritual gifts." And so again, ζηλοῦτε τὰ πνευματικά, "Desire spirituals" (1 Cor. 14:1), that is, gifts. For so it is explained, ζηλοῦτε τὰ χαρίσματα τὰ κρείττονα, "Covet earnestly the best gifts" (1 Cor. 12:31). Whenever, therefore, they are called πνευματικά,[5] there χαρίσματα,[6] denoting their general nature, is to be supplied. And where they are called χαρίσματα only, πνευματικά is to be understood, as expressing their special difference from all others. They are neither natural nor moral, but spiritual endowments. For both their author, nature, and object, are respected herein. Their author is the Holy Spirit, their nature is spiritual, and the objects about which they are exercised are spiritual things.

Again; with respect unto the manner of their communication, they are called μερισμοί τοῦ πνεύματος ἁγίου, "distributions," or partitions, "of the Holy Ghost" (Heb. 2:4). Not whereof the Holy Ghost is the subject, as though he were parted or divided, as the Socinians dream on this place, but whereof he is the author [of] the distributions which he makes. And they are thus called divisions, partitions, or distributions, because they are of divers sorts and kinds, according as the edification of the church did require. And they were not at any time all of them given out unto any one person, at least so as that others should not be made partakers of the same sort. From the same inexhaustible treasure of bounty, grace, and power, these gifts are variously distributed unto men. And this variety, as the apostle proves, gives both ornament and advantage to the church: "If the whole body were an eye, where were the hearing?" etc. (1 Cor. 12:14–25). It is this μερισμός, this various distribution of gifts, that makes the church an organic body; and in this composure, with the peculiar uses of the members of the body, consist the harmony, beauty, and safety of the whole. Were there no more but one gift, or gifts of one sort, the whole body would be but one member; as where there is none, there is no animated body, but a dead carcass.

And this various distribution, as it is an act of the Holy Spirit, produces διαίρεσιν;[7] διαιρέσεις χαρισμάτων εἰσί, "There are diversities of gifts" (1 Cor. 12:4). The gifts thus distributed in the church are divers as to their sorts and kinds, one of one kind, another of another. An account hereof is given by the apostle particularly, in a distinct enumeration of the sorts or kinds of them (1 Cor. 12:8–10). The edification of the church is the general end of them all, but divers, distinct, different gifts are required thereunto.[8]

5   Gk. "spirituals."
6   Gk. "gifts."
7   Gk. "diversity."
8   I.e., in order for this to occur.

258 A DISCOURSE OF SPIRITUAL GIFTS

These gifts being bestowed, they are variously expressed, with regard unto the nature and manner of those operations which we are enabled unto by virtue of them. So are they termed διακονίας, "ministrations" (1 Cor. 12:5). That is, powers and abilities whereby some are enabled to administer spiritual things unto the benefit, advantage, and edification of others, and ἐνεργήματα, "effectual workings" (1 Cor. 12:6) or operations, efficaciously producing the effects which they are applied unto. And lastly, they are comprised by the apostle in that expression, φανέρωσις τοῦ πνεύματος, "The manifestation of the Spirit" (1 Cor. 12:7). In and by them does the Holy Spirit evidence and manifest his power. For the effects produced by them, and themselves in their own nature, especially some of them, do evince[9] that the Holy Spirit is in them, that they are given and wrought by him, and are the ways whereby he acts his own power and grace.

These things are spoken in the Scripture as to the name of these spiritual gifts. And it is evident that if we part with our interest and concern in them, we must part with no small portion of the New Testament. For the mention of them, directions about them, their use and abuse, do so frequently occur, that if we are not concerned in them we are not so in the gospel.

9 I.e., provide evidence for.

2

Differences between Spiritual
Gifts and Saving Grace

THEIR NATURE IN GENERAL, which in the next place we inquire into, will be much discovered in the consideration of those things wherein these gifts do agree with saving graces, and wherein they differ from them.

THREE SIMILARITIES

There are three things wherein spiritual gifts and saving graces do agree—

1. They are, both sorts of them, the purchase of Christ for his church, the special fruit of his mediation. We speak not of such gifts or endowments of men's minds as consist merely in the improvement of their natural faculties. Such are wisdom, learning, skill in arts and sciences, which those may abound and excel in whom are utter strangers to the church of Christ, and frequently they do so, to their own exaltation and contempt of others. Nor do I intend abilities for actions moral, civil, or political, as fortitude, skill in government or rule, and the like. For although these are gifts of the power of the Spirit of God, yet they do belong unto those operations which he exercises in upholding or ruling of the world, or the old creation as such, whereof I have treated before.[1] But I intend those alone which are conversant about

---

1 See Πνευματολογια, or, A Discourse concerning the Holy Spirit: Wherein an Account Is Given of His Name, Nature, Personality, Dispensation, Operations, and Effects; His Whole Work in the Old and New Creation Is Explained; the Doctrine concerning It Vindicated from Oppositions and Reproaches. The Nature Also and Necessity of Gospel Holiness; the Difference between Grace and Morality, or a Spiritual Life unto God in Evangelical Obedience and a Course of Moral Virtues, Are Stated and Declared (1674).

the gospel, the things and duties of it, the administration of its ordinances, the propagation of its doctrine, and profession of its ways. And herein also I put a difference between them and all those gifts of the Spirit about sacred things which any of the people of God enjoyed under the Old Testament. For we speak only of those which are powers of the world to come. Those others were suited to the economy of the old covenant and confined with the light which God was pleased then to communicate unto his church. Unto the gospel state they were not suited, nor would be useful in it. Hence the prophets, who had the most eminent gifts, did yet all of them come short of John the Baptist, because they had not, by virtue of their gifts, that acquaintance with the person of Christ and insight into his work of mediation that he had. And yet also he came short of him that is least in the kingdom of heaven, because his gifts were not purely evangelical. Wherefore, those gifts whereof we treat are such as belong unto the kingdom of God erected in a special manner by Jesus Christ after his ascension into heaven, for he was exalted that he might fill "all things,"[2] τὰ πάντα, that is, the whole church, with these effects of his power and grace.¶[3]

The power, therefore, of communicating these gifts was granted unto the Lord Christ as mediator, by the Father, for the foundation and edification of his church, as it is expressed (Acts 2:33). And by them was his kingdom both set up and propagated and is preserved in the world. These were the weapons of warfare which he furnished his disciples with when he gave them commission to go forth and subdue the world unto the obedience of the gospel (Acts 1:4, 8). And mighty were they through God unto that purpose (2 Cor. 10:3–6). In the use and exercise of them did the gospel run, and was glorified, to the ruin of the kingdom of Satan and darkness in the world. And that he was ever able to erect it again, under another form than that of Gentilism, as he has done in the anti-Christian apostasy of the church visible, it was from a neglect and contempt of these gifts, with their due use and improvement. When men began to neglect the attaining of these spiritual gifts, and the exercise of them, in praying, in preaching, in interpretation of the Scripture, in all the administrations and whole worship of the church, betaking themselves wholly to their own abilities and inventions, accommodated unto their ease and secular interest, it was an easy thing for Satan to erect again his kingdom, though not in the old manner, because of the light of the Scripture, which had made an impression on the minds of men

---

2   Eph. 4:10.
3   The ¶ symbol indicates that a paragraph break has been added to Owen's original text.

which he could not obliterate. Wherefore he never attempted openly any more to set up heathenism or paganism, with the gods of the old world and their worship, but he insensibly raised another kingdom, which pretended some likeness unto and compliance with the letter of the word, though it came at last to be in all things expressly contrary thereunto. This was his kingdom of apostasy and darkness, under the papal anti-Christianism and woeful degeneracy of other Christians in the world. For when men who pretend themselves entrusted with the preservation of the kingdom of Christ did willfully cast away those weapons of their warfare whereby the world was subdued unto him, and ought to have been kept in subjection by them, what else could ensue?

By these gifts, I say, does the Lord Christ demonstrate his power and exercise his rule. External force and carnal weapons were far from his thoughts, as unbecoming his absolute sovereignty over the souls of men, his infinite power and holiness. Neither did any ever betake themselves unto them in the affairs of Christ's kingdom, but either when they had utterly lost and abandoned these spiritual weapons, or did not believe that they are sufficient to maintain the interest of the gospel, though originally they were so to introduce and fix it in the world. That is, that although the gifts of the Holy Ghost were sufficient and effectual to bring in the truth and doctrine of the gospel against all opposition, yet are they not so to maintain it, which they may do well once more to consider. Herein, therefore, they agree with saving graces. For that they are peculiarly from Jesus Christ the mediator is confessed by all, unless it be by such as by whom all real internal grace is denied. But the sanctifying operations of the Holy Spirit, with their respect unto the Lord Christ as mediator, have been sufficiently before confirmed.[4]

2. There is an agreement between saving graces and spiritual gifts with respect unto their immediate efficient cause. They are, both sorts of them, wrought by the power of the Holy Ghost. As to what concerns the former, or saving grace, I have already treated of that argument at large; nor will any deny that the Holy Ghost is the author of these graces but those that deny that there are any such. That these gifts are so wrought by him is expressly declared wherever there is mention of them, in general or particular. Wherefore, when they acknowledge that there were such gifts, all confess him to be their author. By whom he is denied so to be, it is only because they deny the continuance of any such gifts in the church of God. But this is that which we shall disprove.

---

4   E.g., Πνευματολογια, or, A Discourse concerning the Holy Spirit, bk. 2, chaps. 3–4.

3. Herein also they agree, that both sorts of them are designed unto the good, benefit, ornament, and glory of the church. The church is the proper seat and subject of them, to it are they granted, and in it do they reside. For Christ is given to be the "head over all things to the church, which is his body, the fullness of him that filleth all in all" (Eph. 1:22–23). But this church falls under a double consideration. First, as it is believing; secondly, as it is professing. In the first respect absolutely it is invisible, and as such is the peculiar subject of saving grace. This is that church which "Christ loved and gave himself for, that he might sanctify and cleanse it, and present it unto himself a glorious church, not having spot, or wrinkle, or any such thing, but that it should be holy and without blemish" (Eph. 5:26–27).[5] This is the work of saving grace, and by a participation thereof do men become members of this church, and not otherwise. And hereby is the professing church quickened and enabled unto profession in an acceptable manner. For the elect receive grace unto this end in this world, that they may glorify Christ and the gospel in the exercise of it (Col. 1:6; John 15:8). But gifts are bestowed on the professing church to render it visible in such a way as whereby God is glorified. Grace gives an invisible life to the church, gifts give it a visible profession. For hence does the church become organic, and disposed into that order which is beautiful and comely. Where any church is organized merely by outward rules, perhaps of their own devising, and makes profession only in an attendance unto outward order, not following the leading of the Spirit in the communication of his gifts, both as to order and discharge of the duties of profession, it is but the image of a church, wanting an animating principle and form. That profession which renders a church visible according to the mind of Christ, is the orderly exercise of the spiritual gifts bestowed on it, in a conversation evidencing the invisible principle of saving grace. Now, these gifts are conferred on the church in order unto "the edification of itself in love" (Eph. 4:16), as also for the propagation of its profession in the world, as shall be declared afterward. Wherefore, both of these sorts have in general the same end, or are given by Christ unto the same purpose, namely, the good and benefit of the church, as they are respectively suited to promote them.

It may also be added, that they agree herein, that they have both the same respect unto the bounty of Christ. Hence every grace is a gift, that which is given and freely bestowed on them that have it (Matt. 13:11; Phil. 1:29). And although, on the other side, every gift be not a grace, yet, proceeding from gracious favor and bounty, they are so called (Rom. 12:6; Eph. 4:7). How, in their due exercise, they are mutually helpful and assistant unto each other, shall be declared afterward.

---

5   The correct reference is Eph. 5:25–27.

SEVEN DIFFERENCES

Secondly, we may consider wherein the difference lies or does consist which is between these spiritual gifts and sanctifying graces. And this may be seen in sundry instances. As,

1. Saving graces are καρπός, the "fruit" or fruits "of the Spirit" (Gal. 5:22; Eph. 5:9; Phil. 1:11). Now, fruits proceed from an abiding root and stock, of whose nature they do partake. There must be a "good tree" to bring forth "good fruit" (Matt. 12:33). No external watering or applications unto the earth will cause it to bring forth useful fruits, unless there are roots from which they spring and are educed.[6] The Holy Spirit is as the root unto these fruits, the root which bears them, and which they do not bear (Rom. 11:18). Therefore, in order of nature, is he given unto men before the production of any of these fruits. Thereby are they engrafted into the olive, are made such branches in Christ, the true vine, as derive vital juice, nourishment, and fructifying[7] virtue from him, even by the Spirit. So is he "a well of water springing up into everlasting life" (John 4:14). He is a spring in believers. And all saving graces are but waters arising from that living, overflowing spring. From him, as a root or spring, as an eternal virtue, power, or principle, do all these fruits come. To this end does he dwell in them and abide with them, according to the promise of our Lord Jesus Christ (John 14:17; Rom. 8:11; 1 Cor. 3:16), whereby the Lord Christ effects his purpose in "ordaining his disciples to bring forth fruit" that should "remain" (John 15:16). In the place of his holy residence, he works these effects freely, according to his own will. And there is nothing that has the true nature of saving grace but what is so a *fruit of the Spirit*. We have not first these graces, and then by virtue of them receive the Spirit, for whence[8] should we have them of ourselves? But the Spirit bestowed on us works them in us, and gives them a spiritual, divine nature, in conformity unto his own.

With gifts, singly considered, it is otherwise. They are indeed works and effects, but not properly fruits of the Spirit, nor are they anywhere so called. They are effects of his operation upon men, not fruits of his working in them; and, therefore, many receive these gifts who never receive the Spirit as to the principal end for which he is promised. They receive him not to sanctify and make them temples unto God, though metonymically,[9] with respect unto his

6 I.e., developed; inferred.
7 I.e., fruit-bearing.
8 I.e., where.
9 I.e., using the name of one thing for another because an attribute of it is associated with it.

outward effects, they may be said to be made partakers of him. This renders them of a different nature and kind from saving graces. For whereas there is an agreement and coincidence between them in the respects before mentioned, and whereas the seat and subject of them—that is, of gifts absolutely, and principally of graces also—is the mind, the difference of their nature proceeds from the different manner of their communication from the Holy Spirit.

2. Saving grace proceeds from, or is the effect and fruit of, electing love. This I have proved before, in our inquiry into the nature of holiness.[10] See it directly asserted (Eph. 1:3–4; 2 Thess. 2:13; Acts 2:47; 13:48). Whom God graciously chooses and designs unto eternal life, them he prepares for it by the communication of the means which are necessary unto that end (Rom. 8:28–30). Hereof sanctification, or the communication of saving grace, is comprehensive. For we are "chosen to salvation through sanctification of the Spirit" (2 Thess. 2:13), for this is that whereby we are "made meet to be partakers of the inheritance of the saints in light" (Col. 1:12). The end of God in election is the sonship and salvation of the elect, "to the praise of the glory of his grace" (Eph. 1:5–6). And this cannot be unless his image be renewed in them in holiness or saving graces. These, therefore, he works in them, in pursuit of his eternal purpose therein.¶

But gifts, on the other hand, which are no more but so, and where they are solitary or alone, are only the effects of a temporary election. Thus, God chooses some men unto some office in the church, or unto some work in the world. As this includes a preferring them before or above others, or the using them when others are not used, we call it election. And in itself it is their fitting for and separation unto their office or work. And this temporary election is the cause and rule of the dispensation of gifts. So, he chose Saul to be king over his people, and gave him thereon "another heart,"[11] or gifts fitting him for rule and government. So, our Lord Jesus Christ chose and called at the first twelve to be his apostles, and gave unto them all alike miraculous gifts. His temporary choice of them was the ground of his communication of gifts unto them. By virtue hereof no saving graces were communicated unto them, for one of them never arrived unto a participation of them. "Have not I," says our Savior unto them, "chosen you twelve, and one of you is a devil?" (John 6:70). He had chosen them unto their office, and endowed them with extraordinary gifts for the discharge thereof. But one of them being not "chosen unto salvation before the foundation of the world,"[12] being not ordained

---

10 See, e.g., Πνευματολογια, or, A Discourse concerning the Holy Spirit, bk. 4.

11 1 Sam. 10:9.

12 Eph. 1:4.

unto eternal life, but, on the other side, being the son of perdition, or one certainly appointed unto destruction, or before of old ordained unto that condemnation, he continued void of all sanctifying graces, so as, unto any acceptation with God, he was in no better condition than the devil himself, whose work he was to do. Yet was he, by virtue of this choice unto the office of apostleship for a season, endowed with the same spiritual gifts that the others were. And this distinction our Savior himself does plainly lay down. For whereas he says, "Have not I chosen you twelve" (John 6:70)—that is, with a temporary choice unto office—he says, "I speak not of you all; I know whom I have chosen" (John 13:18), so excepting Judas from that number, as is afterward expressly declared. For the election which here he intends is that which is accompanied with an infallible ordination unto abiding fruit-bearing, that is, eternal election, wherein Judas had no interest (John 15:16).

And thus, it is in general, and in other instances. When God chooses anyone to eternal life, he will, in pursuit of that purpose of his, communicate saving grace unto them. And although all believers have gifts also sufficient to enable them unto the discharge of their duty in their station or condition in the church, yet they do not depend on the decree of election. And where God calls any, or chooses any, unto an office, charge, or work in the church, he always furnishes him with gifts suited unto the end of them. He does not so, indeed, unto all that will take any office unto themselves, but he does so unto all whom he calls thereunto. Yea, his call is no otherwise known but by the gifts which he communicates for the discharge of the work or office whereunto any are called. In common use, I confess, all things run contrary hereunto. Most men greatly insist on the necessity of an outward call unto the office of the ministry, and so far, no doubt, they do well, for "God is the God of order,"[13] that is, of his own. But whereas they limit this outward call of theirs unto certain persons, ways, modes, and ceremonies of their own, without which they will not allow that any man is rightly called unto the ministry, they do but contend to oppress the consciences of others by their power and with their inventions. But their most pernicious mistake is yet remaining. So that persons have, or do receive, an outward call in their mode and way, which what it has of a call in it I know not, they are not solicitous[14] whether they are called of God or not. For they continually admit them unto their outward call on whom God has bestowed no spiritual gifts to fit them for their office; whence it is as evident as if written with the beams of the sun,

13   1 Cor. 14:33.
14   I.e., meticulous; careful.

that he never called them thereunto. They are as watchful as they are able that God himself shall impose none on them besides their way and order, or their call. For let a man be furnished with ministerial gifts never so excellent, yet if he will not come up to their call, they will do what lies in them forever to shut him out of the ministry. But they will impose upon God without his call every day. For if they ordain anyone in their way unto an office, though he have no more of spiritual gifts than Balaam's ass, yet, if you will believe them, Christ must accept of him for a minister of his, whether he will or not. But let men dispose of things as they please, and as it seems good unto them, Christ has no other order in this matter, but "As everyone hath received the gift, so let them minister, as good stewards of the manifold grace of God" (1 Pet. 4:10; Rom. 12:6–8). It is true that no man ought to take upon him the office of the ministry but he that is, and until he be, solemnly called and set apart thereunto by the church. But it is no less true that no church has either rule or right so to call or set apart anyone to the ministry whom Christ has not previously called by the communication of spiritual gifts necessary to the discharge of his office. And these things must be largely insisted on afterward.

3. Saving grace is an effect of the covenant, and bestowed in the accomplishment and by virtue of the promises thereof. This has been declared elsewhere at large, where we treated of regeneration and sanctification.[15] All that are taken into this covenant are sanctified and made holy. There is no grace designed unto any in the eternal purpose of God, none purchased or procured by the mediation of Christ, but it is comprised in and exhibited by the promises of the covenant. Wherefore, they only who are taken into that covenant are made partakers of saving grace, and they are all so.¶

Things are not absolutely so with respect unto spiritual gifts, although they also in some sense belong unto the covenant. For the promises of the covenant are of two sorts. (1) Such as belong unto the internal form and essence of it. (2) Such as belong unto its outward administration, that is, the ways and means whereby its internal grace is made effectual. Saving grace proceeds from the former, gifts relate unto the latter. For all the promises of the plentiful effusion of the Spirit under the New Testament, which are frequently applied unto him as he works and effects evangelical gifts, extraordinary and ordinary, in men, do belong unto the new covenant—not as unto its internal essence and form, but as unto its outward administration. And if you overthrow this distinction, that the covenant is considered either with respect unto its internal grace or its external administration, everything in religion will be

---

15   Owen is referring to *Πνευματολογια, or, A Discourse concerning the Holy Spirit*, bks. 3–4.

cast into confusion. Take away internal grace, as some do, and the whole is rendered a mere outside appearance. Take away the outward administration, and all spiritual gifts and order thereon depending must cease. But as it is possible that some may belong unto the covenant with respect unto internal grace who are no way taken into the external administration of it, as elect infants who die before they are baptized, so it is frequent that some may belong to the covenant with respect to its outward administration, by virtue of spiritual gifts, who are not made partakers of its inward effectual grace.

4. Saving grace has an immediate respect unto the priestly office of Jesus Christ, with the discharge thereof in his oblation and intercession. There is, I acknowledge, no gracious communication unto men that respects any one office of Christ exclusively unto the other. For his whole mediation has an influence into all that we receive from God in a way of favor or grace. And it is his person, as vested with all his offices, that is the immediate fountain of all grace unto us. But yet something may, yea, sundry things do, peculiarly respect some one of his offices, and are the immediate effects of the virtue and efficacy thereof. So is our reconciliation and peace with God the peculiar effect of his oblation, which as a priest he offered unto God. And so in like manner is our sanctification also, wherein we are washed and cleansed from our sins in his blood (Eph. 5:25–26; Titus 2:14). And although grace be wrought in us by the administration of the kingly power of Christ, yet it is in the pursuit of what he has done for us as a priest, and for the making of it effectual unto us. For by his kingly power he makes effectual the fruits of his oblation and intercession.¶

But gifts proceed solely from the regal office and power of Christ. They have a remote respect unto and foundation in the death of Christ, in that they are all given and distributed unto and for the good of that church which he purchased with his own blood. But immediately they are effects only of his kingly power. Hence authority to give and dispose them is commonly placed as a consequent of his exaltation at the right hand of God, or with respect thereunto (Matt. 28:18; Acts 2:33). This the apostle declares at large (Eph. 4:7–8, 11–12). Christ being exalted at the right hand of God, all power in heaven and earth being given unto him, and he being given to be head over all things unto the church, and having for that end received the promise of the Spirit from the Father, he gives out these gifts as it seems good unto him. And the continuation of their communication is not the least evidence of the continuance of the exercise of his kingdom.¶

For besides the faithful testimony of the word to that purpose, there is a threefold evidence thereof, giving us experience of it. (1) His communication of saving grace in the regeneration, conversion, and sanctification of the elect.

268 A DISCOURSE OF SPIRITUAL GIFTS

For these things he works immediately by his kingly power. And while there are any in the world savingly called and sanctified, he leaves not himself without witness as to his kingly power over all flesh, whereon, he "gives eternal life unto as many as the Father hath given him" (John 17:2). But this evidence is wholly invisible unto the world, neither is it capable of receiving it when tendered, because it cannot receive the Spirit, nor sees him, nor knows him (John 14:17). Nor are the things thereof exposed to the judgment of sense or reason (1 Cor. 2:9–10). (2) Another evidence hereof is given in the judgments that he executes in the world, and the outward protection which he affords unto his church. On both these there are evident impressions of the continued actual exercise of his divine power and authority. For in the judgments that he executes on persons and nations that either reject the gospel or persecute it, especially in some signal and uncontrollable instance, as also in the guidance, deliverance, and protection of his church, he manifests that though he was dead, yet he is alive, and has the keys of hell and of death. But yet because he is, on the one hand, pleased to exercise great patience toward many of his open, stubborn adversaries, yea, the greatest of them, suffering them to walk and prosper in their own ways. And to leave his church unto various trials and distresses, his power is much hid from the world at present in these dispensations. (3) The third evidence of the continuance of the administration of his mediatory kingdom consists in his dispensation, of these spiritual gifts, which are properly the powers of the new world. For such is the nature of them and their use, such the sovereignty that appears in their distribution, such their distinction and difference from all natural endowments, that even the world cannot but take notice of them, though it violently hate and persecute them, and the church is abundantly satisfied with the sense of the power of Christ in them. Moreover, the principal end of these gifts is to enable the officers of the church unto the due administration of all the laws and ordinances of Christ unto its edification. But all these laws and ordinances, these offices and officers, he gives unto the church as the Lord over his own house, as the sole sovereign lawgiver and ruler thereof.

5. They differ as unto the event even in this world they may come unto, and ofttimes actually do so accordingly. For all gifts, the best of them, and that in the highest degree wherein they may be attained in this life, may be utterly lost or taken away. The law of their communication is, that he who improves not that talent or measure of them which he has received, it shall be taken from him. For whereas they are given for no other end but to trade with, according to the several capacities and opportunities that men have in the church, or their families, or their own private exercise, if that be utterly

neglected, to what end should they be left unto rust and uselessness in the minds of any? Accordingly, we find it to come to pass. Some neglect them, some reject them, and from both sorts they are judicially taken away. Such we have among us. Some there are who had received considerable spiritual abilities for evangelical administrations, but after a while they have fallen into an outward state of things wherein, as they suppose, they shall have no advantage by them, yea, that their exercise would turn to their disadvantage, and thereon do wholly neglect them. By this means they have insensibly decayed, until they become as devoid of spiritual abilities as if they never had experience of any assistance in that kind. They can no more either pray, or speak, or evidence the power of the Spirit of God in anything unto the edification of the church. "Their arm is dried up, and their right eye is utterly darkened" (Zech. 11:17). And this sometimes they come to be sensible of, yea, ashamed of, and yet cannot retrieve themselves. But, for the most part, they fall into such a state as wherein the profession and use of them become, as they suppose, inconsistent with their present interest, and so they openly renounce all concern in them. Neither, for the most part, do they stay here, but after they have rejected them in themselves, and espoused lazy, profitable, outward helps in their room, they blaspheme the author of them in others, and declare them all to be delusions, fancies, and imaginations. And if anyone has the confidence to own the assistance of the Holy Spirit in the discharge of the duties of the gospel unto the edification of the church, he becomes unto them a scorn and reproach. These are branches cut off from the Vine, whom men gather, or those whose miserable condition is described by the apostle (Heb. 6:4–6). But one way or other these gifts may be utterly lost or taken away from them who have once received them, and that whether they be ordinary or extraordinary. There is no kind of them, no degree of them, that can give us any security that they shall be always continued with us, or at all beyond our diligent attendance unto their use and exercise.¶

With saving grace, it is not so. It is, indeed, subject unto various decays in us, and its thriving or flourishing in our souls depends upon and answers unto our diligent endeavor in the use of all means of holiness ordinarily (2 Pet. 1:5–10). For besides that no man can have the least evidence of anything of this grace in him if he be totally negligent in its exercise and improvement, so no man ought to expect that it will thrive or abound in him unless he constantly and diligently attend unto it, and give up himself in all things to its conduct—but yet, as to the continuance of it in the souls of the elect, as to the life and being of its principle, and its principal effect in habitual conformity unto God and his will, it is secured in the covenant of grace.

6. On whomsoever saving grace is bestowed, it is so firstly and principally for himself and his own good. It is a fruit of the special love and kindness of God unto his own soul (Jer. 31:3). This both the nature and all the ends of it do declare. For it is given unto us to renew the image of God in us, to make us like unto him, to restore our nature, enable us unto obedience, and to make us meet[16] for the inheritance of the saints in light. But yet we must take heed that we think not that grace is bestowed on any merely for themselves. For, indeed, it is that wherein God designs a good unto all: *Vir bonus commune bonum,* "A good man is a good to all" ([see] Mic. 5:7).⁋

And, therefore, God in the communication of saving grace unto any has a threefold respect unto others, which it is the duty of them that receive it diligently to consider and attend unto. (1) He intends to give an example by it of what is his will, and what he approves of. And, therefore, he requires of them in whom it is such fruits in holy obedience as may express the example of a holy life in the world, according to the will of God and unto his glory. Hereby does he further the salvation of the elect (1 Pet. 3:1–2; 1 Cor. 7:16). Convince the unbelieving world at present (1 Pet. 2:12, 15; 3:16). And condemn it hereafter (Heb. 11:7). And himself is glorified (Matt 5:16). Let no man, therefore, think that because grace is firstly and principally given him for himself and his own spiritual advantage, he must not account for it also with respect unto those other designs of God. Yea, he who, in the exercise of what he esteems grace, has respect only unto himself, gives an evidence that he never had any that was genuine and of the right kind. (2) Fruitfulness unto the benefiting of others is hence also expected. Holy obedience, the effect of saving grace, is frequently expressed in the Scripture by fruits and fruitfulness (Col. 1:10). And these fruits, or the things which others are to feed upon and to be sustained by, are to be borne by the plants of the Lord, the trees of righteousness. The fruits of love, charity, bounty, mercy, wisdom, are those whereby grace is rendered useful in the world, and is taken notice of as that which is lovely and desirable (Eph. 2:10). (3) God requires that by the exercise of grace the doctrine of the gospel be adorned and propagated. This doctrine is from God; our profession is our avowing of it so to be. What it is the world knows not, but takes its measure of it from what it observes in them by whom it is professed. And it is the unprofitable, flagitious[17] lives of Christians that have almost thrust the gospel out of the world with contempt. But the care that it be adorned, that it be glorified, is committed of God unto

---

16   I.e., fitting; proper.
17   I.e., villainous.

everyone on whom he bestows the least of saving grace. And this is to be done only by the guidance of a holy conversation in conformity thereunto. And many other such blessed ends there are, wherein God has respect unto the good and advantage of other men in the collation[18] of saving grace upon any. And if gracious persons are not more useful than others in all things that may have a real benefit in them unto mankind, it is their sin and shame. But yet, after all, grace is principally and in the first place given unto men for themselves, their own good and spiritual advantage, out of love to their souls, and in order unto their eternal blessedness. All other effects are but secondary ends of it.¶

But as unto these spiritual gifts it is quite otherwise. They are not in the first place bestowed on any for their own sakes or their own good, but for the good and benefit of others. So, the apostle expressly declares, "The manifestation of the Spirit is given to every man to profit withal" (1 Cor. 12:7). These gifts, whereby the Spirit evidences and manifests his power, are bestowed on men for this very end, that they may profit and benefit others in their edification. And yet, also, where they are duly improved, they tend much to the spiritual advantage of them on whom they are bestowed, as we shall see afterward. Wherefore, as grace is primarily given unto us for ourselves, and secondarily for the good of others, so gifts are bestowed in the first place for the edification of others, and secondly for our own spiritual advantage also.

7. The principal difference between them is in their nature and kind, discovering itself in the different subjects, operations, and effects. For those already insisted on are principally from external causes and considerations. (1) As to the different subjects of them, spiritual gifts are placed and seated in the mind or understanding only, whether they are ordinary or extraordinary, they have no other hold or residence in the soul. And they are in the mind as it is notional and theoretical, rather than as it is practical. They are intellectual abilities, and no more. I speak of them which have any residence in us. For some gifts, as miracles and tongues, consisted only in a transient operation of an extraordinary power. Of all others, illumination is the foundation, and spiritual light their matter. So the apostle declares in his order of expression (Heb. 6:4). The will, and the affections, and the conscience are unconcerned in them. Wherefore, they change not the heart with power, although they may reform the life by the efficacy of light. And although God does not ordinarily bestow them on flagitious persons, nor continue them with such as after the reception of them become flagitious, yet they may be in those who

18   I.e., institution; placing in proper order.

are unrenewed, and have nothing in them to preserve men absolutely from the worst of sins. But saving grace possesses the whole soul. Men are thereby sanctified throughout, in the whole "spirit and soul and body" (1 Thess. 5:23), as has been at large declared. Not only is the mind savingly enlightened, but there is a principle of spiritual life infused into the whole soul, enabling it in all its powers and faculties to act obedientially unto God, whose nature has been fully explained elsewhere. Hence (2) they differ in their operations. For grace changes and transforms the whole soul into its own nature (Isa. 11:6–8; Rom. 6:17; 12:2; 2 Cor. 3:18). It is a new, a divine nature unto the soul, and is in it a habit disposing, inclining, and enabling of it unto obedience. It acts itself in faith, love, and holiness in all things. But gifts of themselves have not this power nor these operations. They may and do, in those who are possessed of them in and under their exercise, make great impression on their own affections, but they change not the heart, they renew not the mind, they transform not the soul into the image of God. Hence, where grace is predominant, every notion of light and truth which is communicated unto the mind is immediately turned into practice, by having the whole soul cast into the mold of it. Where only gifts bear sway, the use of it in duties unto edification is best, whereunto it is designed. (3) As to effects or consequents, the great difference is that on the part of Christ. Christ does thereby dwell and reside in our hearts, when concerning many of those who have been made partakers of these other spiritual endowments, he will say, "Depart from me, I never knew you,"[19] which he will not say of anyone whose soul he has inhabited.

These are some of the principal agreements and differences between saving graces and spiritual gifts, both sorts of them being wrought in believers by "that one and the self-same Spirit, which divideth to everyone severally as he will."[20] And for a close of this discourse I shall only add, that where these graces and gifts, in any eminency or good degree, are bestowed on the same persons, they are exceedingly helpful unto each other. A soul sanctified by saving grace is the only proper soil for gifts to flourish in. Grace influences gifts unto a due exercise, prevents their abuse, stirs them up unto proper occasions, keeps them from being a matter of pride or contention, and subordinates them in all things unto the glory of God. When the actings of grace and gifts are inseparable, as when in prayer the Spirit is a Spirit of grace and supplication, the grace and gift of it working together, when utterance in

19 Matt. 7:23.
20 1 Cor. 12:11.

other duties is always accompanied with faith and love, then is God glorified and our own salvation promoted. Then have edifying gifts a beauty and luster upon them, and generally are most successful, when they are clothed and adorned with humility, meekness, a reverence of God, and compassion for the souls of men. Yea, when there is no evidence, no manifestation of their being accompanied with these and the like graces, they are but as a parable or wise saying in the mouth of a fool. Gifts, on the other side, excite and stir up grace unto its proper exercise and operation. How often is faith, love, and delight in God, excited and drawn forth unto special exercise in believers by the use of their own gifts.¶

And thus much may suffice as to the nature of these gifts in general. We next consider them under their most general distributions.

3

Of Gifts and Offices Extraordinary; and First of Offices

THE SPIRITUAL GIFTS whereof we treat respect either powers and duties in the church, or duties only. Gifts that respect powers and duties are of two sorts, or there have been, or are at any time, two sorts of such powers and duties, the first whereof was extraordinary, the latter ordinary, and consequently the gifts subservient unto them must be of two sorts also, which must further be cleared.

Wherever power is given by Christ unto his churches, and duties are required in the execution of that power, unto the ends of his spiritual kingdom, to be performed by virtue thereof, there is an office in the church. For an ecclesiastical office is a special power given by Christ unto any person or persons for the performance of special duties belonging unto the edification of the church in a special manner. And these offices have been of two sorts. First, extraordinary; secondly, ordinary. Some seem to deny that there was ever any such thing as extraordinary power or extraordinary offices in the church. For they do provide successors unto all who are pleaded to have been of that kind, and those such as look how far short they come of them in other things, do exceed them in power and rule. I shall not contend about words, and shall therefore only inquire what it was that constituted them to be officers of Christ in his church whom thence we call extraordinary. And then, if others can duly lay claim unto them, they may be allowed to pass for their successors.

There are four things which constitute an extraordinary officer in the church of God, and consequently are required in and do constitute an extraordinary office. (1) An extraordinary call unto an office, such as none other has or can have, by virtue of any law, order, or constitution whatever. (2) An extraordinary power communicated unto persons so called, enabling them to act what they are so called unto, wherein the essence of any office does consist. (3) Extraordinary gifts for the exercise and discharge of that power. (4) Extraordinary employment as to its extent and measure, requiring extraordinary labor, travail, zeal, and self-denial. All these do and must concur in that office and unto those offices which we call extraordinary.

Thus was it with the apostles, prophets, and evangelists at the first, which were all extraordinary teaching officers in the church, and all that ever were so (1 Cor. 12:28; Eph. 4:11). Besides these, there were, at the first planting of the church, persons endued with extraordinary gifts, as of miracles, healing, and tongues, which did not of themselves constitute them officers, but do belong to the second head of gifts, which concern duties only. Howbeit these gifts were always most eminently bestowed on them who were called unto the extraordinary offices mentioned: "I thank my God, I speak with tongues more than ye all" (1 Cor. 14:18). They had the same gift some of them, but the apostle had it in a more eminent degree (Matt. 10:8). And we may treat briefly in our passage of these several sorts of extraordinary officers.

APOSTLES

First, for the apostles, they had a double call, mission, and commission, or a twofold apostleship. Their first call was unto a subserviency unto the personal ministry of Jesus Christ. For he was a "minister of the circumcision for the truth of God, to confirm the promises made unto the fathers" (Rom. 15:8). In the discharge of this his personal ministry, it was necessary that he should have peculiar servants and officers under him, to prepare his way and work, and to attend him therein. So "he ordained twelve, that they should be with him, and that he might send them forth to preach" (Mark 3:14). This was the substance of their first call and work, namely, to attend the presence of Christ, and to go forth to preach as he gave them order. Hence because he was in his own person, as to his prophetical office, the "minister only of the circumcision," being therein, according to all the promises, sent only to the "lost sheep of the house of Israel," he confined those who were to be thus assistant unto him in that his special work and ministry, and while they were so, unto the same persons and people, expressly prohibiting them to extend their line or measure any further. "Go not," says he, "into the way of the Gentiles, and into any city of the Samaritans enter ye not; but go rather to the lost sheep of the house of Israel" (Matt. 10:5).[1] This "rather" was absolutely exclusive of the others during his personal

---

1 The correct reference is Matt. 10:5–6.

ministry, and afterward included only the preeminence of the Israelites, that they were to have the gospel offered unto them in the first place: "It was necessary that the Word of God should first have been spoken to you" (Acts 13:46).

And this, it may be, occasioned that difference which was afterward among them, whether their ministry extended unto the Gentiles or not; as we may see (Acts 10 and 11). But whereas our Savior, in that commission by virtue whereof they were to act after his resurrection, had extended their office and power expressly to "all nations" (Matt. 28:19), or to "every creature in all the world" (Mark 16:15), a man would wonder whence that uncertainty should arise. I am persuaded that God suffered it so to be that the calling of the Gentiles might be more signalized, or made more eminent thereby. For whereas this was the great "mystery which in other ages was not made known," but "hid in God," namely, "that the Gentiles should be fellow-heirs, and of the same body, and partakers of his promise in Christ," that is, of the promise made unto Abraham, "by the gospel" (Eph. 3:3, 5–11), it being now to be laid open and displayed, he would by their hesitation about it have it searched into, examined, tried, and proved, that the faith of the church might never be shaken about it in after ages. And, in like manner, when God at any time suffers differences and doubts about the truth or his worship to arise in the church, he does it for holy ends, although for the present we may not be able to discover them. But this ministry of the apostles, with its powers and duties, this apostleship, which extended only unto the church of the Jews, ceased at the death of Christ, or at the end of his own personal ministry in this world. Nor can any, I suppose, pretend unto a succession to them therein. Who or what peculiar instruments he will use and employ for the final recovery of that miserable, lost people, whether he will do it by an ordinary or an extraordinary ministry, by gifts miraculous, or by the naked efficacy of the gospel, is known only in his own holy wisdom and counsel. The conjectures of men about these things are vain and fruitless; for although the promises under the Old Testament for the calling of the Gentiles were far more clear and numerous than those which remain concerning the recalling of the Jews, yet because the manner, way, and all other circumstances, were obscured, the whole is called a mystery hid in God from all the former ages of the church. Much more, therefore, may the way and manner of the recalling of the Jews be esteemed a hidden mystery; as indeed it is, notwithstanding the dreams and conjectures of too many.[2]

---

2   For Puritan eschatology, see Crawford Gribben, *The Puritan Millennium: Literature and Theology, 1550–1682*, rev. ed., Studies in Christian History and Thought (Milton Keynes, UK: Paternoster,

But these same apostles, the same individual persons, Judas only excepted, had another call, unto that office of apostleship which had respect unto the whole work and interest of Christ in the world. They were now to be made princes in all lands, rulers, leaders in spiritual things of all the inhabitants of the earth (Ps. 45:16). And to make this call the more conspicuous and evident, as also because it includes in it the institution and nature of the office itself whereunto they were called, our blessed Savior proceeds in it by sundry degrees. For (1) he gave unto them a promise of power for their office, or office-power (Matt 16:19). So, he promised unto them, in the person of Peter, the "keys of the kingdom of heaven," or a power of spiritual binding and loosing of sinners, of remitting or retaining sin, by the doctrine of the gospel (Matt. 18:18; John 20:23). (2) He actually collated a right unto that power upon them, expressed by an outward pledge:

> Then said Jesus to them again, "Peace be unto you: as my Father hath sent me, even so send I you." And when he had said this, he breathed on them, and saith unto them, "Receive ye the Holy Ghost: whose soever sins ye remit, they are remitted unto them; and whose soever sins ye retain, they are retained." (John 20:21–23)

And this communication of the Holy Ghost was such as gave them a peculiar right and title unto their office, but not a right and power unto its exercise. (3) He sealed, as it were, their commission which they had for the discharge of their office, containing the whole warranty they had to enter upon the world, and subdue it unto the obedience of the gospel: "Go teach, baptize, command" (Matt. 28:18–20). But yet, (4) all these things did not absolutely give them a present power for the exercise of that office whereunto they were called, or at least a limitation was put for a season upon it. For under all this provision and furniture,[3] they are commanded to stay at Jerusalem, and not address themselves unto the discharge of their office, until that were fulfilled which gave it its completeness and perfection (Acts 1:4, 8). Wherefore it is said, that after his ascension into heaven, he "gave some to be apostles" (Eph. 4:8, 11). He gave not any completely to be apostles until then.¶

He had before appointed the office, designed the persons, given them their commission, with the visible pledge of the power they should afterward receive. But there yet remained the communication of extraordinary gifts unto

---

2008); Iain H. Murray, *The Puritan Hope: Revival and the Interpretation of Prophecy* (Edinburgh: Banner of Truth, 1971).

3   I.e., equipment that is necessary, useful, or desirable.

them, to enable them unto the discharge of their office. And this was that which, after the ascension of Christ, they received on the day of Pentecost, as it is related (Acts 2). And this was so essentially necessary unto their office that the Lord Christ is said therein to give some to be apostles. For without these gifts they were not so, nor could discharge that office unto his honor and glory. And these things all concurred to the constitution of this office, with the call of any persons to the discharge of it. The office itself was instituted by Christ, the designation and call of the persons unto this office was an immediate act of Christ. So also was their commission and power, and the extraordinary gifts which he endowed them with. And whereas the Lord Christ is said to give this office and these officers after his ascension, namely, in the communication of the gifts of the Holy Ghost unto those officers for the discharge of that office, it is evident that all office-power depends on the communication of gifts, whether extraordinary or ordinary. But where any of these is wanting, there is no apostle, nor any successor of one apostle. Therefore, when Paul was afterward added unto the twelve in the same power and office, he was careful to declare how he received both call, commission, and power immediately from Jesus Christ: "Paul an apostle, not of men, neither by man, but by Jesus Christ, and God the Father, who raised him from the dead" (Gal. 1:1). Whereas those who pretend to be their successors, if they will speak the truth, must say that they are what they are neither of Jesus Christ nor God the Father, but of men and by man. However, they neither dare nor will pretend so to be of God and Christ as not to be called by the ministry of man, which evacuates the pretense of succession in this office.

Furthermore, unto the office described there belongs the measure and extent of its power objectively, and the power itself intensively or subjectively. For the first, the object of apostolical power was twofold: First, the world to be converted; second, the churches gathered of those that were converted, whether Jews or Gentiles.

Objective Power

1. For the first, their commission extended to all the world; and every apostle had right, power, and authority to "preach the gospel to every creature under heaven," as he had opportunity so to do (Matt. 28:18–20; Mark 16:15; Rom. 10:14–18). Now, whereas it was impossible that any one person should pass through the whole world in the pursuit of this right and power; and whereas, for that cause, our Lord had ordained twelve to that purpose, that the work might the more effectually be carried on by their endeavors, it is highly probable that they did by agreement distribute the nations into certain lots

and portions, which they singly took upon them to instruct. So there was an agreement between Paul on the one hand with Barnabas, and Peter, James, and John, on the other, that they should go to the Gentiles, and the other take more special care of the Jews (Gal. 2:7–9). And the same apostle afterward designed, to avoid the line or allotment of others, to preach the gospel where the people were not allotted unto the special charge of any other (2 Cor. 10:16). But yet this was not so appointed as if their power was limited thereby, or that any of them came short in his apostolical power in any other place in the world, as well as that wherein for conveniency he particularly exercised his ministry. For the power of everyone still equally extended unto all nations, although they could not always exercise it in all places alike. Nor did that express agreement that was between Peter and Paul, about the Gentiles and the circumcision, discharge them of their duty, that the one should have more regard unto the circumcision or the other unto the Gentiles, nor did it limit their power or bound their apostolical authority, but only directed the exercise of it as unto the principal intention and design. Wherefore, as to the right and authority of preaching the gospel and converting persons unto the faith, the whole world fell equally under the care, and was in the commission of every apostle, although they applied themselves unto the discharge of this work in particular according to their own wisdom and choice, under the guidance and disposal of the providence of God. And, as I will not deny but that it is the duty of every Christian, and much more of every minister of the gospel, to promote the knowledge of Christ unto all mankind, as they have opportunities and advantages so to do, yet I must say, if there be any who pretend to be successors of the apostles as to the extent of their office-power unto all nations, notwithstanding whatever they may pretend of such an agreement to take up with a portion accommodated unto their ease and interest, while so many nations of the earth lie unattempted as to the preaching of the gospel, they will one day be found transgressors of their own profession, and will be dealt with accordingly.

2. Out of the world, by the preaching of the gospel, persons were called, converted, and thereon gathered into holy societies or churches, for the celebration of gospel worship and their own mutual edification. All these churches, wherever they were called and planted in the whole world, were equally under the authority of every apostle. Where any church was called and planted by any particular apostle, there was a peculiar relation between him and them, and so a peculiar mutual care and love; nor could it otherwise be. So, the apostle Paul pleads a special interest in the Corinthians and others, unto whom he had been a spiritual father in their conversion, and

the instrument of forming Christ in them. Such churches, therefore, as were of their own peculiar calling and planting, it is probable they did everyone take care of in a peculiar manner. But yet no limitation of the apostolical power ensued hereon. Every apostle had still the care of all the churches on him, and apostolic authority in every church in the world equally, which he might exercise as occasion did require. Thus Paul affirms that the "care of all the churches came upon him daily" (2 Cor. 11:28). And it was the crime of Diotrephes, for which he is branded, that he opposed the apostolical power of John in that church where probably he was the teacher (3 John 9–10). But what power, now, over all churches, or authority in all churches, some may fancy or claim to themselves, I know not. But it were to be wished that men would reckon that care and labor are as extensive in this case as power and authority.

Subjective Power

Again, the power of this extraordinary office may be considered intensively or formally what it was. And this, in one word, was all the power that the Lord Christ has given or thought meet to make use of for the edification of the church. I shall give a brief description of it in some few general instances.¶

1. It was a power of administering all the ordinances of Christ in the way and manner of his appointment. Every apostle in all places had power to preach the word, to administer the sacraments, to ordain elders, and to do whatever else belonged unto the worship of the gospel. But yet they had not power to do any of these things any otherwise but as the Lord Christ had appointed them to be done. They could not baptize any but believers and their seed (Acts 8:36–38; 16:15). They could not administer the Lord's Supper to any but the church and in the church (1 Cor. 10:16–17; 11:17–34). They could not ordain elders but by the suffrage and election of the people (Acts 14:23). Those, indeed, who pretend to be their successors plead for such a right in themselves unto some, if not all, gospel administrations, as that they may take liberty to dispose of them at their pleasure, by their sole authority, without any regard unto the rule of all holy duties in particular.¶

2. It was a power of executing all the laws of Christ, with the penalties annexed unto their disobedience. "We have," says the apostle, "in a readiness wherewith to revenge all disobedience" (2 Cor. 10:6). And this principally consisted in the power of excommunication, or the judiciary excision[4] of any person or persons from the society of the faithful and visible body of Christ in

---

4   I.e., removal.

the world. Now, although this power were absolutely in each apostle toward all offenders in every church, whence Paul affirms that he had himself "delivered Hymeneus and Alexander unto Satan" (1 Tim. 1:20), yet did they not exercise this power without the concurrence and consent of the church from whence an offender was to be cut off, because that was the mind of Christ, and that which the nature of the ordinance did require (1 Cor. 5:3–5).¶

3. Their whole power was spiritual, and not carnal. It respected the souls, minds, and consciences of men alone as its object, and not their bodies, or goods, or liberties in this world. Those extraordinary instances of Ananias and Sapphira in their sudden death, of Elymas in his blindness, were only miraculous operations of God in testifying against their sin, and proceeded not from any apostolical power in the discharge of their office. But as unto that kind of power which now has devoured all other appearances of church authority, and in the sense of the most is only significant, namely, to fine, punish, imprison, banish, kill, and destroy men and women, Christians, believers, persons of an unblamable, useful conversation, with the worst of carnal weapons and savage cruelty of mind, as they were never entrusted with it nor anything of the like kind, so they have sufficiently manifested how their holy souls did abhor the thoughts of such anti-Christian power and practices, though in others the mystery of iniquity began to work in their days.

EVANGELISTS

The ministry of the seventy, also, which the Lord Christ sent forth afterward, to "go two and two before his face into every city and place, whither he himself would come" (Luke 10:1–3), was in like manner temporary, that is, it was subservient and commensurate unto his own personal ministry in the flesh. These are commonly called evangelists from the general nature of their work, but were not those extraordinary officers which were afterward in the Christian church under that title and appellation. But there was some analogy and proportion between the one and the other. For as these first seventy seem to have had an inferior work, and subordinate unto that of the twelve in their ministry unto the church of the Jews, during the time of the Lord Christ's converse among them, so those evangelists that afterward were appointed were subordinate unto them in their evangelical apostleship. And these also, as they were immediately called unto their employment by the Lord Jesus, so their work being extraordinary, they were endued with extraordinary gifts of the Holy Ghost (Luke 10:9, 17, 19).

In the gospel church state[5] there were evangelists also, as they are men-tioned (Eph. 4:11; Acts 21:8; 2 Tim. 4:5): "gospellers," preachers of the gospel, distinct from the ordinary teachers of the churches. Things, I confess, are but obscurely delivered concerning this sort of men in Scripture, their office being not designed unto a continuance. Probably the institution of it was traduced[6] from the temporary ministry of the seventy before mentioned. That they were the same persons continued in their first office, as the apostles were, is uncertain and improbable, though it be not that some of them might be called thereunto; as Philip, and Timothy, and Titus were evangelists that were not of that first number. Their special call is not mentioned, nor their number anywhere intimated. That their call was extraordinary is hence apparent, in that no rules are anywhere given or prescribed about their choice or ordina-tion, no qualification of their persons expressed, nor any direction given the church as to its future proceeding about them, no more than about new or other apostles. They seem to have been called by the apostles, by the direction of a spirit of prophecy or immediate revelation from Christ. So it is said of Timothy, who is expressly called an evangelist (2 Tim. 4:5), that he received that gift "by prophecy" (1 Tim. 4:14), that is, the gift of the office—as when Christ ascended, he "gave gifts unto men, some to be evangelists" (Eph. 4:8, 11)—for this way did the Holy Ghost design men unto extraordinary offices and employments (Acts 13:1–3). And when they were so designed by prophecy, or immediate revelation from Christ by the Holy Ghost, then the church in compliance therewith, both "prayed for them" and "laid their hands on them." So when the Holy Ghost had revealed his choosing of Paul and Barnabas unto a special work, the prophets and teachers of the church of Antioch, where they then were, "fasted and prayed, and laid their hands on them," so sending them away (Acts 13:3). And when Timothy was called to be an evangelist by special revelation or prophecy, the apostle laid his hands on him, whereby he received the Holy Ghost in his extraordinary gifts: "The gift of God, which is in thee by the putting on of my hands" (2 Tim. 1:6). And as it was usual with him to join others with himself in those epistles which he wrote by immediate divine inspiration, so in this act of laying his hands on an evangelist, as a sign of the communication of extraordinary gifts, he joined the ordinary presbytery of the church with him that were present in the place where he was so called. It is evident, therefore, that both their call and their gifts were extraordinary, and therefore so also was their office: For

---

5   Owen's use of "gospel church state" here is a reference to the period of early church history
    when all New Testament offices were functioning.
6   I.e., criticized; maligned.

although men who have only an ordinary call to office may have extraordinary gifts, and many had so in primitive times, and although some might have extraordinary gifts who were never called unto office at all, as some of those who spoke with tongues and wrought miracles, yet where there is a concurrence of an extraordinary call and extraordinary gifts, there the office is extraordinary.

The power that these officers in the church were entrusted with was extraordinary. For this is a certain consequent of an extraordinary call and extraordinary gifts. And this power respected all churches in the world equally, yea, and all persons, as the apostles also did. But whereas their ministry was subordinate unto that of the apostles, they were by them guided as to the particular places wherein they were to exercise their power and discharge their office for a season. This is evident from Paul's disposal of Titus as to his work and time (Titus 1:5; 3:12). But yet their power did at no time depend on their relation unto any particular place or church, nor were they ever ordained to any one place or see more than another, but the extent of their employment was every way as large as that of the apostles, both as to the world and as to the churches; only in their present particular disposal of themselves, they were, as it is probable, for the most part under the guidance of the apostles, although sometimes they had particular revelations and directions from the Holy Ghost, or by the ministry of angels, for their special employment, as Philip had (Acts 8:26).

And as for their work, it may be reduced unto three heads:

1. To preach the gospel in all places and unto all persons, as they had occasion. So, Philip went down to Samaria and "preached Christ" (Acts 8:5). And when the apostle Paul charges Timothy to "do the work of an evangelist" (2 Tim. 4:5), he prescribes unto him "preaching the Word in season and out of season" (2 Tim. 4:2). And whereas this was incumbent in like manner on the ordinary teachers of every church, the teaching of these evangelists differed from theirs in two things. (1) In the extent of their work, which, as we showed before, was equal unto that of the apostles. Whereas ordinary bishops, pastors, or teachers were to feed, teach, and take care of the special flocks only which they were set over (Acts 20:17, 28; 1 Pet. 5:2). (2) They were obliged to labor in their work in a more than ordinary manner, as it should seem from 2 Timothy 4:5.¶

2. The second part of their work was to confirm the doctrine of the gospel by miraculous operations, as occasion did require. So Philip the evangelist wrought many miracles of sundry sorts at Samaria, in the confirmation of the doctrine which he taught (Acts 8:6–7, 13). And, in like manner, there

is no question but that the rest of the evangelists had the power or gift of miraculous operations, to be exercised as occasion did require, and as they were guided by the Holy Ghost.¶

3. They were employed in the settling and completing of those churches whose foundations were laid by the apostles. For whereas they had the great work upon them of "preaching the gospel unto all nations,"[7] they could not continue long or reside in any one place or church. And yet when persons were newly converted to the faith, and disposed only into an imperfect order, without any special peculiar officers, guides, or rulers of their own, it was not safe leaving them unto themselves, lest they should be too much at a loss as to gospel order and worship. Wherefore, in such places where any churches were planted but not completed, nor would the design of the apostles suffer them to continue any longer there, they left these evangelists among them for a season, who had power, by virtue of their office, to dispose of things in the churches until they came unto completeness and perfection. When this end was attained, and the churches were settled under ordinary elders of their own, the evangelists removed unto other places, according as they were directed or disposed. These things are evident from the instructions given by Paul unto Timothy and Titus, which have all of them respect unto this order.

Some there are who plead for the continuance of this office, some in express terms and under the same name, others for successors unto them at least in that part of their work which consists in power over many churches. Some say that bishops succeed to the apostles, and presbyters unto those evangelists. But this is scarce defensible in any tolerable manner by them whose interest it is to defend it. For Timothy, whom they would have to be a bishop, is expressly called an evangelist. That which is pleaded with most probability for their continuance is the necessity of the work wherein they were employed, in the rule and settlement of the churches. But the truth is, if their whole work as before described be consulted, as none can perform some parts of it, so it may be very few would overearnestly press after a participation of their office. For to preach the word continually, and that with a peculiar labor and travail, and to move up and down according as the necessity of the edification of the churches does require, doing nothing in them but according to the rule and appointment of Christ, are things that not many will earnestly covet to be engaged in. But there is an apprehension that there was something more than ordinary power belonging unto

7   Mark 16:15.

286 A DISCOURSE OF SPIRITUAL GIFTS

this office, that those who enjoyed it were not obliged always to labor in any particular church, but had the rule of many churches committed unto them. Now, whereas this power is apt to draw other desirable things unto it, or carry them along with it, this is that which some pretend a succession unto. Though they are neither called like them, nor gifted like them, nor labor like them, nor have the same object of their employment, much less the same power of extraordinary operations with them, yet as to the rule over sundry churches they must needs be their successors. I shall, therefore, briefly do these two things. First, show that there are no such officers as these evangelists continued by the will of Christ in the ordinary state and course of the church; second, that there is no need of their continuance from any work applied unto them.

1. And (1) the things that are essential unto the office of an evangelist are unattainable at present unto the church. For where no command, no rule, no authority, no directions are given for the calling of any officer, there that office must cease, as does that of the apostles, who could not be called but by Jesus Christ. What is required unto the call of an evangelist was before declared; and unless it can be manifested, either by institution or example, how anyone may be otherwise called unto that office, no such office can be continued, for a call by prophecy or immediate revelation none now will pretend unto. And other call the evangelists of old had none.

Nor is there in the Scripture the least mention of the call or appointment of anyone to be an ecclesiastical officer in an ordinary stated church, but with relation unto that church whereof he was, or was to be, an officer. But an evangelist, as such, was not especially related unto any one church more than another, though, as the apostles themselves, they might for a time attend unto the work in one place or church rather or more than another. Wherefore, without a call from the Holy Ghost, either immediate by prophecy and revelation, or by the direction of persons infallibly inspired, as the apostles were, none can be called to be evangelists, nor yet to succeed them under any other name in that office. Wherefore, the primitive church after the apostles' time never once took upon them to constitute or ordain an evangelist, as knowing it a thing beyond their rule and out of their power. Men may invade an office when they please, but unless they be called unto it, they must account for their usurpation. And as for those who have erected an office in the church, or an episcopacy, principally if not solely out of what is ascribed unto these evangelists, namely, to Timothy and Titus, they may be further attended unto in their claim when they lay the least pretense unto the whole of what is ascribed unto them. But this "doing the work of an evangelist"[8] is that which few men care for or delight in; only their power and authority, in a new kind of mannagery,[9] many would willingly possess themselves of.

(2) The evangelists we read of had extraordinary gifts of the Holy Spirit, without which they could not warrantably undertake their office. This we have manifested before. Now, these extraordinary gifts, differing not only in degree but in kind from all those of the ordinary ministry of the church, are not at present by any pretended unto. And if any should make such a pretense, it would be an easy matter to convince them of their folly. But without these gifts, men must content themselves with such offices in the church as are stated with respect unto every particular congregation (Acts 14:23; 20:28; Titus 1:5; 1 Pet. 5:1–2; Phil. 1:1).

Some, indeed, seem not satisfied whether to derive their claim from Timothy and Titus as evangelists, or from the bishops that were ordained by them or described unto them. But whereas those bishops were no other but elders of particular churches, as is evident, beyond a modest denial (from Acts 20:28; Phil. 1:1; 1 Tim. 3:1–2, 8; Titus 1:5–9), so certainly they cannot be of both sorts, the one being apparently superior unto the other. If they are such bishops as Titus and Timothy ordained, it is well enough known both what is their office, their work, and their duty. If such as they pretend Timothy and Titus to be, they must manifest it in the like call, gifts, and employment, as they had.

(3) For there are not any now who do pretend unto their principal employment by virtue of office, nor can so do. For it is certain that the principal work of the evangelists was to go up and down, from one place and nation unto another, to preach the gospel unto Jews and Gentiles as yet unconverted, and their commission unto this purpose was as large and extensive as that of the apostles. But who shall now empower anyone hereunto? What church, what persons, have received authority to ordain anyone to be such an evangelist? Or what rules or directions are given as to their qualifications, power, or duty, or how they should be so ordained? It is true, those who are ordained ministers of the gospel, and others also that are the disciples of Christ, may and ought to preach the gospel to unconverted persons and nations as they have opportunity, and are particularly guided by the providence of God. But that any church or person has power or authority to ordain a person unto this office and work cannot be proved.

8   2 Tim. 4:5.
9   I.e., managerial authority.

2. Lastly, the continuance of the employment as unto the settling of new planted churches is no way necessary. For every church, being planted and settled, is entrusted with power for its own preservation and continuance in due order according to the mind of Christ, and is enabled to do all those things in itself which at first were done under the guidance of the evangelists, nor can any one instance be given wherein they are defective. And where any church was called and gathered in the name of Christ, which had some things yet wanting unto its perfection and complete order, which the evangelists were to finish and settle, they did it not but in and by the power of the church itself, only presiding and directing in the things to be done. And if any churches, through their own default, have lost that order and power which they were once established in, as they shall never want power in themselves to recover their pristine estate and condition, who will attend unto their duty according unto rule to that purpose, so this would rather prove a necessity of raising up new evangelists, of a new extraordinary ministry, on the defection of churches, than the continuance of them in the church rightly stated and settled.

PROPHETS

Besides these evangelists there were prophets also, who had a temporary, extraordinary ministry in the church. Their grant from Christ, or institution in the church, is mentioned (1 Cor. 12:28; Eph. 4:11), and the exercise of their ministry is declared (Acts 13:1–2). But the names of prophets and prophecy are used variously in the New Testament. For sometimes an extraordinary office and extraordinary gifts are signified by them; and sometimes extraordinary gifts only; and sometimes an ordinary office with ordinary gifts, and sometimes ordinary gifts only. And unto one of these heads may the use of the word be everywhere reduced.¶

1. In the places mentioned, extraordinary officers endued with extraordinary gifts are intended. For they are said to be "set in the church," and are placed in the second rank of officers, next to the apostles, "first apostles, secondarily prophets" (1 Cor. 12:28), between them and evangelists (Eph. 4:11). And two things are ascribed unto them. (1) That they received immediate revelations and directions from the Holy Ghost in things that belonged unto the present duty of the church. Unto them it was that the Holy Ghost revealed his mind, and gave commands concerning the separation of Barnabas and Saul unto their work (Acts 13:2). (2) They foretold things to come, by the inspiration of the Holy Ghost, wherein the duty or edification of the church was concerned. So Agabus the prophet foretold the famine in the

days of Claudius Caesar, whereon provision was made for "the poor saints at Jerusalem," that they might not suffer by it (Acts 11:28–30). And the same person afterward prophesied of the bonds and sufferings of Paul at Jerusalem (Acts 21:10–11). And the same thing, it being of the highest concern unto the church, was, as it should seem, revealed unto the prophets that were in most churches, for so himself gives an account hereof: "And now, behold, I go bound in the spirit unto Jerusalem, not knowing the things that shall befall me there, save that the Holy Ghost witnesseth in every city, saying that bonds and afflictions abide me" (Acts 20:22–23). That is, in all the cities he passed through where there were churches planted and prophets in them. These things the churches then stood in need of, for their confirmation, direction, and comfort, and were, therefore, I suppose, most of them supplied with such officers for a season, that is, while they were needful. And unto this office, though expressly affirmed to be "set in the church," and placed between the apostles and the evangelists, none, that I know of, do pretend a succession. All grant that they were extraordinary, because their gift and work were so. But so were those of evangelists also. But there is no mention of the power and rule of those prophets, or else undoubtedly, we should have had, on one pretense or other, successors provided for them.

2. Sometimes an extraordinary gift without office is intended in this expression. So it is said that Philip the evangelist "had four daughters, virgins, which did prophesy" (Acts 21:9). It is not said that they were prophetesses, as there were some under the Old Testament, only that "they did prophesy," that is, they had revelations from the Holy Ghost occasionally for the use of the church. For to prophesy is nothing but to declare hidden and secret things by virtue of immediate revelation, be they of what nature they will. And so is the word commonly used (Matt. 26:68; Luke 22:64). So an extraordinary gift without office is expressed, "When Paul had laid his hands upon them, the Holy Ghost came on them; and they spake with tongues, and prophesied" (Acts 19:6). Their prophesying, which was their declaration of spiritual things by immediate revelation, was of the same nature with their speaking with tongues. Both were extraordinary gifts and operations of the Holy Ghost. And of this sort were those miracles, healings, and tongues, which God for a time set in the church, which did not constitute distinct officers in the church, but they were only sundry persons in each church which were endued with these extraordinary gifts for its edification. And therefore are they placed after teachers, comprising both, which were the principal sort of the ordinary continuing officers of the church (1 Cor. 12:28). And of this sort do I reckon those prophets to

be who are treated of (1 Cor. 14:29–33). For that they were neither stated officers in the churches nor yet the brethren of the church promiscuously,[10] but such as had received a special extraordinary gift, is evident from the context (1 Cor. 14:30, 37).

3. Again, an ordinary office with ordinary gifts is intended by this expression: "Having then gifts differing according to the grace that is given to us, whether prophecy, let us prophesy according to the proportion of faith" (Rom. 12:6). Prophecy here can intend nothing but teaching or preaching, in the exposition and application of the word. For an external rule is given unto it, in that it must be done according to the "proportion of faith," or the sound doctrine of faith revealed in the Scripture. And this ever was, and will ever continue to be, the work and duty of the ordinary teachers of the church, whereunto they are enabled by the gifts of Christ, which they receive by the Holy Ghost (Eph. 4:7), as we shall see more afterward. And hence also those who are not called unto office, who have yet received a gift enabling them to declare the mind of God in the Scripture unto the edification of others, may be said to "prophesy."

CONCLUSION

And these things I thought meet to interpose, with a brief description of those officers which the Lord Jesus Christ granted unto his church for a season, at its first planting and establishment, with what belonged unto their office, and the necessity of their work. For the collation of them on the church, and their whole furniture with spiritual gifts, was the immediate work of the Holy Ghost, which we are in the declaration of. And withal it was my design to manifest how vain is the pretense of some unto a kind of succession unto these officers, who have neither an extraordinary call, nor extraordinary gifts, nor extraordinary employment, but only are pleased to assume an extraordinary power unto themselves over the churches and disciples of Christ, and that such as neither evangelists, nor prophets, nor apostles, did ever claim or make use of. But this matter of power is fuel in itself unto the proud, ambitious minds of Diotrephists,[11] and as now circumstanced, with other advantages, is useful to the corrupt lusts of men. And, therefore, it is no wonder if it be pretended unto and greedily reached after, by such as really have neither call to the ministry, nor gifts for it, nor do

10 I.e., in a widespread fashion, generally.
11 *Diotrephes*: the opponent of the apostle John mentioned in 3 John 9.

employ themselves in it. And, therefore, as in these extraordinary officers and their gifts did consist the original glory and honor of the churches in a special manner, and by them was their edification carried on and perfected. So by an empty pretense unto their power, without their order and spirit, the churches have been stained, and deformed, and brought to destruction. But we must return unto the consideration of extraordinary spiritual gifts, which is the special work before us.

4

Of Extraordinary Spiritual Gifts

1 Corinthians 12:4–11

EXTRAORDINARY SPIRITUAL GIFTS were of two sorts. First, such as absolutely exceed the whole power and faculties of our minds and souls. These,
therefore, did not consist in an abiding principle or faculty always resident
in them that received them, so as that they could exercise them by virtue of
any inherent power and ability. They were so granted unto some persons,
in the execution of their office, as that, so often as was needful, they could
produce their effects by virtue of an immediate extraordinary influence of
divine power, transiently affecting their minds. Such was the gift of miracles,
healing, and the like. There were no extraordinary officers, but they had
these gifts. But yet they could work or operate by virtue of them only as the
Holy Ghost gave them special direction for the putting forth of his power in
them. So, it is said that Paul and Barnabas preaching at Iconium, "the Lord
gave testimony unto the word of his grace, and granted signs and wonders
to be done by their hands" (Acts 14:3). The working of signs and miracles is
the immediate operation of the Spirit of God, nor can any power or faculty
efficiently productive of such effects abide in the souls or minds of men.
These miraculous operations were the witness of the Holy Ghost sent down
from heaven, which he gave to the truth of the gospel. See Hebrews 2:4, with
our exposition thereon.[1] Wherefore, there was no more in these gifts, which

1 *Exercitations on the Epistle to the Hebrews Also concerning the Messiah Wherein the Promises
   concerning Him to Be a Spiritual Redeemer of Mankind Are Explained and Vindicated, His Coming
   and Accomplishment of His Work according to the Promises Is Proved and Confirmed, the Person,
   or Who He Is, Is Declared, the Whole Oeconomy of the Mosaical Law, Rites, Worship, and Sacrifice
   Is Explained: And in All the Doctrine of the Person, Office, and Work of the Messiah Is Opened,*

absolutely exceed the whole faculties of our natures, but the designing of certain persons by the Holy Ghost, in and with whose ministry he would himself effect miraculous operations.

Secondly, they were such as consisted in extraordinary endowments and improvements of the faculties of the souls or minds of men, such as wisdom, knowledge, utterance, and the like. Now, where these were bestowed on any in an extraordinary manner, as they were on the apostles and evangelists, they differed only in degree from them that are ordinary and still continued, but are of the same kind with them; whereof we shall treat afterward. Now, whereas all these gifts of both sorts are expressly and distinctly enumerated and set down by our apostle in one place, I shall consider them as they are there proposed by him.

The manifestation of the Spirit is given to every man to profit withal. For to one is given by the Spirit the word of wisdom; to another the word of knowledge by the same Spirit; to another faith by the same Spirit; to another the gifts of healing by the same Spirit; to another the working of miracles; to another prophecy; to another discerning of spirits; to another divers kinds of tongues; to another the interpretation of tongues: but all these worketh that one and the self-same Spirit, dividing to every man severally as he will. (1 Cor. 12:7–11)

The general concerns of this passage in the apostle were declared, and the context opened, at the beginning of our discourse on this subject. I shall only now consider the special spiritual gifts that are here enumerated by the apostle, which are nine in number, laid down promiscuously without respect unto any order or dependence of one upon another, although it is probable that those first placed were the principal, or of principal use in the church.

WORD OF WISDOM

The first is λόγος σοφίας, the "word of wisdom." Λόγος here is of the same signification with דבר in the Hebrew, which often signifies a "thing" or "matter." Wherefore the "word of wisdom" is nothing but wisdom itself. And our

---

the Nature and Demerit of the First Sin Is Unfolded, the Opinions and Traditions of the Antient and Modern Jews Are Examined, Their Objections against the Lord Christ and the Gospel Are Answered, the Time of the Coming of the Messiah Is Stated, and the Great Fundamental Truths of the Gospel Vindicated: With an Exposition and Discourses on the Two First Chapters of the Said Epistle to the Hebrews (1668), bk. 2, on Heb. 2:2–4.

inquiry is, what was that wisdom which was in those days a peculiar and a special gift of the Holy Ghost? Our Lord Jesus Christ promised unto his disciples that he would give them "a mouth and wisdom, which all their adversaries should not be able to gainsay nor resist" (Luke 21:15). This will be our rule in the declaration of the nature of this gift. That which he has respect unto is the defense of the gospel and its truth against powerful persecuting adversaries. For although they had the truth on their side, yet being men ignorant and unlearned, they might justly fear that when they were brought before kings, and rulers, and priests, they should be baffled in their profession, and not be able to defend the truth. Wherefore this promise of a "mouth and wisdom" respects spiritual ability and utterance in the defense of the truth of the gospel, when they were called into question about it. Spiritual ability of mind is the wisdom, and utterance or freedom of speech is the mouth here promised.¶

An eminent instance of the accomplishment hereof we have in Peter and John (Acts 4). For upon their making a defense of the resurrection of Christ, and the truth of the gospel therein, such as their adversaries were not able to gainsay nor resist, it is said that when the rulers and elders saw their παῤῥη-σίαν, that is, their "utterance" in defense of their cause with boldness, and so the wisdom wherewith[2] it was accompanied, considering that they were "unlearned and ignorant," they were astonished, and only considered "that they had been with Jesus" (Acts 4:13). And he it was who, in the accomplishment of his promise, had given them that spiritual wisdom and utterance which they were not able to resist. So it is said expressly of Stephen that his adversaries "were not able to resist the wisdom and the spirit by which he spake" (Acts 6:10). Wherefore, this gift of wisdom, in the first place, was a spiritual skill and ability to defend the truths of the gospel, when questioned, opposed, or blasphemed. And this gift was eminent in those primitive times, when a company of unlearned men were able upon all occasions to maintain and defend the truth which they believed and professed before and against doctors, scribes, lawyers, rulers of synagogues, yea, princes and kings, continually so confounding their adversaries, as that, being obstinate in their unbelief, they were forced to cover their shame by betaking themselves unto rage and bestial fury (Acts 6:10–14; 7:54; 22:22–23), as has been the manner of all their successors ever since.

Now, although this be a special kind of wisdom, an eminent gift of the Holy Ghost, wherein the glory of Christ and honor of the gospel are greatly concerned, namely, an ability to manage and defend the truth in times of

---

2 I.e., by which.

trial and danger, to the confusion of its adversaries, yet I suppose the wisdom here intended is not absolutely confined thereunto, though it be principally intended. Peter, speaking of Paul's epistles, affirms that they were written "according to the wisdom given unto him" (2 Pet. 3:15). That is, that special gift of spiritual wisdom for the management of gospel truths unto the edification of the church of Christ which he had received. And he that would understand what this wisdom is must be thoroughly conversant in the writings of that apostle. For, indeed, the wisdom that he uses in the management of the doctrine of the gospel—in the due consideration of all persons, occasions, circumstances, temptations of men and churches, of their state, condition, strength or weakness, growth or decays, obedience or failings, their capacities and progress, with the holy accommodation of himself in what he teaches or delivers, in meekness, in vehemency, in tenderness, in sharpness, in severe arguings and pathetic expostulations, with all other ways and means suited unto his holy ends, in the propagation of the gospel and edification of the church—is inexpressibly glorious and excellent. All this did he do according to the singular gift of wisdom that was bestowed on him. Wherefore, I take the "word of wisdom" here mentioned to be a peculiar spiritual skill and ability wisely to manage the gospel in its administration unto the advantage and furtherance of the truth, especially in the defense of it when called unto the trial with its adversaries.¶

This was an eminent gift of the Holy Ghost, which, considering the persons employed by him in the ministry for the most part were known to be unlearned and ignorant, filled the world with amazement, and was an effectual means for the subduing of multitudes unto the obedience of faith. And so eminent was the apostle Paul in this gift, and so successful in the management of it, that his adversaries had nothing to say but that he was subtle and took men by craft and guile (2 Cor. 12:16). The sweetness, condescension, self-denial, holy compliance, with all which he made use of, mixed with truth, gravity, and authority, they would have had to be all craft and guile. And this gift, when it is in any measure continued unto any minister of the gospel, is of singular use unto the church of God. Yea, I doubt not but that the apostle fixed it here in the first place, as that which was eminent above all the rest. And as, where it is too much wanting, we see what woeful mistakes and miscarriages men otherwise good and holy will run themselves into, unto the great disadvantage of the gospel, so the real enjoyment and exercise of it in any competent measure is the life and grace of the ministry. As God filled Bezaleel and Aholiab with wisdom for the building of the tabernacle of old, so unless he give this spiritual wisdom unto the ministers of the gospel, no tabernacle of his will be erected where it is fallen down, nor kept up where it stands. I intend not secular wisdom or civil wisdom, much less carnal wisdom, but a spiritual ability to discharge all our duties aright in the ministry committed unto us. And, as was said, where this is wanting, we shall quickly see woeful and shameful work made in churches themselves.

I cannot pass by the consideration of this gift without offering something that may guide us either in the obtaining or the due exercise of it. And hereunto the things ensuing may be subservient. As,

1. A sense of our own insufficiency as of ourselves, as unto any end for which this wisdom is requisite. As it is declared that we have no sufficiency in ourselves for anything that is good, all our sufficiency being of God, so in particular it is denied that we have any for the work of the ministry, in that interrogation, containing a negative proposition, "Who is sufficient for these things?" (2 Cor. 2:16). A sense hereof is the first step toward this wisdom, as our apostle expressly declares: "Let no man deceive himself. If any man among you seemeth to be wise in this world, let him become a fool, that he may be wise" (1 Cor. 3:18). Until we discover and are sensible of our own folly, we are fit neither to receive nor to use this spiritual wisdom. And the want hereof proves the ruin of many that pretend unto the ministry. And it were to be wished that it were only their own. They come to the work of it full of pride, self-conceit, and foolish elation of mind, in an apprehension of their own abilities, which yet, for the most part, are mean and contemptible. This keeps them sufficiently estranged from a sense of that spiritual wisdom we treat of. Hence there is nothing of a gospel ministry nor its work found among them, but an empty name. And as for those who have reduced all ecclesiastical administrations to canons, laws, acts, courts, and legal processes in them, they seem to do it with a design to cast off all use of spiritual gifts, yea, to exclude both them and their Author, name and thing, out of the church of God. Is this the wisdom given by the Holy Ghost for the due management of gospel administrations, namely, that men should get a little skill in some of the worst of human laws and uncomely artifices of intriguing, secular courts, which they pride themselves in, and terrify poor creatures with mulcts[3] and penalties that are any way obnoxious unto them? What use these things may be of in the world I know not; unto the church of God they do not belong.

2. Being sensible of our own insufficiency, earnest prayers for a supply of this wisdom are required in us: "If any of you lack wisdom, let him ask

3   I.e., fines.

of God, that giveth to all men liberally, and upbraideth not, and it shall be given him" (James 1:5). There is both a precept and a promise to enforce this duty. That we all want wisdom in ourselves is unquestionable, I mean, as to our concern in the gospel, either to bear testimony unto it in difficulties or to manage the truths of it unto edification. The way for our supply lies plain and open before us, neither is there any other that we can take one step in toward it: "Let us ask it of God, who giveth liberally," and we shall receive it. This was that which rendered Solomon so great and glorious; when he had his choice given him of all desirable things, he made his request for wisdom to the discharge of the office and duties of it that God had called him unto. Though it was a whole kingdom that he was to rule, yet was his work carnal and of this world, compared with the spiritual administrations of the gospel. And hereunto a worldly ministry is no less averse than unto a sense of their own insufficiency. The fruits do sufficiently manifest how much this duty is contemned[4] by them. But the neglect of it, I say, the neglect of praying for wisdom to be enabled unto the discharge of the work of the ministry, and the due management of the truths of the gospel, according as occasions do require, in them who pretend thereunto, is a fruit of unbelief, yea, of atheism and contempt of God.

3. Due meditation on our great pattern, the Lord Jesus Christ, and the apostles, being followers of them as they were of him, is also required hereunto. As in all other things, so, especially in his ministry for the revelation of the truth, and giving testimony thereunto, the Lord Jesus was the great pattern and example, God in him representing unto us that perfection in wisdom which we ought to aim at. I shall not here in particular look into this heavenly treasury, but only say, that he who would be really and truly wise in spiritual things, who would either rightly receive or duly improve this gift of the Holy Ghost, he ought continually to bear in his heart, his mind, and affections, this great exemplar and idea of it, even the Lord Jesus Christ in his ministry, namely, what he did, what he spoke, how on all occasions his condescension, meekness, and authority did manifest themselves, until he be changed into the same image and likeness by the Spirit of the Lord. The same is to be done, in their place and sphere, toward the apostles, as the principal followers of Christ, and who do most lively represent his graces and wisdom unto us. Their writings, and what is written of them, are to be searched and studied unto this very end, that, considering how they behaved themselves in all instances, on

4 I.e., treated or regarded with contempt.

all occasions, in their testimony, and all administrations of the truth, we may endeavor after a conformity unto them, in the participation of the same Spirit with them. It would be no small stay and guidance unto us, if on all occasions we would diligently search and consider what the apostles did in such circumstances, or what they would have done, in answer to what is recorded of their spirit and actings. For although this wisdom be a gift of the Holy Spirit, yet as we now consider it as it is continued in the church, it may be in part obtained and greatly improved in the due use of the means which are subservient thereunto, provided that in all we depend solely on God for the giving of it, who has also prescribed these means unto us for the same end.

4. Let them who design a participation of this gift take heed it be not stifled with such vicious habits of mind as are expressly contrary unto it and destructive of it. Such are self-fullness or confidence, hastiness of spirit, promptness to speak and slowness to hear, which are the great means which make many abound in their own sense and folly, to be wise in their own conceits, and contemptible in the judgment of all that are truly so. Ability of speech in time and season is a special gift of God, and that eminently with respect unto the spiritual things of the gospel. But a profluency[5] of speech, venting itself on all occasions and on no occasions, making men open their mouths wide when indeed they should shut them and open their ears, and to pour out all that they know and what they do not know, making them angry if they are not heard and impatient if they are contradicted, is an unconquerable fortification against all true spiritual wisdom.

5. Let those who would be sharers herein follow after those gifts and graces which do accompany it, promote it, and are inseparable from it. Such are humility, meekness, patience, constancy, with boldness and confidence in profession, without which we shall be fools in every trial. Wisdom, indeed, is none of all these, but it is that which cannot be without them, nor will it thrive in any mind that is not cultivated by them. And he who thinks it is not worth his pains and travail, nor that it will quit cost, to seek after this spiritual wisdom, by a constant watchfulness against the opposite vices mentioned, and attendance unto those concomitant[6] duties and graces, must be content to go without it. This is the first instance given by our apostle of the spiritual gifts of the primitive times: "To one is given by the Spirit the word of wisdom."

---

5   I.e., flowing copiously or smoothly.
6   I.e., accompanying.

WORD OF KNOWLEDGE

"To another the word of knowledge by the same Spirit"—λόγος γνώσεως. I showed before that λόγος may denote the thing itself, the "word of knowledge," that is knowledge. But if any shall suppose that because this knowledge was to be expressed unto the church for its edification, it is therefore called a "word of knowledge," as a "word of exhortation," or a "word of consolation," that is, exhortation or consolation administered by words, I shall not contend to the contrary. It is knowledge that is the gift peculiarly intended in this second place. And we must inquire both how it is a special gift, and of what sort it is. And it should seem that it cannot have the nature of a special gift, seeing it is that which was common to all. For so says the apostle, speaking unto the whole church of the Corinthians: "We know that we all have knowledge" (1 Cor. 8:1). And not only so, but he also adds that this knowledge is a thing which either in its own nature tends unto an ill issue or is very apt to be abused thereunto. For says he, "Knowledge puffeth up," for which cause he frequently reflects upon it in other places. But yet we shall find that it is a peculiar gift, and in itself singularly useful, however it may be abused, as the best things may be, yea, are most liable thereunto. The knowledge mentioned in that place by the apostle, which he ascribes in common unto all the church, was only that which concerned "things sacrificed unto idols." And if we should extend it further, unto an understanding of the "mystery of the gospel," which was in the community of believers, yet is there place remaining for an eminency therein by virtue of a special spiritual gift. And as to what he adds about "knowledge puffing up," he expounds in the next words: "If any man think that he knoweth anything, he knoweth nothing yet as he ought to know" (1 Cor. 8:2). It is not men's knowledge, but the vain and proud conceit of ignorant men, supposing themselves knowing and wise, that so puffs up and hinders edification.

Wherefore (1) by this "word of knowledge," not that degree of it which is required in all Christians, in all the members of the church, is intended. Such a measure of knowledge there is necessary both unto faith and confession. Men can believe nothing of that whereof they know nothing, nor can they confess with their mouths what they apprehend not in their minds. But it is somewhat singular, eminent, and not common to all. (2) Neither does that eminency or singularity consist in this, that it is saving and sanctifying knowledge which is intended, that there is such a peculiar knowledge, whereby "God shines in the heart of believers"[7] with a spiritual, saving

---

7 2 Cor. 4:6.

insight into spiritual things, transforming the mind into the likeness of them, I have at large elsewhere declared.[8] For it is reckoned among gifts, whereas that other is a saving grace, whose difference has been declared before. It is expressed by the apostle by "understanding all mysteries and all knowledge" (1 Cor. 13:2); that is, having an understanding in, and the knowledge of, all mysteries. This knowledge he calls a gift which "shall vanish away" (1 Cor. 13:8), and so not belonging absolutely unto that grace which, being a part of the image of God in us, shall go over into eternity. And "knowledge" in 1 Corinthians 13:2, is taken for the thing known: "Though I understand all knowledge," which is the same with "all mysteries." Wherefore the knowledge here intended is such a peculiar and special insight into the mysteries of the gospel, as whereby those in whom it was were enabled to teach and instruct others. Thus, the apostle Paul, who had received all these gifts in the highest degree and measure, affirms that by his writing, those to whom he wrote might perceive his "skill and understanding in the mystery of Christ."[9]

And this was in a special manner necessary unto those first dispensers of the gospel; for how else should the church have been instructed in the knowledge of it? This they prayed for them, namely, that they might be filled with the knowledge of the will of God "in all wisdom and understanding" (Col. 1:9; Eph. 1:15–20; 3:14–19; Col. 2:1–2). The means whereby they might come hereunto was by their instruction, who therefore were to be skilled in a peculiar manner in the knowledge of those mysteries which they were to impart unto others, and to do it accordingly. And so it was with them (Acts 20:27; Eph. 3:8–9; Col. 4:2–4). Now, although this gift, as to that excellent degree wherein it was in the apostles and those who received the knowledge of Christ and the gospel by immediate revelation, be withheld, yet it is still communicated in such a measure unto the ministers of the church as is necessary unto its edification. And for anyone to undertake an office in the church who has not received this gift in some good measure of the knowledge of the mystery of God and the gospel, is to impose himself on that service in the house of God, which he is neither called unto nor fitted for. And whereas we have lived to see all endeavors after a special acquaintance with the mysteries of the gospel despised or derided by some, it is an evidence of that fatal and fearful apostasy whereinto the generality of Christians are fallen.

8   *The Causes, Ways, and Means of Understanding the Mind of God as Revealed in His Word, with Assurance Therein* (1678), chap. 4, which is included in vol. 7.
9   This is possibly a reference to 1 Cor. 2 or 2 Cor. 11.

FAITH

Faith is added in the third place: "To another faith by the same Spirit."[10] That the saving grace of faith, which is common unto all true believers, is not here intended, is manifest from the context. There is a faith in Scripture which is commonly called the "faith of miracles," mentioned by our apostle in this epistle as a principal, extraordinary, spiritual gift: "Though I have all faith, so that I could remove mountains" (1 Cor. 13:2)—that is, the highest degree of a faith of miracles, or such as would effect miraculous operations of the highest nature. This I should readily admit to be here intended, but that there is mention made of working miracles in the next verse, as a gift distinct from this faith. Yet whereas this working of miracles is everywhere ascribed to faith, and could not be anywhere but where the peculiar faith from which those operations did proceed was first imparted, it is not unlikely but that by "faith" the principle of all miraculous operations may be intended, and by the other expressions the operations themselves. But if the distinction of these gifts is to be preserved, as I rather judge that it ought to be, considering the placing of "faith" immediately upon "wisdom" and "knowledge," I should judge that a peculiar confidence, boldness, and assurance of mind in the profession of the gospel and the administration of its ordinances is here intended. "Faith," therefore, is that παρρησία ἐν πίστει, that freedom, confidence, and "boldness in the faith," or profession of the faith, "which is in Christ Jesus," mentioned by the apostle (1 Tim. 3:13). That is, our ὑπόστασις, or "confidence" in profession, whose "beginning we are to hold steadfast unto the end" (Heb. 3:14). And we do see how excellent a gift this is on all occasions.¶

When troubles and trials do befall the church upon the account of its profession, many, even true believers, are very ready to faint and despond, and some to draw back, at least for a season, as others do utterly, to the perdition of their souls. In this state the eminent usefulness of this gift of boldness in the faith, of an assured confidence in profession, of a special faith, to go through troubles and trials, is known unto all. Ofttimes the eminence of it in one single person has been the means to preserve a whole church from coldness, backsliding, or sinful compliances with the world. And where God stirs up anyone unto some great or singular work in his church, he constantly endows them with this gift of faith. So was it with Luther, whose undaunted courage and resolution in profession, or boldness in the faith, was one of the principal means of succeeding his great undertaking. And there is no more certain sign of churches being forsaken of Christ in a time of trial than if

10 1 Cor. 12:9.

this gift be withheld from them, and pusillanimity,[11] fearfulness, with carnal wisdom, do spring up in the room of it. The work and effects of this faith are expressed, "Watch ye, stand fast in the faith, quit you like men, be strong" (1 Cor. 16:13; so also Eph. 6:10; 2 Tim. 2:1). And the special way whereby it may be attained or improved, is by a diligent, careful discharge, at all times, of all the duties of the places we hold in the church (1 Pet. 5:1–4).

GIFTS OF HEALING

The "gifts of healing" are nextly mentioned: χαρίσματα ἰαμάτων. "To another the gifts of healing by the same Spirit" (1 Cor. 12:28). So, they are again expressed, in the plural number, because of their free communication unto many persons. These healings respected those that were sick, in their sudden and miraculous recovery from long or deadly distempers, by the imposition of hands in the name of the Lord Jesus. And as many of the "mighty works" of Christ himself, for the reasons that shall be mentioned, consisted in these "healings," so it was one of the first things which he gave in commission to his apostles, and furnished them with power for, while they attended on him in his personal ministry (Matt. 10:1). So also did he to the seventy, making it the principal sign of the approach of the kingdom of God (Luke 10:9). And the same power and virtue he promised to believers, namely, that they should "lay hands on the sick and recover them,"[12] after his ascension. Of the accomplishment of this promise and the exercise of this power, the story of the Acts of the Apostles gives us many instances (Acts 3:7; 5:15; 9:33–34). And two things are observed singular in the exercise of this gift. As first, that many were cured by the shadow of Peter as he passed by (Acts 5:15). And again, many were so by handkerchiefs or aprons carried from the body of Paul (Acts 19:12). And the reason of these extraordinary operations in extraordinary cases seems to have been, the encouragement of that great faith which was then stirred up in them that beheld those miraculous operations, which was of singular advantage unto the propagation of the gospel, as the magical superstition of the Roman church, sundry ways endeavoring to imitate these inimitable[13] actings of sovereign divine power, has been a dishonor to Christian religion.

But whereas these "healings" were miraculous operations, it may be inquired why the gift of them is constantly distinguished from "miracles," and

11 I.e., cowardliness; the state of being weak and afraid of danger.
12 Mark 16:18.
13 I.e., incapable of being imitated.

placed as a distinct effect of the Holy Ghost by itself. For that so it is, is evident both in the commission of Christ granting this power unto his disciples, and in the annumeration of these gifts in this and other places. I answer, this seems to be done on a threefold account.

1. Because miracles absolutely were a sign unto them that believed not, as the apostle speaks of "tongues," they were "a sign, not unto them that believed, but unto them that believed not" (1 Cor. 14:22). That is, they served for their conviction. But this work of healing was a sign unto believers themselves, and that on a double account. (1) The pouring out of this gift of the Holy Ghost was a peculiar sign and token of the coming of the kingdom of God. So says our Savior to his disciples, "Heal the sick, and say unto them, 'The kingdom of God is come nigh unto you'" (Luke 10:9). This gift of healing being a token and pledge thereof. This sign did our Savior give of it himself when John sent his disciples unto him to inquire, for their own satisfaction, not his, whether he were the Messiah or no: "Go," says he, "and show John again those things which ye do hear and see: The blind receive their sight, and the lame walk, and the lepers are cleansed, and the deaf hear, the dead are raised up, and the poor have the gospel preached to them" (Matt. 11:4–5), which was the evidence of his own being the Messiah, and bringing in the kingdom of God. The Jews have an ancient tradition, that in the days of the Messiah all things shall be healed but the serpent. And there is a truth in what they say, although for their parts they understand it not. For all are healed by Christ but the serpent and his seed, the wicked, unbelieving world. And hereof, namely, of the healing and recovery of all things by Christ, was this gift a sign unto the church. Wherefore he began his ministry, after his first miracle, with "healing all manner of sickness, and all manner of disease among the people" (Matt. 4:23–25). (2) It was a sign that Christ had borne and taken away sin, which was the cause, root, and spring of diseases and sicknesses, without which no one could have been miraculously cured. Hence that place of Isaiah, "Surely, he hath borne our griefs, and carried our sorrows" (Isa. 53:4); which is afterward interpreted by being "wounded for our transgressions," and being "bruised for our iniquities" (Isa. 53:5). As also by Peter, by his "bearing our sins in his own body on the tree" (1 Pet. 2:24), is applied by Matthew unto the curing of diseases and sicknesses (Matt 8:16–17). Now, this was for no other reason but because this healing of diseases was a sign and effect of his bearing our sins, the causes of them, without a supposition whereof healing would have been a false witness unto men. It was, therefore, on these accounts, a sign unto believers also.

2. Because it had a peculiar goodness, relief and benignity[14] toward mankind in it, which other miraculous operations had not, at least not unto the same degree. Indeed, this was one great difference between the miraculous operations that were wrought under the Old Testament and those under the New, that the former generally consisted in dreadful and tremendous works, bringing astonishment and ofttimes ruin to mankind, but those others were generally useful and beneficial unto all. But this of healing had a peculiar evidence of love, kindness, compassion, benignity, and was suited greatly to affect the minds of men with regard and gratitude. For long afflictive distempers or violent pains, such as were the diseases cured by this gift, do prepare the minds of men, and those concerned in them, greatly to value their deliverance. This, therefore, in a special manner, declared and evidenced the goodness, love, and compassion of him that was the author of this gospel, and gave this sign of healing spiritual diseases by healing of bodily distempers. And, doubtless, many who were made partakers of the benefit hereof were greatly affected with it. And that not only unto "walking, and leaping, and praising God," as the cripple did who was cured by Peter and John (Acts 3:8), but also unto faith and boldness in profession, as it was with the blind man healed by our Savior himself (John 9:30–33, 38, etc.). But yet no outward effects of themselves can work upon the hearts of men, so as that all who are made partakers of them should be brought unto faith, thankfulness, and obedience. Hence did not only our Savior himself observe, that of ten at once cleansed by him from their leprosy, but one returned to give glory to God (Luke 17:17). But he whom he cured of a disease that he had suffered under eight and thirty years, notwithstanding a solemn admonition given him by our blessed Savior, turned informer against him, and endeavored to betray him unto the Jews (John 5:5–16). It is effectual grace alone which can change the heart, without which it will continue obstinate and unbelieving, under not only the sight and consideration of the most miraculous outward operations, but also the participation in ourselves of the benefits and fruits of them. Men may have their bodies cured by miracles when their souls are not cured by grace.

3. It is thus placed distinctly by itself, and not cast under the common head of "miracles," because ordinarily there were some outward means and tokens of it, that were to be made use of in the exercise of this gift. Such were (1) imposition of hands. Our Savior himself in healing of the sick did generally "lay his hands on them" (Matt. 9:18; Luke 4:40). And he gave the same

14 I.e., kindness; tolerance.

order unto his disciples, that they should "lay their hands on those that were sick, and heal them,"[15] which was practiced by them accordingly. (2) Anointing with oil: "They anointed with oil many that were sick, and healed them" (Mark 6:13). And the elders of the church, with whom this gift was continued, were to come to him that was sick, and praying over him, "anoint him with oil in the name of the Lord," and he should be saved (James 5:14–15). Some do contend for the continuance of this ceremony, or the anointing of them that are sick by the elders of the church, but without ground or warrant. For although it be their duty to pray in a particular manner for those that are sick of their flocks, and it be the duty of them who are sick, to call for them unto that purpose, yet the application of the outward ceremony being instituted, not as a means of an uncertain cure, as all are which work naturally unto that end, but as a pledge and token of a certain healing and recovery, where there is not an infallible faith thereof, when the healing may not ensue, it is to turn an ordinance into a lie. For if a recovery follow ten times on this anointing, if it once fall out otherwise, the institution is rendered a lie, a false testimony, and the other recoveries manifested to have had no dependence on the observation of it. For these reasons, I judge that this gift of healing, though belonging unto miraculous operations in general, is everywhere reckoned as a distinct gift by itself. And from that place of James I am apt to think that this gift was communicated in a special manner unto the elders of churches, even that were ordinary and fixed, it being of so great use and such singular comfort unto them that were poor and persecuted, which was the condition of many churches and their members in those days.

MIRACLES

Miracles ensue in the fifth place: ἐνεργήματα δυνάμεων—"Effectual working of mighty powers," or "powerful works." For the signification of this word, here rendered "miracles," the reader may consult our exposition on Hebrews 2:4.[16] I shall not then transcribe what is already declared, nor is anything necessary to be added thereunto. Concerning this gift of miracles, we have also spoken before in general, so that we shall not much further here insist upon it. Neither is it necessary that we should here treat of the nature, end, and use of miracles in general, which in part also has been done before. Wherefore I shall only observe some few things as to the gift itself, and the use of it in the church, which alone are our present concern. And,

15 Mark 16:18.
16 *Exercitations on the Epistle to the Hebrews Also concerning the Messiah.*

1. As we before observed, this gift did not consist in any inherent power or faculty of the mind, so as that those who had received it should have an ability of their own to work or effect such miracles when and as they saw good. As this is disclaimed by the apostles (Acts 3:12), so a supposition of it would overthrow the very nature of miracles. For a miracle is an immediate effect of divine power, exceeding all created abilities. And what is not so, though it may be strange or wonderful, is no miracle. Only Jesus Christ had in his own person a power of working miracles when, and where, and how he pleased, because "God was with him," or "the fullness of the God head dwelt in him bodily."[17]

2. Unto the working of every miracle in particular, there was a peculiar act of faith required in them that wrought it. This is that faith which is called the faith of miracles: "Though I have all faith, so that I could remove mountains" (1 Cor. 13:2). Now, this faith was not a strong fixing of the imagination that such a thing should be done, as some have blasphemously dreamed, nor was it a faith resting merely on the promises of the word, making particular application of them unto times, seasons, and occasions, wherein it no way differs from the ordinary grace of faith, but this was the true nature of it, that as it was in general resolved into the promises of the word, and power of Christ declared therein, that such and such things should be wrought in general, so it had always a peculiar, immediate revelation for its warranty and security in the working of any miracle. And without such an immediate revelation or divine impulse and impression, all attempts of miraculous operations are vain, and means only for Satan to insinuate his delusions by.

No man, therefore, could work any miracle, nor attempt in faith so to do, without an immediate revelation that divine power should be therein exerted, and put forth in its operation. Yet do I not suppose that it was necessary that this inspiration and revelation should in order of time precede the acting of this faith, though it did the operation of the miracle itself. Yea, the inspiration itself consisted in the elevation of faith to apprehend divine power in such a case for such an end, which the Holy Ghost granted not to any but when he designed so to work. Thus, Paul at once acted faith, apprehended divine power, and at the same time struck Elymas the sorcerer blind by a miraculous operation (Acts 13:9–11). Being "filled with the Holy Ghost" (Acts 13:9), that is, having received an impression and warranty from him, he put forth that act of faith at whose presence the Holy Spirit would affect that miraculous operation which he believed. Wherefore this was the nature of this gift. Some

---

17 Col. 2:9.

persons were by the Holy Ghost endowed with that special faith which was prepared to receive impressions and intimations of his putting forth his power in this or that miraculous operation. Those who had this faith could not work miracles when, and where, and how they pleased; only they could infallibly signify what the Holy Ghost would do, and so were the outward instruments of the execution of his power.

3. Although the apostles had all gifts of the Spirit in an eminent degree and manner, above all others, as Paul says, "I thank my God, I speak with tongues more than ye all,"[18] yet it appears that there were some other persons distinct from them who had this gift of working miracles in a peculiar manner. For it is not only here reckoned as a peculiar, distinct gift of the Holy Ghost, but also the persons who had received it are reckoned as distinct from the apostles and other officers of the church (1 Cor. 12:28–29). Not that I think this gift did constitute them officers in the church, enabling them to exercise power in gospel administrations therein; only they were brethren of the church, made eminent by a participation of this gift, for the end whereunto it was ordained. By these persons' ministry did the Holy Spirit, on such occasions as seemed meet to his infinite wisdom, effect miraculous operations, besides what was done in the same kind by the apostles and evangelists all the world over.

4. The use of this gift in the church at that time and season was manifold. For the principles which believers proceeded on, and the doctrines they professed, were new and strange to the world, and such as had mighty prejudices raised against them in the minds of men. The persons by whom they were maintained and asserted were generally, as to their outward condition, poor and contemptible in the world. The churches themselves, as to their members, few in number, encompassed with multitudes of scoffers and persecuting idolaters, themselves also newly converted, and many of them but weak in the faith. In this state of things, this gift of miracles was exceedingly useful, and necessary unto the propagation of the gospel, the vindication of the truth, and the establishment of them that did believe. For,¶

(1) by miracles occasionally wrought, the people round about who yet believed not were called in, as it were, unto a due consideration of what was done and what was designed thereby. Thus when the noise was first spread abroad of the apostles speaking with tongues, the "multitude came together, and were confounded" (Acts 2:6). So the multitude gathered together at Lystra upon the curing of the cripple by Paul and Barnabas, thinking them to have been gods (Acts 14:11). When, therefore, any were so amazed with seeing the

---

18   1 Cor. 14:18.

miracles that were wrought, hearing that they were so in the confirmation of the doctrine of the gospel, they could not but inquire with diligence into it, and cast out those prejudices which before they had entertained against it.¶

(2) They gave authority unto the ministers of the church, for whereas on outward accounts they were despised by the great, wise, and learned men of the world, it was made evident by these divine operations that their ministry was of God, and what they taught approved by him. And where these two things were effected, namely, that a sufficient, yea, an eminently cogent ground and reason was given why men should impartially inquire into the doctrine of the gospel, and an evidence given that the teachers of it were approved of God, unless men were signally captivated under the power of Satan (2 Cor. 4:4), or given up of God judicially unto blindness and hardness of heart, it could not be but that the prejudices which they had of themselves, or might receive from others, against the gospel, must of necessity be prevailed against and conquered. And as many of the Jews were so hardened and blinded at that time (Rom. 11:7–10; 1 Thess. 2:14–16), so it is marvelous to consider with what artifices Satan bestirred himself among the Gentiles, by false and lying signs and wonders, with many other ways, to take off from the testimony given unto the gospel by these miraculous operations. And this was that which miracles were designed unto toward unbelievers, namely, to take away prejudices from the doctrine of the gospel and the persons by whom it was taught, so disposing the minds of men unto an attendance unto it and the reception of it. For they were never means instituted of God for the ingenerating of faith in any, but only to provoke and prevail with men to attend unprejudicately[19] unto that whereby it was to be wrought. For "faith cometh by hearing, and hearing by the Word of God" (Rom. 10:17). And, therefore, whatever miracles were wrought, if the word preached was not received, if that did not accompany them in its powerful operation, they were but despised. Thus, whereas some, upon hearing the apostles speak with tongues, mocked, and said, "These men are full of new wine" (Acts 2:13), yet upon preaching of the word, which ensued, they were converted unto God. And the apostle Paul tells us that if there were nothing but miraculous speaking with tongues in the church, an unbeliever coming in would say they were all mad (1 Cor. 14:23), who by the word of prophecy would be convinced, judged, and converted unto God (1 Cor. 14:24–25).¶

(3) They were of singular use to confirm and establish in the faith those who were weak and newly converted. For whereas they were assaulted on

---

19 I.e., in an unbiased manner; without prejudice.

every hand by Satan, the world, and, it may be, their dearest relations, and that with contempt, scorn, and cruel mocking, it was a singular confirmation and establishment, to behold the miraculous operations which were wrought in the approbation of the doctrine which they did profess. Hereby was a sense of it more and more let into and impressed on their minds, until, by a habitual experience of its goodness, power, and efficacy they were established in the truth.

PROPHECY

Prophecy is added in the sixth place. Ἄλλῳ δὲ προφητεία, "To another prophecy," that is, is given by the same Spirit. Of this gift of prophecy, we have sufficiently treated before.[20] Only, I take it here in its largest sense, both as it signifies a faculty of prediction, or foretelling things future upon divine revelation, or an ability to declare the mind of God from the word, by the special and immediate revelation of the Holy Ghost. The first of these was more rare, the latter more ordinary and common. And it may be there were few churches wherein, besides their elders and teachers, by virtue of their office, there were not some of these prophets. So of those who had this gift of prophecy, enabling them in an eminent manner to declare the mind of God from the Scriptures unto the edification of the church, it is expressed that there were some of them in the church at Antioch (Acts 13:1–2), and many of them in the church at Corinth (1 Cor. 14). For this gift was of singular use in the church, and, therefore, as to the end of the edification thereof, is preferred by our apostle above all other gifts of the Spirit whatever (1 Cor. 12:31; 14:1, 39). For it had a double use. First, the conviction and conversion of such as came in occasionally into their church assemblies. Those unto whom the propagation of the gospel was principally committed went up and down the world, laying hold on all occasions to preach it unto Jews and Gentiles as yet unconverted. And where churches were gathered and settled, the principal work of their teachers was to edify them that did believe. But whereas some would come in among them into their church assemblies, perhaps out of curiosity, perhaps out of worse designs, the apostle declares that of all the ordinances of the church, this of prophecy was suited unto the conviction and conversion of all unbelievers, and is ofttimes blessed thereunto, whereby this and that man are born in Zion. Second, this exposition and application of the word by many, and that by virtue of an extraordinary

20 Owen is likely referring to chap. 3 of this treatise.

assistance of the Spirit of God, was of singular use in the church itself. For if all Scripture given by inspiration from God, so expounded and applied, be "profitable for doctrine, for reproof, for correction, for instruction in righteousness,"[21] the more the church enjoys thereof, the more will its faith, love, obedience, and consolation be increased.⁋

Lastly, the manner of the exercise of this gift in the church unto edification is prescribed and limited by our apostle (1 Cor. 14:29–33). And first, he would not have the church burdened even with the most profitable gift or its exercise, and therefore determines that at one time not above two or three be suffered to speak, that is, one after another, that the church be neither wearied nor burdened (1 Cor. 14:29). Secondly, because it was possible that some of them who had this gift might mix somewhat of their own spirits in their word and ministry, and therein mistake and err from the truth, he requires that the others who had the like gift, and so were understanding in the mind of God, should judge of what was spoken by them, so as that the church might not be led into any error by them: "Let the other judge."[22] Thirdly, that order be observed in their exercise, and especially that way be given unto any immediate revelation, and no confusion be brought into the church by many speaking at the same time. And this direction manifests that the gift was extraordinary and is now ceased; though there be a continuance of ordinary gifts of the same kind, and to the same end, in the church, as we shall see afterward (1 Cor. 14:30). Fourthly, by the observation of this order, the apostle shows that all the prophets might exercise their gift unto the instruction and consolation of the church in a proper season, such as their frequent assemblies would afford them (1 Cor. 14:31).⁋

And whereas it may be objected that these things coming in an extraordinary, immediate manner from the Holy Ghost, it was not in the power of them who received them to confine them unto the order prescribed, which would seem to limit the Holy Spirit in his operations, whereas they were all to speak as the Spirit gave them ability and utterance, let what would ensue, the apostle assures them by a general principle that no such thing would follow on a due use and exercise of this gift: "For God," says he, "is not the author of confusion, but of peace, as in all churches of the saints" (1 Cor. 14:33). As if he should have said, "If such a course should be taken, that anyone should speak and prophesy as he pretended himself to be moved by the Spirit, and to have none to judge of what he said, all confusion, tumult, and disorder, would

21 2 Tim. 3:16.
22 1 Cor. 14:29.

ensue thereon. But God is the author of no such thing, gives no such gifts, appoints no such exercise of them, as would tend thereunto." But how shall this be prevented, seeing these things are extraordinary, and not in our own power? Yea, says he, "The spirits of the prophets are subject to the prophets" (1 Cor. 14:32). By "the spirits of the prophets," that their spiritual gift and ability for its exercise are intended, none does question. And whereas the apostle had taught two things concerning the exercise of this gift: (1) That it ought to be orderly, to avoid confusion. (2) That what proceeds from it ought to be judged by others. He manifests that both these may be observed, "because the spirits of the prophets are subject to the prophets," that is, both their spiritual gift is so in their own power as that they might dispose themselves unto its exercise with choice and judgment, so as to preserve order and peace, not being acted as with an enthusiastic afflation,[23] and carried out of their own power. This gift in its exercise was subject unto their own judgment, choice, and understanding. So what they expressed by virtue of their spiritual gift was subject to be judged of by the other prophets that were in the church. Thus were the peace and order of the church to be preserved, and the edification of it to be promoted.

DISCERNING OF SPIRITS

Discerning of spirits is the next gift of the Spirit here enumerated: ἄλλῳ δὲ διακρίσεις πνευμάτων, "To another discerning of spirits," the ability and faculty of judging of spirits, the dijudication[24] of spirits. This gift I have, upon another occasion, formerly given an account of, and therefore shall here but briefly touch upon it.[25] All gospel administrations were in those days avowedly executed by virtue of spiritual gifts. No man then durst[26] set his hand unto this work but such as either really had or highly pretended unto a participation of the Holy Ghost, for the administration of the gospel is the dispensation of the Spirit. This, therefore, was pleaded by all in the preaching of the word, whether in private assemblies or publicly to the world.¶

But it came also then to pass, as it did in all ages of the church, that where God gave unto any the extraordinary gifts of his Spirit, for the reformation or edification of the church, there Satan suborned[27] some to make a

---

23 I.e., inspiration.
24 I.e., the act of making a judicial decision.
25 *Πνευματολογια, or, A Discourse concerning the Holy Spirit*, bk. 1, chap. 1.
26 I.e., dared.
27 I.e., induced; bribed.

pretense thereunto, unto its trouble and destruction. So was it under the Old Testament, and so was it foretold that it should be under the New. So the apostle Peter, having declared the nature and excellency, use and certainty, of that prophecy which was of old (2 Pet. 1:19–21), adds thereunto, "But there were false prophets also among the people" (2 Pet. 2:1). That is, when God granted that signal privilege unto the church of the immediate revelation of his will unto them by the inspiration of the Holy Ghost, which constituted men true prophets of the Lord, Satan stirred up others to pretend unto the same spirit of prophecy for his own malicious ends, whereby "there were false prophets also among the people." But it may be it will be otherwise now, under the gospel church state. "No," says he, "there shall be false teachers among you," that is, persons pretending to the same spiritual gift that the apostles and evangelists had, yet bringing in thereby "damnable heresies." Now, all their damnable opinions they fathered upon immediate revelations of the Spirit. This gave occasion to the holy apostle John to give that caution, with his reason of it, which is expressed (1 John 4:1–3), which words we have opened before. And this false pretense unto extraordinary spiritual gifts the church was tried and pestered with so long as there was any occasion to give it countenance, namely, while such gifts were really continued unto any therein.¶

What way, then, had God ordained for the preservation and safety of the church, that it should not be imposed upon by any of these delusions? I answer, there was a standing rule in the church, whereby whatsoever was or could be offered doctrinally unto it might certainly and infallibly be tried, judged, and determined on. And this was the rule of the written word, according to that everlasting ordinance, "To the law and to the testimony, if they speak not according to this word, it is because there is no light in them" (Isa. 8:20). This, in all ages, was sufficient for the preservation of the church from all errors and heresies, or damnable doctrines, which it never fell into, nor shall do so, but in the sinful neglect and contempt hereof. Moreover, the apostle further directs the application of this rule unto present occasions, by advising us to fix on some fundamental principles which are likely to be opposed, and if they are not owned and avowed, to avoid such teachers, whatever spiritual gift they pretend unto (1 John 4:2–3; 2 John 9–11).¶

But yet, because many in those days were weak in the faith, and might be surprised with such pretenses, God had graciously provided and bestowed the gift here mentioned on some, it may be in every church, namely, of discerning of spirits. They could, by virtue of the extraordinary gift and aid therein of the Holy Ghost, make a true judgment of the spirits that men pretended to act and to be acted by, whether they were of God or not. And this was of singular use and benefit unto the church in those days. For as spiritual gifts abounded, so did a pretense unto them, which was always accompanied with pernicious designs. Herein, therefore, did God grant relief for them who were either less skillful, or less wary, or less able on any account to make a right judgment between those who were really endowed with extraordinary gifts of the Spirit and those who falsely pretended thereunto. For these persons received this gift, and were placed in the church for this very end, that they might guide and help them in making a right judgment in this matter. And whereas the communication of these gifts is ceased, and consequently all pretenses unto them, unless by some persons phrenetic[28] and enthusiastic, whose madness is manifest to all, there is no need of the continuance of this gift of "discerning of spirits," that standing infallible rule of the word, and ordinary assistance of the Spirit, being every way sufficient for our preservation in the truth, unless we give up ourselves to the conduct of corrupt lusts, pride, self-conceit, carnal interest, passions, and temptations, which ruin the souls of men.

TONGUES AND THEIR INTERPRETATION

The two spiritual gifts here remaining are speaking with tongues and their interpretation. The first communication of this "gift of tongues" unto the apostles is particularly described (Acts 2:1–4, etc.). And although they were at that time endued with all other gifts of the Holy Ghost, called "power from above" (Acts 1:8), yet was this "gift of tongues" signalized by the visible pledge of it, the joint participation of the same gift by all, and the notoriety of the matter thereon, as in that place of the Acts is at large described. And God seems to have laid the foundation of preaching the gospel in this gift for two reasons. First, to signify that the grace and mercy of the covenant was now no longer to be confined unto one nation, language, or people, but to be extended unto all nations, tongues, and languages of people under heaven. Second, to testify by what means he would subdue the souls and consciences of men unto the obedience of Christ and the gospel, and by what means he would maintain his kingdom in the world. Now, this was not by force and might, by external power or armies, but by the preaching of the word, whereof the tongue is the only instrument. And the outward sign of this gift, in tongues of fire, evidenced the light and efficacy wherewith

---

28 I.e., frenetic; frenzied; frantic.

the Holy Ghost designed to accompany the dispensation of the gospel. Wherefore, although this gift began with the apostles, yet was it afterward very much diffused unto the generality of them that did believe (Acts 10:46; 19:6; 1 Cor. 14:1–27).¶

And some few things we may observe concerning this gift. (1) The special matter that was expressed by this gift seems to have been the praises of God for his wonderful works of grace by Christ. Although I doubt not but that the apostles were enabled, by virtue of this gift, to declare the gospel unto any people unto whom they came in their own language, yet, ordinarily, they did not preach nor instruct the people by virtue of this gift, but only spoke forth the praises of God, to the admiration and astonishment of them who were yet strangers to the faith. So, when they first received the gift, they were heard "speaking the wonderful works of God" (Acts 2:11). And the Gentiles who first believed "spake with tongues, and magnified God" (Acts 10:46). (2) These tongues were so given "for a sign unto them that believed not" (1 Cor. 14:22), that sometimes those that spoke with tongues understood not the sense and meaning of the words delivered by themselves, nor were they understood by the church itself wherein they were uttered (1 Cor. 14:2, 6–11, etc.). But this, I suppose, was only sometimes, and that, it may be, mostly when this gift was unnecessarily used. For I doubt not but the apostles understood full well the things delivered by themselves in divers tongues. And all who had this gift, though they might not apprehend the meaning of what themselves spoke and uttered, yet were so absolutely, in the exercise of it, under the conduct of the Holy Spirit, that they neither did nor could speak anything by virtue thereof but what was according unto the mind of God, and tended unto his praise (1 Cor. 14:2, 14, 17). (3) Although this gift was excellent in itself, and singularly effectual in the propagation of the gospel unto unbelievers, yet in the assemblies of the church it was of little or no use, but only with respect unto the things themselves that were uttered. For as to the principal end of it, to be a sign unto unbelievers, it was finished and accomplished toward them, so as they had no further need or use of it.¶

But now, whereas many unbelievers came occasionally into the assemblies of the church, especially at some freer seasons, for whose conviction the Holy Ghost would for a season continue this gift among believers, that the church might not be disadvantaged thereby, he added the other gift here mentioned, namely, "the interpretation of tongues." He endowed either those persons themselves who spoke with tongues, or some others in the same assembly, with an ability to interpret and declare to the church the things that were spoken and uttered in that miraculous manner, which is the last gift here mentioned. But the nature, use, and abuse of these gifts is so largely and distinctly spoken unto by the apostle (1 Cor. 14:1–27), that as I need not insist on them, so I cannot fully do it without an entire exposition of that whole chapter, which the nature of my design will not permit.

Of the Origin, Duration, Use, and End of Extraordinary Spiritual Gifts

THIS SUMMARY ACCOUNT does the apostle give of these extraordinary gifts of the Holy Ghost which then flourished in the church and were the life of its extraordinary ministry. It may be, mention may occur of some such gifts under other names, but they are such as may be reduced unto some one of those here expressed. Wherefore this may be admitted as a perfect catalogue of them, and comprehensive of that power from above which the Lord Christ promised unto his apostles and disciples upon his ascension into heaven (Acts 1:8). For he "ascended up far above all heavens, that he might fill all things" (Eph. 4:10), that is, the church with officers and gifts, unto the perfection of the saints, by the work of the ministry, and the edification of his body (Eph. 4:12). For being by the right hand of God exalted, and having received of the Father the promise of the Holy Ghost, he shed forth, or abundantly poured out, those things whereof we speak (Acts 2:33). And as they were the great evidences of his acceptation with God, and exaltation, seeing in them the Spirit "convinced the world of sin, of righteousness, and of judgment,"[1] so they were the great means whereby he carried on his work among men, as shall afterward be declared.

There was no certain limited time for the cessation of these gifts. Those peculiar unto the apostles were commensurate unto their lives. None after their decease had either apostolic office, power, or gifts. The like may be said of the evangelists. Nor have we any undoubted testimony that any of those gifts which were truly miraculous, and every way above the faculties of men,

---

1   John 16:8.

were communicated unto any after the expiration of the generation of them who conversed with Christ in the flesh, or those who received the Holy Ghost by their ministry. It is not unlikely but that God might on some occasions, for a longer season, put forth his power in some miraculous operations, and so he yet may do, and perhaps does sometimes. But the superstition and folly of some ensuing ages, inventing and divulging innumerable miracles false and foolish, proved a most disadvantageous prejudice unto the gospel, and a means to open a way unto Satan to impose endless delusions upon Christians. For as true and real miracles, with becoming circumstances, were the great means that won and reconciled a regard and honor unto Christian religion in the world, so the pretense of such as either were absolutely false, or such as whose occasions, ends, matter, or manner were unbecoming the greatness and holiness of him who is the true author of all miraculous operations, is the greatest dishonor unto religion that anyone can invent. But although all these gifts and operations ceased in some respect, some of them absolutely, and some of them as to the immediate manner of communication and degree of excellency, yet so far as the edification of the church was concerned in them, something that is analogous unto them was and is continued. He who gave "some apostles, and some prophets, and some evangelists," gave also "some pastors and teachers."[2] And as he furnished the former with extraordinary gifts, so as far as anything of the like kind is needful for the continual edification of the church, he bestows it on the latter also, as shall be declared.

THE EARLY CHURCH

And these gifts of the Spirit, added unto his grace in real holiness, were the glory, honor, and beauty of the church of old. Men have but deceived themselves and others when they have feigned a glory and beauty of the church in other things. And whatever any think or say, where these gifts of the Holy Ghost, which are the ornaments of the church, her clothing of wrought gold, and her raiment of needlework, are neglected and lost, and they think to adorn her with the meretricious[3] paint of pompous ceremonies, with outward grandeur, wealth, and power, she is utterly fallen from her chastity, purity, and integrity. But it is evident that this is the state of many churches in the world, which are therefore worldly and carnal, not spiritual or evangelical. Power, and force, and wealth—the gifts, in this case, of another spirit—under

2 Eph. 4:11.
3 I.e., pretentious; gaudy; characteristic of a prostitute.

various pretenses and names, are their life and glory, indeed, their death and shame. I deny not but that it is lawful for ministers of the gospel to enjoy earthly possessions, which they do attain by any commendable way among other men. Neither are they required, unless in extraordinary cases, to part with the right and use of their temporal goods because they are so ministers of Christ, though those who are so indeed will not deny but that they ought to use them in a peculiar manner unto the glory of Christ and honor of the gospel, beyond other men. Neither shall I ever question that wherein the Scripture is so express, namely, that those who "labour in the Word and doctrine"[4] should have a convenient, yea, an honorable subsistence provided for them, according to the best ability of the church, for their work's sake.¶

It is in like manner also granted that the Lord Christ has committed all that power which, with respect unto the edification of the church, he will exercise in this world unto the church itself, as it cannot, without a virtual renunciation of the gospel and faith in Christ Jesus as the head and king of the church, be supposed that this power is any other but spiritual, over the souls and consciences of men. And therefore this power cannot be exercised, or be any way made effectual, but by virtue of the spiritual gifts we treat of. But for men to turn this spiritual power, to be exercised only by virtue of spiritual gifts, into an external coercive power over the persons, bodies, liberties, and lives of men, to be exercised by law courts, in ways, forms, manners, utterly foreign to the gospel and all evangelical administrations, without the least pretense unto or appearance of the exercise of the gifts of the Holy Ghost therein, yea, and by persons by whom they are hated and derided, acting with pride, scorn, and contempt of the disciples of Christ and over them, being utterly ignorant of the true nature and use of all gospel administrations, this is to disorder the church, and instead of a house of spiritual worship, in some instances to turn it into "a den of thieves."[5] Where hereunto there are, moreover, annexed earthly revenues, containing all food and fuel of corrupt lusts, with all things satisfactory unto the minds of worldly, sensual men, as a meet reward of these carnal administrations, as it is at this day in the Church of Rome, there all use of the gifts of the Holy Ghost is excluded, and the church is brought into extreme desolation. And although these things are as contrary to the gospel as darkness is to light, yet the world, for many reasons not now to be insisted on, being willing to be deceived in this matter, it is generally apprehended that there is nothing

4   1 Tim. 5:17.
5   Matt. 21:13.

so pernicious unto the church, so justly to be watched against and rooted out, as a dislike of their horrible apostasies, in the corrupt depravation of all evangelical administrations. This was not the state, this was not the condition, of the primitive churches. Their life consisted in the grace of the Spirit, and their glory in his gifts. None of their leaders once dreamed of that new kind of beauty, glory, and power consisting in numberless superstitious ceremonies, instead of religious worship; worldly grandeur, instead of humility and self-denial; and open tyranny over the consciences and persons of men, in the room of spiritual authority, effectual in the power of Christ, and by virtue of the gifts of the Holy Ghost.

There are many sore divisions at this day in the world among and between the professors of Christian religion, both about the doctrine and worship of the gospel, as also the discipline thereof. That these divisions are evil in themselves, and the cause of great evils, hindrances of the gospel, and all the effects thereof in the world, is acknowledged by all. And it is a thing, doubtless, to be greatly lamented, that the generality of them who are called Christians are departed from the great rule of "keeping the unity of the Spirit in the bond of peace."[6] He who does not pray always, who is not ready with his utmost endeavor to remedy this evil, to remove this great obstruction of the benefit of the gospel, is scarce worthy the name of a Christian. The common way insisted on unto this end is that those who have most force and power should set up standards and measures of agreement, compelling others, by all ways of severity and violence, to a compliance therewith, judging them the highest offenders who shall refuse so to do, because the determining and settling of this matter is committed unto them. This is the way of Antichrist and those who follow him therein.¶

Others, with more moderation and wisdom, but with as little success, do or have endeavored the reconciliation of the parties at variance, some, more or all of them, by certain middle ways of mutual condescension which they have found out. Some things they blame, and some things they commend in all; some things they would have them do, and some things omit, all for the sake of peace and love. And this design carries with it so fair and pleadable a pretense, that those who are once engaged in it are apt to think that they alone are the true lovers of Christianity in general, the only sober and indifferent persons, fit to umpire all the differences in the world, in a few propositions which they have framed. And so wedded are some wise and holy men unto these apprehensions of reconciling Christians by their conceived methods,

6   Eph. 4:3.

that no experience of endless disappointments and of increasing new differences and digladiations,[7] of forming new parties, of reviving old animosities, all which roll in upon them continually, will discourage them in their design. "What then," will some say, "would you have these divisions and differences that are among us continued and perpetuated, when you acknowledge them so evil and pernicious?" I say, God forbid. Yea, we pray for, and always will endeavor, their removal and taking away.¶

But yet this I say, on the other hand, whether men will hear or whether they will forbear, there is but one way of effecting this so blessed and desirable a work, which until it be engaged in, let men talk what they please of reconciliation, the worst of men will be reviling and persecuting those who are better than themselves unto the end of the world. And this way is, that all churches should endeavor to reduce themselves unto the primitive pattern. Let us all but consider what was the life and spirit of those churches, wherein their honor, glory, and order did consist, making it our joint design to walk in the principle of that grace of the Spirit wherein they walked, in the exercise and use of those gifts of the Spirit which were the spring of and gave virtue unto all their administrations, renouncing whatever is foreign unto and inconsistent with these things, and that grace and unity will quickly enter into professors which Christ has purchased for them. But these things are here only occasionally mentioned, and are not further to be pursued.

THE KINGDOM OF CHRIST

These spiritual gifts the apostle calls the "powers of the world to come" (Heb. 6:4–5), that is, those effectual powerful principles and operations which peculiarly belong unto the kingdom of Christ and administration of the gospel, whereby they were to be set up, planted, advanced, and propagated in the world. The Lord Christ came and wrought out the mighty work of our salvation in his own person, and thereon laid the foundation of his church on himself, by the confession of him as the Son of God. Concerning himself and his work he preached, and caused to be preached, a doctrine that was opposed by all the world, because of its truth, mystery, and holiness; yet was it the design of God to break through all those oppositions, to cause this doctrine to be received and submitted unto, and Jesus Christ to be believed in, unto the ruin and destruction of the kingdom of Satan in the world. Now, this was a work that could not be wrought without the putting forth and exercise of

---

7   I.e., fights with swords or hand to hand.

mighty power, concerning which nothing remains to be inquired into but of what sort it ought to be.¶

Now, the conquest that the Lord Christ aimed at was spiritual, over the souls and consciences of men; the enemies he had to conflict with were spiritual, even principalities and powers, and spiritual wickednesses in high places, the god of this world, the prince of it, which ruled in the children of disobedience. The kingdom which he had to erect was spiritual, and not of this world; all the laws and rules of it, with their administrations and ends, were spiritual and heavenly. The gospel that was to be propagated was a doctrine not concerning this world, nor the things of it, nor of anything natural or political, but as they were merely subordinate unto other ends, but heavenly and mysterious, directing men only in a tendency according to the mind of God, unto the eternal enjoyment of him. Hereon it will easily appear what kind of power is necessary unto this work and for the attaining of these ends. He that, at the speaking of one word, could have engaged "more than twelve legions of angels"[8] in his work and unto his assistance, could have easily, by outward force and arms, subdued the whole world into an external observance of him and his commands, and thereon have ruled men at his pleasure. As this he could have done, and may do when he pleases, so if he had done it, it had tended nothing unto the ends which he designed. He might, indeed, have had a glorious empire in the world, comprehensive of all dominions that ever were or can be on the earth; but yet it would have been of the same kind and nature with that which Nero had, the greatest monster of villainy in nature. Neither had it been any great matter for the Son of God to have outdone the Romans or the Turks, or such like conspiracies of wicked oppressors.¶

And all those who yet think meet to use external force over the persons, lives, and bodies of men, in order unto the reducing of them unto the obedience of Christ and the gospel, do put the greatest dishonor upon him imaginable, and change the whole nature of his design and kingdom. He will neither own nor accept of any subject but whose obedience is a free act of his own will, and who is so made willing by himself in the day of his power. His design, and his only design, in this world, unto the glory of God, is to erect a kingdom, throne, and rule in the souls and consciences of men, to have an obedience from them in faith, love, and spiritual delight, proceeding from their own choice, understandings, wills, and affections, an obedience that should be internal, spiritual, mystical, heavenly, with respect solely unto things unseen and eternal, wherein himself and his laws should be infinitely

8   Matt. 26:53.

preferred before all earthly things and considerations. Now, this is a matter that all earthly powers and empires could never desire, design, or put a hand unto, and that which renders the kingdom of Christ as of another nature, so more excellent and better than all earthly kingdoms, as liberty is better than bondage, the mind more excellent than the outward carcass, spiritual and eternal things than things carnal and temporary, as the wisdom and holiness of God are more excellent than the folly and lusts of men.

Seeing, therefore, this was the design of Christ, this was the nature and work of the gospel which was to be propagated, wherein carnal power and outward force could be of no use, yea, whose exercise was inconsistent with, dishonorable unto, and destructive of the whole design, and wherein the work to be accomplished on the minds and souls of men is incomparably greater than the conquering of worlds with force and arms, it is inquired what power the Lord Christ did employ herein, what means and instruments he used for the accomplishment of his design, and the erecting of that kingdom or church state which, being promised of old, was called "the world to come," or the "new world," "a new heavens and a new earth, wherein dwelleth righteousness."[9] And I say, it was those gifts of the Holy Ghost whereof we have treated, which were those "powers" of this "world to come." By them it was, or in their exercise, that the Lord Christ erected his empire over the souls and consciences of men, destroying both the work and kingdom of the devil. It is true, it is the word of the gospel itself that is the rod of his strength, which is sent out of Zion to erect and dispense his rule; but that hidden power which made the word effectual in the dispensation of it consisted in those gifts of the Holy Ghost. Men may despise them or think light of them while they please, they are those powers which the Lord Christ in his wisdom thought meet alone to engage in the propagation of the gospel, and the setting up of his kingdom in the world.

The recovery and return of the people from the captivity of Babylon was a type of the spiritual redemption of the church by Jesus Christ. And how God effected that as a type hereof he declares, "'Not by army, nor by power, but by my Spirit,' saith the Lord of hosts" (Zech. 4:6). So, much more, was this work to be effected. So, after his resurrection, the Lord Christ tells his apostles that they were to be his "witnesses in Jerusalem, and in all Judea, and in Samaria, and unto the uttermost part of the earth," that is, all the world over (Acts 1:8). But how shall they be able so to bear testimony unto them as that their witness shall be received and become effectual? Says he, "Ye shall

---

9   Luke 18:30; Matt. 19:28; 2 Pet. 3:13.

receive power for this end. I have given you authority to preach the Word before, and now I will give you such an ability for it as none shall be able to withstand or resist, and this is after the Holy Ghost is come upon you, that is, in the communication of those gifts whereby ye may be enabled unto your work."[10] In them consisted that "mouth and wisdom" which he promised he would give them, "which all their adversaries were not able to gainsay nor resist" (Luke 21:15).¶

ESTABLISHMENT OF THE CHURCH

Wherefore, that which I shall close this discourse with shall be a brief endeavor to declare how those gifts were the spiritual powers of the gospel unto all the ends we have before mentioned, as designed by Jesus Christ; whence it will appear how little there was of the wisdom, skill, power, or authority of men in the whole work of propagating the gospel and planting the church of Christ, as we shall afterward manifest how, by the dispensation of the other more ordinary gifts of the Spirit, both the gospel and the church are continued and preserved in the world.

First, the persons whom the Lord Christ chose, called, and designed unto this work, were by those gifts enabled thereunto. As no mortal men had of themselves any sufficiency for such a work, so the persons particularly called unto it by Jesus Christ lay under all the disadvantages that any persons could possibly be liable unto in such an undertaking. For (1) they were all of them unlearned and ignorant, which the Jews took notice of (Acts 4:13), and which the Gentiles despised them for. (2) They were poor, and of no reputation in the world, which made them contemned by all sorts of persons. And (3) they seem in many instances to have been pusillanimous and fearful, which they all manifested when they so shamefully fled and left their Master in his distresses, the chief of them also swearing that he knew him not. Now, it is easily understood what great disadvantages these were unto the undertaking of so great a work as they were called unto, yea, how impossible it was for them, under these qualifications, to do anything in the pursuit of it. Wherefore, by the communication of these gifts unto them, all these impediments arising from themselves were removed, and they were furnished with endowments of quite another nature, whereby they were eminently filled with that spiritual wisdom, knowledge, and understanding, which surpassed all the wisdom that was of the world or in it, by what ways or means soever it were attained.¶

---

10 This is Owen's interpretation of Acts 1:8.

They both had and declared a wisdom which none of the princes of this world were acquainted with (1 Cor. 2:1–8, 13). Those who, during the abode of Christ in the flesh with them, could not understand a plain parable, and were ever and anon[11] at no small loss about the sense and meaning of their master, having very low and carnal apprehensions about his person, work, and office, were now filled with a knowledge of all heavenly mysteries, and with wisdom to declare, manage, and maintain them against all opposers. Kings, princes, rulers of synagogues, were now all one to them. They had a mouth and wisdom given them which none of their adversaries could resist. Wherever they came, in all nations, to all sorts of people, of all languages, they were now enabled, in their own tongue and speech, to declare and preach the gospel unto them, being always filled with a treasure of wisdom and spiritual mysteries, whence they could draw forth as every occasion did require.¶

Whereas they were poor, the difficulties wherewith such a condition is attended were also by this means utterly taken away. For although they had neither silver nor gold by their work or employment, but their outward wants and distresses were rather increased thereby, yet their minds and souls were by this communication of the Spirit so raised above the world, and filled with such a contempt of all the desirable things in it, and of all the pride of men upon their account, as that their want of possessions and outward enjoyments made them only the more ready and expedite for their work, whence also such of them as had possessions, sold them, gave their price to the poor, that they might be no hindrance unto them in their design. And hence also it was that those who, even after the resurrection of Christ, were inquiring after a temporal kingdom, wherein, no doubt, a good part of its glory, power, and advantages would fall to their shares, as most do who yet continue to dream of such a kingdom in this world, immediately upon the communication of these gifts rejoiced that they were counted worthy of shame for the name of Christ, when they were imprisoned, whipped, and despitefully used (Acts 5:40–41).¶

They had boldness, courage, and constancy given unto them, in the room of that pusillanimity and fear which before they had discovered. This the Jews took notice of and were astonished at (Acts 4:13). And they had reason so to be, if we consider the power and authority of that work wherein they were then assaulted, with the speech of Peter unto them (Acts 4:8–12), which he spoke as filled with the Holy Ghost (see also Acts 5:28–32). And in the whole course of their ministry throughout the world, the like undaunted

---

11 I.e., occasionally.

courage, resolution, and constancy, did always and in all things accompany them. Wherefore, these gifts, in the first place, may be esteemed the "powers of the world to come,"[12] inasmuch as by them those unto whom the work of preaching the gospel, propagating the mystery of it, the conversion of nations, the planting of churches, and in all the erection of the kingdom of Christ, was committed, were enabled by them, unto the utmost capacity of human nature, to discharge, effect, and accomplish the work committed unto them.¶

By virtue and in the strength of these spiritual abilities did they set upon the whole kingdom of Satan and darkness in the world, contending with the gates of hell and all the powers of the earth, attempting the wisdom of the Greeks and the religion of the Jews, with success against both. They went not forth with force and arms, or carnal power. They threatened no man, menaced no man, with the carnal weapons of force or penalties. They had no baits or allurements of wealth, power, or honor, to inveigle[13] the minds of corrupt and sensual men. But, as was said, in the warranty and power of these spiritual gifts, they both attempted and accomplished this work. And things continue still in the same condition, according unto their proportion. Such as is the furniture of men with spiritual abilities and gifts of the Holy Ghost, such is their fitness for the work of the ministry, and no other. And if any shall undertake this work without this provision of abilities for it, they will neither ever be owned by Christ nor be of the least use in the employment they take upon them. A ministry devoid of spiritual gifts is a sufficient evidence of a church under a degenerating apostasy. But these things will be further spoken unto afterward.

Secondly, by these gifts were all their administrations, especially their preaching the gospel, rendered effectual unto their proper end. The preaching of the word, which is the "sword of the Spirit,"[14] was the great instrument whereby they wrought out and accomplished their designed work in the conviction and conversion of the souls of men. It may therefore be inquired what it was that gave efficacy and success unto the word as preached or dispensed by them. Now, this, as it should seem, must be either that the subject matter of it was so suited unto the reasons and understandings of men as that they could not but admit of it upon its proposal; or that the manner whereby they declared it was with such persuasive artifices as were meet to prevail with the minds of men unto an assent, or to impose upon them against the best of their defenses. But the apostle declares that it was utterly otherwise

12 Heb. 6:5.
13 I.e., entice.
14 Eph. 6:17.

in both these regards. For the matter of the doctrine of the gospel, unto the minds of carnal men, such as all men are until renewed by the gospel itself, is folly, and that which is every way meet to be despised (1 Cor. 1:18). And for the manner of its declaration, they did not therein, neither would they, use the enticing words of human wisdom, any arts of oratory, or dresses of rhetoric or eloquence, lest the effects which were wrought by the word should have seemed in any measure to have proceeded from them (1 Cor. 2:4–5). Wherefore, not to mention that internal efficacious power of grace which God secretly puts forth for the conversion of his elect, the consideration whereof belongs not unto our present design, and I say that it was by virtue of those gifts that the administration of the gospel was so efficacious and successful.¶

For from them proceeded that authority over the minds of men wherewith the word was accompanied. When the Lord Christ was anointed by the Spirit to preach the gospel, it is said, "He taught as one having authority, and not as the scribes" (Matt. 7:29). Whatever was his outward appearance in the flesh, the word, as administered by him, was attended with such an authority over the minds and consciences of men as they could not but be sensible of. And so was it with the primitive dispensers of the gospel. By virtue of these spiritual gifts, they preached the word "in the demonstration of the Spirit and of power" (1 Cor. 2:4). There was accompanying of their preaching an evidence or demonstration of a power and authority that was from God and his Spirit. Men could not but conclude that there was something in it which was over them or above them, and which they must yield or submit unto as that which was not for them to contend with. It is true, the power of the gospel was hid unto them that were to perish, whose minds the god of this world had effectually blinded, "lest the light of the glorious gospel of Christ should shine unto them" (2 Cor. 4:3–4), whence it came to pass that the word was rejected by many, yet wherever God was pleased to make it effectual, it was by a sense of a divine authority accompanying its administration, by virtue of those spiritual gifts. And therefore our apostle shows that when men prophesied, or declared the mind of God from the word by the gift of prophecy, unbelievers did "fall down, and, worshipping God, reported that God was in them of a truth" (1 Cor. 14:24–25). They were sensible of a divine authority, which they could not stand before, or withstand.¶

From here also proceeded that life and power for conviction which the word was accompanied with in their dispensation of it. It became shortly to be the arrows of Christ, which were sharp in the hearts of men. As men found an authority in the dispensation of the word, so they felt and experienced an efficacy in the truths dispensed. By it were their minds enlightened, their consciences

328 A DISCOURSE OF SPIRITUAL GIFTS

awakened, their minds convinced, their lives judged, the secrets of their hearts made manifest (as 1 Cor. 14:24–25), until they cried out in multitudes, "Men and brethren, what shall we do?"[15] Hereby did the Lord Christ in his kingdom and majesty ride prosperously, conquering and to conquer, with the Word of truth, meekness, and righteousness, subduing the souls of men unto his obedience, making them free, ready, willing, in the day of his power. These were the forces and weapons that he used in the establishing of his kingdom, which were "mighty through God to the pulling down of strongholds, casting down of imaginations, and every high thing that exalted itself against the knowledge of God, and bringing into captivity every thought to the obedience of Christ" (2 Cor. 10:4–5). So does the apostle describe the success of these administrations as an absolute conquest, wherein all opposition is broken, all strongholds and fortifications are demolished, and the whole reduced unto due obedience. For by this means were all things effected. All the strongholds of sin in the minds of men, in their natural darkness, blindness, and obstinacy, all the high fortifications of prejudices, and vain, proud, lofty imaginations, raised in them by Satan, were all cast down by and before gospel administrations, managed by virtue and authority of these spiritual gifts, which the Lord Christ ordained to be the powers of his kingdom.

Thirdly, those of them which consisted in miraculous operations were suited to fill the world with an apprehension of a divine power accompanying the word and them by whom it was administered. And sundry things unto the furtherance of the gospel depended hereon.¶

1. The world, which was stupid, asleep in sin and security, satisfied with their lusts and idolatries, regardless of anything but present enjoyments, was awakened hereby to an attendance unto and inquiry into this new doctrine that was proposed unto them. They could not but take notice that there was something more than ordinary in that sermon which they were summoned unto by a miracle. And this was the first and principal use of these miraculous operations. They awakened the dull, stupid world unto a consideration of the doctrine of the gospel, which otherwise they would have securely neglected and despised.¶

2. They weakened and took off those mighty prejudices which their minds were possessed with by tradition and secular enjoyments. What these prejudices were I shall not here declare, I have done it elsewhere.[16] It is enough to observe that they were as great, as many, as effectual, as human nature in

---

15 Acts 2:37.
16 Owen seems to be referring to the previous chapter in this treatise.

any case is capable of. But yet although they were sufficiently of proof against all other means of conviction, they could not but sink and weaken before the manifest evidence of present divine power, such as these miraculous operations were accompanied with. For although all the things which they cleaved unto, and intended to do so inseparably, were, as they thought, to be preferred above anything that could be offered unto them, yet when the divine power appeared against them, they were not able to give them defense. Hence, upon these operations one of these two effects ensued. (1) Those that were shut up under their obstinacy and unbelief were filled with tormenting convictions and knew not what to do to relieve themselves. The evidence of miracles they could not withstand, and yet would not admit of what they tendered and confirmed. Whence they were filled with disquietments and perplexities. So, the rulers of the Jews manifested themselves to have been upon the curing of the impotent person at the gate of the temple. "What shall we do," say they, "to these men? For that indeed a notable miracle hath been done by them we cannot deny" (Acts 4:16). (2) The minds of others were exceedingly prepared for the reception of the truth, the advantages unto that purpose being too many to be here insisted on.¶

3. They were a great means of taking off the scandal of the cross. That this was that which the world was principally offended at in the gospel is sufficiently known. Christ crucified was to the Jews a stumbling block, and unto the Greeks foolishness. Nothing could possibly be or have been a matter of so high offense unto the Jews as to offer them a crucified Messiah, whom they expected as a glorious king to subdue all their enemies; nor ever will they receive him, in the mind wherein they are, upon any other terms. And it seemed a part of the most extreme folly unto the Grecians to propose such great and immortal things in the name of one that was himself crucified as a malefactor.[17] And a shame it was thought, on all hands, for any wise man to profess or own such a religion as came from the cross. But yet, after all this blustering of weakness and folly, when they saw this doctrine of the cross owned by God, and witnessed unto by manifest effects of divine power, they could not but begin to think that men need not be much ashamed of that which God so openly avowed. And all these things made way to let in the word into the minds and consciences of men, where, by its own efficacy, it gave them satisfying experience of its truth and power.

From these few instances, whereunto many of an alike nature might be added, it is manifest how these spiritual gifts were the powers of the world

17 I.e., lawbreaker.

to come, the means, weapons, arms, that the Lord Christ made use of for the subduing of the world, destruction of the kingdom of Satan and darkness, with the planting and establishment of his own church on the earth. And as they were alone suited unto his design, so his accomplishment of it by them is a glorious evidence of his divine power and wisdom, as might easily be demonstrated.

6

Of Ordinary Gifts of the Spirit

The Grant, Institution, Use, Benefit, End,
and Continuance of the Ministry

THE CONSIDERATION OF THOSE ordinary gifts of the Spirit which are
annexed unto the ordinary powers and duties of the church does in the next
place lie before us. And they are called ordinary, not as if they were absolutely
common unto all, or were not much to be esteemed, or as if that were any
way a diminishing term. But we call them so upon a double account. (1) In
distinction from those gifts which, being absolutely extraordinary, did exceed
the whole power and faculties of the souls of men, as healings, tongues, and
miracles. For otherwise they are of the same nature with most of those gifts
which were bestowed on the apostles and evangelists, differing only in degree.
Every true gospel ministry has now gifts of the same kind with the apostles,
in a degree and measure sufficient to their work, excepting those mentioned.
(2) Because of their continuance in the ordinary state of the church, which
also they shall do unto the consummation of all things.¶

CHRIST'S GIFT OF THE MINISTRY

Now, my design is to treat peculiarly of the gifts of the Holy Spirit, but because there is a gift of Christ which is the foundation and subject of them,
something must be spoken briefly unto that in the first place. And this gift of
Christ is that of the ministry of the church, the nature of which office I shall
not consider at large, but only speak unto it as it is a gift of Christ. And this
I shall do by some little illustration given unto that passage of the apostle
where this gift and the communication of it is declared:

But unto everyone of us is given grace according to the measure of the gift of Christ. Wherefore he saith, "When he ascended up on high, he led captivity captive, and gave gifts unto men." Now that he ascended, what is it but that he also descended first into the lower parts of the earth? He that descended is the same also that ascended up far above all heavens, that he might fill all things. And he gave some, apostles; and some, prophets; and some, evangelists; and some, pastors and teachers; for the perfecting of the saints, for the work of the ministry, for the edifying of the body of Christ; till we all come in the unity of the faith, and of the knowledge of the Son of God, unto a perfect man, unto the measure of the stature of the fullness of Christ. That we henceforth be no more tossed to and fro, and carried about with every wind of doctrine, by the sleight of men, and cunning craftiness, whereby they lie in wait to deceive; but speaking the truth in love, may grow up into him in all things, which is the head, even Christ. From whom the whole body fitly joined together and compacted by that which every joint supplieth, according to the effectual working in the measure of every part, maketh increase of the body unto the edifying of itself in love. (Eph. 4:7–16)

There is no other place of Scripture wherein at one view the grant, institution, use, benefit, end, and continuance of the ministry is so clearly and fully represented. And the end of this whole discourse is, to declare that the gift and grant of the ministry and ministers, of the office and the persons to discharge it, is an eminent, most useful fruit and effect of the mediatory power of Christ, with his love and care toward his church. And those of whom the apostle speaks, "Unto everyone of us," are the officers or ministers whom he does afterward enumerate, although the words may in some sense be extended unto all believers. But principally the ministry and ministers of the church are intended. And it is said, unto them is "grace given." It is evident that by "grace" here, not sanctifying, saving grace is intended, but a participation of a gracious favor with respect to a special end. So, the word is frequently used in this case by our apostle (Rom. 15:15; Gal. 2:9; Eph. 3:8). This gracious favor we are made partakers of, this trust is freely, in a way of grace, committed unto us. And that "according to the measure of the gift of Christ," unto everyone, according as the Lord Christ does measure the gift of it freely out unto them. Thus in general was the ministry granted unto the church, the particular account whereof is given in the ensuing verses. And,

First,[1] it is declared to be a gift of Christ. Καὶ αὐτὸς ἔδωκε, "And he himself gave" (Eph. 4:11). It is the great fundamental of all church order, power, and worship, that the gift and grant of Christ is the origin of the ministry. If it

---

1   Owen does not delineate the second point that follows this first one.

had not been so given of Christ, it had not been lawful for any of the sons of men to institute such an office or appoint such officers. If any had attempted so to do, as there would have been a nullity in what they did, so their attempt would have been expressly against the headship of Christ, or his supreme authority over the church. Wherefore, that he would thus give ministers of the church was promised of old (Jer. 3:15), as well as signally foretold in the psalm from whence these words are taken. And as his doing of it is an act of his mediatory power, as it is declared in this place, and Matthew 28:18, so it was a fruit of his care, love, and bounty (1 Cor. 12:28). And it will hence follow, not only that offices in the church which are not of Christ's giving by institution, and officers that are not of his gift, grant, by provision and furnishment, have indeed no place therein, but also that they are set up in opposition unto his authority and in contempt of his care and bounty. For the doing so arises out of an apprehension both that men have a power in the church which is not derived from Christ, and that to impose servants upon him in his house without his consent, as also that they have more care of the church than he had, who made not such provision for them. And if an examination might be admitted by this rule, as it will one day come on whether men will or no, some great names now in the church would scarce be able to preserve their station. Popes, cardinals, metropolitans, diocesan prelates, archdeacons, commissaries, officials, and I know not what other monstrous products of an incestuous conjunction between secular pride and ecclesiastical degeneracy, would think themselves severely treated to be tried by this rule. But so it must be at last, and that unavoidably. Yea, and that no man shall be so hardy as once to dare attempt the setting up of officers in the church, without the authority of Christ, the eminency of this gift and grant of his is declared in sundry particular instances, wherein neither the wisdom, nor skill, nor power of any or all of the sons of men, can have the least interest, or in anything alike unto them. And this appears,

THE EMINENCY OF THE MINISTRY

1. From the grandeur of its introduction, or the great and solemn preparation that was made for the giving out of this gift. It was given by Christ "when he ascended up on high, and led captivity captive" (Eph. 4:8). The words are taken from Psalm 68:17–18, "The chariots of God are twenty thousand, even thousands of angels, the Lord is among them, as in Sinai, in the holy place. Thou hast ascended on high, thou hast led captivity captive, thou hast received gifts for men, yea, for the rebellious also, that the Lord God might dwell

among them." In the first place, the glorious appearance of God on Mount Sinai in giving of the law, his descending and ascending unto that purpose, is intended. But they are applied here unto Christ, because all the glorious works of God in and toward the church of old were either representatory or gradually introductory of Christ and the gospel. Thus the glorious ascending of God from Mount Sinai, after the giving of the law, was a representation of his "ascending up far above all heavens, that he might fill all things" (as Eph. 4:10). And as God then "led captivity captive" in the destruction of Pharaoh and the Egyptians, who had long held his people in captivity and under cruel bondage, so dealt the Lord Christ now in the destruction and captivity of Satan and all his powers (Col. 2:15). Only, whereas it is said in the Psalm that "he received gifts for men," here it is said that "he gave gifts to men," wherein no small mystery is couched. For although Christ is God, and is so gloriously represented in the psalm, yet an intimation is given that he should act what is here mentioned in a condition wherein he was capable to receive from another, as he did in this matter (Acts 2:33). And so the phrase in the original does more than insinuate: לָקַחְתָּ מַתָּנוֹת בָּאָדָם, "Thou hast received gifts in Adam," in the man, or human nature. And רקח[2] signifies as well to give as to receive, especially when anything is received to be given. Christ received this gift in the human nature to give it unto others. Now, to what end is this glorious theater, as it were, prepared, and all this preparation made, all men being called to the preparation of it? It was to set out the greatness of the gift he would bestow, and the glory of the work which he would effect. And this was to furnish the church with ministers, and ministers with gifts for the discharge of their office and duty. And it will one day appear that there is more glory, more excellency, in giving one poor minister unto a congregation, by furnishing him with spiritual gifts for the discharge of his duty, than in the pompous installment of a thousand popes, cardinals, or metropolitans. The worst of men, in the observance of a few outward rites and ceremonies, can do the latter; Christ only can do the former, and that as he is ascended up on high to that purpose.

2. It appears to be such an eminent gift from its original acquisition. There was a power acquired by Christ for this great donation, which the apostle declares, "Now that he ascended, what is it but that he also descended first into the lower parts of the earth?" (Eph. 4:9). Having mentioned the ascension of Christ as the immediate cause or fountain of the communication of this gift (Eph. 4:8), he found it necessary to trace it unto its first origin. He does not,

---

2 The Hebrew is לָקַח.

therefore, make mention of the descending into the lower parts of the earth occasionally upon that of his ascending, as if he catched at an advantage of a word, nor does he speak of the humiliation of Christ absolutely in itself, which he had no occasion for. But he introduces it to show what respect this gift of the ministry and ministers, of the office, gifts, and persons, had thereunto. And Christ's descending into the lower parts of the earth may be taken two ways, according as that expression, "The lower parts of the earth," may be diversely understood. For the τὰ κατώτερα μέρη τῆς γῆς, "The lower parts of the earth," are either the whole earth, that is, those lower parts of the creation, or some part of it. For the word "lower" includes a comparison either with the whole creation or with some part of itself. In the first sense, Christ's state of humiliation is intended, wherein he came down from heaven into these lower parts of God's creation, conversing on the earth. In the latter, his grave and burial are intended, for the grave is the lowest part of the earth into which mankind does descend. And both of these, or his humiliation as it ended in his death and burial, may be respected in the words. And that which the apostle designs to manifest is that the deep humiliation and the death of Christ are the fountain and origin of the ministry of the church, by way of acquisition and procurement. It is a fruit whose root is in the grave of Christ. For in those things, in the humiliation and death of Christ, lay the foundation of his mediatory authority, whereof the ministry is an effect (Phil. 2:6–11). And it was appointed by him to be the ministry of that peace between God and man which was made therein and thereby (Eph. 2:14, 16–17). For when he had made this peace by the blood of the cross, he preached it in the giving these gifts unto men for its solemn declaration (2 Cor. 5:18–21). Wherefore, because the authority from whence this gift proceeded was granted unto Christ upon his descending into the lower parts of the earth, and the end of the gift is to declare and preach the peace which he made between God and man by his so doing, this gift relates thereunto also. Hereon does the honor and excellency of the ministry depend, with respect hereunto is it to be esteemed and valued, namely, its relation unto the spiritual humiliation of Christ, and not from the carnal or secular exaltation of those that take it upon them.

3. It appears to be an eminent and signal gift from the immediate cause of its actual communication, or the present qualification of the Lord Christ for the bestowing of it; and this was his glorious exaltation upon his ascension. A right unto it was acquired by him in his death, but his actual investiture with all glorious power was to precede its communication (Eph. 4:8, 10). He was first to ascend up on high, to triumph over all his and our adversaries,

put now under him into absolute and eternal captivity, before he gave out this gift. And he is said here to "ascend far above all heavens," that is, these visible and aspectable heavens, which he passed through when he went into the glorious presence of God, or unto the right hand of the Majesty on high (see Heb. 4:14, with our exposition thereon).[3] It is also added why he was thus gloriously exalted, and this was that he might "fill up all things"; not φυσικῶς,[4] but ἐνεργητικῶς[5]—not in the essence of his nature, but in the exercise of his power. He had laid the foundation of his church on himself in his death and resurrection, but now the whole fabric of it was to be filled with its utensils and beautified with its ornaments. This he ascended to accomplish, and did it principally in the collation of this gift of the ministry upon it. This was the first exercise of that glorious power which the Lord Christ was vested with upon his exaltation, the first effect of his wisdom and love, in filling all things, unto the glory of God and the salvation of his elect. And these things are mentioned, that in the contemplation of their greatness and order we may learn and judge how excellent this donation of Christ is. And it will also appear from hence how contemptible a thing the most pompous ministry in the world is, which does not proceed from this origin.

4. The same is manifest from the nature of the gift itself. For this gift consists in gifts: "He gave gifts" (Eph. 4:8). There is an active giving expressed: "He gave." And the thing given, that is, "gifts." Wherefore the ministry is a gift of Christ, not only because freely and bountifully given by him to the church, but also because spiritual gifts do essentially belong unto it, are indeed its life, and inseparable from its being. A ministry without gifts is no ministry of Christ's giving, nor is of any other use in the church but to deceive the souls of men. To set up such a ministry is both to despise Christ and utterly to frustrate the ends of the ministry, those for which Christ gave it, and which are here expressed. For, (1) Ministerial gifts and graces are the great evidence that the Lord Christ takes care of his church and provides for it, as called into the order and unto the duties of a church. To set up a ministry which may be continued by outward forms and orders of men only, without any communication of gifts from Christ, is to despise his authority and care. Neither is it his mind that any church should continue in order any longer or otherwise than as he bestows

---

3   *Exercitations on the Epistle to the Hebrews, concerning the Priesthood of Christ Wherein the Original, Causes, Nature, Prefigurations, and Discharge of That Holy Office, Are Explained and Vindicated: With a Continuation of the Exposition on the Third, Fourth, and Fifth Chapters of Said Epistle to the Hebrews* (1674), bk. 2, on Heb. 4:14.

4   Gk. "naturally."

5   Gk. "effectively."

these gifts for the ministry. (2) That these gifts are the only means and instruments whereby the work of the ministry may be performed, and the ends of the ministry attained, shall be further declared immediately. The ends of the ministry here mentioned, called its "work," are the "perfecting of the saints, and the edifying of the body of Christ, until we all come unto a perfect man."[6] Hereof nothing at all can be done without these spiritual gifts. And therefore, a ministry devoid of them is a mock ministry, and no ordinance of Christ.

5. The eminency of this gift appears in the variety and diversity of the offices and officers which Christ gave in giving of the ministry. He knew there would, and had appointed there should, be a twofold estate of the church (Eph. 4:11). (1) Of its first election and foundation. (2) Of its building and edification. And different both offices and gifts were necessary unto these different states. For, (1) Two things were extraordinary in the first erection of his church. [1] An extraordinary aggression was to be made upon the kingdom of Satan in the world, as upheld by all the potentates of the earth, the concurrent suffrage of mankind, with the interest of sin and prejudices in them. [2] The casting of men into a new order, under a new rule and law, for the worship of God, that is, the planting and erecting of churches all the world over. With respect unto these ends, extraordinary officers, with extraordinary authority, power, and abilities, were requisite. Unto this end, therefore, he "gave some apostles, and some prophets, and some evangelists," of the nature of whose offices and their gifts we have spoken before. I shall here only add, that it was necessary that these officers should have their immediate call and authority from Christ, antecedent unto all order and power in the church, for the very being of the church depended on their power of office. But this, without such an immediate power from Christ, no man can pretend unto. And what was done originally by their persons is now done by their word and doctrine. For the church is "built upon the foundation of the apostles and prophets, Jesus Christ himself being the chief corner-stone" (Eph. 2:20). (2) There was a state of the church in its edification, which was to be carried on, according to the rules and laws given by Christ, in the ordinary administration of all the ordinances and institutions of the gospel. To this end Christ gives ordinary officers, "pastors and teachers," who by his direction were "ordained in every church" (Acts 14:23). And these are all the teaching officers that he has given unto his church. Or if any shall think that in the enumeration of them in this place, as also 1 Corinthians 12:28, our apostle forgot popes and diocesan bishops, with some others, who certainly cannot

---

6 Eph. 4:12–13.

but laugh to themselves that they should be admitted in the world as church officers, he must speak for himself.

THE CALLING OF THE MINISTRY

But whereas the other sort of officers were given by Christ, by his immediate call and communication of power unto them, it does not appear how he gives these ordinary officers or ministers unto it. I answer, he did it originally, and continues to do it, by the ways and means ensuing.

1. He does it by the law and rule of the gospel, wherein he has appointed this office of the ministry in his church, and so always to be continued. Were there not such a standing ordinance and institution of his, it were not in the power of all the churches in the world to appoint any such among them, whatever appearance there may be of a necessity thereof. And if any should have attempted any such thing, no blessing from God would have accompanied their endeavor, so that they would but set up an idol of their own. Hereon we lay the continuance of the ministry in the church. If there be not an ordinance and institution of Christ unto this purpose, or if, such being granted, yet the force of it be now expired, we must and will readily confess that the whole office is a mere usurpation. But if he has given "pastors and teachers" unto his church, to continue until all his saints in all ages "come unto a perfect man, unto the measure of the stature of the fullness of Christ" (Eph. 4:11–13), and has promised to be with them, as such, unto the consummation of all things (Matt. 28:18–20); if the apostles by his authority ordained elders in every church and city (Acts 14:23; Titus 1:5), and who therein were made overseers of the flocks by the Holy Ghost (Acts 20:28), having the charge of feeding and overseeing the flock that is among them always, until the chief shepherd shall appear (1 Pet. 5:1–5); if believers, or the disciples of Christ, are obliged by him always to yield obedience unto them (Heb. 13:7, 17); with other such plain declarations of the will of the Lord Christ in the constitution and continuance of this office—this foundation stands firm and unshaken as the ordinances of heaven that shall not be changed.¶

And whereas there is not in the Scripture the least intimation of any such time, state, or condition of the church, as wherein the disciples of Christ may or ought to live from under the orderly conduct and guidance of the ministers, it is vain to imagine that any defect in other men, any apostasy of the greatest part of any or all visible churches, should cast them into an incapacity of erecting a regular ministry among them and over them. For whereas the warranty and authority of the ministry depends on this institution of Christ, which is accompanied with a command for its observance (Matt. 28:18–20), all his disciples being obliged to yield obedience thereunto, their doing so in the order and manner also by him approved is sufficient to constitute a lawful ministry among them. To suppose that because the Church of Rome and those adhering unto it have, by their apostasy, utterly lost an evangelical ministry among them, that therefore others unto whom the word of God is come, and has been effectual unto their conversion, have not sufficient warranty from the word to yield obedience unto all the commands of Christ, which, when we have talked of power and authority while we please, is all that is left unto us in this world, or that in so doing he will not accept them and approve of what they have done, is an assertion fit for men to maintain who have a trade to drive in religion unto their own special advantage.

2. The Lord Christ gives and continues this office by giving spiritual gifts and abilities unto men, to enable them to discharge the duties and perform the work of it. This is that which I principally design to confirm in its proper place, which will immediately ensue. All I shall say at present is, that spiritual gifts of themselves make no man actually a minister; yet no man can be made a minister according to the mind of Christ who is not partaker of them. Wherefore, supposing the continuance of the law and institution mentioned, if the Lord Christ does at any time, or in any place, cease to give out spiritual gifts unto men, enabling them in some good measure unto the discharge of the ministry, then and in that place the ministry itself must cease and come to an end. To erect a ministry by virtue of outward order, rites, and ceremonies, without gifts for the edification of the church, is but to hew a block with axes, and smooth it with planes, and set it up for an image to be adored. To make a man a minister who can do nothing of the proper peculiar work of the ministry, nothing toward the only end of it in the church, is to set up a dead carcass, fastening it to a post, and expecting it should do you work and service.

3. He does it by giving power unto his church in all ages to call and separate unto the work of the ministry such as he has fitted and gifted for it. The things before mentioned are essentially constituent of the ministry; this belongs unto the outward order of their entrance into the ministry who are by him called thereunto. And concerning this we may observe the things following.¶

(1) That this power in the church is not despotic or lordly, but consists in a faculty, right, and ability to act in this matter obedientially unto the command of Christ. Hence all the acting of the church in this matter is nothing but an instituted means of conveying authority and office from Christ unto persons called thereunto. The church does not give them any authority of its own or resident in itself, but only, in a way of obedience unto Christ, does

transmit power from him unto them who are called. Hence do they become the ministers of Christ, and not of the bishops, or churches, or men, holding their office and authority from Christ himself, by the law and rule of the gospel; so that whosoever despises them, despises him also in them. Some would have ministers of the gospel to receive all their authority from the people that choose them, and some from the bishops who ordain them, and whence they have theirs I know not. But this is to make them ministers of men and servants of men, and to constitute other masters between them and Christ. And whereas all church power is originally and absolutely vested in Christ, and in him solely, so that none can be partaker of the least interest in it or share of it without a communication of it from him unto them, neither popes, nor prelates, nor people are able to produce any such grant or concession of power unto them from him as that they should have an authority residing in them and in their power, to dispose unto others as they see cause, so as they should hold it from them as a part or efflux[7] of the power vested in them. It is obedience unto the law of Christ, and following the guidance of his previous communication of gifts as a means to communicate his power unto them who are called to the ministry, that is the whole of what is committed unto any in this kind.¶

(2) The church has no power to call any unto the office of the ministry, where the Lord Christ has not gone before it in the designation of him by an endowment with spiritual gifts. For if the whole authority of the ministry be from Christ, and if he never gives it but where he bestows these gifts with it for its discharge (as in Eph. 4:7–8, etc.), then to call any to the ministry whom he has not so previously gifted is to set him aside, and to act in our own name and authority. And by reason of these things the Holy Ghost is said to make men overseers of the flocks who are thus called thereunto, because both the communication of power in the constitution of the law, and of spiritual gifts by internal effectual operation, are from him alone (Acts 20:28).¶

(3) The outward way and order whereby a church may call any person unto the office of the ministry among them and over them, is by their joint solemn submission unto him in the Lord, as unto all the powers and duties of this office, testified by their choice and election of him. It is concerning this outward order that all the world is filled with disputes, about the call of men unto the ministry, which yet, in truth, is of the least concern therein. For whatever manner or order be observed herein, if the things before mentioned be not premised thereunto, it is of no validity or authority. On the other hand,

---

7   I.e., a passing away; expiration.

grant that the authority of the ministry depends on the law, ordinance, and institution of Christ, that he calls men unto this office by the collation of spiritual gifts unto them, and that the actings of the church herein are but an instituted moral means of communicating office-power from Christ himself unto any, and let but such other things be observed as the light and law of nature requires in cases of an alike kind, and the outward mode of the church's acting herein need not much be contended about. It may be proved to be a beam of truth from the light of nature, that no man should be imposed on a church for their minister against their wills or without their express consent, considering that his whole work is to be conversant about their understandings, judgments, wills, and affections; and that this should be done by their choice and election, as the Scripture does manifestly declare (Num. 8:9–10; Acts 1:23, 26; 6:3–6; 14:23), so that it was for some ages observed sacredly in the primitive churches, cannot modestly be denied. But how far any people or church may commit over this power of declaring their consent and acquiescency[8] unto others to act for them, and as it were in their stead, so as that the call to office should yet be valid, and provided the former rules be observed, I will not much dispute with any, though I approve only of what makes the nearest approaches to the primitive pattern that the circumstances of things are capable of.¶

(4) The Lord Christ continues his bestowing of this gift by the solemn ordinance of setting apart those who are called in the manner declared, by "fasting and prayer, and imposition of hands" (Acts 13:2–3; 14:23; 1 Tim. 4:14). By these means, I say, does the Lord Christ continue to declare that he accounts men faithful, and puts them into the ministry, as the apostle speaks (1 Tim. 1:12).

THE END OF THE MINISTRY

There are yet remaining sundry things in the passage of the apostle which we now insist on, that declare the eminency of this gift of Christ, which may yet be further briefly considered. As the end why it is bestowed; and this is expressed, first, positively, as to the good and advantage of the church thereby (Eph. 4:12); second, negatively, as to its prohibition and hindrance of evil (Eph. 4:14).¶

1. In the end of it as positively expressed three things may be considered. (1) That it is πρὸς τὸν καταρτισμὸν τῶν ἁγίων, that is, for the gathering

---

8 I.e., complicity.

of the saints into complete church order. The subject matter of this part of their duty is the saints, that is, by calling and profession, such as are all the disciples of Christ. And that which is effected toward them is καταρτισμὸς, their coagmentation,[9] jointing, or compacting into order. So the word signifies (Gal. 6:1). And this effect is here declared (Eph. 4:16). It is true, the saints mentioned may come together into some initial church order by their consent and agreement to walk together in all the ways of Christ, and in obedience unto all his institutions, and so become a church essentially before they have any ordinary pastor or teacher, either by the conduct of extraordinary officers, as at first, or through obedience unto the word, hence elders were ordained among those who were in church state, that is, thus far, before (Acts 14:23). But they cannot come to that perfection and completeness which is designed unto them. That which renders a church completely organic, the proper seat and subject of all gospel worship and ordinances, is this gift of Christ in the ministry.

But it may be asked, whether a church before it comes unto this καταρτισμός, or "completeness," before it has any minister in office, or has by any means lost the ministry among them, may not delegate and appoint some one or more from among themselves to administer all the ordinances of the gospel among them and unto them, and by that means make up their own perfection?

(2) The church being so completed, these officers are given unto it "for the work of the ministry."[10] This expression is comprehensive, and the particulars included in it are not in this place to be inquired into. It may suffice unto our present purpose to consider that it is a work, not a preferment;[11] and a work they shall find it who design to give up a comfortable account of what is committed unto them. It is usually observed that all the words whereby the work of the ministry is expressed in the Scripture do denote a peculiar industrious kind of labor, though some have found out ways of honor and ease to be signified by them.¶

(3) Both these are directed unto one general issue. It is all εἰς οἰκοδομὴν τοῦ σώματος τοῦ χριστοῦ, "unto the edification of the body of Christ." Not to insist on the metaphors that are in this expression, the excellency of the ministry is declared, in that the object of its duty and work is no other but the body of Christ himself; and its end, the edification of this body, or its increase in faith and obedience, in all the graces and gifts of

9   I.e., uniting together.
10 Eph. 4:12.
11 I.e., promotion; advancement.

the Spirit, until it come unto conformity unto him and the enjoyment of him. And a ministry which has not this object and end is not of the giving or grant of Christ.

2. The end of the ministry is expressed negatively, or with respect unto the evils which it is ordained for our deliverance from (Eph. 4:14). (1) The evil which we are hereby delivered from is the danger of being perniciously and destructively deceived by false doctrines, errors, and heresies, which then began, and have ever since, in all ages, continued to infest the churches of God. These the apostle describes from the design of their authors, which is "to deceive," their diligence in that design, "They lie in wait to accomplish it," [and] the means they use to compass their end, which are "sleights and cunning craftiness," managed sometimes with impetuous violence, and thus called a "wind of doctrine." (2) The means hereof is our deliverance out of a childlike state, accompanied with weakness, instability, and willfulness. And sad is the condition of those churches which either have such ministers as will themselves toss them up and down by false and pernicious doctrines, or are not able by sound instructions to deliver them from such a condition of weakness and instability as wherein they are not able to preserve themselves from being in these things imposed on by the "cunning sleights of men that lie in wait to deceive." And as this ministry is always to continue in the church (Eph. 4:13), so it is the great means of influencing the whole body, and every member of it, unto a due discharge of their duty, unto their edification in love (Eph. 4:15–16).

Designing to treat of the spiritual gifts bestowed on the ministry of the church, I have thus far diverted unto the consideration of the ministry itself as it is a gift of Christ and shall shut it up with a few corollaries. (1) Where there is any office erected in the church that is not in particular of the gift and institution of Christ, there is a nullity in the whole office, and in all administrations by virtue of it. (2) Where the office is appointed, but gifts are not communicated unto the person called unto it, there is a nullity as to his person, and a disorder in the church. (3) It is the duty of the church to look on the ministry as an eminent grant of Christ, with valuation, thankfulness, and improvement. (4) Those who are called unto this office in due order labor to approve themselves as a gift of Christ; which it is a shameless impudence for some to own who go under that name. (5) This they may do in laboring to be furnished with gracious qualifications, useful endowments, diligence and laborious travail in this work, by an exemplary conversation, in love, meekness, self-denial, readiness for the cross, etc.

7

Of Spiritual Gifts Enabling the Ministry to the Exercise and Discharge of Their Trust and Office

UNTO THE MINISTRY so given unto the church, as has been declared, the Holy Ghost gives spiritual gifts enabling them unto the exercise and discharge of the power, trust, and office committed unto them. Now, although I am not thoroughly satisfied what men will grant or allow in these days, such uncouth and bold principles are continually advanced among us, yet I suppose it will not, in words at least, be denied by many but that ministers have, or ought to have, gifts for the due discharge of their office. To some, indeed, the very name and word is a derision, because it is a name and notion peculiar to the Scripture. Nothing is more contemptible unto them than the very mention of "the gifts of the Holy Ghost." At present I deal not with such directly, though what we shall prove will be sufficient for their rebuke, though not for their conviction.[1] Wherefore our inquiry is, whether the Spirit of God does effectually collate on the ministers of the gospel spiritual gifts, enabling them to perform and effect evangelical administrations, according to the power committed unto them and duly required of them, unto the glory of Christ and edification of the church. It is moreover inquired, whether the endowment of men with these spiritual gifts, in a degree and measure suited unto public edification, be not that which does materially constitute them ministers of the gospel, as being antecedently necessary unto their call unto their office.

---

1 Owen was convinced that neglect of the spiritual gifts gave rise to the Roman Catholic sacramental system with all of its rituals. See the full introduction in vol. 7 regarding the Church of Rome and this discourse.

These things, I say, are to be inquired into, because, in opposition unto the first, it is affirmed that these supposed gifts are nothing but mere natural abilities, attained by diligence and improved by exercise, without any special respect unto the working of the Holy Ghost, at least otherwise than what is necessary unto the attaining of skill and ability in any human art or science, which is the ordinary blessing of God on man's honest endeavors. And to the other it is opposed, that a lawful, ordinary, outward call is sufficient to constitute any man a lawful minister, whether he have received any such gifts as those inquired after or no.¶

Wherefore, the substance of what we have to declare and confirm is, that there is a special dispensation and work of the Holy Ghost in providing able ministers of the New Testament for the edification of the church, wherein the continuance of the ministry and being of the church, as to its outward order, does depend; and that herein he does exert his power and exercise his authority in the communication of spiritual gifts unto men, without a participation whereof no man has de jure,[2] any lot or portion in this ministration. Herein consists no small part of that work of the Spirit which belongs unto his promised dispensation in all ages, which to deny is to renounce all faith in the promise of Christ, all regard unto his continued love and care toward the church in the world, or at least the principal pleadable testimony given thereunto, and under pretense of exalting and preserving the church, totally to overthrow it. Now, the evidence which we shall give unto this truth is contained in the ensuing assertions, with their confirmation.

1. The Lord Jesus Christ has faithfully promised to be present with his church "unto the end of the world."[3] It is his temple and his tabernacle, wherein he will dwell and walk continually. And this presence of Christ is that which makes the church to be what it is, a congregation essentially distinct from all other societies and assemblies of men. Let men be formed into what order you please, according unto any outward rules and measures that are either given in the Scripture or found out by themselves, let them derive power and authority by what claim soever they shall think fit, yet if Christ be not present with them, they are no church, nor can all the powers under heaven make them so to be. And when any church loses the special presence of Christ, it ceases so to be. It is, I suppose, confessed with and among whom Christ is thus present, or it may be easily proved. See his promises to this purpose (Matt. 28:20; Rev. 21:3). And those churches do exceedingly mistake their

---

2   I.e., by right.
3   Matt. 28:20.

interest who are solicitous about other things but make little inquiry after the evidences of the presence of Christ among them. Some walk as if they supposed they had him sure enough, as it were, immured[4] in their walls, while they keep up the name of a church, and an outward order that pleases and advantages themselves. But outward order, be it what it will, is so far from being the only evidence of the presence of Christ in a church, that when it is alone, or when it is principally required, it is none at all. And therefore, whereas preaching of the word and the right administration of the sacraments are assigned as the notes of a true church, if the outward acts and order of them only be regarded, there is nothing of evidence unto this purpose in them.

2. This promised presence of Christ is by his Spirit. This I have sufficiently proved formerly, so that here I shall be brief in its rehearsal, though it be the next foundation of what we have further to offer in this case.[5] We speak not of the essential presence of Christ with respect unto the immensity of his divine nature, whereby he is equally present in or equally indistant from all places, manifesting his glory when, where, and how he pleases. Nor does it respect his human nature; for when he promised this his presence, he told his disciples that therein he must leave and depart from them (John 16:5–8), whereon they were filled with sorrow and trouble, until they knew how he would make good the promise of his presence with them, and who or what it was that should unto their advantage supply his bodily absence. And this he did in his visible ascension, when "he was taken up, and a cloud received him out of their sight" (Acts 1:9), when also it was given in charge unto them not to expect his return until his coming unto judgment (Acts 1:11). And, accordingly, Peter tells us that the "heaven must receive him until the times of restitution of all things" (Acts 3:21), when he will appear again "in the glory of his Father" (Matt. 16:27), even that glory which the Father gave him upon his exaltation (Phil. 2:9–11), joined unto "that glory which he had with him before the world was" (John 17:5). In and upon this his departure from them, he taught his disciples how they should understand his promise of being present and abiding "with them unto the end of the world," and this was by sending of his Holy Spirit in his name, place, and stead, to do all to them and for them which he had yet to do with them and for them (see John 14:16–18, 26–28; 15:26; 16:7–15).¶

And other vicar in the church Christ has none, nor does stand in need of any, nor can any mortal man supply that charge and office. Nor was any such

---

4 I.e., enclosed.
5 E.g., Πνευματολογια, or, A Discourse concerning the Holy Spirit, bk. 2, chap. 5.

ever thought of in the world until men grew weary of the conduct and rule of the Holy Spirit, by various ways taking his work out of his hand, leaving him nothing to do in that which they called "the church." But I suppose I need not handle this principle as a thing in dispute or controversy. If I greatly mistake not, this presence of Christ in his church by his Spirit is an article of faith unto the catholic[6] church, and such a fundamental truth as whoever denies it overthrows the whole gospel. And I have so confirmed it in our former discourses concerning the dispensation and operations of the Holy Ghost, as that I fear not nor expect any direct opposition thereunto.[7] But yet I acknowledge that some begin to talk as if they owned no other presence of Christ but by the word and sacraments. Whatever else remains to be done lies wholly in ourselves. It is acknowledged that the Lord Christ is present in and by his word and ordinances; but if he is not otherwise present, or is present only by their external administration, there will no more church state among men ensue thereon[8] than there is among the Jews, who enjoy the letter of the Old Testament and the institutions of Moses. But when men rise up in express contradiction unto the promises of Christ and the faith of the catholic church in all ages, we shall not contend with them.

3. This presence of the Spirit is secured unto the church by an everlasting, unchangeable covenant: "'As for me, this is my covenant with them,' saith the Lord; 'My Spirit that is upon thee, and my words which I have put in thy mouth, shall not depart out of thy mouth, nor out of the mouth of thy seed, nor out of the mouth of thy seed's seed,' saith the Lord, 'from henceforth and forever'" (Isa. 59:21). This is God's covenant with the gospel church, to be erected then when "the Redeemer should come to Zion, and unto them that turn from transgression in Jacob" (Isa. 59:20). This is a part of the covenant that God has made in Christ the Redeemer. And as the continuance of the word unto the church in all ages is by this promise secured, without which it would cease and come to nothing, seeing it is "built on the foundation of the apostles and prophets" (Eph. 2:20), so is the presence of the Spirit in like manner secured unto it, and that on the same terms with the word, so as that if he be not present with it, all covenant relation between God and it does cease. Where this promise does not take place, there is no church, no ordinances, no acceptable worship, because no covenant relation. In brief, then, where there is no participation of the promise of Christ to send the Spirit to abide with us always, no interest in that covenant wherein God engages that his Spirit shall not depart from

6 I.e., universal.
7 Πνευματολογια, or, *A Discourse concerning the Holy Spirit.*
8 I.e., as a result.

us forever, and so no presence of Christ to make the word and ordinances of worship living, useful, effectual in their administration, unto their proper ends, there is no church state, whatever outward order there may be.

4. The gospel is called the ministration of the Spirit, and the ministers of it the ministers of the Spirit: "Who hath also made us able ministers of the new testament; not of the letter, but of the Spirit" (2 Cor. 3:6); not of the "ministration of death," but of that of the "Spirit," which is "glorious" (2 Cor. 3:7–8). There never was, nor ever shall be, any but these two ministrations in the church: that of the letter and of death and that of the Spirit and of life. If there be a ministration in any church, it must belong to one of these. And all ministers must be so either of the letter or of the Spirit. If there be a ministry pretended unto that is neither of the letter nor of the Spirit, it is anti-Christian. The ministry which was carnal, of the letter and death, was a true ministry, and in its place glorious, because it was appointed of God, and was efficacious as unto its proper end. That of the gospel is of the Spirit, and much more glorious. But if there be a ministration that has the outward form of either, but indeed is neither of them, it is no ministration at all. And where it is so, there is really no ministration but that of the Bible, that is, God by his providence continuing the Bible among them, makes use of it as he sees good for the conviction and conversion of sinners, wherein there is a secret manifestation of the Spirit also.¶

We may, therefore, inquire in what sense the ministration of the gospel is called the "ministry of the Spirit." Now, this cannot be because the laws, institutions, and ordinances of its worship were revealed by the Spirit, for so were all the ordinances and institutions of the Old Testament, as has been proved before, and yet the ministration of them was the ministration of the letter and of death, in a worldly sanctuary, by carnal ordinances. Wherefore it must be so called in one of these respects. Either (1) because it is the peculiar aid and assistance of the Spirit whereby any are enabled to administer the gospel and its institutions of worship according to the mind of God, unto the edification of the church. In this sense men are said to be made "able ministers of the new testament," that is, ministers able to administer the gospel in due order. Thus in that expression, "ministers of the Spirit," the "Spirit" denotes the efficient cause of the ministry, and he that quickens it (2 Cor. 3:6). Or (2) it may be said to be the "ministration of the Spirit," because in and by the ministry of the gospel the Spirit is in all ages administered and communicated unto the disciples of Christ, unto all the ends for which he is promised. So Galatians 3:2, the Spirit is received by "the teaching of faith." Take it either way, and the whole of what we plead for is confirmed. That he alone enables men unto the discharge of the work of the ministry, by the spiritual gifts which he communicates unto them, is the first sense, and expressly that which we contend for; and if, in and by the ministration of the gospel in all ages, the Spirit is communicated and administered unto men, then does he abide with the church forever, and for what ends we must further inquire.

5. The great end for which the Spirit is thus promised, administered, and communicated under the gospel, is the continuance and preservation of the church in the world. God has promised unto the Lord Christ that his kingdom in this world should endure "throughout all generations," with the course of the sun and moon (Ps. 72:5), and that "of the increase of his government there should be no end" (Isa. 9:7). And the Lord Christ himself has declared his preservation of his church, so as that "the gates of hell should not prevail against it" (Matt. 16:18). It may therefore be inquired whereon the infallible accomplishment of these promises, and others innumerable unto the same end, does depend, or what is that means whereby they shall be certainly executed. Now, this must be either some work of God or man. If it be of men, and it consist of their wills and obedience, then that which is said amounts hereunto, namely, that where men have once received the gospel, and professed subjection thereunto, they will infallibly abide therein in a succession from one generation unto another. But besides that, it must be granted that what so depends on the wills of men can have no more certainty than the undetermined wills of men can give security of, which indeed is none at all, so there are confessed instances without number of such persons and places as have lost the gospel and the profession thereof. And what has fallen out in one place may do so in another, and consequently in all places where the reasons and causes of things are the same. On this supposition, therefore, there is no security that the promises mentioned shall be infallibly accomplished. Wherefore the event must depend on some work of God and Christ. Now, this is no other but the dispensation and communication of the Spirit. Hereon alone does the continuance of the church and of the kingdom of Christ in the world depend.¶

And whereas the church falls under a double consideration, namely, of its internal and external form, of its internal spiritual union with Christ and its outward profession of obedience unto him, the calling, gathering, preservation, and edification of it in both respects belong unto the Holy Spirit. The first he does, as has been proved at large, by his communicating effectual saving grace unto the elect.[9] The latter, by the communication of

---

9   Πνευματολογια, *or, A Discourse concerning the Holy Spirit*, bk. 3, chap. 5.

gifts unto the guides, rulers, officers, and ministers of it, with all its members, according unto its place and capacity. Suppose, then, his communication of internal saving grace to cease, and the church must absolutely cease as to its internal form. For we are united unto the Lord Christ as our mystical head by the Spirit, the one and self-same Spirit dwelling in him and them that do believe. Union unto Christ without saving grace, and saving grace without the Holy Spirit, are strangers unto the gospel and Christian religion. So is it to have a church that is holy and catholic which is not united unto Christ as a mystical head. Wherefore the very being of the church, as unto its internal form, depends on the Spirit in his dispensation of grace, which if you suppose an intercision[10] of, the church must cease. It has the same dependence on him as to its outward form and profession, upon his communication of gifts. For "no man can say that Jesus is the Lord," or profess subjection and obedience unto him in a due manner, "but by the Holy Ghost" (1 Cor. 12:3). Suppose this work of his to cease, and there can be no professing church. Let men mold and cast themselves into what order and form they please, and let them pretend that their right and title unto their church power and station is derived unto them from their progenitors or predecessors, if they are not furnished with the gifts of the Spirit, to enable their guides unto gospel administrations, they are no orderly gospel church.

6. The communication of such gifts unto the ordinary ministry of the church in all ages is plainly asserted in sundry places of the Scripture, some whereof may be briefly considered. The whole nature of this work is declared in the parable of the talents (Matt. 25:14–30). The state of the church from the ascension of Christ unto his coming again unto judgment, that is, in its whole course on the earth, is represented in this parable. In this season he has servants whom he entrusts in the affairs of his kingdom, in the care of his church, and the propagation of the gospel. That they may, in their several generations, places, and circumstances, be enabled hereunto, he gives them, in various distributions, talents to trade with, the least whereof was sufficient to encourage them who received them unto their use and exercise. The trade they had to drive was that of the administration of the gospel, its doctrine, worship, and ordinances to others. Talents are abilities to trade, which may also comprise opportunities and other advantages, but abilities are chiefly intended. These were the gifts whereof we speak. Nor did it ever enter into the minds of any to apprehend otherwise of them. And they are abilities which Christ, as the king and head of his church, gives unto men in a special

---

10 I.e., interruption.

manner, as they are employed under him in the service of his house and work of the gospel. The servants mentioned are such as are called, appointed, and employed in the service of the house of Christ, that is, all ministers of the gospel, from first to last. And their talents are the gifts which he endows them with, by his own immediate power and authority, for their work.¶

And hence these three things follow. (1) That wherever there is a ministry that the Lord Christ sets up, appoints, or owns, he furnishes all those whom he employs therein with gifts and abilities suitable to their work, which he does by the Holy Spirit. He will never fail to own his institutions, with gracious supplies, to render them effectual. (2) That where any have not received talents to trade with, it is the highest presumption in them, and casts the greatest dishonor on the Lord Christ, as though he requires work where he gave no strength, or trade where he gave no stock, for anyone to undertake the work of the ministry. Where the Lord Christ gives no gifts, he has no work to do. He will require of none any special duty where he does not give a special ability. And for any to think themselves meet for this work and service in the strength of their own natural parts and endowments, however acquired, is to despise both his authority and his work. (3) For those who have received of these talents, either not to trade at all, or to pretend the managing of their trade on another stock, that is, either not sedulously[11] and duly to exercise their ministerial gifts, or to discharge their ministry by other helps and means, is to set up their own wisdom in opposition unto his, and his authority. In brief, that which the whole parable teaches is, that wherever there is a ministry in the church that Christ owns or regards, as used and employed by him, there persons are furnished with spiritual gifts from Christ by the Spirit, enabling them unto the discharge of that ministry; and where there are no such spiritual gifts dispensed by him, there is no ministry that he either accepts or approves.

"As we have many members in one body, and all members have not the same office; so we, being many, are one body in Christ, and everyone members one of another. Having then gifts differing according to the grace that is given to us, whether prophecy," etc. (Rom. 12:4–8). It is indifferent, as to our present purpose, whether the apostle treats here of offices or of duties only. The things ensuing, which are plain and obvious in the text, are sufficient unto the confirmation of what we plead for. (1) It is the ordinary state of the church, its continuance being planted, its preservation and edification, that the apostle discourses about; wherefore what he speaks is necessary unto the church in all

---

11   I.e., dedicatedly or diligently.

ages and conditions. To suppose a church devoid of the gifts here mentioned, is to overthrow the whole nature and end of a gospel church. (2) That the principle of all administrations in the church state described is gifts received from Jesus Christ by his Spirit. For declaring the way whereby the church may be edified, he lays the foundation of it in this, that to everyone of us is given grace according to the measure of the gift of Christ. For the apostle exhorts those unto whom he speaks to attend unto those duties whereby the church may be edified, and that by virtue of the gifts which they had received. All the whole duty of anyone in the church lies in this, that he act according to the χάρισμα[12] that he is made partaker of. And what these χαρίσματα[13] are, as also by whom they are bestowed, has been already fully declared. (3) That these gifts give not only ability for duty, but rule and measure unto all works of service that are to be performed in the church. Everyone is to act therein according to his gift, and no otherwise. To say that this state of the church is now ceased, and that another state is introduced, wherein all gospel administrations may be managed without spiritual gifts, or not by virtue of them, is to say that which, de facto,[14] is true in most places; but whether the true nature of the church is not overthrown thereby is left unto consideration. First Peter 4:10–11 is a parallel testimony hereunto, and many others to the same purpose might be pleaded, together with that which is the foundation of this whole discourse (Eph. 4:7–16; etc.). Only let it be remembered, that in this whole discourse, by "gifts" I do understand those χαρίαματα πνευματικὰ, those "spiritual largesses," which are neither absolutely natural endowments nor attainable by our own industry and diligence.

7. These gifts, as they are bestowed unto that end, so they are indispensably necessary unto gospel administrations. For, as we have proved, they are spiritual, and not legal or carnal. And spiritual administrations cannot be exercised in a due manner without spiritual gifts, yea, one reason why they are spiritual, and so called, is, because they cannot be performed without the aid and assistance of the Holy Spirit in and by these gifts of his. Had the Lord Christ appointed administrations of another nature, such as were every way suited unto the reason of men, and to be exercised by the powers thereof, there had been no need of these spiritual gifts. For the spirit of a man knows the things of a man and will both guide and act him therein. And whereas these administrations are, in their nature, use, signification, and efficacy, spiritual, it is by spiritual gifts alone that they may be managed. Hence these things do

12 Gk. "gift."
13 Gk. "gifts."
14 Lat. "in reality."

live and die together; where the one is not, there neither will the other be. Thus, when many, perhaps the most who were outwardly called unto office in the church, began to be carnal in their hearts and lives, and to neglect the use of these gifts, neither applying themselves unto the attaining of them, nor endeavoring to excite or increase what they had received by diligence or constant exercise, refusing to trade with the talent committed unto them, they quickly began to wax weary of spiritual administrations also. Hereon, in compliance with many corrupt affections, they betook themselves unto an outward, carnal, ceremonious worship and administration of ordinances, which they might discharge and perform without the least aid or assistance of the Holy Ghost or supply of spiritual gifts. So, in the neglect of these gifts, and the loss of them which ensued thereon, lay the beginning of the apostasy of the Christian church as to its outward profession, which was quickly completed by the neglect of the grace of the Spirit, whereby it lost both truth and holiness. Nor could it be otherwise. For, as we have proved, the outward form and being of the church, as to its visible profession, depend on the reception and use of them. On their decay, therefore, the church must decay as to its profession, and in their loss is its ruin. And we have an instance in the Church of Rome, what various, extravagant, and endless inventions the minds of men will put them upon to keep up a show of worship, when, by the loss of spiritual gifts, spiritual administrations are lost also. This is that which their innumerable forms, modes, sets of rites and ceremonies, seasons of worship, are invented to supply, but to no purpose at all, but only the aggravation of their sin and folly.

8. In the last place, we plead the event, even in the days wherein we live. For the Holy Ghost does continue to dispense spiritual gifts for gospel administrations in great variety unto those ministers of the gospel who are called unto their office according unto his mind and will. The opposition that is made hereunto by profane scoffers is not to be valued. The experience of those who are humble and wise, who, fearing God, do inquire into these things, is appealed unto. Have they not an experiment of this administration? Do they not find the presence of the Spirit himself, by his various gifts in them, by whom spiritual things are administered unto them? Have they not a proof of Christ speaking in them by the assistance of his Spirit, making the word mighty unto all its proper ends? And as the thing itself, so the variety of his dispensations manifest themselves also unto the experience of believers. Who sees not how different are the gifts of men, the Holy Ghost dividing unto everyone as he will? And the experience which they have themselves who have received these gifts, of the special assistance which they receive

in the exercise of them, may also be pleaded. Indeed, the profaneness of a contrary apprehension is intolerable among such as profess themselves to be Christians. For any to boast themselves they are sufficient of themselves for the stewardly dispensation of the mysteries of the gospel by their own endowments, natural or acquired, and the exercise of them, without a participation of any peculiar spiritual gift from the Holy Ghost, is a presumption which contains in it a renunciation of all or any interest in the promises of Christ made unto the church for the continuance of his presence therein. Let men be never so well persuaded of their own abilities, let them pride themselves in their performances, in reflection of applauses from persons unacquainted with the mystery of these things; let them frame to themselves such a work of the ministry as whose discharge stands in little or no need of these gifts; yet it will at length appear that where the gifts of the Holy Ghost are excluded from their administration, the Lord Christ is so, and the Spirit himself is so, and all true edification of the church is so, and so are all the real concerns of the gospel.¶

And so have we, as I hope, confirmed the second part of the work of the Holy Ghost with respect unto spiritual gifts—namely, his continuance to distribute and communicate unto the church to the end of the world, according unto the powers and duties which he has erected in it or required of it.

8

Of the Gifts of the Spirit with Respect unto Doctrine, Rule, and Worship

How Attained and Improved

THERE REMAIN YET two things to be spoken unto with respect unto the gifts which the Holy Ghost bestows on the ministers of the gospel, to qualify them unto their office, and to enable them unto their work. And these are—First, what they are; second, how they are to be attained and improved.⁋

THE MINISTERIAL GIFTS

In our inquiry after the first, or what are the gifts whereby men are fitted and enabled for the ministry, we wholly set aside the consideration of all those gracious qualifications of faith, love, zeal, compassion, careful tender watchfulness, and the like, whereon the holy use of their ministry does depend. For our inquiry is only after those gifts whereon depends the very being of the ministry. There may be a true ministry in some cases where there is no sanctifying grace; but where there are no spiritual gifts, there is no ministry at all. They are, in general, abilities for the due management of the spiritual administrations of the gospel, in its doctrine, worship, and discipline, unto the edification of the church. It is not easy, nay, it may be, unto us it is not possible, to enumerate in particular all the various gifts which the Holy Ghost endows the ministers of the gospel with. But whereas all the concerns of the church may be referred unto these three heads, of doctrine, worship, and rule, we may inquire what are the principal spiritual gifts of the Holy Ghost with respect unto them distinctly.

Gifts concerning Doctrine

The first great duty of the ministry, with reference unto the church, is the dispensation of the doctrine of the gospel unto it, for its edification. As this is the duty of the church continually to attend unto (Acts 2:42), so it is the principal work of the ministry, the foundation of all other duties, which the apostles themselves gave themselves unto in a special manner (Acts 6:4). Hence is it given in charge unto all ministers of the gospel (Acts 20:28; 1 Pet. 5:2; 1 Tim. 1:3; 4:13, 16; 5:17; 2 Tim. 4:1–3). For this is the principal means appointed by Christ for the edification of his church, that whereby spiritual life is begotten and preserved. Where this work is neglected or carelessly attended unto, there the whole work of the ministry is despised. And with respect unto this ministerial duty there are three spiritual gifts that the Holy Ghost endows men with, which must be considered.

1. The first is wisdom, or knowledge, or understanding in the mysteries of the gospel, the revelation of the mystery of God in Christ, with his mind and will toward us therein. These things may be distinguished, and they seem to be so in the Scripture sometimes. I put them together, as all of them denote that acquaintance with and comprehension of the doctrine of the gospel which is indispensably necessary unto them who are called to preach it unto the church. This some imagine an easy matter to be attained; at least, that there is no more, nor the use of any other means, required thereunto, than what is necessary to the acquisition of skill in any other art or science. And it were well if some, otherwise concerned in point of duty, would but lay out so much of their strength and time in the obtaining of this knowledge as they do about other things which will not turn much unto their account. But the cursory perusal of a few books is thought sufficient to make any man wise enough to be a minister. And not a few undertake ordinarily to be teachers of others who would scarcely be admitted as tolerable disciples in a well-ordered church. But there belongs more unto this wisdom, knowledge, and understanding than most men are aware of. Were the nature of it duly considered, and with the necessity of it unto the ministry of the gospel, probably some would not so rush on that work as they do, which they have no provision of ability for the performance of. It is, in brief, such a comprehension of the scope and end of the Scripture, of the revelation of God therein, such an acquaintance with the systems of particular doctrinal truths, in their rise, tendency, and use, such a habit of mind in judging of spiritual things, and comparing them one with another, such a distinct insight into the springs and course of the mystery of the love, grace, and will of God in Christ, as enables them in whom it is

to declare the counsel of God, to make known the way of life, of faith and obedience unto others, and to instruct them in their whole duty to God and man thereon. This the apostle calls his "knowledge in the mystery of Christ," which he manifested in his writings (Eph. 3:4).¶

For as the gospel, the dispensation and declaration whereof is committed unto the ministers of the church, is the "wisdom of God in a mystery" (1 Cor. 2:7), so their principal duty is to become so wise and understanding in that mystery as that they may be able to declare it unto others, without which they have no ministry committed unto them by Jesus Christ (see Eph. 1:8–9; 3:3–6, 18–19; Col. 4:3). The sole inquiry is, whence we may have this wisdom, seeing it is abundantly evident that we have it not of ourselves. That in general it is from God, that it is to be asked of him, the Scripture everywhere declares (Col. 1:9; 2:1–2; 2 Tim. 2:7; James 1:5; 1 John 5:20). And in particular it is plainly affirmed to be the special gift of the Holy Ghost. He gives the "word of wisdom" (1 Cor. 12:8), which place has been opened before. And it is the first ministerial gift that he bestows on any. Where this is not in some measure, to look for a ministry is to look for the living among the dead. And they will deceive their own souls in the end, as they do those of others in the meantime, who on any other grounds do undertake to be preachers of the gospel. But I shall not here divert unto the full description of this spiritual gift, because I have discoursed concerning it elsewhere.[1]

2. With respect unto the doctrine of the gospel, there is required unto the ministry of the church skill to divide the word aright, which is also a peculiar gift of the Holy Ghost: "Study to show thyself approved unto God, a workman that needeth not to be ashamed, rightly dividing the Word of truth" (2 Tim. 2:15). Both the former clauses depend on the latter. If a minister would be accepted with God in his work, if he would be found at the last day "a workman that needeth not to be ashamed," that is, such a builder of the house of God as whose work is meet, proper, and useful, he must take care to "divide the Word of truth," which is committed unto his dispensation, "rightly," or in a due manner. Ministers are stewards in the house of God, and dispensers of the mysteries thereof. And therefore, it is required of them that they give unto all the servants that are in the house, or do belong unto it, a meet portion, according unto their wants, occasions, and services, suitable unto the will and wisdom of their Lord and Master: "Who is that faithful and wise steward, whom his master shall make ruler over his household, to give them their portion of meat in due season?" (Luke 12:42–43). For this giving of provision

---

1 See chap. 4 of this treatise.

and a portion of meat unto the household of Christ consists principally in the right dividing and distribution of the word of truth. It is the taking out from those great stores of it in the Scripture, and, as it were, cutting off a portion suitable unto the various conditions of those in the family. Herein consists the principal skill of a scribe furnished for the kingdom of heaven with the wisdom before described. And without this, a common course of dispensing or preaching the word, without differencing of persons and truths, however it may be gilded over with a flourish of words and oratory, is shameful work in the house of God.¶

Now, unto this skill sundry things are required.¶

(1) A sound judgment in general concerning the state and condition of those unto whom anyone is so dispensing the word. It is the duty of a shepherd to know the state of his flock; and unless he does so, he will never feed them profitably. He must know whether they are babes, or young men, or old; whether they need milk or strong meat; whether they are skillful or unskillful in the word of righteousness; whether they have their senses exercised to discern good and evil, or not; or whether his hearers are mixed with all these sorts, whether, in the judgment of charity, they are converted unto God, or are yet in an unregenerate condition, what probably are their principal temptations, their hindrances and furtherances; what is their growth or decay in religion. He that is not able to make a competent judgment concerning these things, and the other circumstances of the flock, so as to be steered thereby in his work, will never evidence himself to be "a workman that needeth not to be ashamed."¶

(2) An acquaintance with the ways and methods of the work of God's grace on the minds and hearts of men, that he may pursue and comply with its design in the ministry of the word. Nothing is by many more despised than an understanding hereof; yet is nothing more necessary to the work of the ministry. The word of the gospel as preached is *vehiculum gratiae*,[2] and ought to be ordered so as it may comply with its design in its whole work on the souls of men. He, therefore, who is unacquainted with the ordinary methods of the operation of grace fights uncertainly in his preaching of the word, like a man beating the air. It is true, God can, and often does, direct a word of truth, spoken as it were at random, unto a proper effect of grace on some or other, as it was when the man drew a bow at a venture, and smote the king of Israel between the joints of the harness.[3] But ordinarily a man is not likely to hit a joint who knows not how to take his aim.¶

2   Lat. "the vehicle of grace."
3   Here Owen is alluding to 1 Kings 22:34.

(3) An acquaintance with the nature of temptation, with the special hindrances of faith and obedience, which may befall those unto whom the word is dispensed, is in like manner required hereunto. Many things might be added on this head, seeing a principal part of ministerial skill does consist herein.¶

(4) A right understanding of the nature of spiritual diseases, distempers, and sicknesses, with their proper cures and remedies, belongs hereunto. For the want hereof, the hearts of the wicked are oftentimes made glad in the preaching of the word, and those of the righteous filled with sorrow. The hands of sinners are strengthened, and those who are looking toward God are discouraged or turned out of the way. And where men either know not these things, or do not or cannot apply themselves skillfully to distribute the word according to this variety of occasion, they cannot give the household its portion of meat in due season. And he that wants this spiritual gift will never divide the word aright, unto its proper ends (2 Tim. 3:16–17). And it is lamentable to consider what shameful work is made for want hereof in the preaching of some men, yea, how the whole gift is lost, as to its power, use, and benefit.

3. The gift of utterance also belongs unto this part of the ministerial duty in the dispensation of the doctrine of the gospel. This is particularly reckoned by the apostle among the gifts of the Spirit (1 Cor. 1:5; 2 Cor. 8:7). And he desires the prayers of the church that the gift may abide with himself and abound in him (Eph. 6:19). And he there declares that the nature of it consists in the "opening of the mouth boldly, to make known the mysteries of the gospel" (as also Col. 4:3). Now, this utterance does not consist in a natural volubility of speech, which, taken alone by itself, is so far from being a gift of the Spirit, or a thing to be earnestly prayed for, as that it is usually a snare to them that have it, and a trouble to them that hear them. Nor does it consist in a rhetorical ability to set off discourses with a flourish of words, be they never so plausible or enticing, much less in a bold corrupting of the ordinance of preaching by a foolish affectation[4] of words, in supposed elegancies of speech, quaint expressions, and the like effects of wit, that is, fancy and vanity.¶

But four things do concur hereunto. (1) Παῤῥησία, or *dicendi libertas*.[5] The word we translate "utterance" is λογος, that is, speech. But that not speech in general, but a certain kind of speech is intended, is evident from

---

4   I.e., design to impress; artificiality.
5   Gk., Lat. "freedom of speech."

the places mentioned, and the application of them. And it is such a speech as is elsewhere called παρρησία, that is, a freedom and liberty in the declaration of the truth conceived. This a man has when he is not, from any internal defect, or from any outward consideration, straitened in the declaration of those things which he ought to speak. This frame and ability the apostle expresses in himself: "O ye Corinthians, our mouth is open unto you, our heart is enlarged" (2 Cor. 6:11). A free, enlarged spirit, attended with an ability of speech suited unto the matter in hand, with its occasions, belong to this gift. (2) So also does boldness and holy confidence. So, we often render παρρησία, wherein this utterance does much consist. When the Spirit of God, in the midst of difficulties, oppositions, and discouragements, strengthens the minds of ministers, so as that they are not terrified with any amazement, but discharge their work freely, as considering whose word and message it is that they do deliver, belongs to this gift of utterance. (3) So also does gravity in expression, becoming the sacred majesty of Christ and his truths, in the delivery of them. He that speaks is to "speak as the oracles of God" (1 Pet. 4:11), that is, not only as to truth, preaching the word of God and nothing else, but doing it with that gravity and soundness of speech which become them who speak the oracles of God. For as we are to deliver "sound doctrine," and nothing else (Titus 1:9), so we are to use "sound speech, that cannot be condemned" (Titus 2:7–8). (4) Hereunto, also, belongs that authority which accompanies the delivery of the word when preached in demonstration of these spiritual abilities. For all these things are necessary that the hearers may receive the word, "not as the word of man, but, as it is in truth, the Word of God."[6]

These are the principal spiritual gifts wherewith the Holy Ghost endows the ministers of the church with respect unto the effectual dispensation of the word, or the doctrine of the gospel, which is committed unto them. And where they are communicated in any such degree as is necessary unto the due discharge of that office, they will evidence themselves to the consciences of them that do believe. The dispensation of the word by virtue of them, though under great variety from the various degrees wherein they are communicated, and the different natural abilities of them that do receive them, will be sufficiently distinguished and remote from that empty, wordy, sapless way of discoursing of spiritual things, which is the mere effect of the wit, fancy, invention, and projection of men destitute of the saving knowledge of our Lord Jesus Christ and the mysteries of the gospel.

6   1 Thess. 2:13.

Gifts concerning Worship

The second head of duties belonging unto the ministerial office respects the worship of God. By the worship of God here, I understand only that special part thereof whereof himself is the immediate object. For, absolutely, the preaching and hearing of the word is a part of sacred worship, as that wherein we act the obedience of faith unto the commands of God, and submit ourselves unto his institution. And, indeed, as unto those that hear, it is God declaring himself by his Word that is the immediate object of their worship. But the dispensation of the word which we have considered is the acting of men, upon the authority and command of God, toward others. But, as was said, by that we inquire into, I intend that alone whereof God himself was the immediate object. Such are all the remaining offices and duties of the church, those only excepted which belong to its rule. And this worship has various acts, according to the variety of Christ's institutions and the church's occasions. Yet, as to the manner of its performance, it is comprised in prayer. For by prayer we understand all the confessions, supplications, thanksgivings, and praises that are made unto God in the church, whether absolutely or in the administration of other ordinances, as the sacraments.¶

Wherefore, in this duty, as comprehensive of all the sacred offices of public worship, as the glory of God is greatly concerned, so it is the principal act of obedience in the church. This, then, as to the performance of it, depends either on the natural abilities of men, or on the aids and operation of the Holy Ghost. By the natural abilities of men, I understand not only what they are able of themselves in every instance to perform, but also whatever assistance they may make use of, either of their own finding out or of others'. And by the aids of the Holy Ghost, I intend a special spiritual gift bestowed on men to this purpose. Now, to suppose that the whole duty of the church herein should consist in the actings of men in their own strength and power, without any special assistance of the Holy Spirit, is to exclude the consideration of him from those things with respect whereunto he is principally promised by our Lord Jesus Christ. But what concerns this gift of the Holy Ghost has been at large handled by itself already and must not here be again insisted on. Taking for granted what is therein sufficiently confirmed, I shall only add that those who have not received this gift are utterly unfit to undertake the office of the ministry, wherein it is their duty to go before the church in the administration of all ordinances, by virtue of these abilities. In things civil or secular, it would be esteemed an intolerable solecism[7] to call and choose

---

7   I.e., breaching of good manners.

a man to the discharge of an office or duty whose execution depended solely on such a peculiar faculty or skill as he who is so called has no interest in or acquaintance with. And it will one day appear to be so also in things sacred and religious, yea, much more.

Gifts concerning the Rule of the Church

Thirdly, the rule of the church belongs unto the ministers of it. God has established rule in the church (Rom. 12:8; 1 Cor. 12:28; 1 Tim. 5:17; 1 Thess. 5:12; Heb. 13:7, 17). I dispute not now of what sort this ministry is, nor whether the rule belongs unto one sort alone. It is enough unto my present design that it is committed by Christ unto the ministers of the church, which are its guides, rulers, and overseers. Nor shall I at present inquire into the particular powers, acts, and duties of this rule; I have done it elsewhere.[8] I am only now to consider it so far as its exercise requires a special ministerial gift to be communicated by the Holy Ghost. And in order thereunto the things ensuing must be premised.¶

1. That this rule is spiritual and has nothing in common with the administration of the powers of the world. It has, I say, no agreement with secular power and its exercise, unless it be in some natural circumstances that inseparably attend rulers and ruled in any kind. It belongs unto the kingdom of Christ and the administration of it, which are "not of this world." And as this is well pleaded by some against those who would erect a kingdom for him in the world, and, as far as I can understand, of this world, framed in their own imaginations unto a fancied interest of their own. So, it is as pleadable against them who pretend to exercise the rule and power of his present kingdom after the manner of the potestative[9] administrations of the world. When our Savior forbade all rule unto his disciples after the manner of the Gentiles, who then possessed all sovereign power in the world, and told them that it should not be so with them, that some should be great and exercise dominion over others, but that they should serve one another in love, the greatest condescension unto service being required of them who are otherwise most eminent, he did not intend to take from them or divest them of that spiritual power and authority in the government of the church which he intended to commit unto them. His design, therefore, was to declare what that authority

---

8 E.g., *An Enquiry into the Original, Nature, Institution, Power, Order, and Communion of Evangelical Churches. The First Part. With an Answer to the Discourse of the Unreasonableness of Separation, Written by Dr. Edward Stillingfleet, Dean of Paul's; and in Defense of the Vindication of the Nonconformists from the Guilt of Schism* (1681).

9 I.e., authoritative.

was not, and how it should not be exercised. A lordly or despotical power it was not to be, nor was it to be exercised by penal laws, courts, and coercive jurisdiction, which was the way of the administration of all power among the Gentiles. And if that kind of power and rule in the church which is for the most part exercised in the world is not forbidden by our Savior, no man living can tell what is so. For as to meekness, moderation, patience, equity, righteousness, they were more easy to be found in the legal administrations of power among the Gentiles than in those used in many churches. But such a rule is signified unto them, the authority whereof, from whence it proceeds, was spiritual, its object the minds and souls of men only, and the way of whose administration was to consist in a humble, holy, spiritual application of the word of God or rules of the gospel unto them.¶

2. The end of this rule is merely and solely the edification of the church. All the power that the apostles themselves had, either in or over the church, was but unto their edification (2 Cor. 10:8). And the edification of the church consists in the increase of faith and obedience in all the members thereof, in the subduing and mortifying of sin, in fruitfulness in good works, in the confirmation and consolation of them that stand, in the raising up of them that are fallen, and the recovery of them that wander, in the growth and flourishing of mutual love and peace; and whatever rule is exercised in the church unto any other end is foreign to the gospel, and tends only to the destruction of the church itself.¶

3. In the way and manner of the administration of this rule and government two things may be considered. (1) What is internal, in the qualifications of the minds of them by whom it is to be exercised, such are wisdom, diligence, love, meekness, patience, and the like evangelical endowments. (2) What is external, or what is the outward rule of it, and this is the word and law of Christ alone, as we have elsewhere declared.[10]

From these things, it may appear what is the nature, in general, of that skill in the rule of the church which we assert to be a peculiar gift of the Holy Ghost. If it were only an ability or skill in the canon or civil law, or rules of men; if only an acquaintance with the nature and course of some courts, proceeding litigiously, by citations, processes, legal pleadings, issuing in pecuniary mulcts, outward coercions, or imprisonments, I should willingly acknowledge that there is no peculiar gift of the Spirit of God required thereunto. But the nature of it being as we have declared, it is impossible it should be exercised

---

10 E.g., *An Enquiry into the Original, Nature, Institution, Power, Order, and Communion of Evangelical Churches.*

aright without special assistance of the Holy Ghost. Is any man of himself sufficient for these things? Will any man undertake of himself to know the mind of Christ in all the occasions of the church, and to administer the power of Christ in them and about them? Wherefore the apostle, in many places, teaches that wisdom, skill, and understanding to administer the authority of Christ in the church unto its edification, with faithfulness and diligence, are a special gift of the Holy Ghost (Rom. 12:6, 8; 1 Cor. 12:28). It is the Holy Ghost which makes the elders of the church its bishops or overseers, by calling them to their office (Acts 20:28). And what he calls any man unto, that he furnishes him with abilities for the discharge of.¶

And so have we given a brief account of those ordinary gifts which the Holy Ghost communicates unto the constant ministry of the church, and will do so unto the consummation of all things, having, moreover, in our passage manifested the dependence of the ministry on this work of his; so that we need no addition of pains to demonstrate that where he goes not before in the communication of them, no outward order, call, or constitution is sufficient to make anyone a minister of the gospel.

Ministry Gifts for All Church Members

There are gifts which respect duties only. Such are those which the Holy Ghost continues to communicate unto all the members of the church in a great variety of degrees, according to the places and conditions which they are in, unto their own and the church's edification. There is no need that we should insist upon them in particular, seeing they are of the same nature with them which are continued unto the ministers of the church, who are required to excel in them, so as to be able to go before the whole church in their exercise. The Spirit of the gospel was promised by Christ unto all his disciples, unto all believers, unto the whole church, and not unto the guides of it only. To them he is so in a special manner, with respect unto their office, power, and duty, but not absolutely or only. As he is the Spirit of grace, he quickens, animates, and unites the whole body of the church, and all the members of it, in and unto Christ Jesus (1 Cor. 12:12–13). And as he is the administrator of all supernatural gifts, he furnishes the whole body and all its members with spiritual abilities unto its edification (Eph. 4:15–16; Col. 2:19). And without them, in some measure or degree, ordinarily, we are not able to discharge our duty unto the glory of God. For,

1. These gifts are a great means and help to excite and exercise grace itself, without which it will be lifeless and apt to decay. Men grow in grace by the due exercise of their own gifts in duties. Wherefore, every individual person

on his own account does stand in need of them with respect unto the exercise and improvement of grace (Zech. 12:10).¶

2. Most men have, it may be, such duties incumbent on them with respect unto others as they cannot discharge aright without the special aid of the Spirit of God in this kind. So is it with all them who have families to take care of and provide for. For ordinarily they are bound to instruct their children and servants in the knowledge of the Lord, and to go before them in that worship which God requires of them, as Abraham did, the "father of the faithful."[11] And hereunto some spiritual abilities are requisite. For none can teach others more than they know themselves, nor perform spiritual worship without some spiritual gifts, unless they will betake themselves unto such shifts as we have before on good grounds rejected.¶

3. Every member of a church in order according to the mind of Christ possesses some place, use, and office in the body, which it cannot fill up unto the benefit and ornament of the whole without some spiritual gift. These places are various, some of greater use than others, and of more necessity unto the edification of the church, but all are useful in their kind. This our apostle disputes at large (1 Cor. 12:12–20, etc.). All believers in due order do become one body, by the participation of the same Spirit and union unto the same head. Those who do not so partake of the one Spirit, who are not united unto the head, do not properly belong to the body, whatever place they seem to hold therein. Of those that do so, some are as it were an eye, some as a hand, and some as a foot. All these are useful in their several places, and needful unto one another. None of them is so highly exalted as to have the least occasion of being lifted up, as though he had no need of the rest, for the Spirit distributes unto everyone severally as he will, not all unto anyone, save only unto the head, our Lord Jesus, from whom we all receive grace according to the measure of his gift. Nor is any so depressed or useless as to say it is not of the body, nor that the body has no need of it, but everyone in his place and station concurs to the unity, strength, beauty, and growth of the body, which things our apostle disputes at large in the place mentioned.¶

4. Hereby are supplies communicated unto the whole from the head (Eph. 4:15–16; Col. 2:19). It is of the body, that is, of the church under the conduct of its officers, that the apostle discourses in those places. And the duty of the whole it is to speak the truth in love, everyone in his several place and station. And herein God has so ordered the union of the whole church in itself, unto and in dependence on its head, as that through and by not only the

11 Rom. 4:16.

supply of every joint, which may express either the officers or more eminent members of it, but the effectual working of every part, in the exercise of the graces and gifts which the Spirit does impart to the whole, the body may edify itself and be increased.¶

5. The Scripture is express that the Holy Ghost does communicate of those gifts unto private believers and directs them in that duty wherein they are to be exercised (1 Pet. 4:10). Everyone, that is, every believer, walking in the order and fellowship of the gospel, is to attend unto the discharge of his duty, according as he has received spiritual ability. So was it in the church of Corinth (1 Cor. 1:5–7), and in that of the Romans (Rom. 15:14), as they all of them knew that it was their duty to covet the best gifts, which they did with success (1 Cor. 12:31). And hereon depend the commands for the exercise of those duties which, in the ability of these gifts received, they were to perform. So were they all to admonish one another, to exhort one another, to build up one another in their most holy faith. And it is the loss of those spiritual gifts which has introduced among many an utter neglect of these duties, so as that they are scarce heard of among the generality of them that are called Christians. But, blessed be God, we have large and full experience of the continuance of this dispensation of the Spirit, in the eminent abilities of a multitude of private Christians, however they may be despised by them who know them not. By some, I confess, they have been abused. Some have presumed on them beyond the line and measure which they have received. Some have been puffed up with them. Some have used them disorderly in churches and to their hurt. Some have boasted of what they have not received. All which miscarriages also befell the primitive churches. And I had rather have the order, rule, spirit, and practice of those churches that were planted by the apostles, with all their troubles and disadvantages, than the carnal peace of others in their open degeneracy from all those things.

HOW MINISTERIAL GIFTS ARE ATTAINED

It remains only that we inquire how men may come unto or attain a participation of these gifts, whether ministerial or more private. And unto this end we may observe,

1. That they are not communicated unto any by a sudden afflatus[12] or extraordinary infusion, as were the gifts of miracles and tongues, which were bestowed on the apostles and many of the first converts. That dispensation

---

12 I.e., revelation.

of the Spirit is long since ceased, and where it is now pretended unto by any, it may justly be suspected as an enthusiastic delusion. For as the end of those gifts, which in their own nature exceed the whole power of all our faculties, is ceased, so is their communication, and the manner of it also. Yet this I must say, that the infusion of spiritual light into the mind, which is the foundation of all gifts, as has been proved, being wrought sometimes suddenly or in a short season, the concomitancy[13] of gifts in some good measure is oftentimes sudden, with an appearance of something extraordinary, as might be manifested in instances of several sorts.¶

2. These gifts are not absolutely attainable by our own diligence and endeavors in the use of means, without respect unto the sovereign will and pleasure of the Holy Ghost. Suppose there are such means of the attainment and improvement of them, and that several persons do, with the same measures of natural abilities and diligence, use those means for that end, yet it will not follow that all must be equally partakers of them. They are not the immediate product of our own endeavors, no, not as under an ordinary blessing upon them. For they are χαρίσματα, arbitrary largesses or gifts, which the Holy Spirit works in all persons severally as he will. Hence, we see the different events that are among them who are exercised in the same studies and endeavors. Some are endued with eminent gifts, some scarce attain unto any that are useful, and some despise them, name and thing. There is, therefore, an immediate operation of the Spirit of God in the collation of these spiritual abilities, which is unaccountable by the measures of natural parts and industry. Yet I say,¶

3. That ordinarily they are both attained and increased by the due use of means suited thereunto, as grace is also, which none but Pelagians[14] affirm to be absolutely in the power of our own wills. And the naming of these means shall put an issue unto this discourse. (1) Among them, in the first place, is required a due preparation of soul, by humility, meekness, and teachableness. The Holy Spirit takes no delight to impart of his special gifts unto proud, self-conceited men, to men vainly puffed up in their own fleshly minds. The same must be said concerning other vicious and depraved habits of mind, by which, moreover, they are ofttimes expelled and cast out after they have been in some measure received. And in this case I need not mention those by whom all these gifts are despised. It would be a wonder indeed if they

---

13 I.e., existence or occurrence together.

14 Pelagians are those who hold to the heterodox teachings of Pelagius (ca. 354–418), who denied original sin and believed that human beings had the free will to achieve perfection without the aid of divine grace.

370 A DISCOURSE OF SPIRITUAL GIFTS

should be made partakers of them, or at least if they should abide with them. (2) Prayer is a principal means for their attainment. This the apostle directs unto when he enjoins us earnestly to desire the best gifts. For this desire is to be acted by prayer, and not otherwise. (3) Diligence in the things about which these gifts are conversant. Study and meditation on the word of God, with the due use of means for the attaining a right understanding of his mind and will therein, is that which I intend. For in this course, conscientiously attended unto, it is that, for the most part, the Holy Spirit comes in and joins his aid and assistance for furnishing of the mind with those spiritual endowments. (4) The growth, increase, and improvement of these gifts depend on their faithful use according as our duty does require. It is trade alone that increases talents, and exercise in a way of duty that improves gifts. Without this they will first wither and then perish. And by a neglect hereof are they lost every day, in some partially, in some totally, and in some to a contempt, hatred, and blasphemy of what themselves had received. (5) Men's natural endowments, with elocution, memory, judgment, and the like, improved by reading, learning, and diligent study, do enlarge, set off, and adorn these gifts, where they are received.[15]

---

15   In the first published edition (1693), between this treatise on spiritual gifts and the application section appended appeared a list of books also sold by William Marshall, including more titles by Owen as well as other well-known Dissenters, such as Hanserd Knollys and John Bunyan.

The Application of the
Foregoing Discourse

WITH RESPECT UNTO the dispensation of the Spirit toward believers, and
his holy operations in them and upon them, there are sundry particular duties, whereof he is the immediate object, prescribed unto them. And they are
those whereby on our part we comply with him in his work of grace, whereby
it is carried on and rendered useful unto us. Now, whereas this Holy Spirit is
a divine person, and he acts in all things toward us as a free agent, according
unto his own will, the things enjoined us with respect unto him are those
whereby we may carry ourselves aright toward such a one, namely, as he is a
holy, divine, intelligent person, working freely in and toward us for our good.
And they are of two sorts, the first whereof are expressed in prohibitions of
those things which are unsuited unto him and his dealings with us, the latter
in commands for our attendance unto such duties as are peculiarly suited
unto a compliance with him in his operations; in both which our obedience
is to be exercised with a peculiar regard unto him. I shall begin with the first
sort and go over them in the instances given us in the Scripture.

GRIEVING THE HOLY SPIRIT

First, we have a negative precept to this purpose: μὴ λυπεῖτε τὸ πνεῦμα τὸ
ἅγιον, "Grieve not the holy Spirit" (Eph. 4:30). Consider who he is, what he
has done for you, how great your concern is in his continuance with you, and
withal that he is a free, infinitely wise, and holy agent in all that he does, who
came freely unto you, and can withdraw from you, and grieve him not. It is
the person of the Holy Spirit that is intended in the words, as appears, first,
from the manner of the expression, τὸ πνεῦμα τὸ ἅγιον, "that holy Spirit."
Second, by the work assigned unto him; for by him we are "sealed unto the

day of redemption." Him we are not to "grieve." The expression seems to be borrowed from Isaiah 63:10, where mention is made of the sin and evil here prohibited: והמה מדו ועצביאח רוח קדש,[1] "But they rebelled, and vexed his holy Spirit." קָצֵב[2] is to "trouble" and to "grieve," and it is used when it is done unto a great degree. The LXX renders it here by παροξύνω, which is "so to grieve as also to irritate and provoke to anger and indignation," because it has respect unto the rebellions of the people in the wilderness, which our apostle expresses by παραπικραίνω and παραπικρασμὸς, words of the same signification. To vex, therefore, is the heightening of grieving by a provocation unto anger and indignation; which sense is suited to the place and matter treated of, though the word signifies no more but to "grieve," and so it is rendered by λυπέω (Gen. 45:5; 2 Sam. 19:2).

Now, grief is here ascribed unto the Holy Spirit as it is elsewhere unto God absolutely: "It repented the Lord that he had made man on the earth, and it grieved him at his heart" (Gen. 6:6). Such affections and perturbations[3] of mind are not ascribed unto God or the Spirit but metaphorically. That intended in such ascriptions is to give us an apprehension of things as we are able to receive it. And the measure we take of them is their nature and effects in ourselves. What may justly grieve a good man, and what he will do when he is unjustly or undeservedly grieved, represent unto us what we are to understand of our own condition with respect unto the Holy Ghost when he is said to be grieved by us. And grief in the sense here intended is a trouble of mind arising from an apprehension of unkindness not deserved, of disappointments not expected, on the account of a near concern in those by whom we are grieved. We may, therefore, see hence what it is we are warned of when we are enjoined not to grieve the Holy Spirit. As,

1. There must be unkindness in what we do. Sin has various respects toward God, of guilt, and filth, and the like. These several considerations of it have several effects. But that which is denoted when it is said to "grieve him" is unkindness, or that defect of an answerable love unto the fruits and testimonies of his love which we have received, that it is accompanied with. He is the Spirit of love; he is love. All his actings toward us and in us are fruits of love, and they all of them leave an impression of love upon our souls. All the joy and consolation we are made partakers of in this world arise from a

---

1   *Biblia Hebraica Stuttgartensia* reads, וְהֵמָּה מָרוּ וְעִצְּבוּ אֶת־רוּחַ קָדְשׁוֹ. *Biblia Hebraica Stuttgartensia*, ed. Karl Elliger and Wilhelm Rudolph (Stuttgart: Deutsche Bibelgesellschaft, 1983); hereafter cited as *BHS*.

2   *BHS* reads, וְעִצְּבוּ.

3   I.e., worries.

sense of the love of God, communicated in an endearing way of love unto our souls. This requires a return of love and delight in all duties of obedience on our part. When instead hereof, by our negligence and carelessness, or otherwise, we fall into those things or ways which he most abhors, he greatly respects the unkindness and ingratitude which is therein, and is therefore said to be grieved by us.

2. Disappointment in expectation. It is known that no disappointment properly can befall the Spirit of God. It is utterly inconsistent with his prescience and omniscience. But we are disappointed when things fall not out according as we justly expected they would, in answer unto the means used by us for their accomplishment. And when the means that God uses toward us do not, by reason of our sin, produce the effect they are suited unto, God proposes himself as under a disappointment. So, he speaks of his vineyard: "I looked that it should bring forth grapes, and it brought forth wild grapes" (Isa. 5:4). Now, disappointment causes grief: as when a father has used all means for the education of a child in any honest way or course, and expended much of his estate therein, if he, through dissoluteness or idleness, fail his expectation and disappoint him, it fills him with grief. They are great things which are done for us by the Spirit of God. These all of them have their tendency unto an increase in holiness, light, and love. Where they are not answered, where there is not a suitable effect, there is that disappointment that causes grief. Especially is this so with respect unto some signal mercies. A return in holy obedience is justly expected on their account. And where this is not, it is a thing causing grief. This are we here minded of, "Grieve not the holy Spirit of God, whereby ye are sealed unto the day of redemption."[4] So great a kindness should have produced other effects than those there mentioned by the apostle.

3. The concern of the Holy Spirit in us concurs to his being said to be grieved by us. For we are grieved by them in whom we are particularly concerned. The miscarriages of others we can pass over without any such trouble. And there are two things that give us a special concern in others. (1) Relation, as that of a father, a husband, a brother. This makes us to be concerned in, and consequently to be grieved for, the miscarriages of them that are related unto us. So is it with the Holy Spirit. He has undertaken the office of a comforter toward us and stands in that relation to us. Hence, he is so concerned in us as that he is said to be grieved with our sins, when he is not so at the sins of them unto whom he stands not in special relation. (2) Love gives concern and makes way for grief upon occasion of it. Those

4 Eph. 4:30.

whom we love we are grieved for and by. Others may provoke indignation, but they cause not grief. I mean on their own account; for otherwise we ought to grieve for the sins of all. And what is the special love of the Holy Ghost toward us has been declared.

HOW WE GRIEVE THE SPIRIT

From what has been spoken, it is evident what we are warned of, what is enjoined unto us, when we are cautioned not to grieve the Holy Spirit, and how we may do so. For we do it,

1. When we are not influenced by his love and kindness to answer his mind and will in all holy obedience, accompanied with joy, love, and delight. This he deserves at our hands, this he expects from us. And when it is neglected, because of his concern in us, we are said to grieve him. For he looks not only for our obedience, but also that it be filled up with joy, love, and delight. When we attend unto duties with an unwilling mind, when we apply ourselves unto any acts of obedience in a bondage or servile frame, we grieve him, who has deserved other things of us.

2. When we lose and forget the sense and impression of signal mercies received by him. So the apostle, to give efficacy unto his prohibition, adds the signal benefit which we receive by him, in that he seals us to the day of redemption; which, what it is, and wherein it does consist, has been declared.[5] And hence it is evident that he speaks of the Holy Spirit as dwelling in believers; for as such he seals them. Whereas, therefore, in and by sin we forget the great grace, kindness, and condescension of the Holy Spirit in his dwelling in us, and by various ways communicating of the love and grace of God unto us, we may be well said to grieve him. And certainly this consideration, together with that of the vile ingratitude and horrible folly there are in neglecting and defiling his dwelling place, with the danger of his withdrawing from us on the continuance of our provocation, ought to be as effectual a motive unto universal holiness and constant watchfulness therein as any that can be proposed unto us.

3. Some sins there are which in a special manner above others do grieve the Holy Spirit. These our apostle expressly discourses of (1 Cor. 6:15–20). And, by the connection of the words in this place, he seems to make "corrupt communication," which always has a tendency unto corruption of conversation, to be a sin of this nature (Eph. 4:29–30).

---

5   This is a reference to the previous treatise in this volume, *The Holy Spirit as a Comforter* (1693).

VEXING THE HOLY SPIRIT

Secondly, that which we have rendered to "vex him" (Isa. 63:10), is but the heightening and aggravation of his being grieved by our continuance, and, it may be, obstinacy, in those ways whereby he is grieved. For this is the progress in these things. If those whom we are concerned in, as children or other relations, do fall into miscarriages and sins, we are first grieved by it. This grief in ourselves is attended with pity and compassion toward them, with an earnest endeavor for their recovery. But if, notwithstanding all our endeavors, and the application of means for their reducement, they continue to go on frowardly in their ways, then are we vexed at them, which includes an addition of anger and indignation unto our former sorrow or grief. Yet in this posture of things we cease not to attempt their cure for a season, which if it succeeds not, but they continue in their obstinacy, then we resolve to treat with them no more, but to leave them to themselves. And not only so, but upon our satisfaction of their resolution for a continuance in ways of sin and debauchery, we deal with them as their enemies, and labor to bring them unto punishment. And for our better understanding of the nature of our sin and provocation, this whole scheme of things is ascribed unto the Holy Ghost with respect unto them. How he is said to be "grieved," and on what occasion, has been declared. Upon a continuance in those ways wherewith he is grieved, he is said to be "vexed," that we may understand there is also anger and displeasure toward us. Yet he forsakes us not, yet he takes not from us the means of grace and recovery. But if we discover an obstinacy in our ways, and an untractable perverseness, then he will cast us off, and deal with us no more for our recovery; and woe unto us when he shall depart from us!¶

So when the old world would not be brought to repentance by the dispensation of the Spirit of Christ in the preaching of Noah (1 Pet. 3:19–20), God said thereon that his Spirit should give over, and "not always strive with man" (Gen. 6:3). Now, the cessation of the operations of the Spirit toward men obstinate in ways of sin, after he has been long grieved and vexed, comprises three things. First, a subduction[6] from them of the means of grace, either totally, by the removal of their light and candlestick, all ways of the revelation of the mind and will of God unto them (Rev. 2:5). Or as unto the efficacy of the word toward them, where the outward dispensation of it is continued, so that "hearing they shall hear, but not understand" (Isa. 6:9; John 12:40). For by the word it is that he strives with the souls and minds of men. Second, a forbearance of all chastisement, out of a gracious design to heal and recover

6   I.e., process of pulling something down.

them (Isa. 1:5). Third, a giving of them up unto themselves, or leaving them unto their own ways; which although it seems only a consequent of the two former, and to be included in them, yet is there indeed in it a positive act of the anger and displeasure of God, which directly influences the event of things, for they shall be so given up unto their own hearts' lusts as to be bound in them as in "chains of darkness" unto following vengeance (Rom. 1:26, 28).¶

But this is not all. He becomes at length a professed enemy unto such obstinate sinners: "They rebelled, and vexed his holy Spirit, therefore he was turned to be their enemy, and he fought against them" (Isa. 63:10). This is the length of his proceeding against obstinate sinners in this world. And herein also four things are included. 1. He comes upon them as an enemy, to spoil them. This is the first thing that an enemy does when he comes to fight against any; he spoils them of what they have. Have such persons had any light or conviction, any gift or spiritual abilities, the Holy Spirit being now become their professed enemy, he spoils them of it all. "From him that has not shall be taken away even that which he seems to have."[7] Seeing he neither had nor used his gifts or talent unto any saving end, being now at an open enmity with him who lent it him, it shall be taken away. 2. He will come upon them with spiritual judgments, smiting them with blindness of mind and obstinacy of will, filling them with folly, giddiness,[8] and madness in their ways of sin, which sometimes shall produce most doleful[9] effects in themselves and others. 3. He will cast them out of his territories. If they have been members of churches, he will order that they shall be cut off, and cast out of them. 4. He frequently gives them in this world a foretaste of that everlasting vengeance which is prepared for them. Such are those horrors of conscience, and other terrible effects of an utter desperation, which he justly, righteously, and holily sends upon the minds and souls of some of them. And these things will he do, as to demonstrate the greatness and holiness of his nature, so also that all may know what it is to despise his goodness, kindness, and love.

TAKING STOCK OF OURSELVES

And the consideration of these things belongs unto us. It is our wisdom and duty to consider as well the ways and degrees of the Spirit's departure from provoking sinners, as those of his approach unto us with love and grace.

---

7 Luke 8:18.
8 I.e., playfulness and silliness.
9 I.e., mournful; causing grief or affliction.

These latter have been much considered by many, as to all his great works toward us, and that unto the great advantage and edification of those concerned in them. For thence have they learned both their own state and condition, as also what particular duties they were on all occasions to apply themselves unto, as in part we have manifested before, in our discourses about regeneration and sanctification.[10]

Firstly,[11] and it is of no less concern unto us to consider aright the ways and degrees of his departure, which are expressed to give us that godly fear and reverence wherewith we ought to consider and observe him. David, on his sin, feared nothing more than that God would take his holy Spirit from him (Ps. 51:11). And the fear hereof should influence us unto the utmost care and diligence against sin. For although he should not utterly forsake us, which, as to those who are true believers, is contrary to the tenor, promise, and grace of the new covenant, yet he may so withdraw his presence from us as that we may spend the remainder of our days in trouble, and our years in darkness and sorrow. "Let him," therefore, "that thinketh he standeth," on this account also "take heed lest he fall."[12] And as for them with whom he is, as it were, but in the entrance of his work, producing such effects in their minds as, being followed and attended unto, might have a saving event, he may, upon their provocations, utterly forsake them, in the way and by the degrees before mentioned. It is therefore the duty of all to serve him with fear and trembling on this account. And,

Secondly, it is so to take heed of the very entrances of the course described. Have there been such evils in any of us as wherein it is evident that the Spirit is grieved? As we love our souls, we are to take care that we do not vex him by a continuance in them. And if we do not diligently and speedily recover ourselves from the first, the second will ensue. Has he been grieved by our negligence in or of duties, by our indulgence unto any lust, by compliance with or conformity to the world? Let not our continuance in so doing make it his vexation. Remember that while he is but grieved, he continues to supply us with all due means for our healing and recovery. He will do so also when he is yet vexed. But he will do it with such a mixture of anger and displeasure as shall make us know that what we have done is an evil thing and bitter. But have any proceeded further, and continued long thus to vex him, and have refused his instructions, when accompanied, it may be, with sore afflictions or inward distresses, that have been evident tokens of his displeasure? Let

---

10   E.g., *Πνευματολογια, or, A Discourse concerning the Holy Spirit*, bks. 3–5.
11   Although Owen does not include "Firstly," that is clearly his intention.
12   1 Cor. 10:12.

such souls rouse up themselves to lay hold on him, for he is ready to depart, it may be forever. And,

Thirdly, we may do well to consider much the miserable condition of those who are thus utterly forsaken by him. When we see a man who has lived in a plentiful and flourishing condition, brought to extreme penury[13] and want, seeking his bread in rags from door to door, the spectacle is sad, although we know he brought this misery on himself by profuseness or debauchery of life. But how sad is it to think of a man whom, it may be, we knew to have had a great light and conviction, to have made an amiable profession, to have been adorned with sundry useful spiritual gifts, and had in estimation on this account, now to be despoiled of all his ornaments, to have lost light, and life, and gifts, and profession, and to lie as a poor withered branch on the dunghill of the world! And the sadness hereof will be increased when we shall consider, not only that the Spirit of God is departed from him, but also is become his enemy, and fights against him, whereby he is devoted unto irrecoverable ruin.

---

13 I.e., the state of being very poor; extreme poverty.

General Index

provided for the edification of the church, 346

"ministration of the Spirit," 224, 254

ministry of the church
  calling of, 338–41
  eminency of, 333–38
  as gift of Christ, 331–33
  for the good and advantage of the church, 341–43
  for the prohibition and hindrance of evil, 341, 343
  outward call to, 265
  without spiritual gifts, 326

"ministry of the Spirit," 349

ministry to the Gentiles, 277, 280

miracles, 293, 306–10
  cessation of, 368–69

misery, of those forsaken by the Spirit, 378

Missal, 3, 29, 35, 38

modesty, 67

Mohammed, 30

Mohammedans, 161

mother, comfort of, 196–97

natural conscience, 76, 82

natural endowments
  distinct from spiritual gifts, 268, 353, 370
  and prayer, 6, 70–71, 112, 116–17, 125, 140, 361, 370

New Testament
  miracles of, 305
  no set forms of prayer in, 164
  ordinances of, 254
  plentiful and rich effusion of the Spirit in, 61–62
  richer communication of grace in, 61

Noah, preaching of, 375

obedience, 373

obstinate in the ways of sin, 375–76

oil, anointing with, 223

Old Testament
  miracles of, 305

no set forms of prayer, 164

ordinances of, 254

prayers in, 155

promises of the Spirit, 216

ordinances and institutions of the gospel, 337, 338

ordinary gifts of the Spirit, 266, 331–43

Origen, 90

ornaments, in worship, 36

Papacy
  on spiritual anointing, 231
  stranger to the true nature of prayer, 107
  superstition in prayer, 131
  see also Roman Catholic Church

parable of the talents, 351–52

paraclete, 182–91

parents, duty to pray, 123

pastors and teachers, 318, 332, 337, 338

pater-noster, 113

peace of God, 101, 335

Pelagians, 42, 83, 172, 369

Pelagius, 172

Pentecost, 60, 279

Peter, preaching on Pentecost, 188

Philip
  daughters as prophetesses without office, 289
  as evangelist, 283

pleading with God, 121

pledge, 241–43

Pliny the Elder, 135n5

Plotinus, 142–43

Plutarch, 242

Ponder, Nathaniel, 1n1

pouring out of the Holy Spirit, 3, 51–52, 128–29

powers of the world to come, 321, 326

practical atheism, 48

prayer
  according to one's ability, 70, 105, 112, 113, 114
  aids in, 2, 28
  benefits others, 7, 138

Scripture Index